The Militia and the Right to Arms,

OR, HOW THE SECOND AMENDMENT FELL SILENT

Constitutional Conflicts

A SERIES WITH THE INSTITUTE OF BILL OF RIGHTS LAW

AT THE COLLEGE OF WILLIAM AND MARY

Series Editors: Neal Devins and Mark Graber

The Militia and the Right to Arms,

OR, HOW THE SECOND AMENDMENT FELL SILENT

H. Richard Uviller and William G. Merkel

DUKE UNIVERSITY PRESS   DURHAM AND LONDON 2002

© 2002 Duke University Press   All rights reserved
Printed in the United States of America on acid-free paper ∞
Designed by Rebecca Giménez   Typeset in Monotype Garamond
by Tseng Information Systems, Inc.   Library of Congress Cataloging-
in-Publication Data appear on the last printed page of this book.
We are grateful to the Anne S. K. Brown Collection at Brown University
Library for permission to use the two militia caricatures in chapter 4.

To Daphne and Sacha in joy and gratitude.

H. R. U.

For my parents with love and appreciation.

W. G. M.

I acknowledge the helpful comments of my erudite colleagues, Professors Barbara Black and Henry Monaghan, on an earlier draft of this work. And I express my particular appreciation for the loving support of my wife, Rena.

H. R. U.

I would like to acknowledge the generous assistance of several friends and colleagues. Dr. Gareth Davies (St. Anne's College, Oxford) reviewed sections on twentieth century history and offered helpful commentary. Dr. Christopher B. Howard (U.S.A.F. Reserves) shared freely of his abundant knowledge of military affairs. Dr. Lelia Roeckell (Molloy College, New York) provided much encouragement, and a friendly place to stay during numerous trips to New York. Dr. Andrew King (University College, Cork) helped refine my understanding of the sixteenth and seventeenth century English cultural background. In myriad ways, our copanelists and presenters at the April 2000 Chicago-Kent College of Law conference on the Second Amendment influenced both my own and Professor Uviller's thinking as we set about the task of revising a conference paper and expanding it into a book. All told, this Second Amendment project took nearly seven years to bring to completion. Along the way, Dr. David Lecomber and Dr. Alan Iwi assisted with my computing in Oxford, Eleni Canellos lent me her laptop, and Victoria Wilson made sure I hadn't wholly forgotten my Latin. My coauthor showed equal parts forbearance and resolve, and always a perfect sense of judgment. Were it not for Professor Uviller, I fear I might have gone hopelessly off course long before the happy conclusion of our odyssey. My D. Phil. supervisors at Oxford, Professor D. W. Howe and the late Dr. Duncan MacLeod, furnished invaluable suggestions and support related to this project, even as it distracted repeatedly from my appointed doctoral labors. Finally, appreciation is due the incomparable and incorrigible Dr. Sarah A. Swash, absent whose sense of mystery and cheer I would have laughed and smiled much less often while working on this book. Except for coauthors Uviller and Merkel, none of the above-named individuals bears any responsibility for the opinions and conclusions expressed herein, some of which, doubtless, some of them do not share.

W. G. M.

The Militia and the Right to Arms,

OR, HOW THE SECOND AMENDMENT FELL SILENT

"A well-regulated militia being necessary to the security of a free state, we need cheap, available handguns."

Few Americans can confront the question of private ownership of firearms dispassionately. And the Constitution's Second Amendment is to some the sacred text that raises the emotional issue to the lofty plane of basic rights and traditions of American freedom. While many of us regard guns in private hands as the scourge of our times, and favor government imposition of controls and punitive deterrence of all sorts, many others think of possession of firearms — the handguns and assault weapons along with the hunting rifles — as the gift of the Founders, immune to government restriction and regulation. The gun people and their friends point to the ringing language of the Second Amendment, "the right of the people to keep and bear arms shall not be infringed," as well as the early ethic of self-reliance — and distrust of government — as support for the notion that the Constitution itself assures the people free access to firearms. And many commentators, some dedicated practitioners, some single-topic academics, and some others with genuine scholarly credentials have come forward to support this position.

For our part, we take no position on the question of whether guns in private hands are good or bad for society as a whole, nor do we opine on whether government-imposed gun control measures will be likely to reduce the extraordinary infliction of bullet wounds — as well as the rate of gun-assisted felonies — that have become the shame of American culture. It is possible, as John Lott and others have argued,[1] that wider handgun ownership by sane and law-abiding citizens will actually reduce the incidence of violent crime. On the other hand, Lott's statistical methods have been challenged, and the debate does not lack vocal advocates of the contrary view.[2] Our only thesis here is that for better or for worse, the Constitution, and the Second Amendment in particular, have nothing whatever to contribute to the question. While the Second Amendment surely did once speak loudly and clearly to the issue of arms in private hands, we will conclude from an examination of the language of the provision, as understood by the ratifiers, and from the history of the militia since the eighteenth century, that the "right of the people" has become a vacant and meaningless sequence of words. It is not easy to take an unequivocal pronouncement of the Great Text and declare it null, but a fair examination of the original meaning of the clause and the historical development of its ingredients compels our conclusion.[3]

This, then, is our plan of argument. In part I we introduce the conceptual and political roots of the Second Amendment. Much of what we set forth here is familiar ground to scholars of the eighteenth century. In the light of the high-decibel controversy surrounding the modern import of the constitutional provision, it is reassuring — if somewhat surprising — to find such general accord regarding the seventeenth- and eighteenth-century antecedents of the provision, and the function of arms and the militia in the design of the new American political experiment. We describe the understanding of the founding generation as derived from the political thought that impressed itself on the minds of those concerned with the nature of just and enduring government and, in particular, the place of a military organization within it. Here we draw not only upon the influential sources in America in the late eighteenth century, but also upon the collateral expressions of the founders and their contemporaries to find the most likely purposes and assumptions underlying the text. This will constitute the web of historical context from which the meaning of the text may be read.

Specifically, in chapter 1 we identify and describe the two competing schools of thought on the meaning of the Second Amendment and analyze the four decisions of the United States Supreme Court interpreting the constitutional right to arms. Although these cases are old and, in some respects, flawed, we argue that they were correctly decided. We will here sound the first theme of the book: that in the Framers' minds, and in the text they left as a record of their purpose, the right to arms was indissolubly linked to a "well-regulated militia," an institution with clearly understood historical, ideological, political, and legal meaning in late eighteenth-century America.

Chapter 2 examines the political and constitutional history of the Anglo-American militia from the eve of English colonization until the War of Independence. It pays particular attention to the politically charged distinction between the citizen militia and the professional "standing army," a distinction with which early American republicans were nothing less than obsessed. Chapter 3 turns to the efforts of the newly independent Americans to forge an effective system of national defense and to frame a workable constitutional structure of government. Both of these tasks required striking a just balance between the rival claims of an effective but potentially dangerous regular army on the one side of the scale and the politically favored but historically unreliable citizen militia on the other.

Resolution of these dilemmas, many republicans insisted, required revitalization of the militia as a universal, amateur, occasional obligation of citizenship in the best classical tradition. Meanwhile, veteran government officers and strong military men — George Washington, among them — hoped for a large army and lobbied for reorganization, regulation, and nationalization of the militia. Both of these competing visions found expression in the Constitution of 1787. But anti-federalist opponents of strong national government feared the sweeping military powers granted to the central authority and demanded express assurances that the federal government could not disarm the people's militia as a pretext for installing a large and dangerous standing army. These urgent concerns were answered in the Second Amendment. Drafted by James Madison, the provision passed the First Congress with the rest of the Bill of Rights in 1789, and was ratified by the requisite three-fourths of the states in 1791.

In the second part of the book, we trace the evolution of the militia as a military organization from the earliest days of the Republic to the present time. Part II yields the second theme of the work: times change, and even once-cherished components of a written constitution may sometimes lose vitality. Thus, in chapter 4, we explore the beginnings of the end of the Framers' militia. One year after ratification of the Second Amendment and the rest of the Bill of Rights, Congress passed the Militia Act of 1792, designed to breathe life into the militia of several states and to set national standards. But as the decades unfolded, more and more Americans lost interest in the old militia. Though service was (at least in theory) still obligatory, by the 1830s the parade grounds and muster points were empty, and the militia of such importance to the founding generation was no more.

Chapter 5 carries the evolution of the amateur military unit through a new phase: the era of the volunteer soldier. From the 1840s through the close of the nineteenth century, volunteer companies rather than the defunct common militia constituted the bulk of America's military strength. Supplementing a smallish regular army, it was the volunteers who pulled the laboring oar in the imperialist conflicts with Mexico and Spain. And in the blood-drenched struggle to save the Union and bring an end to slavery, volunteers predominated in the northern forces. In chapter 6 we meet the modern form of the militia, the federalized National Guard, and trace its evolution through the twentieth century. The Guard, we will show, became a military organization utterly unlike the militia contemplated by the Framers: a component of the regular army rather than a counterweight to the federal military establishment, select rather than universal, and armed by the central government rather than by the citizens themselves.

With this history behind us, we encounter, in part III, the problem of interpreting ancient texts for faithful modern application. Here, the third major theme emerges: meaning should be permitted to swing only a few degrees on its mooring to language. Interpretation—a legitimate device for understanding—can shade meaning as context, technology, and social custom change, but only to a limited extent. Wide adjustments distort meaning and ultimately alter text. We do not believe in amendment by radical reinterpretation. In chapter 7 we explore the ingredients of meaning and the obligations of fidelity. We will stress that because the operative language of the Second Amendment recognizing the right to keep and bear arms was expressly predicated on the importance of an amateur, self-armed military organization, it cannot be read in our new century without a frank assessment of the extent to which a well-regulated militia is today necessary to the security of a free state. Indeed, we must ask whether there is today any military institution whatsoever on the landscape that resembles the militia of old. If, as we contend, the predicate institution for the acknowledged right has vanished, leaving no recognizable descendants, the right dependent upon it is deprived of its essence and becomes a vacant, silent relic.[4]

When we arrive, finally, at the twenty-first century, we explore further the ghost of this once-proud right. We then test our thesis, in chapter 8, against a few of the many competing interpretations. To this we have appended a postscript, chapter 9, in which we describe and comment on the most recent—indeed, the only recent—decision upholding a challenge to a gun control law on the basis of the Second Amendment, *United States v. Emerson*. In our Conclusion, the Second Amendment reemerges in its original contours, as a declaration protecting rights fundamental to the vitality of the militia, the constitutionally preferred system of national defense. But as the Second Amendment resurfaces with the shape and substance with which it was invested over two hundred years ago, it enters a modern America in which its voice has been stilled by the erosion of the meaning of its message.

I

ARMS, THE MAN, AND THE MILITIA:

THE HISTORY OF A CONCEPT

A well regulated Militia, being necessary to the
security of a free State, the right of the people
to keep and bear Arms, shall not be infringed.
— *United States Constitution, Amendment II*

1

The Gun in the American Self-Portrait

Owning and carrying personal firearms—or at least the unbridled right to do so—has become a freighted metaphor of American individualism with obvious linkage to the muscular frontier hero of myth and experience. To survive, the pioneer required self-sufficiency and self-protection. Thus, survival meant having the instruments of the hunt as well as the means to repel the occasional invading bandit or savage. On the supposition that they were the most effective and available weapons, our imagination has provided this American prototype with unrestricted access to firearms. Assisted by visual myth-enhancers, our folklore has etched on our national self-image the lone explorer, trapper, or adventurer, along with the stalwart farmer and family guardian who kept his powder dry and his flintlock well-oiled for regular employment to protect and provide for self, dependents, and neighbors. That image of the eighteenth- or nineteenth-century man—or woman—with the gun continues to exert considerable influence on many twenty-first-century Americans as they expound the meaning of the Second Amendment entitlement to arms.

However well this picture may accord with the history of early American settlers, the legacy of our pioneer heritage transmits a surge of national pride in the virtues of individual enterprise and mutual assistance. These virtues draw nourishment also from a largely unsuspected source far from the supposed—or actual—life of the pioneers spread across the wilderness. A message was heard by American colonists that can be traced to Renaissance Florence and the English revolution of the mid-seventeenth century. Renaissance versions of classical Greek and Roman society were adopted by pamphleteers in John Locke's time, and, nearly a century later, their pamphlets became popular in Revolutionary America. These political tracts extolled the incorruptibly independent citizen-in-arms serving public purposes. The only durable classical republics, these political prophets asserted, were founded on the virtue of the citizen, voluntarily contributing his energy to the common weal and, by his courage and personal armament, assuring the safety of all.[1] Personal arms, in the classical configuration, served community interests of order and stability when the able-bodied amateurs assembled in military ranks as a militia.

Today, when we think of "the militia," we cannot put from our minds the little we know of the small armed bands of libertarians and self-styled patriots. In some ways, today's phantom of the armed pioneer limns the true American patriot as loyal to great quasi-religious principles thought to be the Founders' creed. Emboldened by his proclaimed stance of sturdy independent autonomy, this present-day hero is scornful of the accretions of social enlightenment of the past 200 years and is animated by a hearty distrust of government, which he sees as having betrayed the grand design of the sainted Founders in favor of a debilitating social ethic. The modern militiamen have reinvented personal responsibility and taken upon themselves the basic obligation of defense of body, land, and family against vaguely defined intruders of any stripe—including the forces of government itself. In notable contrast with the classical republican militia, however, today's neo-frontiersmen do not profess to even rudimentary communitarian ideals in taking up arms. They are insular cells of self-righteousness. Among other things, it is the absence of a settled, broad-scale, socially rooted public dimension to their arms-bearing that separates today's armed autonomists from the militia contemplated in the Second Amendment.

Despite his disturbing xenophobia, however, our contemporary militiaman marches to a drumbeat not altogether repugnant to patriotic American values. We do, as a nation, extol the principle of individual responsibility.[2] Indeed, an argument might be made that we have maintained democracy as successfully as we have because of the egalitarian ideals and skeptical attitudes toward authority that derive in part from the colonial and early national experience. While our idea of the frontier has been colored by generations of Hollywood scriptwriters, the legend remains a vital component of contemporary notions of civic courage and individual virtue. And, to the extent that the gun figures in our image of the responsible, liberty-loving, family protector who stands at the center of our cherished self-image today, it cannot be lightly dismissed. Symbols count.

With the resurgence of the militant individualist, interest has been rekindled in the constitutional precept most closely associated with the credo: the Second Amendment. Roused from a peaceful rest alongside its slumbering companion, the Third Amendment (which forbids the government to quarter troops in private homes),[3] the proclaimed right of the individual to keep and bear arms has been stitched like an icon into the center of the banner around which our contemporary frontiersmen rally. Largely ignoring the introductory language: *"A well-regulated Militia being necessary to the security of a free state,"* the individual rights brigade emphasizes the ringing language of the main clause: *"the right of the people to keep and bear Arms, shall not be infringed."*[4] These people see in the provision, engraved in parchment, a recognition of the basic liberty of each individual citizen, in his or her private capacity, to possess lethal weapons without government interference. It is, they claim, an entitlement written into the text of the fundamental civic charter to add a stroke to the definition of the freedom of the individual citizen, a stroke every bit as important as the security against unreasonable searches and seizures or the right not to be forced to cooperate in one's own prosecution.[5]

Opposed to the individualists, another contingent takes the position that the Second Amendment was adopted only to assure the states control over their local militias. Their position was aptly summarized by Laurence Tribe: "The central concern of the Second Amendment's framers was to prevent such federal interferences with the state militias as would permit the establishment of a standing national army and the consequent destruction of local autonomy."[6] This cohort refuses to acknowledge any purpose or effect in the provision to assure individuals the absolute right to keep guns. They argue that the newly liberated colonists, still mistrustful of central government and its standing armies, wrote the Second Amendment into the Bill of Rights out of concern over the powers granted the new federal government in Article 1, Section 8, powers expressly allowing Congress to "call forth the Militia to execute the Laws of the Union, suppress Insurrections and repel Invasions" as well as to organize, arm, and discipline the citizen soldiery. It was not enough that Clause 16 of Section 8 expressly reserves to the states the "Appointment of the Officers" and the "Authority of training the Militia according to the discipline prescribed by Congress." Fearing federal control—even use of state militias against rebellious citizens—anti-federalists insisted on the Second Amendment (so this contingent insists) to make sure Congress would not take away the essential power of the local troops by depriving them of their weapons. This take on the Second Amendment is often labeled the "collectivist" approach by adherents and detractors alike. As will become apparent, we are not insensitive to the primacy accorded to the militia in the phrasing and the explicit purpose of the Second Amendment. But we find ourselves unable to ignore the clear language concerning the "right of the people," or to deem the reference to "the people" to be but an alternate phrasing of "the militia."

THE SUPREME COURT SPEAKS (FAINTLY)

In this raging hermeneutic controversy, the Supreme Court has been, if not silent, strangely Delphic. In recent decades, there have been some stray comments from individual Justices. For example, back in 1974, Justice William O. Douglas had this to say in a dissent:

> A powerful lobby dins into the ears of our citizenry that these gun purchases are constitutional rights protected by the Second Amendment. . . . There is under our decisions no reason why stiff state laws governing the purchase and possession of pistols may not be enacted. . . . There is no reason why all pistols should not be barred to everyone except the police. The leading case is *United States v. Miller*, 307 U.S. 174 [discussed below] upholding a federal law making criminal the shipment in interstate commerce of a sawed-off shotgun. . . . The Second Amendment, it was held, "must be interpreted and applied" with the view of maintaining a "militia. . . ." Critics say that proposals [for gun control] water down the Second Amendment. Our decisions belie that argument, for the Second Amendment, as noted, was designed to keep alive the militia.[7]

In a PBS television interview in 1991, Chief Justice Warren Burger was uncharacteristically outspoken (though his feelings may have messed up his syntax somewhat). He said:

> If I were writing the Bill of Rights now there wouldn't be any such thing as the Second Amendment. . . . This has been the subject of one of the greatest pieces of fraud, I repeat the word "fraud," on the American public by special interest groups that I have ever seen in my lifetime. Now just look at those words. There are only three lines to that amendment. A well regulated militia—if the militia, which was going to be the state army, was going to be well regulated, why shouldn't 16 and 17 and 18 or any other age persons be regulated in the use of arms the way an automobile is regulated? It's got to be registered, that you can't just deal with at will. . . . I don't want to get sued for slander, but I repeat that they [the NRA] have had far too much influence on the Congress of the United States than as a citizen I would like to see—and I am a gun man. I have guns. I've been a hunter ever since I was a boy.[8]

In a concurrence in 1997, Justice Clarence Thomas became the only Justice of the Supreme Court to reject in an opinion the collectivist reading of the Second Amendment, supporting his position by noting that the "growing body of scholarly commentary" favors an individual rights approach.[9]

But apart from these occasional—and individual—comments, the Court as such has spoken only four times on the subject of the Second Amendment.[10] The decisions, *Cruikshank* (1876), *Presser* (1886), *Miller v. Texas* (1894), and *United States v. Miller* (1939), are old, flawed in some respects, and, in the most critical instance (and the most recent), insolubly ambiguous. Yet, until the recent decision in a maverick Texas case called *United States v. Emerson,* federal courts have read the opinions consistently down to the present day.

The single exception to this virtual unanimity upheld a constitutional challenge to a federal gun law.[11] The United States District Court opinion and the opinion of the United States Court of Appeals for the Fifth Circuit are discussed more fully in chapter 9. Apart from the Fifth Circuit, every federal circuit court has relied on *United States v. Miller* at least once in rejecting a Second Amendment challenge to firearms regulations. No fewer than seven circuits have done so since 1995.[12]

The two Supreme Court cases exercising the most influence on lower courts have been the first and last in the series, *United States v. Cruikshank* and *United States v. Miller*. In essence *Cruikshank* teaches that the Second Amendment is not binding on the states, and *United States v. Miller* that the Second Amendment does not invalidate all federal laws prohibiting weapons.

The principal holding of *Cruikshank*—notwithstanding problems discussed below—continues to make sense to today's courts. As written, the Second Amendment protected the military forces of the co-sovereign states against federal encroachment. Regarding the Second Amendment, the *Cruikshank* Court wrote

[t]he right . . . of "bearing arms for a lawful purpose" . . . is not a right granted by the Constitution. Neither is it in any manner dependent upon that instrument for its existence. The second amendment declares that it shall not be infringed; but this, as has been seen, means no more than it shall not be infringed by Congress. This is one of the amendments that has no other effect than to restrict the powers of the national government.[13]

It should probably be noted here (for fuller discussion later) that some scholars, most notably Professor Akhil Amar, have argued that the meaning of the Second Amendment was transformed by the adoption of the Fourteenth Amendment in 1868. They contend that the Framers of this Reconstruction Amendment intended the phrase "privileges and immunities of citizens of the United States" to include the right to keep and bear arms, which was thus explicitly placed beyond "abridgment" by the states. So, they say, in our time, the "privilege" to keep guns and the "immunity" against state regulation thereof supersede the *Cruikshank* doctrine. Moreover, according to Amar, the rebirth of the Second Amendment as an injunction against state action liberated it from its obsolete link to the militia. Thus magically reborn, the Amendment now expressed a personal right designed primarily to protect individuals and informal collectives of recently liberated slaves.

Perhaps a more sensible construction of the incorporationist thesis would hold that the Fourteenth Amendment applied the Second Amendment, intact, against state governments to assure the newly emancipated citizens that their right to serve in, and be protected by an integrated state militia (in those days the militia was still the state's primary law enforcement mechanism), would not be thwarted by any measure adopted by a state government to disqualify people from militia duty on account of race. It is conceivable, after all, that state governments could by selective arms regulation undermine the democratic base of local militias. And to the extent that there is an implicit right to serve, or at least to have an integrated militia, applying the Second Amendment as written against state governments might further that end. But alas, we are still not persuaded. First, by the Reconstruction period, the idea that militia service required the troops to supply their own arms was long out of date. Moreover, as we shall argue in the pages ahead, for all its allure, Amar's case is weak that the majority of drafters and ratifiers of the Fourteenth Amendment intended the privileges and immunities clause to apply the Bill of Rights (and thus the Second Amendment) against the states.

Moreover, if there was genuine concern among the Framers of the Reconstruction Amendments that a racially integrated militia could be subverted by exclusion of black citizens, the place one would expect to see the proscriptive provision is not the Fourteenth Amendment. Nineteenth-century political thought distinguished between mere civil rights and higher order political rights, to which only full political citizens were entitled. Emblematic of the latter class of rights were voting, office holding, and militia service.[14] Hence, the Fifteenth Amendment, adopted in 1870,[15] guaranteeing the right to vote to former slaves and other African American males, rather than the Fourteenth Amendment, which promised to all citizens equal civil status, would have been the more likely vehicle for expansion of the Second Amendment right to arms. But the Fifteenth Amendment, like the Fourteenth, nowhere mentions the right to arms, gravely undermining the argument that the right to participation in the militia was a political right that the Reconstruction amendments intended to guarantee.

Limitation of the prohibition of the Second Amendment to Congress, announced in *Cruikshank,* was restated at the end of the nineteenth century in *Miller v. Texas,*[16] the third in the series of the Supreme Court's four Second Amendment cases. However, both *Cruikshank* and *Miller v. Texas* came down well before the wave of incorporation decisions by which the Supreme Court applied most of the rights enumerated in the Bill of Rights against the states.[17] In fact, *Miller v. Texas,* like *Cruikshank,* is archetypically pre-incorporationist in tone and style, relying on the now obsolete *Baron v. Baltimore*[18] and *Slaughter-House*[19] cases. One might, therefore, be inclined to ask whether *Cruikshank*'s holding that the Second Amendment does not bind the states, coming at the end of the Reconstruction period, survives the incorporation of most of the Bill of Rights over the course of the twentieth century. But the Supreme Court early and repeatedly rejected the Privileges and Immunities Clause as the vehicle by which to bring all the provisions of the Bill of Rights to the states. Insofar as they are enforceable against the states, they are incorporated in the Due Process Clause of the Fourteenth Amendment. Considering the provisions of the Bill of Rights one at a time pursuant to this policy of "selective incorporation,"[20] no federal court—much less the Supreme Court—has yet thought the provisions of the Second Amendment binding on the states. Thus, it is fair to say that *Cruikshank*—dated as its jurisprudence may seem—has not been overturned by implication through the general triumph of incorporation. Indeed, modern cases state forthrightly that *Cruikshank*'s Second Amendment holding is still the law of the land.[21]

The Second Amendment's right to keep and bear arms is not unique among the rights enumerated in the first eight Amendments; there are three others not binding upon the states.[22] But inasmuch as the Second Amendment addresses the powers of the U.S. Congress expressly to assure the "security of a free state," we do see it as symptomatic of a peculiar concern with federalism. This concern distinguishes the constitutional right to arms from the many aspects of the Bill of Rights that have been applied against the states. Unlike the First,[23] Fourth,[24] Fifth,[25] Sixth,[26] Eighth,[27] and possibly even the Seventh[28] Amendment guarantees of personal liberties, the Second Amendment is aimed directly at preserving the balance of powers between federal and state governments. As such, it lacks a private liberty component that could be applied as a limit to state action against individuals coterminous with the limit on federal action originally enshrined by the Framers.

We want to emphasize that the Second Amendment not only was not, and was not intended to be, but could not have been plausibly applied to the states as most of its fellow Amendments were. The importance of the point is obvious. Indeed, to us, it appears the whole of our thesis is wonderfully encapsulated, like DNA, in this molecular point. For if the Second Amendment as written[29] was really about the right of individual people to have guns, it would essentially be kin to the rights to speak and pray, to be secure in private spaces, to decline to furnish self-inculpatory evidence, to have a lawyer and a fair trial, and the rest. There would be no reason not to apply such a right against states so that state governments could not interfere with this basic right any more than the federal government can. That's the whole point of the due process incorporation process. But the Second Amendment is not, at heart, about personal rights independent of militia obligations, and the passage of the Fourteenth Amendment could not have rewritten it *sub silentio*. As originally adopted, and as it came through the constitutional upheaval of the Reconstruction period, the Second Amendment is about the federal relationships of states to the nation that contains them. The Amendment expresses the deep concern of many of the founding generation that, under the main body of the new Constitution, the central government would be empowered to weaken the capacity of the state governments to protect their citizens by military force—even against the forces of the central government itself, if that extremity became necessary. Following the War of Secession, there simply was no manifest desire outside the radical wing of the Republican Party to protect the strength and universality of the state militia by prohibiting state abridgment of the right to carry arms in the service of the state governments. Thus, despite its date, *Cruikshank* has rightly remained the law of the land.

Legally irrelevant, but morally more vexing than *Cruikshank*'s preincorporation vintage, is the fact that the case worked a shameful perversion of justice which should rightly place it alongside *Dred Scott* in the annals of judicial infamy.[30] *Cruikshank* affirmed a federal circuit court order arresting judgment upon a jury verdict convicting six of several thousand members of the "White League" (a.k.a. the Ku Klux Klan) who in April 1873 banded together in disguise, in violation of the Enforcement Act of 1870, to prevent black citizens from voting and to punish blacks for appearing at the polls and for carrying arms to protect themselves. The activities of the White League that led to the prosecution of Cruikshank climaxed in the Colfax Massacre in which several hundred black people were murdered by the Klan, which was then in the process of "redeeming" Louisiana from Reconstruction rule.[31] *Cruikshank* had been the only successful federal prosecution in the wake of the atrocities, and by arresting judgment in the case, the United States Supreme Court precluded punishment for the massacre.

Of perhaps partially redeeming value, *Cruikshank*—while steeped in the formalism characteristic of the age of pedantic pleading—is still cited for the nobler proposition that due process requires an indictment to set forth with particularity and factual specificity each element of an offense with which a defendant is charged.[32] This is no trivial requirement in the criminal process. Particularity in pleading not only gives the accused clear notice of the charge against which he or she must defend, but it holds the prosecution to the accusation initially brought. Though the principle is grand—and the decision is honored for it—in truth, this aspect of *Cruikshank* reflects less a liberal Court's concern for the trial rights of defendants than a reactionary Court's desire to put the breaks on radical Reconstruction's expansion of civil rights for former slaves and other human citizens.[33]

If *Cruikshank*—its dubious provenance notwithstanding—remains readily understandable purely as Second Amendment precedent, *United States v. Miller* is more problematic from the standpoint of Second Amendment doctrine. The single critical sentence in that decision reads as follows:

> In the absence of any evidence tending to show that possession or use of a "shotgun having a barrel of less than eighteen inches in length" at this time has some reasonable relationship to the preservation or efficiency of a well regulated militia, we cannot say that the Second Amendment guarantees the right to keep and bear such an instrument.[34]

It is read by the individual rights advocates as saying that the weapon in question, a sawed-off shotgun, could be proscribed only because it was not the sort of gun likely to be among the ordnance of a militia.[35] This reading suggests that other types of weapons—handguns, rifles, assault guns, even rocket launchers, and machine guns—are immune from government regulation. Recently, however, a panel of the United States Court of Appeals for the Third Circuit joined the virtually unanimous consensus,[36] affirming that *United States v. Miller* affords no Second Amendment protection to possession of weapons of colorable military description absent proof of lawful use in the legitimate militia. In that case, Judge Sloviter wrote, "However clear the [*Miller*] Court's suggestion that the firearm before it lacked the necessary military character, it did not state that such character alone would be sufficient to secure Second Amendment protection. In fact the *Miller* Court assigned no special importance to the character of the weapon itself, but instead demanded a reasonable relationship between its 'possession or use' and militia-related activity."[37] The maverick *Emerson* case remains the only exception.

Those taking the opposing position read the same language from the *Miller* opinion as confirming the inescapable connection between the right to have arms and the purposes of a collective, lawfully established militia. These people say, in effect, that the proclamation of the major clause of the Second Amendment is dependent on its service to the minor.[38] The unfortunate ambiguity in the holding of *United States v. Miller* is, to some extent, relieved by the Court's recognition in the same opinion that "the obvious purpose" of the Second Amendment is "to assure the continuation and render possible the effectiveness of . . . state militias." The Amendment, the Court wrote, "must be interpreted and applied with that end in view."[39] To many (among them, as we have seen, Justice William O. Douglas), the import of this sentence is plain: The Second Amendment should be interpreted to promote its articulated purpose in assuring the effectiveness of the militia.

Between *Cruikshank* and *United States v. Miller,* the Supreme Court handed down two other Second Amendment opinions. In 1886, the Court produced *Presser v. Illinois,*[40] which one writer has called the most important decision on the Second Amendment.[41] There, the Supreme Court considered constitutional challenges to the Militia Code of Illinois. The case arose from a criminal charge brought under a portion of the Code prohibiting men from "associat[ing] themselves together in a[ny] military company" other than the regularly constituted state militia, or from drilling or parading without permission of the Governor.[42] In upholding Hermann Presser's conviction for leading an armed parade of his Lehr und Wehr Verein[43] through the streets of Chicago without leave from the Governor, the Court made clear that the Second Amendment does not sanctify wholly private militia operating without state license or authority.[44]

The *Presser* decision is the best reasoned of the Supreme Court's Second Amendment cases. But unfortunately for purposes of the present controversy, *Presser* addresses Second Amendment considerations only tangentially. The *Presser* opinion is devoted chiefly to rejecting well thought out (if misplaced) preemption and supremacy arguments by appellant's co-counsel, Lyman Trumbull. The former Senate Judiciary Chairman and moderate Republican leader during Reconstruction[45] maintained that the entire Militia Code of Illinois, consisting largely of the Illinois Militia Act of 1879, was unconstitutional. According to Trumbull, the Illinois Code allowed an organized state militia of no more than 8,000 men, but the federal Militia Act of 1792, by which Congress occupied the field in respect to militia organization, actually required the states to maintain general or common militias, consisting of the entire non-exempted military-aged male population.[46] Because the state act was incompatible with federal law, Trumbull insisted, it must give way in the face of the Supremacy Clause.[47] The Supreme Court, however, invoking the doctrine of severability, held that the only provisions of the code relevant to Presser's indictment — namely those barring armed parades by unlicensed bodies without gubernatorial permission — were clearly constitutional; the Justices therefore declined to pass on the constitutionality of the rest of the state militia code.[48]

Insofar as the Second Amendment was concerned, the *Presser* Court reaffirmed *Cruikshank,* stating that the Amendment restrained only congressional action. The Court also stated that, while Article 1, Section 8, of the Constitution empowered Congress to organize, arm, and discipline (as well as "call forth") the militia, the right to serve in the state militia was a creature of state law, and not a privilege and immunity of national citizenship.

In what appears to be a departure from consistency, the Court expressed the dictum that, in the interests of preserving public security, the states were prohibited from weakening the federal authority by prohibiting the people from keeping arms. It was an aside, to be sure, but any acknowledgment of constitutional restraint upon the states certainly conflicts with the declared exemption of states from the Second Amendment's prohibition of congressional infringement. What the Court actually said in *Presser* was that, because "all citizens capable of bearing arms constitute the reserve military force or reserve militia of the United States as well as the States," the states cannot prohibit the people from keeping and bearing arms "so as to deprive the United States of their rightful resource for maintaining the public security, and disable the people from performing their duty to the general government."[49] In other words, by disarming their people, the states would not only weaken their own military units, but necessarily and by the same stroke weaken federal authority to call out and rely on (state) militia as well, and this they may not do.

The Court attempted to resolve the apparent conflict with *Cruikshank* by stating that the prohibition on state-ordered disarmament of the federal militia reserve did not derive from the Second and Fourteenth Amendments. Instead, it reflected what the Court called "the prerogative of the general government, as well as its general powers" respecting the "reserve militia of the United States." The Court thus invoked the doctrine of federal supremacy[50] attached to the "calling forth" and "providing for" powers belonging to the federal government under Article 1, Section 8, of the Constitution to imply a prohibition against state interference with arms bearing in the militia when called forth into federal service.[51] This implicit "right" of the people to keep and bear arms derived from Article 1 is enforceable against the states, therefore, at the instance of the United States under the Supremacy clause rather than on the complaint of individual citizens under the Second Amendment. *Presser* does not apply the individual right of citizens to bear arms against the states; it only assures that federal interests will not be subverted by state action. And, of course, the decision had no application outside the context of militia service. To the Supreme Court,[52] as well as to Lyman Trumbull,[53] the right to arms protected both the local interests of the states and the federal interests of the nation by enabling a self-armed militia, but served no private purposes whatever.

The other Supreme Court case touching the Second Amendment is the other *Miller* case, *Miller v. Texas*,[54] in which the Court dismissed a Second Amendment claim for want of jurisdiction and lack of a federal question. Beyond refusing to apply the Second and Fourth Amendments against state courts ("it is well settled that the restrictions of these amendments operate only upon the Federal power, and have no reference whatever to proceedings in state courts"),[55] Justice Brown's 1894 opinion says nothing at all about the scope of the Second Amendment protection of the right to bear arms.

In addition to this familiar four, the Supreme Court indirectly expressed an opinion on the subject in a comparatively recent case. In 1995, the Court decided *United States v. Lopez*,[56] appraising the constitutionality under the Commerce Clause (Article I, Section 8, Clause 3 of the Constitution) of the Gun Free School Zones Act of 1990, which outlawed carrying a gun on school property. The decision has been celebrated by scholars as the opening move of the Court's postmodern campaign to revitalize the federal structure of our government by considering critically the too-ready — and, in the past six or seven decades, virtually unchallenged — invocation by Congress of its power to regulate interstate commerce. The Court struck down the antigun statute for failure to articulate any tenable relationship between gun possession in school zones and commerce among the states. Only the reach of the Commerce Clause is discussed by the Court — not a word about the Second Amendment. In a brief dissenting opinion in *Lopez*, Justice Stevens wrote:

> Guns are both articles of commerce and articles that can be used to restrain commerce. Their possession is the consequence, either directly or indirectly, of commercial activity. In my judgment, Congress' power to regulate commerce in firearms includes the power to prohibit possession of guns at any location because of their potential harmful use.[57]

Clearly, Justice Stevens assumes that gun possession lacks any constitutional protection that might render gun prohibition by Congress void — or at least suspect. Similarly, the *Lopez* majority's analysis of the Gun Free School Zone Act implicitly rejected suggestions by a group styling itself "Academics for the Second Amendment *et al.*" who submitted a brief as a "friend of the Court." They urged that the statute be invalidated as a violation of the Second Amendment. So, strongly implicit in these aspects of the decision is the assumption of both majority and dissenter that the Second Amendment is not concerned with gun restrictions enacted by Congress. More importantly, the majority appraisal of the statute under the Commerce Clause assumes federal power to regulate traffic in guns actually in interstate commerce, and this assumption strongly implies that gun trafficking and carrying as such is not a constitutionally protected activity.

A CLOSER LOOK AT TEXT AND OUR EMERGING HYPOTHESIS

The issues joined in the Supreme Court cases, if not well known to more doctrinaire polemicists, have been thoroughly expounded in the growing academic literature on the subject. It is not our intention to provide a comprehensive, critical review of the positions and arguments of all those who have preceded us into the fray, and of the many lower court decisions they cite. We will (in chapter 8) have a fairly close look at the arguments of a few scholars and some of the authorities they rely upon, and (in chapter 9) we will discuss the notorious *Emerson* case. But principally, we mean to submit an interpretation of the Second Amendment less often heard, and to summon textual and historical analysis that we find more persuasive than that offered by most of the protagonists.

In a kernel, the hypothesis we shall advance is this: the Second Amendment cannot be read as a simple guarantee to the states that they will be able to maintain armed troops subject to their command despite what Article 1, Section 8, might appear to say to the contrary. Such a reservation to the states of power not expressly granted to the federal government, if such there were, would more likely be found in the Tenth Amendment (which states just that).[58] From the text as well as a fair understanding of the contemporary ethic regarding arms and liberty, it seems to us overwhelmingly evident that the principal purpose of the Amendment was to secure a personal, individual entitlement to the possession and use of arms. We cannot, however, (as the individual rights contingent generally does) disregard entirely the first part of the text proclaiming a well-regulated militia necessary to the security of a free state. The question becomes, then, how does the introductory phrase effect the scope of the individual right to arms secured in the language of the main clause of the Amendment?

Here, as a matter of textual analysis, we regard it as highly significant that of the several great entitlements enunciated in the first eight Amendments, no other is hedged by a conditional or explanative clause.[59] The Founders could have said, introducing the First Amendment, for example, that free communication being essential to the intelligent exercise of the franchise, Congress shall make no law, etc. If they had, the gloss might have had a different sheen; laws restricting artistic expression, commercial speech, or other communication unrelated to voting might have been tolerated. But they didn't. They could have written in the Fifth that torture being inimical to the dignity of man, and likely to induce false confessions, no one shall be compelled to be a witness against himself.[60] But they didn't. So too, introductory clauses might have altered the impact of the single provision of the Fourth Amendment or the several of the Sixth. The unconditional rights announced in the First, Fourth, Fifth, and Sixth Amendments might then have been construed considerably less generously.

Despite the fact (as Professor Volokh has reminded us[61]) that numerous state constitutions employed introductory provisions, the Second Amendment remains unique among the federal Bill of Rights. In the light of this distinctive introductory language, we understand the Second Amendment as though it read like this: *Inasmuch as a well-regulated Militia shall be necessary to the security of a free state and so long as privately held arms shall be essential to the maintenance thereof, the right of the people to keep and bear such arms shall not be infringed.* By this paraphrase, we part company from the most devoted of the individual rights advocates. The immutable point of difference is that, to us, the language of the Amendment can not support a right to personal weaponry independent of the social value of a regulated organization of armed citizens notwithstanding comments in other contexts by some of the Founders regarding guns and the ideal of personal responsibility.

A BRIEF VISIT TO THE FOUNDERS

To be sure, more than a few utterances by leading figures of the Revolutionary and Constitutional period do endorse shooting and gun possession as tokens of robust and independent character. Perhaps the most cited dictum comes from the quill of none other than Thomas Jefferson, advising his fifteen-year-old nephew of the value of sport shooting for building character:

> A strong body makes the mind strong. As to species of exercises, I advise the gun. While this gives a moderate exercise to the Body, it gives boldness, enterprise and independence to the mind. Games played with the ball, and others of that nature, are too violent for the body and stamp no character on the mind. Let your gun therefore be the constant companion of your walks.[62]

Jefferson's homily, dispatched from Paris in 1785, reveals as much about the eighteenth-century English-speaking aristocracy's distaste for rowdy and plebeian soccer as it does about his constitutionalism. The cultural importance of sport as an enforcer of image and status in late colonial and early national Virginia should not be overlooked. To the Anglican gentry, soccer and cricket were esteemed rather less loathsome than brawling and cockfighting, but were still considered unfit for gentlemen, who preferred riding to hounds, shooting, fowling, (lawn) bowling, croquet, horse racing, and boxing, the later two, incidentally, only in a sponsorship and wagering capacity, with the fisticuffs and jockeying typically left to champion slaves.[63]

Although in this letter, Jefferson was obviously endorsing shooting as an attribute of manly and genteel character, he had earlier been one of the few political leaders of the Revolutionary generation (Samuel Adams was another[64]) to discuss weapons possession outside the context of sport, even labeling guns property worthy of constitutional protection. In Jefferson's 1776 draft Constitution for Virginia, he proposed that "no free man be debarred the use of arms in his own lands or tenements."[65] This proposition, radical as it was, perhaps represented a retreat from an earlier version of the proposed fundamental law for Virginia, which would have guaranteed an unqualified proclamation that no "freeman be debarred the use of arms."[66] Such a right would have extended, presumably, to public, common, and unclaimed lands as well as private property. Neither submission became law in the Old Dominion, a fate shared by a number of other radical provisions of Jefferson's draft constitutions, including a clause guaranteeing fifty-acre land grants to every person not otherwise entitled to vote,[67] thereby elevating the general populace into the propertied electorate, rather than debasing electoral qualifications to the meanest level of the commonest man.[68]

Jefferson's early radicalism respecting constitutional entitlements to gun possession went the way of his land redistribution and emancipation schemes.[69] By the time of the famous avuncular letter, Jefferson's praise of firearms was no longer articulated on constitutional grounds. Two years later, writing Madison from Paris with advice on the desirability of the proposed federal Bill of Rights, Jefferson spoke exclusively of protecting a right against standing armies, and made no mention of arms or weapons at all.[70]

Indeed, save for Jefferson's failed 1776 proposals, and an amendment put forward by Samuel Adams at the Massachusetts Ratifying Convention in 1787 but rejected by that body, we know of no endorsements of private arms possession made by leading figures of the revolutionary generation in the context of drafting or interpreting the Constitution, the Second Amendment, militia legislation, or related state constitutional provisions.[71] Exhortations lauding the virtues of gunmanship, including Jefferson's to his nephew, were invariably made without any reference to legal sanction or other establishment of right.

For Jefferson's peers on the political stage, arms-related discourse in a legislative context focused on securing or organizing the militia rather than protecting a private right to own guns for recreational or other personal purposes. The most telling collateral utterance relating to the language of the Second Amendment is doubtless the Militia Act of 1792. Passed by Congress only one year after the Amendment's ratification, the Militia Act fleshed out the right to arms described in the Amendment. It provided

> That every citizen so enrolled [in the militia] and notified, shall, within six months thereafter, provide himself with a good musket or firelock, a sufficient bayonet and belt, two spare flints, and a knapsack, a pouch with a box therein to contain not less than twenty-four cartridges, suited to the bore of his musket or firelock, each cartridge to contain a proper quantity of powder and ball: or with a good rifle, knapsack, shot-pouch and powder-horn, twenty balls suited to the bore of his rifle, and a quarter of a pound of powder; and shall appear, so armed, accoutered and provided, when called out to exercise, or into service, except, that when called out on company days to exercise only, he may appear without a knapsack.[72]

This statute, the light it sheds on the Second Amendment, and its singular importance to the evolution of the militia are analyzed in detail in the pages ahead. But for now, it is sufficient to compare the language in the statute to that in Jefferson's familial counsel. The statute reflects the military reference of the Framers'obligation-focused "rights talk" in the Second Amendment, while Jefferson's aphorisms on the salubrious nature of shooting not only lack a military reference, but pivotally remain wholly apolitical, extralegal, and unconcerned with rights.

Indeed, it is worth remarking that, unlike the Framers of the Second Amendment, Jefferson spoke not of *bearing arms,* but simply of *a gun* being his nephew's "constant companion [on his] walks." By contrast, the Second Amendment speaks not of *guns,* but of *the right to keep and bear arms.* In late-eighteenth-century parlance, *bearing arms* was a term of art with an obvious military and legal connotation. "Carrying a gun" lacks the implication of *bearing arms* and, of course, the Constitution nowhere mentions a "right to carry a gun."[73] As a review of the Library of Congress's data base of congressional proceedings in the revolutionary and early national periods reveals, the thirty uses of "bear arms" and "bearing arms" in bills, statutes, and debates of the Continental, Confederation, and United States' Congresses between 1774 and 1821 invariably occur in a context exclusively focused on the army or the militia.[74]

State supreme courts had several opportunities during the antebellum years to assess the meaning of the phrase "keep and bear arms" in state constitutional provisions similar in form and words to the federal Second Amendment. For example, interpreting a provision of the Tennessee Constitution that then declared, "The free white men of this state have a right to keep and bear arms for their common defence," Tennessee's highest court wrote:

> Every free white man may *keep and bear arms*. But to keep and bear arms for what? If the history of the subject had left in doubt the object for which the right is secured, the *words* that are employed must completely remove that doubt. It is declared that they may keep and *bear* arms for the common defence. The word "common" here used, means according to Webster; 1. Belonging equally to more than one, or to many indefinitely. 2. Belonging to the public. 3. General. 4. Universal. 5. Public. The object then, for which the right of keeping and bearing arms is secured, is the defence of the *public*. The free white men may keep arms to protect the public liberty, to keep in awe those who are in power, and to maintain the supremacy of the laws and the constitution. The words "bear arms" too, have reference to their military use, and were not employed to mean wearing them about the person as part of the dress. As the object for which the right to keep and bear arms is secured, is of a general and public nature, to be exercised by the people in a body, for the *common defence,* so the arms, the right to keep which is secured, are such as are usually employed in civilized warfare, and that constitute the ordinary military equipment.[75]

Tennessee's interpretation reflected long-established usage, not linguistic innovation.[76]

Ignoring the case from Tennessee, proponents of the individual rights cause like to cite a decision from neighboring Kentucky endorsing a broader right to arms. But, as we shall see, that decision was based on state constitutional language quite different from that of the Second Amendment. In 1822, the Court of Appeals of Kentucky got an appeal from a man named Bliss who had been convicted of carrying a concealed weapon, a sword hidden in a cane.[77] The Kentucky law under which Bliss was convicted—and fined the considerable sum of one hundred dollars—forbade any person to "wear a pocket pistol, dirk, large knife, or sword in a cane, concealed as a weapon, unless when travelling on a journey." That statute, Bliss argued, conflicted with a provision of the Constitution of the Commonwealth of Kentucky that provided: "the right of the citizens to bear arms in defense of themselves and the state, shall not be questioned."[78] Reasoning that the statute, while it did not entirely destroy the right preserved in the state constitution, did restrain its full enjoyment, the Kentucky court struck down the law under which Bliss had been fined. In so doing, individualists are fond of pointing out, the Court of Appeals acknowledged a private, state constitutional right for purposes having nothing to do with militia service.[79] We should remark, however, that the Kentuckians' "right to bear arms in defense of themselves and the state" readily lends itself to a broader—and more privatistic—construction than the Second Amendment's with its syntactical linkage to the well-regulated militia. And it is also worth noting that subsequent versions of the Kentucky Constitution preserved the right of citizens to keep and bear arms in defense of themselves as well as the state, but also expressly allowed the legislature to pass gun control laws and statutes banning bowie knives and other vicious blades of the sort that Bliss had carried hidden in his cane.[80]

Some twenty-four years after Mr. Bliss ran afoul of the Kentucky Code, a man named Hawkins Nunn was charged and convicted in the state of Georgia with the high misdemeanor of having and keeping about his person a pistol other than a "horseman's pistol," contrary to state law.[81] Unlike Bliss, Nunn argued that the law under which he was convicted violated not only the constitution of the State of Georgia, but the Second Amendment of the U.S. Constitution as well. Reluctant but unflinching, the Supreme Court of Georgia took on the question of the constitutionality of the law in question under federal precepts. Pronouncing himself fully aware that the Second Amendment, like other 1789 amendments, had been held to be restrictions on the federal government only, Judge Lumpkin nonetheless confessed: "I am inclined to the opinion that the article in question [the Second Amendment] does extend to all judicial tribunals, whether constituted by the Congress of the United States or the States individually." The provision is "general in its nature . . . broad enough to embrace both Federal and State governments."[82]

Judge Lumpkin's expansive understanding of the ambit of Amendment II stands out in the literature, coming as it does decades and a great and tragic war before any higher court began the slow process of "incorporation"—application to state governments of the Bill of Rights, one by one, through the medium of the Due Process Clause of the postwar Fourteenth Amendment—a process that never did reach the Second Amendment. Moreover, in his studied naiveté, Judge Lumpkin makes no direct reference to an opinion of Chief Justice John Marshall thirteen years before. Perhaps he means a nod to it with his vague "I am aware that it has been decided," but he immediately juxtaposes a contrary opinion of the state court. He surely sees no obstacle in such decision to his "inclination" to read the Second Amendment as binding on the states.

The Marshall opinion accorded such light treatment came in a case that considered the question whether the provision of the Fifth Amendment decreeing just compensation for governmental takings of property applies to state governments.[83] A question, the revered Chief thought, "of great importance, but not of much difficulty." The limitations of power expressed in the U.S. Constitution "are naturally, and, we think, necessarily applicable to the government created by the instrument," Marshall wrote. Look to state constitutions, Marshall instructed us, for powers of, and restraints against, state governments. Marshall's opinion in this case, *Barron v. Baltimore,* stood for nearly a century as the definitive federal judgment that the U.S. Bill of Rights bound only Congress and not the legislatures of the states.

The independence of state courts to choose to be bound by provisions of the federal Bill of Rights was not much discussed—nor authoritatively decided—in the first half of the nineteenth century. But it certainly sounds odd to modern ears to hear a judge of a state high court holding that the Second Amendment *seems* to apply to all governments because, by restraining the power of the central government to deprive citizens of their arms, the founding generation did not intend to empower state government to do so. Therefore—

without reference to the state constitution or any express acknowledgment that the Supreme Court of the United States had reached a contrary opinion—the state court employs the federal provision to strike down a state law. Needless to say, the *Nunn* case is much cited by those who share Judge Lumpkin's understanding of the right to keep and bear arms. However, it remains a sport in the jurisprudence of federalism, to say nothing of the judicial literature of the Second Amendment itself. For those who relish oddities, it is a little gem. But for those who seek a coherent doctrine, *Nunn v. Georgia* is a case of no importance whatever.

The most authoritative antebellum analysis of the right to arms emerged not from the chambers of any state supreme court, but from the pen of an eminent Supreme Court Justice and constitutional scholar, Joseph Story. Usefully for our purposes, Justice Story wrote not about state provisions, but about the Second Amendment itself. In his *Commentaries on the Constitution,* Story wrote under his entry on the Second Amendment, that "[t]he right of citizens to keep and bear arms has been justly considered as the palladium of the liberties of a republic; since it offers a strong moral check against the usurpation and arbitrary power of rulers." [84] This description, standing on its own, has become a favorite of individualist interpreters of the Second Amendment. Numerous commentators rely on the just-quoted language to support an argument that Justice Story supported (and in his famous textbook asserted) the principle that individual citizens should have the right to keep weapons for private purposes, the most important of which was to keep the government in check, and, if necessary, to furnish the means for individual defense against a usurpatory and oppressive state. These commentators, including the confident tandem of Don B. Kates and Randy Barnett,[85] badly miss the mark.

Story's much quoted panegyric occurs in the context of a much longer morose lamentation on the failure of the states to enforce militia regulations and the consequent decay of the venerable citizens' militia into disuse and derision. In the same passage so admired by Kates and Barnett, Story goes on to say:

> though . . . the importance of a well regulated militia would seem so undeniable, it cannot be disguised that, among the American people, there is a growing indifference to any system of militia

discipline, and a strong disposition, from a sense of its burthens, to be rid of all regulations. How it is practicable to keep the people duly armed, without some organization, it is difficult to see. There is certainly no small danger that indifference may lead to disgust, and disgust to contempt; and thus gradually undermine all the protection intended by this clause of the national bill of rights."[86]

Thus, despite its pleasant ring, the "palladium of liberties" line cannot be read in isolation to support those who would construe the constitutional clause as establishing a purely private right. Rather, Story's discussion of the Second Amendment treats unambiguously of a liberty to arms existing wholly in the context of the organized, legally established militia.

Story's concern was not that the federal government might seize firearms that citizens held for their own devices. It was that absent a viable and well-regulated militia, necessity would dictate establishment of a large, professional army, and that this army would undermine political liberties. As Story wrote earlier in the same passage "[i]t is against sound policy for a free people to keep up large military establishments and standing armies in time of peace, both from the enormous expenses with which they are attended, and the facile means which they afford to ambitious and unprincipled rulers to subvert the government and trample on the rights of the people." As we shall see in the coming chapters, Story's worries about the dangers of standing armies were firmly rooted in orthodox American political theory stretching back several generations. At the same time, his fears that Americans had lost interest in the virtuous militia of their fathers had become a common lament of the antebellum years.

To return to our central theme, then, the individual right to keep and bear arms that is secured in the Second Amendment in our analysis is a right without application outside the context of service in state or federal militia. As we shall develop more fully in future chapters, the essential military context of the declared right disintegrated as the nation matured. The long decay began in the early years of the Republic when compulsory and universal militia service gave way to the selective, volunteer principle. We will present the historical evidence of the fall of the mythic ideal of the selfless militia-of-the-whole into the proverbial disfavor, disrepute, and desuetude.[87] As we pursue the history of the American militia, we will note that, beginning in 1808, the federal government provided an annual appropriation of $200,000 with which the states could purchase militia arms.[88] By this grant, the national government set off down a long road leading in the early twentieth century to the complete assumption of the responsibility of arming the militia. The federal allocation represented a dramatic reversal of the policy of the Militia Act of 1792, which (it will be recalled) had rested responsibility with the individual able-bodied man.[89] When the Civil War came in 1861, and the nation first confronted the need for mass mobilization under the Constitution, all state enrollees and Volunteer Companies were sworn into federal service, clad in federal uniforms, given federal medical checkups, and paid by the federal paymaster.[90] And after considerable initial confusion regarding the bounds of state and federal authority, all arms used by the 2,666,999 soldiers who served in the Union Armies[91] were procured and issued by the federal government.[92]

ADD A FEW SIGNIFICANT EVENTS
IN THE TWENTIETH CENTURY

The transition out of the Framers' militia system was completed early in the last century, when the Act of 1792, which had never been enforceable, was finally laid to rest, and a more serviceable regime at long last established. In 1903, in the wake of inquiries into the chaos surrounding mobilization of state guard units to fight the Spanish War and suppress the Philippine Insurrection of 1898–1901, Congress acted under pressure from President Theodore Roosevelt to subdivide the by then entirely fictitious militia-of-the-whole into an Active Militia (the National Guard) and Unorganized Militia (the nonenrolled male population between eighteen and forty-five years of age). The Dick Act also standardized state units and equipment and, in return for massive increases in federal funding, the states agreed to accept substantially enhanced federal supervision of militia training.[93]

In 1908, five years after passing the Dick Act, Congress attempted to bypass the problem of the (un)constitutionality of militia service outside the United States that had plagued the President and War Department in the wars of 1812–15, 1846–48, and 1898–1901. Within a few years, however, both the Attorney General and the Judge Advocate General of the Army had written reports finding legislation ostensibly waiving restrictions on extraterritorial deployment of militia unconstitutional,[94] thereby presenting Congress anew with the problem of legally dispatching American reservists for duty on foreign shores.[95]

This issue came to a head during the controversy surrounding the preparedness movement proceeding American entry into the First World War. The bitterly contested National Defense Act of 1916[96] "federalized" the Organized Militia, which was thenceforth known only as the National Guard, and integrated it into the command structure of the War Department and regular army. Upon congressional authorization, the President was empowered to draft guardsmen into federal service for the duration of the emergency specified by Congress, that is, to send guardsmen become soldiers to fight on foreign soil. Thus, in the years before World War I, state militias were integrated into a federally supervised United States Army National Guard, a military organization supplied with standardized, congressionally prescribed arms, purchased with federal funds, and kept in state arsenals that were built to federal specifications and financed increasingly by the national government. By accepting militia funding under the new arrangements, by conforming their units to federal standards, and by agreeing to army supervision, state legislatures acknowledged delegation of the provision of security against foreign enemies to the U.S. Army and the organized reserves, and acquiesced in a new framework of federal relations that allowed the massive mobilization of citizens into soldiers assigned to foreign combat in both world wars.[97]

The amalgamation of militia and army was arrested during the 1920s, but the process of federal integration resumed soon after Franklin Roosevelt entered the White House.[98] In 1933, Congress made the National Guard part of the regular army during peace as well as wartime, justified its administration not under the Militia Clause as theretofore, but under the Army Clause of the Constitution, and erased the word "militia" from the War Department charts, changing the name of the supervisory agency to National Guard Bureau.[99] State adjutant generals and the National Guard lobbyists were able to ensure that state units, which had been dissolved when guardsmen were called up to serve in the Great War, would be kept intact during future conflicts. Pivotally, however, the Act of 1933 imposed upon the states the dual enlistment system that continues in force till this day, whereby guardsmen take simultaneous oaths to serve in their state units and in the regular army when called up to national duty. In the words of Supreme Court Justice John Paul Stevens, "Since 1933 all persons who have enlisted in a State National Guard unit have simultaneously enlisted in the National Guard of the United States. . . . Under the 'dual enlistment' provisions of the statute that have been in effect since 1933, a member of the Guard who is ordered to active duty in the federal service is thereby relieved of his or her status in the State Guard for the entire period of federal service." [100] Thus, although members of the National Guard are now called up to federal duty in the fellowship of their own state brigades and companies, those state Guard units become components of the U.S. Army once called into national service.

Between the world wars, the descendants of the militia lost what small independent identity they retained. Congress delegated to the President power to order Guard units into federal service whenever Congress declared a national emergency, and they authorized troop use in excess of the regular forces. And shortly after World War II, Congress did away with the requirement of the declaration of an emergency, and gave the president blanket authority to call up National Guard units. In the event of overseas service, the call-up remains subject to the consent of the governor of the state whose unit is mobilized,[101] but, as the Supreme Court made clear in 1990, gubernatorial consent cannot be withheld for any reason other than the state's requirement that the unit in question perform vital militia duties at home.[102]

The importance of the organized militia, that is to say, the National Guard, as the nation's principal military reserve, has diminished substantially in the years since World War II. The technical complexity of equipment and tasks required of a thoroughly professionalized modern army, and the deterrent effect of nuclear arsenals, have made a mass war drawing all the manpower reserve of the country increasingly unlikely. The need for a whole nation in arms has — in all likelihood permanently — disappeared. And in the aftermath of Vietnam, conscription has become so unpopular as to border on being politically unfeasible. In this climate, the volunteer principle has again supplanted the draft as the recruiting mechanism for fighting the limited wars which characterize the nuclear age, leaving no shadow of the old militia's universality or compulsory service obligation about today's National Guard.[103]

These historical processes, treated in detail hereafter, have fundamentally changed the militia and the context in which it operates. Taken together, we will argue, historical developments have altered a vital condition for the articulated right to keep and bear arms. While not exactly obsolete, the Second Amendment has become, like the Third, dormant. As it reposes today, it is simply neutral on the power of Congress with regard to gun regulation, and—we maintain—still of no significance on state powers of gun control. It will doze unless or until the conditions of its enactment are revived: until at least one state restores its militia (in some form approaching the original sense of the term), and requires the members to arm themselves. The revival is not likely, but it is not inconceivable.

It might illustrate our position regarding the present recumbent posture of the Second Amendment to imagine a provision of the 1789 Bill of Rights reading as follows: *Commerce within and between the several States being essential to the economy of the Nation, the right of the people to breed and keep horses shall not be infringed.* Should government, at some level that is bound by the provision, enact today a restriction on the number of horses that might be stabled within a designated area, no constitutional challenge would be heard, we will claim, because the right created by the provision had gone into suspension when equine commerce was taken over by the internal combustion engine.

We are proposing that the first clause of the Second Amendment—which cannot be ignored—must be read as a *condition* for the principal clause. And it is significant that—even if rhetoric concerning the virtue of economic self-sufficiency and citizen defense had permeated late-eighteenth-century thinking on this side of the Atlantic—the condition imposed by the text is not: "Self-reliance and the unrestrained access to arms being necessary to the maintenance of personal security, the right of the people to keep and bear arms shall not be infringed." Such a condition, it might be well maintained, would never change and would keep the enunciated right as alive today as it was when enacted. To those who would have it so, we express our regrets but, as they have often said to their gun control opponents, wishing will not make it so. If one side is stuck with one clause, the other is as fully bound to take account of the other.[104]

It should be unnecessary to emphasize that our position says nothing whatever about the legality or wisdom of possessing arms, the types of weapons people may own, or regulation of the manner and purposes of carrying them. We say only that such entitlement or prohibitions as there may be must emanate from a source other than the Second Amendment to the Constitution of the United States. And it is, in our view, entirely fitting that the democratic branch—free of constitutional constraints—should from time to time enact, amend, repeal, and reenact, locally or federally, such rules regarding private access to weapons of various sorts as may seem wise.[105]

In substance, we are merely amending Justice Oliver Wendell Holmes' famous dictum in *Lochner v. New York* that the "Fourteenth Amendment does not enact Mr. Herbert Spencer's *Social Statics*"[106] by adding, "Nor does the Second Amendment enact Mr. Wayne LaPierre's *Guns, Crimes, and Freedom*." As Holmes divorced constitutionalism from social policy, we argue that the Second Amendment should never become a vehicle for judicial imposition of restraints grounded in social theory, however "enlightened." The Second Amendment was intended to prohibit Congress or the President from disarming state militias by disarming their members. Period. It does not encode a general federal policy with regard to gun ownership by which courts may strangle efforts of local legislatures to enact what they deem enlightened social policy.

Perhaps the most difficult component of our argument will be neither the linguistic nor the historical but the theoretical: how do changing times affect the meaning of ancient texts? Here, eschewing the modern, pragmatic Posner,[107] we come closer to Justice Scalia's position that the original intention of the Framers, inferred from text according to a hypothetical contemporary understanding, should govern as long as and insofar as critical assumed underlying social and technological factors remain fundamentally unchanged.[108] Since most such things evolve in some respects, what constitutes an unchanged *critical* factor is obviously a matter of judgment. But it does seem clear that a provision relating to horses enacted in an era of exclusively horse-powered land transportation loses its force when the mode of commerce is utterly altered. To this general theory of construction, we would add that an express recognition in the governing text of the dependence of a right on a particular social condition makes our interpretive model considerably easier to apply.

2

The Militia Ideal in the American Revolutionary Era

ORIGINS OF THE TEXT

Many have been baffled by the language of the single sentence that is the Second Amendment. Just what should we make of the odd—indeed unique—preamble, the language that precedes (but otherwise seems to have no connection to) the ringing declaration of the right to keep and bear arms?[1] To others, the meaning is perfectly clear, though they sharply divide on just what it is. Some emphasize the textual primacy of the militia, and insist that the right to arms belongs exclusively to this constitutionally sanctioned military organization. To these readers, the use of the word "people" in the main clause only restates the prerogatives held collectively by the militia.[2] Still others as vehemently would regard the preamble as nothing but introduction, of no more substantive significance than an indrawn breath before the delivery of the message.[3] And the message, like others in the First, Fourth, Fifth, and Sixth Amendments, is unequivocal: now and forever, in military pursuits and all others, guns are an individual entitlement immune from government curtailment.[4]

To us, however, those academics who profess confusion, along with many who engage in confident dispute, suffer either from reluctance to delve into the ample historical record, or from a highly selective reading of it. Our historical approach is simply this: we take seriously the words chosen by the drafters, and seek their meaning to the ratifying generation. This approach discloses that to the Founders, and indeed to the entire literate polity of new-fledged Americans, the language of the Second Amendment could hardly have been a more felicitous expression of its scope, intent, and purpose. On this record, there seems to us little doubt that the provision protected as an individual right (and in more democratically generous form) the ancient English custom of free, adult citizens to keep and to carry arms, but only in the context and for the advancement of the organized, occasional, communal, military units generally believed to be indispensable to the preservation of political liberty.[5] While recognizing this right, our new democracy firmly rejected the features of the progenitive English Bill of Rights of the seventeenth century that conditioned the right to "have arms" on "station" and loyalty to the Protestant faith.[6]

Commentators writing from the individualist perspective generally take a different view of the Second Amendment. Their reading does not necessarily reject history as a guide to the meaning of eighteenth-century documents. Indeed, many of the individualist writers go beyond the text and evolution of the constitutional provision itself, and call upon a wider range of historical sources including the English Bill of Rights, Blackstone's *Commentaries on the Laws of England,* and Justice Story's *Commentaries on the Constitution.* But writers such as Joyce Lee Malcolm, Don B. Kates, Nelson Lund, and Stephen P. Halbrook typically misread the historical material they rely on, and consistently foist modern, libertarian concepts onto communal Renaissance and Enlightenment constructs which they sever from their natural, historical contexts.[7] These writers have developed an audible voice in law reviews, in the lecture circuits and conference halls, and in trade journals that promote and elaborate their interpretation of history. It has become a self-perpetuating fallacy as the champions of individual rights to arms, joined by advocates and even a judge or two, cite one another and seek to convey their peculiar understanding of the seventeenth- and eighteenth-century history of the right to arms as the "standard model" of Second Amendment scholarship.[8] However, as we will emphasize in the coming chapters, the historical interpretation promoted by this dedicated band of individual rights advocates has been rejected by virtually every historian of recognized stature who has addressed the question.[9]

When it comes to the historical record, the individualists are correct in at least one respect. During the ratification debate, some radical anti-federalists did call for a wider, purely private right to own weapons. But, what the individualists ignore is that—at least outside of New Hampshire[10]—theirs remained distinctly marginal voices.[11] On the other hand, innumerable contemporary utterances, cutting a wide swath across the political spectrum and spanning the full breadth of the nation, support our militia-focused reading of the Second Amendment. For the moment, we choose but one such expression from the Virginia Ratifying Convention. Virginia's recommended constitutional amendments, drafted principally by George Mason and appended to its vote of ratification, include language that is virtually identical to the Second Amendment, but more illuminating:

> Seventeenth, that the people have the right to keep and bear arms; that a well regulated militia composed of the body of the people trained to arms is the proper, natural and safe defence of a free state. That standing armies in time of peace are dangerous to liberty, and therefore ought to be avoided, as far as the circumstances and protection of the community will admit; and that in all cases the military should be under strict subordination to and governed by the Civil power.[12]

Like the framers of the Second Amendment two years later, Virginians at the Ratifying Convention imbedded the right to keep and bear arms in a web of related military principles. In this framework, keeping and bearing arms were two intimately linked, mutually dependent duties and entitlements. Robert Shalhope reminds us that "more often than not, [Americans of the Revolutionary generation] considered these rights inseparable."[13] *Bearing* arms implied making muster, equipped and ready for service; *keeping* entailed steady readiness to serve when called to duty.[14] For the founding generation and for near contemporaries, then, the right to keep and bear arms, far more than others enshrined in the Bill of Rights, brooked, tolerated, invited, and even demanded regulation because of its communal and military context.[15] This is what Justice Story had in mind when he reflected, "How it is practical to keep people duly armed without some organization, it is difficult to see."[16]

As the Virginia Ratifying Convention's conjunction makes plain, the right of arms was not therefore an *individual right* in the same sense as the rights expressed in the Fourth, Fifth, Sixth, and even the First

Amendments to the United States Constitution. These are rights the exercise of which protected *personal integrity,* often at the expense of common interests. They reflect distinctly postclassical ideals, rooted in the principles of the common law but accorded a basis in larger political theory only by the individual rights philosophers of the eighteenth century who forged the first modern conceptions of liberal democracy. They owe as much to the Enlightenment as to the Renaissance. In contrast, the "personal" right expressed in the neoclassical language of the Second Amendment was understood by principal draftsman James Madison to serve the interests of the commonweal by buttressing *community security* and reducing the sway of a dangerous, potentially despotic standing army.[17]

The extent that we are today bound by the understanding of our foreparents, and how far the running sands erode or reshape the governing intent of ancient text are perplexing—though ever-engaging —questions.[18] But we think the significance of dramatically altered context two centuries later is especially loud and clear in the case of the Second Amendment because the Framers explicitly stated their social and ideological premise in the same breath as the right they enunciated. Hence, in this chapter we develop the historical argument that the right expressed belonged to the individual, and that it was enumerated among the fundamentals because, in the republican framework of this particular provision, it was deemed a communal bulwark.

To pursue this inquiry into purpose and meaning, we must return to the frame of mind of the people who thought about these questions in late-eighteenth-century America—which, in those exhilarating days of Revolution and constitution making, was very nearly the entire free adult population. Here, we insist that history is important, that text takes meaning from context, and that the Constitution cannot be remade at will to reflect changing sensibilities. At the same time, we step away from the devoted originalism that would bind us to interpretations that make sense only by ignoring the evolution of ideas and institutions. In this familiar quandary, which afflicts all who would garb ancient texts in modern dress, we find ourselves occupying the delicate balance point between the fixed core of original meaning and the shifting surfaces of subsequent developments, between "application" and "interpretation." To us, the important thing (and the trick) is to accord due deference to both demands, and to find a reconciliation between their apparently contradictory injunctions.

We look first to history. Pulitzer and Bancroft Prize winner Gordon Wood (among others) has argued that the prevailing political climate in this epoch among Americans of all classes and conditions was vigorously intellectual and historicist.[19] The American Revolution was, like the framing and adoption of the Constitution, a revolution of ideas.[20] As Wood explained in *The Creation of the American Republic,* the Revolution aimed to restore the honored old ideas of British constitutionalism, while the written Constitution of 1787 framed revolutionary new structures to serve the familiar goals and purposes of the old paradigm.[21]

In this philosophical climate, "militia" and "bearing arms" were pedigreed terms of art, deeply steeped in meaning which was then as intuitively clear as it is now opaque. Both were central constructs in a system of thought with which the revolutionary generation was intimately familiar, and with which many of its representatives were virtually obsessed. This was the intellectual universe of civic humanism or classical republicanism,[22] the political culture that formed the starting point for constitutional debate in late-eighteenth-century America.

Until the late 1950s, most American historians assumed that the constitutional universe of the founding period could be reduced to a recapitulation of Locke's *Second Treatise on Government.* An outpouring of brilliant scholarship during the next two decades amply demonstrated that the constitutionalism of the Founders and Framers had in fact had a rather different predicate. Locke was not a fundamental figure in their political hagiography, and Americans of the constitutional period were far closer to the radical, civic, and communitarian impulses of the English Commonwealth and the Restoration era opposition than to what twentieth-century writers have wrongly styled "Lockean" individualism. These insights became the central tenets of a new republican paradigm, which in great measure determined the course of writing about early American history from the late 1960s into the early 1980s.[23]

Not only did leaders of the American Revolutionary era absorb the radical thought of the interregnum English Commonwealth and the Restoration opposition, they also applied this republican ideology to the constitutional questions of their own time—including the issues of the relationship of liberty to arms and the role of the military in civil society. In the words of Lance Banning,

> No man's thought is altogether free. Men are born into an intellectual universe where some ideas are native and others are difficult to conceive. Sometimes this intellectual universe is so well structured and has so strong a hold that it can virtually determine not only the ways in which a society will express its hopes and discontents but also the central problems with which it will be concerned. In 1789 Americans lived in such a world. The heritage of classical republicanism and English opposition thought, shaped and hardened in the furnace of a great Revolution, left few men free.[24]

The republican ideology that went so far in defining the political world of Revolutionary America rested on a short set of assumptions about the nature of man and the state. Like their Commonwealth and Whig forbears during and after the English Civil War, Americans of the Revolutionary period assumed that public virtue was both the source and goal of any legitimate exercise of public authority. Public virtue implied a common purpose, a dedication that transcended individual interest.[25] Its antithesis was corruption, both individual and constitutional.[26] Individual corruption could take the most obvious and literal form of soliciting or working improper, self-serving influence in government, or it could manifest itself in economic dependence, which sapped the individual of his independent will and ability to make public-minded choices.[27] Constitutional corruption arose from inter-branch imbalances, or from imbalances in power among social orders, which undid the carefully nourished historical stability of the polity.[28]

The vilest engine of constitutional corruption was the standing army and the system of debt, taxation, and executive bureaucracy upon which it depended. Military power in the hands of a professional band of soldiers—whose loyalty to the government was unleavened by personal commitment to the community, the people, or the concerns of local security—was anathema to the ideals of civic virtue. Expensive, disengaged, brutal, and unthinking (and most likely composed of ne'er-do-wells and foreigners into the bargain), the standing army was corruption of the body politic incarnate.[29] The surest antidote to this sort of corruption was reliance on a militia of independent and virtuous freemen who supplied their own arms for the defense of the Republic. In the words of a seventeenth-century pamphleteer, "[T]he only Ancient and true Strength of the Nation [is] the Legal Militia . . . The Militia must, and can never otherwise be than for English Liberty, because else it doth destroy itself; but a standing Force can be for nothing but [royal] Prerogative, by whom it hath its idle living and Subsistence."[30]

In this system of thought, then, privately kept arms and militia were interlocking, central concepts. Early in the evolution of republican ideology, during the sixteenth and seventeenth centuries, they were perhaps the central concepts.[31] However, as time wore on and republican ideology was shaped more and more by English and eventually by American experience, the relative importance of various components of republicanism underwent adjustment. While independent arms possession long retained symbolic and rhetorical significance, by 1787, Madison's "American science of politics"[32] focused more on structural safeguards for republican government (and hence on the dangers of a standing army) than on the character of the individual best suited to prop up a republic (and hence on the linkage of ownership of arms to virtue).

Whether federalist or anti-federalist, American political theory of the Constitutional period no longer relied principally on an ideal of personal arms possession—even if it descended from ideology that did, and even if it still engendered rhetorical flourishes on the virtues of personal arms similar to those which had informed political thought at an earlier time. This sea change in political principle is developed in detail in the next chapter. There, we examine the evolving role of arms possession in republican political theory, from its origins in the Renaissance up until its last flowering in the anti-federalism of the Bill of Rights and the Second Amendment. What emerges is a Second Amendment expressing a constitutional preference for government independent of standing armies rather than a right to arms existing wholly without public or military context.

CIVIC HUMANISM

At least part of the ideology of the American Revolution had its origins in the Italian Renaissance. As J. G. A. Pocock developed the argument some twenty-five years ago, Renaissance statesmen—especially

Machiavelli in Florence—wrestled with renewed conceptions of the inter-relations of politics, history, and human nature.[33] In the Middle Ages, political systems—even history itself—had seemed relatively stable. The same organic interdependence of prince, clergy, nobles, and people characterized all Christendom, forming an ingrained pattern transferred with slight variations from generation to generation. The Renaissance brought a consciousness of change, of evolution, and the consequent appreciation of the inherent instability of society.[34]

In the Italian city-states where the Renaissance first and most brightly flourished, rediscovery of the history of republican Athens and Rome brought with it a grim realization that these once-vigorous republics had vanished over time. Historically conscious Florentines and Venetians bemoaned the inability of the ancient republican institutions to withstand historical change and decay. In crafting their own republican city-states, Renaissance statesmen sought to create some certainty that their political systems might, unlike their classical predecessors, endure.[35] But Machiavelli more than others understood that the new republics too would inevitably decline because the republican virtue upon which republican governance depended was ultimately incapable of resisting corruption.[36] The goal of public policy and statecraft was therefore to stave off individual and political corruption to prolong the life of the republic to the maximum extent possible. This was best achieved in a climate where selfless public service remained the highest ideal. And in this scheme, of course, the highest public purpose was the military defense of the republic itself.[37]

Yet, according to Machiavelli's *Discourses,* defense achieved by granting a powerful magistrate absolute control of a strong standing army was chimerical.[38] Although that power might repel foreign enemies, it surely corrupted the virtue of the citizen. If it buttressed the republic in the short term, it undermined it over the long haul. Propped up by a standing army, government would no longer flow from deliberation and the individual's sense of duty to the commonweal, but from "placemen," office-seekers, and influence peddlers buying and selling favor with the powerful magistracy necessary to administer the vast military establishment. Access to decision-making authority would become purchasable, and decisions would be made to suit private purposes. The military itself would no longer be employed chiefly in necessary defense, but in elaborate foreign campaigning designed to justify expanding its size, influence, and bankroll. The once virtuous and independent-minded republican citizenry would become politically passive and civicly feeble; the republic would go over to absolutism, and the state itself eventually fall to more robust competitors.[39]

In the classical mode then, republican survival was premised largely on a capacity for defense independent of a standing, professional, full-time, state-financed military establishment. Here, at the center of the civic-humanist paradigm, was the arena in which the citizen-soldier could assert his civic virtue in the service of the republic. The ideal of the citizen-soldier was embodied in the legendary General Cincinnatus, who had been called from the plow to the defense of the Roman Republic. To act in the spirit of Cincinnatus in the early Renaissance era required economic independence: one had to have the wherewithal to carry one's own arms in the service of the republic.[40] Hirelings and mercenaries, paid by the state to carry arms that they could not furnish themselves, represented the very antithesis of the classical republican ideal for these professional soldiers acted not from motives of virtue, but merely at the bidding of the powerful.[41] As developed below, this antiarmy ideal passed through Commonwealth ideology and English political pamphlets into the mainstream of American Revolutionary thought.[42]

THE ENGLISH CIVIL WARS AND
THE CLASSICAL REPUBLICANS

Even as sixteenth-century Italian writers celebrated the virtues of classical citizen soldiers, the nations of continental Europe were experiencing a "military revolution"[43] during which the feudal array yielded to the professional army—the very negation of an armed citizenry.[44] But while Renaissance learning spread from Italy to England during the Tudor period, the military revolution did not.[45] In Elizabethan England, physical separation from Europe, reliance on naval defense against foreign powers, and the conjunction of imported neoclassical ideals with native prejudices against professional soldiers helped engender policies favoring modernization of the historic militia rather than creation of a standing army to guard the Protestant state against Catholic invasion or subversion.[46]

The term "militia" did not enter the English language until 1590.[47] However, an institution analogous to the militia existed as a holdover from the pre-Norman customary duty of male subjects of every social rank to appear in arms whenever the Saxon fyrd was summoned to defend king and country, a species of obligation existing quite apart from the separate Anglo-Norman duty to bear arms in the array. In 1558, the first year of Elizabeth's reign, England's system of military obligation was reorganized, with control of the county forces devolving to members of the local gentry thenceforth called county Lord Lieutenants.[48] This localism was jealously guarded against royal control as long as the militia continued to be a politically relevant institution in England. In 1573, legislation created "trained bands" of selected men to serve as the core of the county militia. A full-time force was assembled to meet the threat of the Spanish Armada in 1588, but it disbanded quickly after the crisis, and thereafter the trained bands and county militia served as England's only army apart from a small force of the Queen's Guards.[49]

Elizabeth's successor James I, ruling in both England and Scotland, took little interest in military affairs for their own sake.[50] But James was greatly concerned with expanding English royal prerogative and expounding theories of absolute monarchical powers,[51] and in this atmosphere, the relatively harmonious relations between Crown and Parliament characteristic of England's first "golden age" decayed.[52] As tensions between Crown and Parliament intensified, seventeenth-century English politics were given up to ideological and political struggles, focusing on issues of religion and separation of powers and, after the coronation of Charles I, on questions of military funding, organization, and control.[53]

Quarrels between King and Parliament over military issues began as altercations about strategy in Europe, but soon merged with constitutionally more explosive questions concerning control of the taxing power, the Crown's attempt to rule without Parliament, and the scope of royal power over the religious establishment and dissenting churches.[54] The pacifist James I long succeeded in ignoring parliamentary pressure for direct British intervention to support the Protestant cause in the Thirty Years' War, but by the close of his reign, the King's favorite, Buckingham, was interjecting English expeditionary forces into French campaigns with disastrous results.[55] Upon the accession of Charles I in 1625, the new King made clear his eagerness to involve England more directly in the continental war. But unlike the haphazard naval privateering undertaken with the Crown's blessing through the early stages of the war, raising a large army for action in Europe required that Parliament create new revenue by imposing taxes. Parliamentarians, jurists, scholars, and the educated realm agreed that the King did not enjoy the power of taxation without parliamentary consent. Yet Parliament suspected that voting high taxes to raise an army would leave Charles virtually unchecked in the exercise of those powers and prerogatives he did legitimately wield. If the King secured the revenue his army required, his opponents feared he could dispense with Parliament by dissolving it and not calling a new one. Without Parliament to pass statutes and voice opposition, Charles' critics argued, the door would open to the King's unpopular High Church religious program.[56]

Exasperated by parliamentary intransigence over the right to control taxation and by the tone of Parliament's Petition of Right of 1628, Charles I did indeed decide to circumvent the legislature, calling no Parliament at all from 1629 to 1640.[57] Charles endeavored to finance his personal rule by imposts and excises, forced loans, billeting soldiers contrary to law, and by imposing an unpopular and unsuccessful levy called the ship money, which attempted to requisition from inland cities and counties a cash equivalent to the ships coastal jurisdictions customarily surrendered for royal service.[58] The final failure of this scheme and the King's desire to raise money to put down uprisings by Presbetyrian Covenanters in Scotland and Catholic Confederates in Ireland led to the begrudging convention of the Short and Long Parliaments in 1640. By September 1642, the inability of King and Parliament to settle the "Constitutional Question" over the power of taxation had unleashed the English Civil War.[59]

Political issues that fueled the English Civil War were not resolved during that conflict or in its immediate aftermath. Images forged and questions raised in the mid-seventeenth century long endured in the minds of English-speaking peoples, and almost 150 years later, these familiar civic dilemmas exercised unrivaled influence on the developing ideology behind the American Revolution, Constitution, and Bill of Rights. The allegorical importance of the English Civil War and of republican thought to George Washington is captured nicely by Gary Wills. According to Wills, Washington was heavily influenced by Addison's drama *Cato* (1707), the most popular play in eighteenth-century America. Indeed, Washington is said to have seen it staged over two hundred times, and he cited from it liberally and often. *Cato* can be understood as an allegory on the Civil War, in which Cromwell appeared in the guise of the great Roman Republican who lent the play its name. Addison's message was of the infinitely greater nobility of republicanism to Caesarism, and according to Wills, Washington's retirement from military command, and his refusal to be king, were consciously patterned after *Cato.*[60]

At the heart of England's seventeenth-century quest for constitutional settlement were questions concerning legislative and executive responsibilities and, specifically, the control of armed individuals, the organized militia, and standing armies. The same issues crystallized again in the 1780s, across the Atlantic, in the efforts to forge what became the Second Amendment to the United States Constitution. Yet the English Civil War and the English Commonwealth left a mixed legacy for the Second Amendment's Framers and interpreters.[61]

To begin with, Commonwealth ideology—the republican principles at the heart of the parliamentary cause—developed into the background of accepted political values that Americans on all sides of revolutionary and constitutional politics took for granted.[62] Thus, during the formative period of the American Revolution, whiggish fidelity to the gospels of the English Commonwealth and to the opposition doctrine of the Restoration era amounted to almost the whole of the American political ideology. Central to this line of thinking were the tenets of legislative supremacy, limits over executive power, and suspicion of standing armies.[63] During the "critical period"[64] before ratification of the American Constitution, the "ancient" English rights and liberties characterizing the Commonwealth ideal informed the beliefs of federalists and anti-federalists alike.[65]

Although Americans in the 1780s universally accepted the fundamental principles of Cromwell's parliamentary cause of the 1640s, the lessons of the English Civil War directly touching the army and citizen soldiers were not unambiguous. Cromwell's victorious Parliamentary Force was a republican army in the sense that it comprised civic minded, independent thinking, politically conscious, citizen-soldiers, fighting expressly for the public good of the Commonwealth.[66] However, the New Model Army was also arguably the first modern regular army.[67] Plowmen and artisans rallied to the Good Old Cause[68] for nonmercenary purposes, but they became full-time, highly regimented, professional soldiers, differentiated according to merit and function, not according to birth and station.[69] More even than being in the service of the state, they became, or endeavored to become, the state.[70] Finally, with the paradigmatic passing (or ossification?) of their virtue and revolutionary idealism, they became something that bore a marked and disturbing resemblance to a standing army on the European model,[71] which Americans of the immediate pre-Revolutionary period firmly eschewed.[72]

In addition to the professionalization of Cromwell's army, the militia and the system of its administration became problematic in the aftermath of the war. Under the rule of the major generals, Cromwell organized all England into full-time militia districts, which were regimented, standardized, and supervised to an extent that, with the waning of revolutionary Puritan zeal, seemed oppressive.[73] As Commonwealth gave way to Protectorate and finally to Restoration, Cromwell's one-time secretary, poet John Milton, was not the only one to muse upon the waning of Republican glory.[74] In 1656, James Harrington published his *Commonwealth of Oceana*, the classical republican parable of England and its political culture. He expounded the ideal of the citizen-soldier-statesman, transposed from the Florentine into the English idiom. Harrington's imagination brought forth a militiaman who might never have won the war, but who nonetheless represented the militia's most stoically civic and communitarian principles.[75] This fantasy of the early Cromwellian Commonwealthsman, rather than the living veteran struggling for political accommodation after the war, passed into the pamphlets of later generations of Real Whig English opposition thinkers, and from thence into the Spirit of '76 and, in transfigured form, into the militia mythos of today.[76]

THE SETTLEMENT AND THE BILL OF RIGHTS OF 1689

The English Commonwealth/Protectorate was a military republic, spending as much as ninety percent of government income on the army, navy, and militia.[77] After the death of Oliver Cromwell in 1658, parliamentary and republican leaders proved unable to resurrect a political consensus in favor of either the military establishment or the administrative and revenue mechanisms necessary to sustain that martial system. In the end, the Protectorate collapsed under the combined weight of its military apparatus and its inability to forge a constitutional consensus settling and legitimizing its own continued existence.[78] But Restoration of the monarchy in 1660 only recast the fundamental military/constitutional questions of the day; it did not submerge them. Old Commonwealthsmen and new Whigs soon perceived familiar abuses in Stuart military policy. Criticism of the Crown and the army became widespread in the 1670s; in the next decade "No Standing Army" became — with "No Popery" — the most prominent mantra of opposition politicians and pamphleteers.[79] At length, the country/Whig/opposition joined forces with William of Orange to thwart the Stuart vision of an absolutist Britain and usher in a constitutional monarchy. The English constitutional settlement achieved with the Glorious Revolution of 1688–89 embodied principles that would remain fundamental to the Framers of the American Constitution and Bill of Rights a hundred years later.[80] The accommodation the Convention Parliament reached with William and Mary after the flight of James II (successor to the Restoration king, Charles II) was memorialized in the Declaration of Rights of February 12, 1689. It consisted of two sections: a written catalogue of grievances against the old executive, and a set of stipulations of parliamentary and individual rights that the new monarchs bound themselves to respect.[81]

The Declaration of Rights spoke to the same concerns over maintenance of standing armies and disarmament of the citizen army that prompted passage of the American Second Amendment exactly a century later. The Declaration reflected Whig resentment of the Stuart government's confiscation of arms in opposition strongholds, where the militia could not be expected to side with the Crown in the event of a new civil war. Likewise, it condemned royal establishment, without full parliamentary authorization, of a large professional army composed disproportionately of Irish Catholics and officered by the Crown's Catholic sympathizers, in clear violation of the Test Act of 1661. As critics of the Stuart Court declaimed throughout the 1670s and 1680s, this new army was designed not to protect English security or even to project English interests abroad, but to provide employment for royal favorites and to bully and harass the parliamentary opposition that considered itself the natural defender of the Protestant nation against royal and papal usurpation.[82]

At the center of the first section of the Declaration of Rights was the charge that "the late King James the Second, by the Assistance of divers Evil Counsellors, Judges, and Ministers Employ'd by Him, did endeavor to subvert and extirpate the Protestant religion, and the laws and liberties of th[e] Kingdom."[83] In its indictment of the old monarchy, the Convention complained that the deposed King conspired to violate religious and political liberties by such abusive means:

> Levying Money for and to the Use of the Crown, by Pretence of Prerogative, for other time, and in other manner, than the same was granted by Parliament[,] [Article 4]
>
> Raising and keeping a standing Army within this Kingdom in time of Peace, without consent of Parliament; and Quartering Soldiers contrary to Law[,] [Article 5] and
>
> Causing several good subjects, being Protestants, to be Disarmed, at the same time when papists were both armed and Imployed contrary to Law. [Article 6]

Among the royal concessions demanded by the Convention Parliament in the second section of the Declaration of Rights were stipulations

> That levying of Money for or to the Use of the Crown, by pretence of Prerogative, without Grant of Parliament, for longer time, or in other manner, than the same is or shall be granted, is Illegal[,] [Article 4]
>
> That the raising or keeping a standing Army within the Kingdom in time of Peace, unless it be with Consent of Parliament, is against Law[,] [Article 6] and
>
> That the Subjects which are Protestants, may have Arms for their Defence suitable to their Condition, and as allowed by Law. [Article 7]

With these last three provisions, the Convention secured legal protection for the English polity against royal funding of standing armies by illegal taxes, against royal maintenance of unfunded standing armies during peacetime without parliamentary consent, and against royal disarmament of those subjects that Parliament deemed suited to bearing arms in the militia. In so doing, it constitutionalized the Whig theory of legislative supremacy that had animated anti-army politics throughout the seventeenth century, and effected a major shift in the locus of sovereignty from Crown to Parliament.

As Lois Schwoerer suggests, the crown that William III accepted in 1689 was hence a very different crown from that for which Charles I raised his standard in 1642, for which he lost his head in 1649, and to which his son, Charles II, was restored in 1660.[84]

Although the Convention Parliament could successfully make a bloodless revolution, it could not technically speak with the sovereign's voice under accepted principles of constitutional law.[85] It was a fundamental axiom of the ancient law that only "the King in Parliament" was sovereign over the English people. The Convention, however, had been elected and convened with the throne "vacant" following James' "abdication."[86] It was therefore with a view to legitimacy that an act of the Convention transformed that body into a constitutionally familiar Parliament soon after William and Mary's coronation, and that Parliament then reduced the Settlement embodied in the Declaration to proper statutory form in the Bill of Rights on December 16, 1689.[87] Changes were made in the statutory language specifying the order of succession to the throne, requiring that the monarch be Protestant, clarifying the prohibition on the dispensing power (by which Charles II and James II authorized individuals to disobey the law), and adding a preamble and connectors, but the language regarding standing armies and the right to arms remained identical to that used in the Declaration of February 12.[88] In that form, the right to arms remains established in Britain to this day. It might be noted that from its inception until modern times, the Bill of Rights has never stood in the way of legislation curtailing private ownership and use of arms in the United Kingdom.[89]

The earliest draft of the Declaration of Rights, known as the Heads of Grievances, said more about arms and the militia than the final versions of the Bill of Rights and the Declaration. The Heads of Grievances, reported by a radical-Whig-dominated Commons Committee on Rights on February 2, 1689, ten days before the Declaration passed, included the statement that "the acts concerning the militia are grievous to the subject,"[90] and further circumscribed the right to arms by stipulating that "[i]t is necessary for the public safety, that the subjects, which are Protestants, should provide and keep arms for the common defence, and that arms which have been seized and taken from them be restored."[91]

Recently, much discussion of the Amendments the American Congress proposed in 1789 has focused on these clauses enacted and rejected by the English Convention Parliament in 1689. One argument favored by Joyce Lee Malcolm (and a growing entourage of individualist interpreters of the Second Amendment) concerns the House of Lords' deletion of the just-quoted language from the arms and militia clauses proposed in the Heads of Grievances. Malcolm argues that striking this language—and in particular deleting the "arms for the common defence" clause—demonstrates that the Convention Parliament was concerned not with protection of the militia, but rather with preserving a private, personal, and individual liberty to keep weapons for any purpose whatsoever.[92] Malcolm's analysis dwells heavily on deleted passages; she pays less attention to the meaning of the enacted text. Moreover, Malcolm's argument fails to take account of the legislative context in which the militia-protecting clause was expunged.

The drafting history is enlightening. The original version submitted by the Commons Committee on Rights called for the protection of two sorts of rights: those which were—at least arguably—already established by English law, and those which would require enactment of new statutes to become part of the *corpus juris*. Responding to suggestions made by the Upper House when it reported back its marked-up copy of the Rights Committee's draft, the full House of Commons first classified enumerated rights based on whether or not their establishment required creation of new law, and then voted to strike each and every clause guaranteeing a right not firmly established under existing law.[93] This "shift to the right" eliminated not only the proposed injunction against militia disarmament containing the "common defence" language, but ten other cherished Whig principles as well.[94] It struck from the Declaration all of the radical Whig assertions as to what new laws the new King should accept, and left intact only the "undisputed" and "ancient" rights which King James stood accused of violating and Prince William was asked to acknowledge before accepting the crown. By curtailing the scope of the rights proffered by the radical Whig-dominated Committee on Rights, party managers hoped to render the constitutional Settlement less revolutionary in appearance, and hence more palatable to moderate Whigs, Tories, conservative elements in the House of Lords, and to Prince William himself.[95]

In this light, elimination of the militia clause and the other putative statutory innovations did not reflect the triumph of privatistic individualism, but rather a concession to corporatist traditionalism.

This was common ground alike to Whigs, Tories, aristocrats, gentry, guild members, and craftsmen, all united in resistance to absolutism. At the same time, the deletion of novel assertions of right helped conciliate parliamentary lawyers who opposed the Stuart's extra-legal rule, but desired scrupulously to stay within the bounds of the law as they indicted the old regime.[96]

The plain meaning of the enacted language, like the legislative context from which that language emerged, also undermines Malcolm's reading. True, the Rights Committee version allowed subjects "to have arms for the common defence," while the enacted language allowed subjects arms only for their "defence suitable to their conditions and as allowed by law."[97] But this statutory language patently stops short of conveying an unfettered general license to carry weapons. And insofar as our ultimate concern remains with text that actually became (or codified or memorialized) law, the insertion rather than the deletion is of course the most significant feature of the Lords' amendment. Instead of guaranteeing arms to all who would mobilize for the common defense as the original draft had it, the ultimate Declaration of Rights confirmed merely a right to those defensive arms to which subjects were entitled by virtue of rank or station. The guns contemplated in the Declaration of Rights were intended to defend against plots, uprisings or invasions that threatened social stability, and thus reflected a sense of the common purpose, which was at the same time generally consonant with the particular interests and responsibilities of the privileged classes. The right to arms of 1689 was intended to serve a stabilizing function. As Sir John Lowther, M.P., commented four years later, an unfettered right to arms "savours of the politics to arm the mob, which . . . is not very safe for any government."[98] Even as Lowther was speaking, the Commons voted, 169 to 65, to strike an amendment to the Game Act of 1693 that would have established the very entitlement to hold weapons for private purposes that Malcolm maintains was already written into the Bill of Rights.[99]

Moreover, as adopted in 1689, the provision codifying the right to arms made clear that even the privileged held their guns subject to law. Article 14 of the Bill of Rights not only incorporated all of the restrictive, class-oriented gun and game laws enacted since Parliament first limited the ownership of small firearms by an Act of 1541,[100] it also invited passage of new laws further clarifying and controlling the right to arms, which invitation the new Parliament quickly accepted.[101] Neither the Declaration nor the Bill of Rights, then, created a new universal right to hold weapons without prior parliamentary or customary license.

In any case, in 1789, the Framers of the American Second Amendment chose not to employ the language of the English Bill of Rights regarding the right to "have Arms." James Madison, who had labored so hard to bring about the separation of church and state in Virginia, had no desire to saddle the American Bill of Rights with religious qualifications.[102] Still, it is interesting to reflect that the language of 1689 resonates with the same powerful suspicions of a potentially subversive military establishment that informed the Second Amendment. Not only did the English Bill of Rights warn against the dangers of a standing army, but it complained that under the closet Catholic, James II, the wrong sort of men—unrepublican men, who took their orders from a foreign prince (the "Bishop of Rome," i.e., the Pope) rather than arriving at political decisions independently—had been entrusted with arms ownership for service to the state.[103] If Americans were by 1789 moving slowly away from anti-Catholicism as the touchstone of republicanism,[104] they had hardly abandoned the belief that there were those whose character and political principles fitted or unfitted them for military service or leadership. Nor had they given up entirely the notion that provisions of the constitutional law might serve to optimize the civic virtue of individuals in military service.[105] But as developed in the pages ahead, a large measure of Madison's innovative genius in the organic Constitution is reflected in his reliance on federalism and formal separation of powers rather than constitutional reification of the republican character to preserve the political stability that came from republican military institutions.[106] As we shall see, under the government established by Madison's seven original articles, armed service by Catholics seemed far less dangerous than in Stuart England, not only because Protestantism's enhanced regional and global security made toleration of Catholics inherently less threatening, but because neither of the political branches of the new national government was given the ready ability or impetus to turn a standing army against the nation. Yet unlike Madison, the anti-federalists remained skeptical of any central power, no matter how circumscribed by checks and balances. They insisted that the survival of republican institutions was linked inexorably to the civic character of individuals, and saw in universal militia service not only a safeguard against the monarchic standing army, but affirmation of the republican character upon which the militia ideal was based.[107]

THE OPPOSITION TRADITION
AND ITS AMERICAN RECEPTION

The parliamentary government that emerged in Britain after the accession of George I in 1714 was based on one-party consensus. Nearly every member of Parliament professed himself a Whig and endorsed the Settlement and Bill of Rights of 1689, parliamentary supremacy, Hanoverian rule, and the (parliamentary) union with Scotland of 1707.[108] Consequently, British opposition of the period was mainly extraparliamentary. "Country" opponents of the administrative style pursued at court by a narrow circle of ministers and parliamentarians under the control of Robert Walpole expressed themselves largely by pseudonymous newspaper and pamphlet denunciations of the government. Pamphleteers of this era — most importantly Viscount Bolingbroke and the tandem of John Trenchard and Thomas Gordon — invoked the republican spirit of the past century to serve as a foil to the corrupt, commercial, administrative ethos of the times.[109] While remaining marginal in England, the writings of the "Real Whig"[110] opposition school resurfaced with renewed vigor in America during the 1760s and 1770s.[111] As Bernard Bailyn demonstrated in his compilation, *Pamphlets of the American Revolution,*[112] this opposition dogma of early Hanoverian England, in the form of reprints, recapitulations, and pseudonymous rehashing, became the driving intellectual engine of the American Revolution.[113]

Antipathy to standing armies was a central precept of Trenchard and Gordon's Real Whiggery that resonated well in American ears.[114] According to Bailyn, American colonists "universally agreed"[115] with Trenchard's famous 1697 *Argument, Shewing, that a Standing Army Is Inconsistent with a Free Government. . . .*[116] There, Trenchard set down how "unhappy nations ha[d] lost that precious jewel *liberty* . . . [because] their necessities or indiscretions ha[d] permitted a standing army to be kept amongst them."[117] Indeed, militarism was widely blamed for the collapse of republican government in Venice, Sweden, and Denmark,[118] and militarism was feared as the most likely cause of the demise of republicanism in British America.[119]

Some pamphleteers used the standing army issue as a springboard for individualistic panegyrics on the virtue of provincial militia, and unfavorable comparisons between these stoic rustics and the decayed, shiftless characters who made up Britain's "mercenary" professional army. Thus, in 1773 a "British Bostonian" admonished the home country not to "make the Americans subject to their *slavery.*" "Americans," this Bostonian fumed,

> will not submit *to be* SLAVES, they know the use of the gun, and military art, as well as any of his Majesty's troops at St. James's, and where his Majesty has one soldier, who art in general the refuse of the earth, America can produce fifty, free men, and all volunteers, and raise a more potent army of men in three weeks, than England can in three years.[120]

In a similar vein, but with less certainty and a greater sense of balance, the Welsh-born nonconformist, economist, and moralist Richard Price commented in the aftermath of the American Revolution that

> Free States ought to be bodies of armed *citizens,* well regulated, and well disciplined, and always ready to turn out, when properly called upon, to execute the laws, to quell riots, and to keep the peace. Such, if I am rightly informed, are the citizens of America.[121]

The eighteenth-century republicanism on which the Revolutionaries drew so heavily focused as much on constitutional balance as on the centrality of arms possession to republican character. In eighteenth-century America, republicanism not only served to champion public over private purposes, the ideology also accommodated itself to a collectivist vision of politics. Thus, in 1774, Josiah Quincy, a future signer of the Declaration of Independence, cautioned that "supreme power is ever possessed by those who have arms in their hands and are disciplined to the use of them."[122] As Bailyn writes with a nod to Jefferson's *Summary View of the Rights of British America,* colonists on the eve of independence agreed "absolute danger to liberty lay in the absolute supremacy of 'a veteran army'—in making 'the civil subordinate to the military . . . instead of subjecting the military to the civil powers.' "[123]

Less visionary than Harrington's 1656 treatise *Oceana,* eighteenth-century republicans rehearsed endless object lessons in the demise of actual historical commonwealths that had gone over to corruption and civic passivity.[124] All the while they stressed institutional balance alongside individual virtue as barriers against corruption and absolutism.[125] The standing army remained their arch symbol of a corrupted polity, but this reflected the standing army's tendency to subvert legislative independence as well as its displacement of virtue from the individual. By the middle of the eighteenth century, fear of power, corruption, and the imperial magistracy were eclipsing the independence of the soldier-statesman as principal icons of republicanism in Anglo-American constitutional discourse.[126]

RETHINKING THE PROVINCIAL MILITIA
DURING THE GREAT WAR FOR EMPIRE

One reason behind the changing role of the militia in American political thought is that the militia was itself declining as a military and indeed as a cultural institution in the pre-Revolutionary years.[127] As the frontier receded westward during the first half of the eighteenth century, the danger of Indian attack became ever more remote in the settled, relatively populous eastern counties. By the time of the French and Indian War (1757–64), compulsory militia service proved unenforceable.[128] According to Professor Lawrence Cress, Americans in

> the middle of the eighteenth century . . . no longer considered defense the responsibility of the entire community. . . . The militia had not disappeared, but it had all but lost its military significance, becoming more a reflection of local political relationships and a lingering symbol of the responsibilities as well as the rights of a citizen in a free society.[129]

Not only had the institutional militia decayed in the established colonies, but many, if not most, easterners no longer possessed that familiarity with firearms and marksmanship that frontier existence reputedly instilled in their grandfathers and great-grandfathers.[130] The numbers are in dispute, and it seems likely that Michael Bellesiles has seriously exaggerated the case that few Americans even owned operable guns in the late eighteenth century.[131] Still, as numerous letters from frustrated militia captains to their royal superiors attest, compliance with regulations mandating that militia members maintain government-issued muskets at home proved impossible for many colonists.[132] And with little immediate stake in imperial rivalries between France and Britain, and no sense of peril from France's Indian allies, few eastern farmers of middling means rallied to the royal cause from 1757 to 1763. Those militiamen who made muster tended to vanish when ordered into long campaigns outside the borders of their home colonies.[133] British and provincial authorities soon realized that success against French arms in North America would depend on Regulars[134]—that is, British soldiers—and long-serving colonial volunteers.[135]

George Washington, a militia colonel and wealthy Virginia squire with considerable speculative and patriotic interests at stake in the French and Indian War, was one Anglo-American who shared British sentiments wholeheartedly.[136] Reflecting on militia units under his command during the early stages of the war, he wrote his British commander:

> Militia, you will find, Sir, will never answer your expectation, no dependence is to be placed upon them; They are obstinate and perverse, they are often egged on by the Officers, who lead them to acts of disobedience, and, when they are ordered to certain posts for the security of stores, or the protection of the Inhabitants, will, on a sudden, resolve to leave *them,* and the united vigilance of their officers can not prevent them.[137]

Indeed, Washington was so dispirited by the performance of his own militia, and so impressed by the British Regulars with whom he served in Braddock's ill-fated campaign and afterward, that he could only hope exposure to the Regulars might help transform the Virginia militia into a respectable and efficient fighting force. "Discipline," he wrote optimistically, "is the soul of an army. It makes small numbers formidable; procures success to the weak, and esteem to all; and may, in a manner peculiar to us, who are in the way to be joined to Regulars in a very short time, . . . [set us apart] from other Provincials."[138]

The French and Indian War ended successfully for Washington and the Americans, with the Treaty of Paris in 1763 securing British sovereignty in Canada and, in the process, severing the connections between hostile frontier Indians and their French allies and arms suppliers. But in the years after the war, Anglo-American colonists became restive in the face of Britain's increasingly aggressive American tax enforcement policies — policies that resulted largely from victory over the French and the consequent burdens of policing an enlarged New World empire.[139]

CONSTITUTIONAL CRISIS AND A STANDING ARMY:
THE REPUBLICAN NIGHTMARE BECOMES REALITY

In 1763, the people of the Thirteen Colonies seemed the most contented, patriotic, and British of George III's subjects.[140] But in the victory over France and the completeness of Britain's conquest of North America lay seeds of discontent that ripened into the old Empire's dissolution, consummated only twenty years after the Treaty of Paris in a second treaty of the same name.

At the root of the impending troubles was the problem of war debt. The conflict of 1757–63, the fourth of seven titanic struggles for empire that kept Britain and France at war more years than not between 1697 and 1815, was the most expensive yet.[141] George III, young, headstrong, friendless save for his tutor Bute, and determined to rule as well as reign, confronted at war's end a truly staggering national debt of £122,603,336.[142] To compound the situation, policy considerations favored maintenance of the wartime army rather than demobilization.[143] Policing the Indian frontier in North America, keeping up garrisons in the strategic towns of Halifax, Quebec, and St. Augustine, and sinking the record debt required revenue.

All this put the King's new Prime Minister, George Grenville, desperately to work seeking new sources of income. A wine tax at home irked Members of Parliament and their kin; a cider tax produced riots. Meanwhile, the American colonies were hardly taxed at all, and inhabited by some of the most prosperous and fortunate people on the face of the globe. To the Ministry, it seemed all too obvious that the Americans should help pay for the army that delivered them from the French and protected them from the Indians.[144] The remaining decade of British rule in America was given up to futile efforts to discover an effective formula for imposing and collecting this American contribution to the Exchequery. Little did Grenville know how deeply he and his successors would offend the colonists' sense of constitutional propriety by imposing imperial taxes.

From the American perspective, the various tax schemes of the 1760s and 1770s—the Sugar Act, the Stamp Act, the Townshend Duties, and the Tea Act—presented, with different degrees of vexatiousness, the same series of problems. Principally, the taxes were deemed unprecedented, usurpatory, and, therefore, illegal.[145] To the provincial lawyers, printers, and political agitators destined to lead a revolution, these tax-related issues appeared fundamentally as problems of constitutionalism. The American sense of constitutionalism, moreover, was more historical than legalistic. It focused, as we have seen, on a whiggish interpretation of seventeenth-century British history, and in particular, on the Glorious Revolution, Settlement, and Bill of Rights of 1689.[146] As Britain essayed ever bolder tax collection schemes, Americans came to realize, with more than a little dismay, that the British ministry did not share the Americans' interpretation of the British Constitution. The more Americans stressed the fundamental Whig maxims at the heart of their understanding of the Settlement, the more they realized British officials did not take their whiggery seriously. In particular, Americans came to the grim realization that British officials did not understand that the Bill of Rights should apply in favor of American provincial legislatures in precisely the same manner that it applied to benefit the Parliament at Westminster.[147] And given the Americans' own unwavering commitment to the proposition that the principles of 1689 protected them as well as those other Englishmen across the water, it was a forgone conclusion that ministerial imposition of taxes for the purpose of maintaining an army and servicing a debt would occasion a constitutional crisis.

It would be difficult to overestimate how whiggish Americans were in the closing days of the old Empire. Reprints of Trenchard and Gordon's *Cato's Letters*—those famous republican denunciations of the Walpole government that ran originally in newspapers of the 1720s—appeared in fully forty percent of the public and private libraries in late colonial British North America, then the most literate society in the world.[148] Cato, of course, laid down a precise, analytic description of the eschatology of a republic's demise.[149] And one by one in the 1760s and 1770s, Cato's stepping stones on the road to subversion surfaced before the colonials' horrified eyes. Not only did the Ministry attempt to enforce internal taxes voted by the Westminster

Parliament in which the Americans were not represented, but it dispatched a swarm of revenue officers to serve in hitherto unknown posts, and established incentives for these officials to seize property, cargo, and even ships for sometimes trivial reasons. The Ministry expanded the role of both provincial and Crown executives in local affairs and sought to free royal governors from provincial legislative control by paying their salaries directly from London.[150] When the New York Assembly hesitated to provide funds to compensate property owners for quartering Regulars, the Ministry ordered the Assembly suspended.[151] And when restive locals embarked on a campaign to intimidate royal administrators in Boston—unlike New York, not an established garrison town—the newly established Colonial Office in Whitehall ordered British Regulars to occupy the city.[152]

No aspect of the imperial taxation regime spawned greater resentment than the employment of a standing army to buttress British authority in the unruly colonies. Historically, Americans had not questioned the army's limited presence in the colonies.[153] Smallish coastal garrisons in Savannah and Charleston were welcomed as deterrents against Spanish or Indian raids and even slave insurrection, and the nearby presence of full regiments at St. Augustine afforded both economic advantage and a sense of security.[154] While some residents of New York complained of crassness and bad manners on the part of soldiers in the town's mid-sized garrison, others welcomed the army and navy's trade. Outside the Deep South and New York City, the army was largely unknown, with the bulk of Britain's American strength stationed in scattered posts in the interior, and large garrisons in Canada and the Caribbean. The standing army was distant, and Americans largely assumed the Bill of Rights and parliamentary supremacy would protect them against the sort of militarist abuses associated with the Stuarts.[155] But attitudes changed drastically in the late 1760s as British officials first questioned the applicability of constitutional guarantees to the colonies, and then redeployed substantial western garrisons to New York and Boston to prop up the new customs collection apparatus.[156]

The arrival of four regiments of Regulars in Boston on October 1, 1768, confirmed the worst fears of whiggish patriots. "It is the indefeasible right of subjects," the Boston Town Meeting swiftly resolved, "to be consulted and to give their free consent in person or by representative of their own free election to the raising and keeping a standing army among them; and the inhabitants of this town, being free subjects, have the same right derived from nature and confirmed by the British constitution as well as . . . [their] royal charter; and therefore the raising or keeping a standing army without their consent in person or by representatives of their own free election would be an infringement of their natural, constitutional, and charter rights."[157]

Although doomsayers had long suspected Governor Bernard would seek the aid of troops from nearby Halifax, few were prepared for the initial sense of dismay and alarm that accompanied the sight of British Regulars disembarking in Boston harbor. "To have a standing army!" Andrew Eliot wrote to Thomas Hollis when he first sighted the troop ships on the horizon, "Good God! What can be worse to a people who have tasted the sweets of liberty! Things are come to an unhappy crisis; there will never be that harmony between Great Britain and her colonies that there had been; all confidence is at an end; and the moment there is any blood shed all affection will cease."[158]

As the ubiquitous republican Cato presciently described the events that would come to pass as an antirepublican conspiracy uncoiled, so too did he set forth in his *Letters* precisely what steps to take to stave off subversion and save the republic.[159] These steps, familiar enough to every sentient colonial, were the very steps taken by the first Whigs in the 1680s, when the party of Shaftesbury and Locke rose in resistance to Stuart usurpation, and articulated the fundamentals of whiggery that in American minds formed the bedrock of English constitutionalism.[160]

The course of resistance to tyranny flowed naturally from loyalty to the true Constitution. And in the face of illegal taxation, executive usurpation, and army occupation, the self-evident constitutionalist remedies included refusal of local courts and juries to enforce Crown directives, reassertion of local legislative supremacy, and revival of the local militia.

The presence of the army in its new, alarming role signaled the need to implement resistance according to this familiar Whig paradigm. Colonists most attuned to politics and ideology took the lead in goading less radical countrymen into a heightened state of political awareness and participation. Following the occupation of Boston, agitators and philosophers unleashed a torrent of republican antiarmy pamphlets celebrating the virtues of the provincial citizen militia and denouncing the perceived depravity of the imperial army.[161] The *Jour-*

nal of the Times, syndicated throughout the colonies, furnished a day-by-day account of Massachusetts "under military rule,"[162] and the circulars distributed by Committees of Correspondence consciously hearkened back to the seventeenth century's radical, insurrectionary opposition.[163] But even though revolutionary theorists and pamphleteers pointed the way toward military confrontation, during the first occupation of Boston (1768–1772), demonstrative resistance to Crown authority remained confined largely to political intimidation, tarring and feathering, rioting, and ransacking of houses.[164] A sizable majority of the population remained committed on some level to reconciliation and reestablishment of civilian rule within the theoretical confines of the old order, and local government nowhere crossed over into organized, armed resistance to the established sovereign.[165]

The army withdrew not long after the acquittal of the soldiers tried for the Boston Massacre, and the repeal of the Townshend Duties restored a kind of calm before the storm in the early seventies.[166] But in December 1773, Sons of Liberty dumped the cargo of three British merchantmen into Boston Harbor to protest the Tea Act by which Westminster reasserted its taxing power over the colonies, and Parliament responded quickly with the Boston Port Act (closing the port to trade), the Administration of Justice Act (removing venue to England for criminal trials of Crown officers), the Massachusetts Government Act (vesting legislative and jury functions with the executive), and the Quartering Act (permitting seizure of unoccupied buildings such as empty warehouses to serve as barracks).[167] Troops returned from Halifax to strengthen the garrison at Castle William in the harbor, and others took up quarters in the town itself.[168]

Intercolonial economic resistance to British occupation and policy resumed according to patterns of cooperative non-importation and non-consumption established during the crises over the Stamp Act and the Townshend Duties. But within Massachusetts itself, political resistance via the traditional, constitutional organs of civil government was now defined as illegal, if not treasonous. As appeals to law and reason proved unavailing, the Lockean moment of dissolution of government and the appeal to Heaven loomed ever more likely.

Thus, the Intolerable Acts inspired Massachusetts' General Court and many of the other provincial legislatures to revitalize their colonies' historic militia to serve as constitutional counterweights to the redcoats. Arms were purchased in Europe,[169] militia laws enforced, and training intensified.[170] By the spring of 1775, when General Gage, commander of the British regiments around Boston and Royal Governor of Massachusetts, issued orders to surrender to central storehouses militia arms previously kept in private homes, and authorized the army to confiscate arms not duly turned over to the government, colonial hostility toward ministerial policy had risen to a fever pitch.[171] In March, the army seized gunpowder in Charlestown and cannon in Cambridge without encountering resistance.[172] But shots were fired on April 19, 1775, when provincial militia at Lexington and Concord confronted British Regulars searching for colonial powder stores.[173] By nightfall, over a hundred soldiers and militiamen lay dead and dying.[174] An eight-year war had begun.

THE CONTINENTAL ARMY AND THE MILITIA DURING THE AMERICAN REVOLUTION

Soon after American protest escalated into armed resistance, republican rumination about standing armies clashed with the hard reality of military campaigning. Given his tastes, sentiments, and especially his unsatisfactory experiences with militia units during the French and Indian War, it is hardly surprising that Washington quickly set about forging a regular army upon his appointment as Commander in Chief by the Continental Congress on June 15, 1775.

"Let us have a respectable Army, and such as will be competent to every contingency," the Commanding General pleaded to Congress.[175] While the effort to create a regular army met with considerable hardships through the course of the war, the performance of militia under his command only intensified Washington's determination to mold a European-style professional force under Continental colors.[176] After the American disasters at Long Island and Brandywine during the summer of 1776, Washington informed Congress that if he were "called upon to declare upon Oath, whether the Militia have been most serviceable or hurtful upon the whole; [he] should subscribe to the latter."[177] The General later reflected that

> Regular troops alone are equal to the exigencies of modern war, as well for defence as for offence. . . . No militia will ever acquire the habits necessary to resist a regular force. . . . The Firmness requisite for the real business of fighting is only to be attained by

a constant course of discipline and service. I have never yet been witness to single instance that would justify a different opinion.[178]

Washington's opinions on the militia, while unforgiving, were hardly idiosyncratic. Indeed, the disillusion of military and political leaders with America's historic militia became general and widespread soon after colonial grievances with Britain erupted into war. Consider as an example Alexander Hamilton's retrospective comments on the reputation of the wartime militia expressed in Federalist 25:

> I expect we shall be told that the militia of the country is its natural bulwark, and would be at all times equal to the national defense. This doctrine, in substance, had like to have lost us our independence. It cost millions to the United States that might have been saved. The facts which from our own experience forbid a reliance of this kind are too recent to permit us to be the dupes of such a suggestion. The steady operations of war against a regular and disciplined army can only be successfully conducted by a force of the same kind. . . . The American militia, in the course of the late war, have, by their valor on numerous occasions, erected eternal monuments to their fame; but the bravest of them feel and know that the liberty of their country could not have been established by their efforts alone, however great and valuable they were. War, like most other things, is a science to be acquired and perfected by diligence, by perseverance, by time, and by practice.[179]

As Hamilton hinted, the militia was not quite so consistently useless as Washington had suggested. In the action at Bunker Hill, for instance, volunteer companies formed in anticipation of hostilities acquitted themselves very well. But they were defending fixed positions. What Washington realized from the start of the war was that no American amateurs, not even elite volunteer units who had devoted long hours to training, could successfully engage mainline British Regulars in pitched battle on open fields.[180] Washington did not have sufficient confidence in his Continentals—even after the institution of systematic European-style drill under Inspector General Steuben—to challenge British strength directly with the best of American regular forces.[181] American success depended on surprise, maneuver, an excellent artillery arm, and taking outnumbered British

detachments at a disadvantage. The principal American victories—
Trenton, Princeton, Saratoga, and Yorktown—were all of this pattern. When American infantry units met the main British Army head-
on, as on Long Island or at Brandywine, the result was invariably a
rout. Final victory owed far more to American perseverance, French
assistance, and the loss of British political will than it did to any
mythical prowess of the backwoods militiaman.[182]

The demands of major war for professional armies contradicted
a firmly rooted republican ideology that favored citizen soldiers.
Reality, leaders reluctantly acknowledged, was not consonant with
their own revolutionary rhetoric, which dwelled heavily on the civic
virtue of citizen soldiers and the abuses of British militarism in order
to justify the American cause. Accordingly, the Revolution demanded
some degree of accommodation between political theory and experience.

To compound matters, the pure republicanism that had ushered
colonials toward separation with relative doctrinal ease suffered serious strains as it passed from mere opposition creed into a principle of
majority government. With the war's end, republican ideology necessarily had to become a philosophy of balanced constitutionalism for
peacetime, as much as a theory of individual civic courage best suited
to moments of military crises.[183] It was therefore inevitable that the
role of the man of arms in American political theory would be rewritten as America settled into independence after the second Peace
of Paris.

Washington, of course, did not desire to see the new nation's security staked on the historic militia system that had proven so inadequate
during wartime. "The Jealousies of a standing Army," he wrote, "and
the Evils to be apprehended from one, are remote; and in my judge-
ment, situated and circumstanced as we are, not at all to be dreaded;
but the consequence of wanting one, according to my Ideas, . . . is certain, and inevitable Ruin."[184] But as a leading historian of the United
States Army has aptly commented, "Washington himself could not
base his prescriptions for the future military policy of the United
States solely upon the combat experience of the Revolution." In the
words of Professor Weigley:

> The nature of a permanent American Army was a political issue,
> the decision of which could influence the larger question of the

nature of the United States. A society of free men had grown up in America partly because at the beginning the citizenry had relied on themselves for their own defense. To establish a standing army would be to accept a European import that had been designed in the first place to buttress monarchy. Even if American circumstances minimized any likelihood that an American standing army would promote a despotism, the creation of such an army might nevertheless contribute to a more centralized and more powerful government than many leaders of the Revolution thought wise.[185]

The tension between republican hostility to standing armies and the desire of strong government men for security flared up again and again through the tumultuous 1780s. It was not even tentatively resolved until a new balance was struck with the adoption of the Second Amendment to the United States Constitution.

3

Madisonian Structuralism: The Place of the Militia in the New American Science of Government

The Second Amendment—and the Bill of Rights as a whole—arose in response to anti-federalist fears of powers either vested in or not expressly withheld from the federal government by the Constitutional Convention in 1787. The convention had lodged in Congress and the executive branch substantial authority over both the army and the militia. While the states expressly retained powers to appoint officers of the militia and to conduct training within congressional prescription,[1] to anti-federalists these concessions did not amount to much.[2] The anti-federalists had reason to be apprehensive. Their anxiety was fortified by the recollection of centrist's efforts to consolidate a powerful national army and militia during the "critical period" before 1787. As early as 1783, nationalists in the Confederation Congress and army leaders such as Washington, Knox, and von Steuben directed their attention to the permanent, peacetime organization of the military in the new nation. In April 1783, Congress appointed a committee, which included Hamilton and Madison, to "consider what arrangements it will be proper to make in the different departments with reference to a peace."[3] At the invitation of Hamilton, General Washington consulted his top aides and drew up his "Sentiments on a Peace Establishment."[4] Washington bid for the largest regular force he thought Congress might conceivably authorize, but bowing to political necessity, he based his proposed system of peace-time defense largely on the militia.

The old commanding general argued that "every citizen who enjoys the protection of a free Government, owes not only a proportion of his property, but even his personal services to the defence of it, and consequently that the Citizens of America (with a few legal and official exceptions) from 18 to 50 years of age should be borne on the Militia Rolls." But this was simply his starting point in political theory. His vision of the militia in action was decidedly more "statist"—more authoritarian, more federal, and more professional. He favored twice yearly musters and inspections of the general body, from which would be winnowed the "Van and Flower of the American Forces," a "Continental Militia," patterned after the Continental Army, and held ready for service, "nearly in the same manner the Minute Men formerly were." Washington's Continental Militia would drill two to four weeks per year, wear federal uniforms, and carry standard equipment supplied from state arsenals. By their shining example, Americans would come to think it "universally reputable to bear Arms and disgraceful to decline having a share in the performance of Military duties."[5]

Actually, Washington would have preferred not to rely on militia at all, but hostility to standing armies was too widespread in and out of Congress to make this a realistic possibility. The best he could hope for was that Congress would authorize a small professional army to be supplemented by a federally supervised militia. The Continental Militia Washington envisioned was, however, no ad hoc militia of the whole, and certainly nothing like the self-proclaimed "Michigan militia"[6] of today, but rather an organized, trained, select reserve part-time army of the United States, equipped with standard issue arms. Washington's Continental Militia would have become the United States' first-order reserve, a bulwark on which the nation could depend to maintain order and to mount initial defenses during the early stages of an invasion, giving the government time to deploy the Regulars, and, if needed, raise an expanded wartime army.

Washington's proposal was but the first in a long, unavailing line of efforts to separate out from the universal militia a more efficient and better trained cadre of citizen soldiers for national service. Plans of this type, labeled select militia schemes, quickly (and understandably) aroused the same sort of republican suspicions as proposals favoring standing armies. A few years later, during the ratification debate, the Federal Farmer, one of the most influential anti-federal pamphleteers, summed up the republican argument against select militias as follows:

> These corps, not much unlike regular troops, will ever produce an inattention to the general militia; and the consequence has ever been, and always must be, that the substantial men, having families and property, will generally be without arms, without knowing the use of them, and defenseless; whereas, to preserve liberty, it is essential that the whole body of the people always possess arms, and be taught alike, especially when young, how to use them; nor does it follow from this, that all promiscuously must go into actual service on every occasion. The mind that aims at a select militia, must be influenced by a truly anti-republican principle.[7]

The Confederation Congress never acted on the original select militia plan set forth in Washington's *Sentiments*. However, congressional inaction in this instance probably reflects indifference and inertia as much as principled rejection. In these lax days after the war, when members yearned to return to private life and the affairs of their own state legislatures, quorums seldom assembled at Princeton, Annapolis, or Philadelphia.[8] That the Articles of Confederation prohibited members of Congress from serving any more than three years out of six only accelerated the retreat of the Revolution's leading lights to state and private affairs.[9] Having served his allotted three years, Madison quit Congress for the General Assembly of Virginia in October 1783,[10] and after the energetic Thomas Jefferson left for France in the spring of 1784, Congress accomplished very little of substance for several years. A plan for militia organization suggested by General Steuben was ignored entirely.[11]

Notwithstanding Steuben's and Washington's earlier rebuffs, Henry Knox submitted a "Plan for the General Arrangement of the Militia of the United States" soon after his appointment as Secretary of War by Congress in 1786.[12] More carefully detailed than Washington's *Sentiments,* Knox's *General Arrangement* served for many years as the standard blueprint for reforming the militia by selection. Knox proposed to retain the militia-of-the-whole in theory, but to divide it up into three corps according to age — an advanced corps aged 18–20, a main corps aged 21–45, and a reserve aged 46–59. The advance corps would train six weeks a year, while demands on the main and reserve corps would be less severe, thereby reducing dislocation to families and the economy. The intensive training required of young militiamen allowed Knox to envision eventual abolition of the regular army, thus holding out some hope that arch-republicans might find the plan palatable. But, like Washington's *Sentiments* three years before, Knox's proposal was neglected by Congress during the remaining months of Confederation government.[13] When the new federal government eventually assembled in New York in 1789, it inherited a small regular army of some six hundred men from the old regime, but no national militia system was in place, and administration of state militia remained still an entirely local affair.[14]

THE MILITARY, THE MILITIA, AND THE PHILADELPHIA CONVENTION

As Gordon Wood has recounted in his *Creation of the American Republic,* the men who would frame the Constitution became increasingly certain in the years after the Paris Peace of 1783 that American domestic politics were headed in the wrong direction.[15] They shared with men who would become anti-federalists a perception that Americans had fallen away from the public virtue of the Revolutionary War days. In fact, almost all commentators of the mid 1780s remarked (in archetypally republican fashion) that the nation was given up to luxury, to money-making, even more to money-spending, and to self-service.[16] If there was no general agreement as to who the best sort of people were, there was general agreement that they were no longer in national politics.[17]

In the 1780s, more than ever before or since, the focus of power was on the states, more precisely on the state legislatures, more precisely still on the lower or popular Houses of the state legislatures. The radical state constitutions of the Revolutionary period generally set up weak executives while according wide latitude to the popular branch of the legislature. They sought to prevent the propertied and commercial classes from concentrating greater influence than their numbers alone justified in lawmaking, appointments, and administration. The "failure" of these post-Revolutionary state governments was illustrated most dramatically by Massachusetts's severe difficulties suppressing Shays' Rebellion, an uprising by irate farmers in the western part of the state demanding debt and tax relief.[18] The insurrectionary activities of the Shaysites focused on preventing creditors from collecting from debtors. The rebels mobbed courts, intimidated jurors and judges, and blocked magistrates and sheriffs from executing judgments.[19] Although the governor called out the militia to protect the integrity of the legal process, western militia either failed to make muster or switched sides, assisting in the capture of the Confederation's arsenal at Springfield.[20]

The slowness of state militia to respond to orders to put down the Shaysites, and the fact that several units went over to the rebels, highlighted the weakness of the executive and the futility of depending on the militia to execute the law. Many future anti-federalists considered this lack of military vigor to be the beauty of the existing system, but to future federalists, the militia's ineffectual forays against Daniel Shays were a disgrace. For those who deplored the government's weakness, the incident became one of the most compelling stimuli to formation of a stronger Union with a more vigorous executive, reliable military, and effective judicial system. Among these was James Madison, the principal architect of the Constitution, who shared with other federalists the opinion that, in the post-Revolutionary climate, government on the state and local level (and there was during the Confederation period little government on the national level) failed to protect the "worthy against the licentious."[21]

Thus, as Madison planned for the Philadelphia Convention, he had several things on his mind. First, he wanted to devise a political system that would not immediately grant debt relief, supply easy money, and allow painless bankruptcy. Fiscal integrity was important. At the same time, Madison understood that the new government could not survive without a functioning judicial system with real power to enforce the law.[22] Most important for our purposes, Madison and other nascent federalists realized that the strong federal regime they favored would require some readjustment of American constitutional theory and the reassessment of the role of the military in a democratic republic.

In 1776, American Revolutionaries widely considered themselves upholders of the traditional "mixed" or English Constitution.[23] Under that system, a theoretical balance and equilibrium derived from the tripartite division of the political nation into Monarch, Lords, and Commons, each allotted their respective political competencies.[24] The requirement that military funding flow from Parliament, and the strong voice of stability and aristocracy issuing from the Lords, served in the English model to check any inclination of the magistracy to turn a military establishment to corruption of the Exchequer or oppression of the nation. The balanced Constitution was a theory highly prized by pamphleteers on both sides of the Atlantic, and became a defining influence on the developing revolutionary sensibilities of colonial Americas.

Crucial was the balanced Constitution's co-dependence on a theoretical preference for the militia. The alternative: a standing army—either under control of the magistracy (as in late colonial Massachusetts) or of the legislature (as during the English Commonwealth)—fatally upset the constitutional balance by placing unlimited authority with a single order of society. But theory, by the late eighteenth century, little mirrored reality. For Britain, imperial conflict with France necessitated a vast military establishment. In England, lowland Scotland, and Wales, the harmful effects of standing armies were mitigated by placing chief reliance on the less dangerous royal navy, and by stationing the majority of the army overseas. However, in the North American colonies of Massachusetts and New York, the antirepublican impact of garrisoning was eventually received with full force.

Meanwhile, in both Britain and in the newly emerging American states, the tripartite structure of the old mixed theory had lost much of its tensile strength. For one thing, democratic impulses in America severed constitutional theory from its basis in the hereditary class system. During the Revolution, the established and propertied social orders largely lacked the clout to endow the newly created upper houses of the legislatures with powers reflecting the elite status of their constituents. In fact, many republicans and the Constitution of Pennsylvania had gone over to unicameralism, while the upper houses that remained lacked the voting and office-holding qualifications to make them effective reserves of aristocratic power.[25] Thus, by 1787, in the minds of proto-federalists, the traditional mixed constitution had either fallen into hopeless disrepair or proven ineffective in lending order to American political culture. To soon-to-be antifederalists, on the other hand, the acknowledged disorder was either desirable or remediable by a return to the civic virtue upon which the old theory was premised.[26]

Gordon Wood's greatest contribution to our understanding of early American political thought arises from his analysis of how radically the constitutionalism of 1787 differed from that of 1776.[27] In little more than a decade, the political theory of the young nation was transformed. The difference between the old understanding and the new rested most fundamentally on the federalists' loss of faith in the attainability, sustainability, and (in the case of Hamilton) even in the political desirability of civic virtue.[28] Inevitably, this federalist change of heart provoked a profound reassessment of the role of the militia, and of that republican archetype, the citizen-soldier, in the newly unfolding system.

Unlike radical republican visionaries, federalists were not fundamentally opposed in all instances to vigorous government.[29] A clear case in point is that they would have found vigorous government useful in suppressing the Shaysites.[30] To federalists, the principal problem was rather that unchecked authority was exercised too severely by the wrong sort of people for the wrong sort of ends. Too powerful state legislatures had fallen under the control of uneducated, unqualified, short-sighted, unprincipled men who pursued easy-money policies that served the immediate interests of debtors, but undermined the long-range interests in stability of the leading social orders of the Revolutionary years.[31] The science of government, federalists thought, must be practiced by experts whose education, experience, and outlook fitted them for the job. They rejected increasingly the republicans' undifferentiated social theory in favor of specialization.[32]

The specialization that explained the fitness and qualifications for leadership of the traditional political class also called into question the wisdom of the republican ideal of an undifferentiated citizen militia of part-time soldiers, part-time plowmen and mechanics, and part-time politicians. In time of crisis especially, order required firmer security than that provided by the decaying and undisciplined arch-democratic militias.

Federalists did not abandon all the goals of civic humanism, however. While the radical republican preference for a democratic and unprofessional militia was at least partially subverted by new federal military powers, other core values of the old ideology lived on in the new constitutionalism, now protected by radically new instrumentalities of balance. The Philadelphia Constitution did recognize the historical Anglo-American preference for a militia, but it also conceded the necessity of at least some professional soldiering to secure external peace and internal stability. These twinned, countervailing goals of military amateurism and professionalism are reflected in the overall Madisonian structure of the new government, and in the militia and military clauses of the organic Constitution.[33]

MILITIA AND MILITARY POWERS
IN THE CONSTITUTION OF 1787

Classical republicans feared unchecked power, and especially absolute, unrepublican control over the military. In large measure, so too did the new federalists. But at the Philadelphia Convention in the summer of 1787, they devised novel safeguards against the ancient abuses. Most significant was the two-tiered division of military control between the executive and legislative federal branches, and between the national and state authorities.

Separation of powers was not in itself a radical innovation. Judicial independence, for example, had informed resistance to the Stuarts as early as 1610 with Lord Coke's famous opinion in Dr. Bonham's Case,[34] and judicial tenure on good behavior was duly guaranteed in the Act of Settlement of 1701.[35] Perhaps still more fundamental to commonwealth philosophy, parliamentary independence from the monarchy developed into the mainstay of English opposition ideology, and was enshrined in the Bill of Rights of 1689.[36] Midway through the eighteenth century, Baron de Montesquieu could look across the Channel with envy and celebrate British separation of powers as the most perfect of political systems.[37]

But the Madisonian model of separation marked a new departure from its European antecedents. Among the branches, the American Constitution saw advantages in blending, allowing each partially to exercise powers normally belonging to others.[38] In addition to lateral overlap, the American version of a federal system provided for a sharing of power vertically, between the states and the federal government.[39] The character of this double-dimensional division is nowhere more evident than in the Constitution's vital military and militia clauses. Article 1, Section 8, provided that Congress shall have the power:

To raise and support Armies, but no Appropriation of Money to that Use shall be for a longer Term than two Years [Clause 12];

To provide and maintain a Navy [Clause 13];

To make Rules for the Government and Regulation of the land and naval Forces [Clause 14];

To provide for calling forth the Militia to execute the Laws of the Union, suppress Insurrections and repel Invasions [Clause 15];

To provide for organizing, arming, and disciplining, the Militia, and for governing such part of them as may be employed in the Service of the United States, reserving to the States respectively, the Appointment of Officers, and the Authority of training the Militia according to the discipline prescribed by Congress [Clause 16].

At the same time, Article 2, Section 2, Clause 1, provided that

The President shall be Commander in Chief of the Army and navy of the United States, and of the Militia of the several States, when called into actual Service of the United States.

Under the Constitution, then, Congress was empowered to raise a professional army, to keep it in the field, but not to finance the army's continuance beyond the two-year term for which the House of Representatives was itself elected. A dangerously large army would presumably not be borne by the people to whom the Representatives were beholden. And since all funding measures were to originate in the lower House, the question of the army's longevity was never far removed from popular control. Moreover, since any army raised by Congress was to take its orders from the President, congressional control would be less than absolute even during the two-year interval between elections. For his part, the President would not, like the early Stuarts, depend directly on the legislature's acquiescence to respond to military crises, for, assuming Congress made such provision under Article 1, Section 8, Clause 15, the President would be empowered to call up the several state militia into the service of the United States to execute the Laws of the Union, suppress Insurrections, and repel Invasions. (Congress provided the required authorization in 1795.) The militia, in turn, unlike its royalist Restoration counterpart, could be counted on to follow solid local civic preferences, for its officers were subject to state appointment.[40]

Thus, the dangers of standing armies, which in the republican paradigm had been linked to fear of executive abuse and legislative corruption, were now tempered by Madison's division of authority among Congress, President, and the states. Madison's solution to the dilemma posed by the need for military power even in a democratic republic was more elaborate, intricate, and structuralist than the British approach of separating the funding and command functions between Parliament and his Majesty's Cabinet in Parliament. With the constitutional system itself now shorn of much of the former potential for absolutist abuse, the individuals who made up the new legislature and magistracy might safely possess less than perfectly virtuous personal constitutions.

At the same time, the federalism and structuralism of the new Constitution aimed to ensure restoration of the right sort of people to leading roles in national policy formation and political stewardship, thereby providing another level of protection against the abusive potential of the standing army.[41] The Electoral College, and the staggered, filtered election of senators, served as assurances that unqualified and vulgar populists would not operate direct control over the military forces. This nod to the importance of public character was not a purely civic humanist concession, for Madison envisioned more than virtue as the hallmark of political fitness. Madison saw suitability for public office as a product of education and outlook. With all the optimism of the late Enlightenment, Madison believed qualifications for public office could be studiously acquired, even as his classically republican predecessors believed public character was fleeting and forever subject to decay.[42]

THE ANTI-FEDERALIST CRITIQUE OF THE FEDERAL MILITARY POWER AND THE CRUSADE FOR A BILL OF RIGHTS

There was a minority who did not share Madison's modern optimistic outlook. Years ago, Cecelia Kenyon called them the men of little faith.[43] Classically republican until the last, they soon rallied against the outline of government drafted in Philadelphia. Ultimately, the diligence of these anti-federalists bore fruit in the recognition of the centrality of the militia in the Second Amendment.

When, in September 1787, the Philadelphia Convention submitted the Constitution to Congress to pass on to the state conventions for approval, heated public debate ensued concerning political theory and the future of the republic.[44] At first, anti-federalists objected both to the surrender of state powers to the national government and to the scant specific securities provided in the proposed Constitution for individual rights. As adoption became more and more likely, however, opposition—principled and strategic alike—focused on securing a bill of rights to set limits to federal powers. Various themes were sounded as federalists and anti-federalists debated the desirability of providing concrete guaranties for rights and struggled over which rights would merit such protection. Fear of standing armies, and in particular of a centrally controlled standing army, became a major—but not the leading—theme during the ratification fight.

National Rifle Association President Charlton Heston has commented that the right to bear arms is the most important of the rights secured in the first ten amendments.[45] Many might dispute his ranking of the Bill of Rights as read today. But there can be little doubt that, as a matter of history, Heston's assessment badly misses the mark. If there is a dominant theme in the commentary and the documents surrounding the creation of the Bill of Rights, it is almost certainly fear of potential federal involvement with organized religion.[46] Although the right to bear arms in a citizen militia was important to many in the founding generation, it was not their prime concern. And, as we shall shortly see, any supposed individual right to possess arms outside the context of collective defense (Heston's prime concern) remained remote and insignificant.

The anti-federalist critique of the Constitution originated even before dissolution of the Philadelphia Convention when George Mason noted down his *Objections*.[47] These were published soon thereafter. Mason was especially concerned that state bills of rights could not protect individuals against incursions by the powerful federal government. He lamented the absence of any federal "Declaration of Rights," and noted particularly the lack of guarantees for freedom of the press, trial by jury in civil cases, and security against standing armies in peacetime. He made no mention of protecting an individual right to arms. When the Constitution arrived before Congress in New York, Virginia's Richard Henry Lee, who had not been at the Convention, endeavored unsuccessfully to attach a set of amendments similar in substance to Mason's *Objections*. Lee proposed guaranteeing freedom of religion, of the press, of assembly and petition, trial by jury in civil and criminal cases, the independence of judges, and free and frequent elections. He also proposed a ban on peacetime standing armies, on excessive bail or fines, and on unreasonable searches and seizures. Like Mason, Lee made no mention of securing to individuals the right to possess weapons for private purposes.[48] From the outset then, two of the most prominent anti-federalist leaders articulated nearly all the major principles that would eventually be written into the Bill of Rights, but neither made any claim for a right resembling the NRA's favorite.

Nor does a review of the ratification debate bear out the individualist contention that a demand to secure a personal right to arms was a driving force behind the anti-federalist movement and the wellspring of the Bill of Rights.[49] Two leading historians of the ratification process, Robert Allen Rutland[50] and Bernard Schwartz,[51] have noted only slight significance in sporadic calls to secure an individualistic right to arms. A third, Jack Rakove, not only marks the infrequency and marginality of invocations of a private right to possess arms free of federal interference, but argues persuasively that those rare claims must be balanced against late-eighteenth-century America's "orthodox understanding of the extent of the police powers of the . . . states, which authorized government to legislate broadly in pursuit of the public health and welfare."[52]

Many leading anti-federal spokesmen during the Critical Period belabored issues relating to security for the militia and preservation of the body politic against the dangers of federal standing armies. One of the more famous opponents of ratification was Luther Martin of Maryland, who, like Mason, had refused to sign the Constitution at Philadelphia. Declaiming on the proposed Constitution before the State Assembly at Annapolis, Martin blasted the militia clauses as part and parcel of a full-scale transfer of sovereignty from the states to the new central government:

> It was urged [at the Constitutional convention] that, if after having retained to the general government the great powers already granted, and among those, that of raising and keeping up regular troops, without limitations, the power over the Militia should be taken away from the States, and also given to the general government, it ought to be considered as the last coup de grace to the State governments; that it must be the most convincing proof,

the advocates of this system design the destruction of the State governments, and that no professions to the contrary ought to be trusted; and that every State in the Union ought to reject such a system with indignation, since, if the general government should attempt to enslave them, they could not have any possible means of self-defense.[53]

Martin's concerns for state sovereignty were typical of anti-federalists. Similar fears of the militia clauses and of the federal military powers were expressed in a minority report by his own state convention, and echoed in four of the official petitions for Amendments published by six states. It was these reports from the state ratifying conventions that eventually persuaded the First Congress to pass the Second Amendment and the rest of the Bill of Rights.[54]

While Martin's classically republican solicitude for the militia characterized the anti-federal mainstream, a small number of anti-federalists supported a more personal right to arms than that needed to provide institutional security for the states and the people against a too powerful federal military. These supporters of constitutional right to own weapons for private purposes were atypical even within the anti-federalist movement, and they remained insignificant within the nation as a whole. More importantly, as we shall see shortly, their voices, unlike Luther Martin's, went unheeded as the Second Amendment was adopted by Congress and ratified by the states. But before we reach the text of the Amendment itself, let us pause briefly to consider some of the calls for a personal right to private arms that were expressed here and there while the controversy over the Constitution raged.

New Hampshire stood out among those states whose conventions appended petitions for a bill of rights to their ratification of the Constitution. As we have noted, the Granite State's convention was the only one to put forward a draft amendment that might be read to support a personal right against federal disarmament even outside the context of militia service. In addition to a suggested amendment prohibiting the quartering of troops in private homes without the owners' consent and barring maintenance of peacetime standing armies absent approval of three-fourths of both Houses of Congress,[55] the New Hampshire convention proposed that "Congress shall never disarm any Citizen unless such as are or have been in Actual

Rebellion."[56] This language is certainly not crystal, and it might support the argument that a private right to gun possession is protected. But to whatever extent New Hampshire's delegates may have proposed an individual right to arms independent of duty to the state, they sought to push the republic further than any of the other states desired to go.

In neighboring Massachusetts, for example, the ratification convention rejected an amendment proposed by Samuel Adams that would have denied Congress power "to prevent the people of the United States who are peaceable citizens from keeping their own arms."[57] The convention did so despite the Bay Colony's charged history of arms and powder seizures that culminated in the outbreak of hostilities at Lexington and Concord in 1775. Delegates to the Ratifying Convention were doubtless swayed more by the recent Shaysite uprising than by past royal abuses, but this was not the first time Massachusetts had declined to heed scattered minority appeals for a constitutional right to keep arms for private purposes. Robert Shalhope has recently emphasized petitions submitted by citizens of Northhampton and Williamsburgh during the period of public comment on John Adams' proposed Massachusetts Constitution of 1780.[58] That Constitution—still in force today—was accepted by the people only after addition of a Bill of Rights and other revisions to a draft rejected in 1778.[59] The Massachusetts Bill of Rights included in Article XVII provisions asserting that "[t]he people have a right to keep and bear arms for the common defense," warning of the dangers of peacetime armies, and urging strict civilian control of the military. The communities of Northhampton and Williamsburgh, Shalhope informs us, were not satisfied with the declaration of these public rights, and sought additional recognition of a right to keep arms for self-defense. Shalhope's point in this context is that the case for the "standard model" is not wholly without supporting evidence. What Shalhope neglects to emphasize for the benefit of his readers is the crucial fact that the Northampton and Williamsburgh petitions were rejected, and that Adams's wording of Article 17 remains on the books to this very day.

Outside of Massachusetts, other marginal voices called out for a private right to arms. It seems safe to assume that in back country North Carolina, elements of the populist, prodebtor, Regulator movement would have supported a purely personal right to arms, in part to facilitate resistance to taxation the Regulators deemed extra-legal.[60] Yet even in the Tar Heel State's assembly, dominated by anti-federal sentiment, advocates of a private right to arms were unable to impress their vision on the state convention as a whole. North Carolina adopted verbatim the proposed Virginia Bill of Rights,[61] except that North Carolina sent its recommendations to Congress with instructions that amendments be adopted before the new Constitution took effect. The Convention refused to ratify the Constitution before federal adoption of a Bill of Rights, and North Carolina did not join the new federal Union until Congress sent the proposed Bill of Rights to the States in 1789. North Carolina's tactics played a crucial role in bolstering momentum for amendments to the Constitution,[62] but the only right to arms that North Carolina endorsed was expressly linked to service in the militia.

Pennsylvania too boasted some radical, libertarian support for an unrestricted right to weapons, but, as elsewhere, those calls were firmly rejected by the majority of the state's voters and legislators. Much has been made[63] of an Address favoring a personal right to arms, circulated by a disaffected minority after the Keystone State's convention concluded its affairs.[64] In addition to reciting standard Whig canons about standing armies and military subordination to the civil authority, the Address proclaimed "[t]hat the people have a right to bear arms for the defence of themselves and their own State, or the United States, or for the purpose of killing game; and no law shall be passed for disarming the people or any of them, unless for crimes committed, or real danger of public injury from individuals."

The Address did not bear the imprimatur of the state convention, and Garry Wills suggests that, on closer inspection, this "minority report" turns out to be no more than the collected ramblings of a single embittered eccentric who departed the convention in disgust when he was unable to scuttle ratification.[65] Wills perhaps overstates his case, for, as Saul Cornell (a noted specialist on Pennsylvania anti-federalism) reminds us, the minority report, though written hastily by a single pen after the convention had already dissolved, was reprinted often and distributed widely throughout the country.[66] Still, Wills' essential point that the Address's view of arms-related rights did not represent majority opinion in Pennsylvania is a sound one. Cornell himself stresses that for mainstream Pennsylvania anti-federalists (let alone federalists), claims to constitutionalize a right to arms remained firmly linked to the official militia firmly under the control of lawful authority. Indeed, in 1788, the state's most respected anti-federalist leaders unequivocally condemned anarchist, antistatist disturbances in Carlisle, and pointedly distanced themselves from insurrectionaries who mobilized ad hoc armed bands, while claiming merely to have summoned the lawfully established local militia.[67]

Some commentators, Professors Cornell and Bellesiles among them, have stressed still another issue in this context. Pennsylvanians' conceptions of the proposed federal right to arms, they point out, must be measured against the background in which the state Constitution's declaration that "[t]he people have a right to bear arms for the defence of themselves and the state" was applied.[68] And, say Cornell and Bellesiles, that declared right coexisted without tension with state test acts that prevented loyalists and other suspect characters (amounting to nearly half the male population of arms-bearing age) from serving in the militia or keeping arms.[69]

Implicit in Cornell's and Bellesiles's analyses is the notion that the late-eighteenth-century right to arms must have been less than iron-clad, because it was not universally applied. While of great historical interest, we are not convinced that this insight is relevant to current endeavors at interpretation of the Second Amendment. All constitutional liberties are applied more widely today than in former times, and exclusions against loyalists, women, Catholics, and blacks are happily long since abandoned and forsaken. The real issue in deciding whether the constitutional protection of a given activity is genuinely rooted in eighteenth-century practice is thus not one of determining what segment of the population was formerly admitted to claim the right in question. If it were, we would have to conclude reluctantly that, by today's fair and inclusive standards, there were no genuine rights in the eighteenth century.

For twenty-first-century Americans interested in the doctrinal scope (rather than the social applicability) of the historically rooted rights set down in 1789, a more instructive inquiry is whether the liberty of acknowledged full citizens (patriotic white Protestant men if you will) to engage in a particular activity was asserted in constitutionalist terms during the Framers' era. In this light, the ratification politics of Pennsylvania are indeed instructive, but not because a closer look at prevailing practice discloses that distrusted minorities were denied the right to arms. Rather, this history is enlightening because it reveals that the assertion of an individual right to arms for purposes beyond service in the lawful state militia may have resonated with some groups of anarchic radicals, but that majority sentiment and enlightened reason failed to embrace constitutional claims for such a right in Pennsylvania.[70]

More representative of national opinion than the unofficial Address of the Pennsylvania minority and (one interpretation of) the official New Hampshire Petition—and more influential in the formation of the Bill of Rights—were the debates and resolutions of the Virginia Ratifying Convention. Eight states had already voted in favor of ratification by the time delegates convened in Richmond in June of 1788, and another, New Hampshire, voted to ratify before the Virginia Convention adjourned, bringing to nine the number of "ayes"—the minimum required by Article VII for the Constitution to take effect among the states approving it. But the support of Virginia, the largest and most populous state, remained critical for the Constitution's ultimate success and for winning over the remaining nonratifying states of New York, North Carolina, and Rhode Island. Thus, the Old Dominion, where opponents of the Constitution were well organized and well-represented,[71] afforded anti-federalists a last clear chance to impress their aspirations on the nation's design. After long and thoughtful discussions, the Virginia Convention, following the lead of Massachusetts, appended a list of proposed amendments to its resolution of ratification.[72] These reflected substantial concessions to the anti-federalists and eventually formed the blueprint Madison used in the First Congress to draft the Bill of Rights.

At the Richmond Convention, George Mason, the anti-federal spokesman whose *Objections* had sounded the opening salvo in the ratification struggle, soon expanded the scope of his opposition to encompass the dangers of federalizing the militia. He feared that Congress might use its power over state forces as a pretext for disarming them. "Congress may neglect to provide for arming and disciplining the militia; and the state governments cannot do it, for Congress has an exclusive right to arm them."[73] The flamboyant Patrick Henry echoed Mason's concerns. "When this power is given up to Congress," he asked, "how will your militia be armed?"[74] Federalists Marshall and Madison countered correctly that the federal power to arm was not exclusive, so that Virginia might independently arm her militia if Congress declined to do so.[75] In the context of this exchange, it is important to note that Mason and Henry were motivated not by fears that the federal government would disarm individuals and thereby prevent them from protecting themselves. Their solicitude was entirely for arming the state militia to protect the community from insurrection and external danger. And they were sensitive to the fact that, by its very existence, an armed and trained local militia protected the community from the political and fiscal hazards of a large federally controlled army.

The ninth, tenth, and eleventh proposed amendments to emerge from the Virginia Convention embodied the delegation's desire to delineate more clearly the scope of respective federal and state military authority. The ninth amendment would have required two-thirds consent from both houses of Congress for maintaining a peacetime standing army, and the tenth would have restricted peacetime enlistments to a maximum of four years. The eleventh—a direct concession to Mason and Henry—expressed each state's power to arm and discipline its militia whenever Congress should neglect to do so, and provided that federal martial law should govern the militia only when duly called to the service of the United States in time of war, invasion, or rebellion.[76]

More significantly, these proposed amendments built on fundamental principles of government set forth in the declaration that accompanied the Virginia ratification resolution. Three of the principles declared by the Virginia Convention bore directly on the future Second Amendment to the United States Constitution. Most important of these was the seventeenth, which held

> That the people have a right to keep and bear arms; that a well regulated Militia composed of the body of the people trained to arms is the proper, natural and safe defence of a free State. That standing armies in time of peace are dangerous to liberty, and therefore ought to be avoided, as far as the circumstances and protection of the Community will admit; and that in all cases the military should be under strict subordination to and governed by the Civil power.[77]

By these terms, the ratifying convention's concern with the right to arms were plainly directed toward the service of a collective purpose. Demanding greater assurances vis-à-vis the new federal government, the delegates in Richmond were not concerned with individual license; they insisted only that trained men under arms, subject to civil control, were far better assurance of political and public liberty than a professional military establishment.

The Virginians did express some concern for individual autonomy in the military context, but this solicitude did not relate to any claimed right to arm oneself for private purposes. What the delegation favored in the way of individual rights were exemptions rather than entitlements. They wanted to protect householders against quartering of troops in private residences (this concern found expression in Amendment III of the Constitution) and to honor religious scruples against coerced performance of military duty. (This concern found its way into Madison's original draft of what became the Second Amendment, but this conscientious objector clause was struck at the insistence of the Senate during conference with the House.)

These two principles were set down as the ninth and tenth articles in Virginia's ratification declaration.[78] Sanctity of the home and liberty of conscience were fundamental values of eighteenth-century political theory that pressed for accommodation with the government's demands for military service. Whether republican society depended on republican character or vice versa was then much debated,[79] but in either case, banning billeting and recognizing conscientious objection made for reassuringly sound policy from the vantage points of both republican and natural rights theory.

The concerns expressed in the Virginia debates — most particularly the preference for a militia over a standing army — echoed numerous pamphlets from all corners of the new nation. Many of these sounded a traditional republican refrain, warning of the dangers of standing armies under absolute control and enfeebled militias unable to restore the political balance. Thus, in the City of Brotherly Love, the pseudonymous "Philadelphiensis" proclaimed:

> Who can deny but the president general will be a king to all intents and purposes, and one of the most dangerous kinds too; a king elected to command a standing army? Thus our laws are to be administered by this tyrant; for the whole, or at least the most important part of the executive department is put in his hands.[80]

Another Philadelphia editorialist, "Centinel," feared not a presidential, but a legislative tyrant.[81] Centinel argued that federalization of state forces through the militia clauses would usher in an era of congressional domination of the states. The militia clauses, Centinel wrote, would

> subject the citizens of these states to the most arbitrary military discipline: even death may be inflicted on the disobedient; in the character of militia, you may be dragged from your families and homes to any part of the continent and for any length of time, at the discretion of the future Congress. . . . The militia of Pennsylvania may be marched to Georgia or New Hampshire, however incompatible with their interests or consciences; in short, they may be made as mere machines as Prussian soldiers.[82]

Centinel's concerns were shared by the Bostonian pamphleteer, "John De Witt." "Let us inquire," he mused, "why they [Congress] have assumed this great power. . . . The nature of the demand . . . forces you to believe that it is . . . for the purpose of consolidating and finally destroying your strength, as your respective governments are to be destroyed." Reflecting on the rising federalist conspiracy, De Witt recalled his republican history. "It is asserted," he remembered, "by the most respectable writers upon government, that a well regulated militia, composed of the yeomanry of the county, have ever been considered as the bulwark of a free people. Tyrants have never placed any confidence on a militia composed of freemen."[83]

Better remembered than even the most familiar anti-federal pamphlets are the opinions from the pen of Publius published in the Federalist papers. The pen was wielded by three heavy hitters of the federalist lineup: Madison, Hamilton, and Jay. These opinions are revealing and powerful, revealing because they take issue with the federalists' most serious concerns, and powerful because they had the greatest impact on the federalists' subsequent constitutional reforms. With the exception of Hamilton's argument that a government of enumerated powers need not be feared—which reassured no anti-federalist—justifications that Publius offered to the opponents of the Constitution would soon inform compromises forged in the First Congress to maintain central military strength while allaying the anti-federalists. The Bill of Rights was written with the placation of anti-federalists in mind, but it was written by federalists. Hence, the rationales employed by leading proponents of ratification remain instructive in understanding the concession federalists ultimately offered to their anti-federal countrymen in the form of the Bill of Rights and the Second Amendment.

A favorite theme of Publius was the necessity of a standing army. Like Washington, Hamilton took from the war an enduring skepticism regarding the fighting effectiveness of the militia. In Federalists 25, 27, 28, and 29, as Publius, he argued that a professional army was the only means to combat a professional army, and thus the only true guarantee of national security and independence. An inefficient militia, in contrast, would be an extravagance without much military value. Since a regular army was a necessity, Hamilton saw no way around accepting its constitutional legitimacy. In his eyes, it was far better to provide for structural safeguards against military dictatorship than to wish away the problem of military necessity.[84]

Happily for Hamilton, the federal system was well designed to guard against military excess. "As far as an army may be considered as a dangerous weapon," Hamilton reflected, "it had better be in those hands of which the people are most likely to be jealous [the federal government] than in those of which they are least likely to be jealous [the state governments]."[85] Thus, vigilance, the classical republican requisite for civil-military balance, would actually be enhanced by the new system.

In Federalist 46, Madison addressed head-on the radical anti-federalist fear that the national army might serve a tyrant's designs of conquest and empire. In so doing, he conceded frankly the checking value of the general militia within the federal system. "Let a regular army, fully equal to the resources of the country, be formed," he argued,

> and let it be entirely at the devotion of the federal government: still it would not be going too far to say that *the State governments with the people on their side would be able to repel the danger.* The highest number to which, according to the best computation, a standing army can be carried in any country does not exceed one hundredth part of the whole number of souls, or one twenty-fifth part of the number able to bear arms. This proportion would not yield, in the United States, any army of more than twenty-five or thirty thousand men. To these would be opposed a militia amounting to near half a million of citizens with arms in their hands, *officered by men chosen from among themselves,* fighting for their common liberties and

united and *conducted by governments possessing their affections and confidence.* It may well be doubted whether a militia thus circumstanced could ever be conquered by such a proportion of regular troops (italics in original).[86]

Thus, while Hamilton thought the army necessary because the militia was ineffective, Madison thought the general militia sufficiently effective — if for no other reason than its size — to nullify the threat of a professional army. To both writers, however, the federal structure itself served to lessen the dangers historically associated with standing armies. Madison in particular seemed to engage openheartedly the fears expressed in the anti-federal pamphlets. Clearly, to anti-federalists, the continued vitality of the militia was the only means of rendering an army palatable. While Madison likely still considered enumeration of powers sufficient protection for the militia's constitutional status, he was quickly coming round to an appreciation of the importance of amendments to secure a consensus behind the new Constitution. Hamilton, for his part, clung to the notion that a government of enumerated powers was inherently harmless until the very end of the federalist series. In Federalist 84, the New Yorker argued:

> It has been several times truly remarked that bills of rights are, in their origin, stipulations between kings and their subjects, abridgements of prerogative in favor of privilege, reservations of rights not surrendered to the prince. Such was MAGNA CHARTA, obtained by the barons, sword in hand from King John. Such were the subsequent confirmations of that charter by succeeding princes. Such was the Petition of Right assented to by Charles I, in the beginning of his reign. Such, also, was the Declaration of Right presented by the Lords and Commons to the Prince of Orange in 1688, and afterwards thrown into the form of an act of Parliament called the Bill of Rights. It is evident, therefore, that, according to their primitive signification, they have no application to constitutions professedly founded upon the power of the people, and executed by their immediate representatives and servants.[87]

But anti-federalists did not trust Hamilton's logic, and they demanded express guarantees for their traditional rights. Beginning with Massachusetts, five of the last six states to ratify did so with the understanding that the First Congress would amend the Constitution to include a federal Bill of Rights. That the First Congress proved willing to do so was a direct concession to the strength and cogency of the anti-federalist opposition, and particularly to the eloquence of Patrick Henry and George Mason in the Virginia Convention.[88] On the whole, anti-federalists had agitated at least as strongly for the principles behind what became the First, Fourth, Fifth, Sixth, Ninth, and Tenth Amendments as they did for those behind the Second.[89] Freedom from religious establishment, free exercise of religion, a free press, free expression, freedom to assemble, common law procedural rights, jury trial (civil and criminal), the inability of the federal government to touch other basic common law rights, such as the right against unreasonable searches and seizures, and the integrity of the states as guarantors of those rights had figured as prominently in anti-federalist pamphleteering as the dangers of standing armies.[90] The subject of individual arms as source or substance of any right or principle other than security against a standing army arose during the ratification debates only sporadically, and on the radical fringe.[91] It is not surprising then that Madison, when he directed his attentions to fulfilling the federalists' commitment to provide a Bill of Rights, did not endeavor to write a guarantee to an unfettered personal right to arms into the amended Constitution.

One further development during the ratification crisis merits serious consideration in our endeavor to understand the mind of the man who served as principal draftsman of the Second Amendment. This is Madison's correspondence with Jefferson concerning the desirability of a bill of rights. Eight years Jefferson's junior, Madison had already entered into the "Great Collaboration"[92] with the author of the Declaration of Independence by the time Jefferson undertook his six-year ministry to France in 1784. By 1787, when Madison led the delegates to the Constitutional Convention in Philadelphia, his relationship with Jefferson had been cemented by his successful stewardship of many of Jefferson's reform bills through the House of Burgesses, including the great Statute of Virginia for Religious Freedom.[93] Yet Madison retained then and always a deferential manner toward his political mentor.[94] When Madison, aged thirty-one and serving in the Congress at Philadelphia, fell hopelessly in love with a fifteen-year-old girl and took to wasting great amounts of time and money at the barbers, it was Jefferson who chastened him to return to hard work in the service of his country.[95] Later, Madison would seek and obtain Jefferson's blessing of his marriage to a stunning young widow, known to posterity as Dolley Madison.[96]

While Jefferson was in Paris, transatlantic correspondence between the two Virginians flowed steadily.[97] Their letters were at once eclectic and erudite. Madison valued Jefferson's encyclopedic knowledge of political philosophy, and while some commentators would rate Madison the weightier and more practical of the pair, the truth is that he usually yielded to Jefferson's political suggestions.[98] The advisability of a bill of rights in the federal Constitution is a case in point. With due regard to the secrecy of the proceedings in Philadelphia, Madison had kept Jefferson abreast of the developing shape of the Constitution throughout the Convention summer of 1787. In reply, Jefferson offered critical analysis and historical perspective.

Jefferson considered Madisonian federalism a stroke of genius. He was especially pleased by the constitutional compromise between the claims of large and small states, and was very favorably disposed toward Madison's system of checks and balances. But, as Jefferson wrote in a letter of December 20, 1787, he did not consider the Constitution to be altogether perfect. "I will now add what I do not like," he declared. "First the omission of a bill of rights providing clearly and without the aid of sophisms for freedom of religion, freedom of the press, protection against standing armies, restriction against monopolies, the eternal and unremitting force of the habeas corpus laws, and trials by jury in all matters of fact triable by the laws of the land and not by the law of Nations."[99]

Thus, protection from standing armies — but not an individual entitlement to arms — numbered among the rights for which Jefferson sought express protection. Six weeks later Jefferson wrote to Madison proposing a mechanism whereby a bill of rights might be secured. "I am glad to hear that the new constitution is received with favor," he began, referring to the prospects for ratification in the upcoming state conventions. "I sincerely wish that the first 9 conventions may receive, and the 4. last reject it. The former will secure it finally, while the latter will oblige them to offer a declaration of rights in order to complete the union. We shall thus have all its good, and cure its principal defect."[100] As we shall shortly see, Jefferson's prognostication approximated very nearly the future course of ratification.

In the ensuing summer of 1788, Jefferson—still in Paris—was expecting imminent arrival of the welcome news that Virginia had assented to the Constitution, and that the constitutionally mandated approval of at least nine states had been achieved.[101] On the last day of July, Jefferson learned that New Hampshire, outpacing the Virginians, had brought up the required nine, thereby bringing the new government into force among the ratifying states. The Minister to Versailles fired off a letter to congratulate Madison on the constitutional achievement, and, at the same time, remind his former colleague of the desirability and demand for a bill of rights. In particular, Jefferson amplified his concerns about standing armies. He wrote of the newly ratified Constitution:

> It is a good canvas on which some strokes only want retouching. . . . It seems pretty generally understood that this should go to Juries, Habeas corpus, Standing armies, Printing, Religion, and Monopolies. . . . If no check can be found to keep the number of standing troops within safe bounds, while they are tolerated as far as necessary, abandon them altogether, discipline well the militia and guard the magazines with them. More than magazine guards will be useless if few, dangerous if many. No European nation can ever send against us such a regular army as we need fear, and it is hard if our militia is not equal to those of Canada or Florida.[102]

Given his recent experiences as a displaced wartime governor of an occupied Virginia,[103] Jefferson doubtless was engaging in wishful thinking about the feebleness of European armies. And given the desperation of the former chief executive's pleas for Continental assistance during that British invasion of Virginia, his confidence in the American militia's ability to protect the nation also seems rather too optimistic.[104] But more importantly for our purposes, it is worth remarking that Jefferson once again made no references whatever to any arms-related rights other than the right of the people to be protected from standing armies. In this light, Jefferson's letters from Paris advocating a bill of rights make an interesting contrast to his letter describing to a young nephew the sporting benefits of shooting, which we discussed in chapter 1. Individualist interpreters of the Second Amendment may be fond of citing such praise of sport shooting as evidence that the Framers favored a right to keep weapons for private purposes, but in a political context, Jefferson's discourse on arms was now focused firmly on the old Whig militia/army paradigm, and hence directed squarely to the collective purpose of preservation of the militia.[105]

Though not intended for public distribution, Jefferson's letters to Madison advocating a bill of rights came into wide circulation at the height of the ratification debate through the efforts of Uriah Forrest, an American who, while traveling in Europe, corresponded with Jefferson concerning the state of developments at home. Jefferson favored Forrest with replies enclosing copies of his letters to Madison commenting on the course of ratification. Thanks to Forrest, the letters were much publicized by the anti-federalist press, and became a godsend to advocates of amendments.[106] Whether by coincidence, or by the force of his wide American influence, Jefferson's hopes first expressed privately to Madison that nine states ratify, and the remaining four withhold their approval pending amendments, proved prescient. The first nine state conventions did approve the Philadelphia design, and while only two of the remaining states rejected the Constitution, it was their rejection—coupled with the amendments proposed by five of the last six ratifying states and in particular those proposed by Virginia—that paved the way for the Bill of Rights.[107]

THE SECOND AMENDMENT: THE LAST ACT OF CLASSICAL REPUBLICAN CONSTITUTIONALISM?

In April 1789, when the First Congress assembled in New York, James Madison took his seat as a representative from Virginia. The emergence of organized parties was still some years off, and there was not in 1789 any equivalent of the Majority Leader of the House, but Madison soon established himself among the representatives as one of the chief architects of legislation. His driving purpose during the spring and summer of 1789 was attainment of a bill of rights. Although originally somewhat hesitant, Madison was by now firmly convinced that a series of amendments would serve felicitously to round out the work begun at Philadelphia. Several events explain his change of heart.

In the first place, his election to Congress had been hard-fought. Arch anti-federalist Patrick Henry had used his influence in the Virginia General Assembly to thwart Madison's bid for the Senate, and then backed the candidacy of James Monroe in Madison's congressional district, all the while branding Madison a foe of amendments.[108] Madison owed his narrow victory in part to assurances he gave his constituents that he would back amendments. More importantly, he felt duty-bound to honor implicit guarantees to anti-federalists made by the Virginia and other ratifying conventions that a bill of rights would follow ratification.[109] More fundamentally still, from the perspective of political theory, the transatlantic exchange of letters with Jefferson described above had brought Madison around to principled belief in the desirability of a bill of rights.[110] And from the standpoint of political tactics, Madison was eager to move forward on the amendments as quickly as possible, fearing that delay would stir discontent among the late anti-federal opposition, and lend credence to calls for a disruptive and perhaps fatal second convention.[111]

Thus, on May 4, 1789, Madison informed the House that he intended "to bring on the subject of amendments to the constitution" on May 25.[112] This shrewd move stole much of the anti-federal thunder, and sapped the urgency from Theodorick Bland's May 5 introduction of an application by the Virginia General Assembly, engineered by Patrick Henry, for a second convention, and a similar application from New York read the following day.[113] But on the whole, Congress was more concerned with legislation setting up the new government and righting the nation's finances than with securing a Bill of Rights. Consequently, members devoted most of their time through the first summer session to wrangling over the future permanent seat of government, establishing executive departments and the judiciary, and hammering out the schedule of tariff rates. As Congressman James Jackson from Georgia reasoned, "Without we pass the collection bill we can get no revenue, and without revenue the wheels of government cannot move."[114]

Madison, however, kept the Bill of Rights firmly in view. With anti-federalists outside Congress again mounting calls for a second convention, Madison intervened decisively on June 8 to redirect Congress's attentions to the amendments. "This day," he reminded the House, "is the day assigned for taking into consideration the subject of amendments to the Constitution. As I consider myself bound in honor and in duty to do what I have done on this subject, I shall proceed to bring the amendments before you as soon as possible, and advocate them until they shall be finally adopted or rejected by a Constitutional majority of this House."[115] Considerable effort was re-

quired for Madison to convince his colleagues to lay aside other pressing business and consider constitutional amendments. But Madison
was a great persuader. As Chief Justice Marshall recalled years later,
if eloquence included the art of "persuasion by convincing, then
Mr. Madison was the most eloquent man I ever heard."[116]

In this spirit, Madison reassured members that he was "sorry to be
accessory to the loss of a single moment of time by the House."[117] He
accommodated them by yielding his motion that Congress go into
Committee of the Whole to consider amendments. In its place, he
urged that "a select committee be appointed to consider and report
such amendments as are proper for Congress to propose to the legislatures of the several States, conformably to the fifth article of the
Constitution."[118] And he pointed out that further delay would spark
suspicion that Congress was not acting in good faith. "It cannot be a
secret to the gentlemen in this House," he reminded members, "that,
notwithstanding the ratification of this system of Government . . .
yet still there is a great number of our constituents who are dissatisfied with it. . . . We ought not to disregard their inclination, but,
on principles of amity and moderation, conform to their wishes and
expressly declare the great rights of mankind."[119]

Madison then read his proposed amendments into the record.[120]
These were based on his review of the long lists of suggested amendments submitted from the state conventions, the bills of rights embodied in the state constitutions, the English Bill of Rights of 1689,
and a stream of letters and reports from citizens and congressmen.
He had access also to a widely circulated pamphlet compiling the
amendments proposed by Virginia, North Carolina, and four other
states, to which he referred in a letter to Jefferson.[121] But he relied
most heavily on the Virginia recommendations.[122] Madison contemplated at this stage a series of clauses integrated into relevant portions
of the organic text of the Constitution, but Roger Sherman's well-
reasoned argument in favor of the separate catalogue we know today
eventually won out before the full House.[123]

Madison's original draft of what we know as the Second Amendment was incorporated along with (in order) the precursors of the
First, Third, Fifth, Eighth, Fourth, Sixth, and Ninth Amendments
in a lengthy provision to be inserted into Article 1, Section 9, between
Clauses 3 and 4, placing further express limitations on the powers of

Congress. It provided: "*The right of the people to keep and bear arms shall not be infringed; a well armed and well regulated militia being the best security of a free country: but no person religiously scrupulous of bearing arms shall be compelled to render military service in person.*"[124]

After renewed debate on the advisability and timing of amendments, the House ignored Madison's tactical concession to form a select committee, and voted instead to go into Committee of the Whole to consider amendments to the Constitution.[125] This appeared finally to short-circuit the drive for a second convention, but another six weeks passed without members taking any action. On July 21, Madison again "begged the House to indulge him in the further consideration of amendments," and go into Committee of the Whole in accordance with the motion of June 8.[126] This time, the House voted instead to send Madison's motion along with the amendments proposed by various states to a Select Committee consisting of one member from each state.[127] Madison was named as the Representative from Virginia, and he exercised persuasive influence over the committee during its week-long proceedings.

The Select Committee reported on July 28, but the report was ordered to lie on the table.[128] It followed Madison's scheme of weaving amendments into the fabric of the seven Articles of 1787, and in substance remained essentially faithful to Madison's original June 8 proposal. The Select Committee did, however, alter the text of the future Second Amendment in four respects. It reversed the order of the militia and right to bear arms clauses, so that the stately endorsement of the "well regulated militia" moved to the beginning of the text, where it remains in the version ratified by the states. The committee also inserted a seven-word qualification of the militia, characterizing it as "composed of the body of the people," and deleted Madison's stipulation that the militia be "well armed." Most significantly, the Select Committee substituted "State" for "country" as the referent of the "best security" clause, so that the proposed amendment now addressed more directly anti-federal concern about state security. Finally, the committee draft dropped the qualifier "in person," from the conscientious objector provision, suggesting that religious pacifists might well have a constitutional right not only to avoid militia duty, but to avoid paying for a substitute as well. Thus, the Select Committee draft provided in full: "*A well regulated militia, composed of the body of the people, being the best security of a free State, the right of the people to keep and bear arms shall not be infringed, but no person religiously scrupulous shall be compelled to bear arms.*"[129]

Not until August 13 did the House finally resolve itself into Committee of the Whole to consider the Select Committee report.[130] The fifteen proposed substantive amendments were parsed, refined, and partitioned in Congress. Ultimately, twelve were approved by both Houses, and ten were ratified by the states.[131] On its course to passage, the draft of the Second Amendment[132] emerged unscathed from debates in the full House, but was pruned by the Senate.[133] Both Chambers rejected other proposed changes. By inference, as well as from the record of debate in the House, the process casts light on the Amendment's intended meaning.

On August 17, 1789, the full House opened debate on the Second Amendment. Elbridge Gerry of Massachusetts, a delegate to the Philadelphia Convention who had refused to sign the Constitution, objected immediately to the conscientious objector clause Madison had drafted.[134] Gerry's hostility arose not from any contempt for those of tender conscience—in fact he proposed replacing the draft language with a clause more narrowly tailored to protect exclusively those belonging to religious sects that were opposed to bearing arms—but from his strong anti-federal and republican principles. Gerry feared that the proposed clause would empower the federal government to declare per se rules as to conscientious ineligibility, thereby excluding whole groups from military service, and effectively disarming the militia. "I am apprehensive," Gerry told the House, "that this clause would give an opportunity to the people in power to destroy the Constitution itself. They can declare who are the religiously scrupulous, and prevent them from bearing arms."[135]

"What, sir, is the use of a militia?" Gerry next asked the Speaker. "It is," he continued in answer to his own question,

> to prevent the establishment of a standing army, the bane of liberty. Now, it must be evident, that, under this provision, together with their other powers, Congress could take such measures with respect to a militia as to make a standing army necessary. Whenever Governments mean to invade the rights and liberties of the people, they always attempt to destroy the militia, in order to raise an army upon their ruins. This was actually done by Great Britain

at the commencement of the late Revolution. . . . The Assembly of Massachusetts, seeing the rapid progress that administration were making to divest them of their inherent privileges, endeavored to counteract them by the organization of the militia; but they were always defeated by the influence of the Crown.[136]

At this point, Gerry's monologue on political theory was interrupted by Mr. Seney of Maryland, who "wished to know what question there was before the committee, in order to ascertain the point upon which the gentleman was speaking." Gerry soon cut to the chase. "Now if we give a discretionary power to exclude those from military duty who have religious scruples, we may as well make no provision on this head [i.e., for preserving the militia from federal destruction]."[137] Discretionary authority to declare whole segments of the population ineligible for service would vitiate the militia, or at the very least undermine its republican character. Gerry wished, therefore, "the words to be altered so as to be confined to persons belonging to a religious sect scrupulous of bearing arms." The motion lost by two votes in the House,[138] which carried the Amendment as reported, but later, at the Senate's insistence, the conscientious objector clause was struck entirely by the House-Senate conference, and it formed no part of the Amendment eventually submitted for ratification.

The whole tenor of the House debates indicates clearly that the Framers' purpose in the drafting of the Second Amendment was to protect the constitutional status of the militia; there is no suggestion of any concern with a personal liberty to carry arms for private purposes. Consider the example of Congressman Benson of New York, who objected to the conscientious objector clause for reasons quite distinct from those articulated by Gerry. "No man can claim this indulgence of right," Benson maintained. "It may be a religious persuasion, but it is no natural right, and therefore ought to be left to the discretion of the Government."[139]

Benson, like Madison, was concerned that the Constitution not become cluttered up with guarantees of rights that were not fundamental to political liberty, and which would therefore routinely require balancing against other rights and the demands of sound government. "If this stands part of the Constitution," Benson continued, "it will be a question before the Judiciary[140] on every regulation you make with respect to the organization of the militia, whether it comports with this declaration or not. It is extremely injudicious to intermix matters of doubt with fundamentals."[141] If the rights of conscientious objectors were not constitutionalized in part because its ambit was a matter of doubt and not clearly fundamental, it goes without saying (or repeating) that the putative right to arm oneself for private purposes—which, although favored by a few radicals outside Congress,[142] was not even reported by the House Committee—remained beyond the scope of the Second Amendment as passed by both Houses and sent to the states for ratification.

A second failed motion by Elbridge Gerry affords additional evidence of the Framers' military construction of the Second Amendment. Gerry thought the first part of the Amendment suffered from uncertainty, and feared that "[a] well regulated militia being the best security of a free State, admitted an idea that a standing army was a secondary one."[143] What Gerry feared, apparently, was *state* standing armies. He was alone in this apprehension, however. Probably, less radical members considered the language of Article 1, Section 10, Clause 3 ("No State shall . . . keep Troops or Ships of War in time of peace")[144] an ample guarantee against states maintaining independent standing armies.

It may also be that Gerry's reference to a standing army as a "State's" secondary source of security invoked in members' eyes a federal rather than a provincial regular force, serving ostensibly to secure either individual member states or the whole Union. If Gerry did mean to imply that neither states nor the Union should have the protection of any federal regulars whatsoever, this was further than any of his colleagues wished to push the antiarmy issue. That principle, at least as a matter of absolutes, had already been settled in favor of the federalists by ratification of the Philadelphia Constitution. For anti-federal members of the First Congress, the real military question on both the constitutional and policy level now centered on ensuring a significant role for the historic militia alongside the army so as to minimize the dangers of the latter. And in this light, Gerry's failed amendment—whether it referred to state or federal armies—only enhances the impression that the issue before Congress was the protection of political liberties from the baneful effects of a military establishment.

Another indication that the House considered the Second Amendment a public surety against the abuses of a large standing army rather than a private allowance to keep weapons for personal purposes emerges from the debate to amend its text to require two-thirds consent by both houses for setting up a standing army during peacetime. While Gerry received no floor support for his thinly veiled suggestion that the Constitution be amended to bar standing armies entirely, Erasmus Burke of South Carolina felt bold enough to essay a slightly less radical proviso. Burke proposed that "[any] standing army in time of peace is dangerous to public liberty, and such shall not be raised or kept up in time of peace, but from necessity, and for security of the people, nor then without the consent of two-thirds of the members present of both Houses; and in all cases the military shall be subordinate to the civil authority."[145]

This amendment to the Amendment failed by a margin of thirteen votes, but no one disagreed with Burke's insistence that the militia served as a hedge against the army establishment. Instead, Hartely of Pennsylvania objected that supermajority provisions were undemocratic,[146] and Vining of Delaware protested that the Amendment had just been approved and thus should no longer be subject to debate.[147]

Notwithstanding the fact that the House had already voted to approve the Select Committee version of the proposed Amendment, debate was revived concerning the conscientious objector clause on August 21. The speeches of two members, Thomas Scott of Pennsylvania, and Elias Boudinot of New Jersey, are memorialized in the *Annals*. Boudinot favored retaining the conscientious objector provision on grounds of religious liberty and out of concern that unwilling citizens not be compelled to go to war. Scott meanwhile returned to the theme sounded four days earlier by Gerry, and expressed fears that under the proposed clause, conscientious objectors could "neither be called upon for services, nor [could] . . . an equivalent be demanded."[148]

Under such circumstances, Scott warned, "a militia can never be depended upon. This would lead to the violation of another article in the Constitution, which secures to the people the right of keeping arms, and in this case recourse must be had to a standing army."[149] Now, if "the right of keeping arms," as Scott calls it, referred to a right of keeping weapons for purposes other than serving in the militia, it is difficult to see how that right could be violated by exempting Quakers and other professing pacifist sectarians from the right and obligation of militia service. At the same time, it is not at all clear that violating a right to weapons possession for private, nonmilitary purposes would so weaken the militia's manpower pool as to require creation of a large standing army to defend the nation. Scott, clearly, must have had militia service in mind when he spoke of the "right of keeping arms."

To be sure, a single legislator's comments cannot define the elusive contours of a legislature's intent.[150] But placing Scott's comments in their proper context is enlightening precisely because Scott's remarks have been cited glibly for the proposition that there is "another article in the constitution, which secures to the people the right of keeping arms" in order to suggest that the militia-focused right enshrined in the Second Amendment can be divorced from an entirely distinct, private right to arms.[151] On closer inspection, this turns out to be a highly contrived construction. Scott differentiates not between separate constitutional protections for rights to arms for public and private purposes, but between the right to arms for public purposes and the proposed right of conscientious objection. His concern was that constitutional protection for objector status would undermine the sense of public duty and obligation that alone rendered the right to arms meaningful. As Scott explained, he did not consider conscientious objection a constitutional right at all, but rather a question of policy for state legislatures:

> I conceive it . . . to be a legislative right altogether. There are many sects I know, who are religiously scrupulous in this respect; I do not mean to deprive them of any indulgence the law affords; my design is to guard against those who are of no religion. It has been urged that religion is on the decline; if so, the argument is more strong in my favor, for when the time comes that all religion should be discarded, the generality of persons shall have recourse to these pretexts to get excused from bearing arms.[152]

Again, one is hard pressed to imagine godless pacifists or shirkers feigning Quakerism in hopes of being excused from the exercise of their constitutional right to keep weapons for hunting or shooting trespassers.

In sum, a review of the House debates makes clear that no issues relating to self-defense or hunting were contemplated in the context of the future Second Amendment. Twelve members spoke,[153] airing their differences over a variety of topics, principally the advisability of affording constitutional protection to religious objection. No one spoke for the unleavened virtue of standing armies, nor for a right to arms for private purposes, nor for a right to carry arms for any purpose other than service in the state militia, or in the federalized militia called up into national service.

Our knowledge of proceedings in the Senate is far more sketchy, since the Senate's affairs were carried on behind closed doors until 1794, and no official record of Senate debates was kept until thereafter. Even Senator William MacLay's Journal, generally a source of useful information and lively opinion on Senate debates during the First Congress, falls silent on the Bill of Rights, as the Pennsylvanian spent much of September 1789 in his sickbed lambasting the federalists and bewailing the Quaker State's fading chances of becoming the permanent seat of government.[154] We do know from the bare-bones account in the Senate Journal[155] that the Senate joined the House in rejecting a motion to restrict the powers of Congress to keep up a standing army during time of peace, and that the Senate parted company with the House in rejecting the conscientious objector provision that had engendered so much debate among the representatives.[156] In addition, the Senate struck the "body of the people" tag that the House Select Committee had appended to its description of the militia as the "best security of a free state,"[157] which description the Senate then recast as "necessary to the security of a free state."[158]

But the Senate also took up at least one proposed change not considered in the other chamber. The Senate considered a motion to insert "for the common defence" between "bear arms" and "shall not" in the major clause.[159] Had this motion carried, the Amendment would have read in full *"A well regulated militia, being necessary to the security of a free State, the right of the people to keep and bear arms for the common defence shall not be infringed."* The motion to insert this four-word qualifier failed,[160] however, and interpreters favoring a private rights reading of the Second Amendment are much inclined to argue that the Senate's decision not to include this "common defence" provision suggests that the drafters had private, individual defense in mind.[161]

There are, however, at least two other explanations for the Senate's decision to reject the proposed insertion, and they more nearly reflect what we know about the Senate's general approach to the Bill of Rights and the anti-federal mandate for Amendments than does the individualists' model. First, the Senate's revision of the House draft of the Bill of Rights focused on brevity. According to the editor of *The Documentary History of the Bill of Rights,* "the Senate performed the important job of tightening up the language of the House version, striking out surplus wording and provisions."[162] Indeed, the Senate trimmed the Bill of Rights from seventeen to twelve Amendments, and in the process cut its overall length by some thirty percent.[163] This concern to prune away excess verbiage from the House-reported Bill of Rights hardly suggests that senators would have wished to burden the pending Second Amendment with surplusage of their own creation, given that invocation of arms bearing in the militia already clearly proclaimed the purpose of common defense to eighteenth-century ears.

Quite apart from these considerations of brevity and avoidance of redundancy, inserting a reference to the "common defence" would have introduced an element of inconsistency into a provision already linked in its first clause to the "security" of a "free State." "Common" defense might well have suggested to the draftsmen national defense. As senators worked over the text of the Second Amendment, they could not have forgotten that in provisions of the Articles of Confederation relating to the militia, the terms "common defence" had been used to mean joint state action under federal control to defend, collectively, the United States.[164] Thus, if arms bearing were qualified as necessary to the "common defence," the very concerns at the heart of the anti-federalist crusade would be frustrated. The anti-federalist mandate, after all, focused on the militia precisely because it served as a protective force on the state level, rather than for the common defense of the nation.[165] Without a record of the Senate debates, any analysis of the Framers' understanding in this regard is even more speculative than these ventures normally are. Still, it is well to keep in mind that senators—then far more than now—considered theirs the states' rather than the peoples' chamber, and senators perceived their primary responsibility as protecting state rather than popular interests.[166]

With this background in mind, a state-militia-focused reading of the Senate's rejection of the "common defence" insertion is reinforced by reference to the above-mentioned substitution of "State" for "country" in the House Select Committee draft of the Second Amendment. When the militia was labeled the best security of a free "country," it seemed to have an exclusively national purpose, but when redefined as the best security of a free "State," its local purpose was clearly preserved. The Senate, of course, rearranged the clause to read "necessary to the security of a free State," thereby retaining, and emphasizing, the pointed local reference. Linked to the House switch from "country" to "State," the Senate's rejection of the "common defence" clause thus reflects an Amendment concerned with federalism, and the preservation of states' capacities to defend themselves against disorder, insurrection, and invasion whenever the national government should refrain from acting, or find itself unable to act under the federal military or militia powers.

Many of these pages have been devoted to exploration of the original meaning and context of the terms of the Second Amendment. "Bearing arms" and "militia," in particular, were freighted in the late eighteenth century with significance not perhaps apparent at a first casual examination in our own time.[167] In large measure, this significance becomes understandable only in the light of detailed examination of the rich, textured intellectual history in which those terms existed. Yet, in the end, only the language written into the final version of the Amendment—passed by both Houses and ratified by the states—remains binding. While little discussion of eighteenth-century context and theory will be entirely off point, many of the ideas long associated with arms or the militia did not work their way into the words finally expressing the "right to bear arms" that comes down to us today. And notwithstanding citations by "standard modelers"[168] to English game law cases[169] and the "Dissent of the Minority of the Convention of Pennsylvania,"[170] one of these related constructs not codified into the Second Amendment was the right to keep arms for private purposes.

Some radicals out of Congress, such as Samuel Adams in the Massachusetts Convention, had sought to join that very issue.[171] Formulations that would have constitutionalized such a right were readily available.[172] Yet they were not only rejected by the drafters,[173] they were not even raised in the House debates. We are left instead with the single sentence of Madison's formulation, rearranged,[174] culled,[175] and, in two instances, altered,[176] yielding ultimately the familiar Second Amendment ratified in 1791. Understanding its terms, and its terms only, in the light of then familiar usage and theory, a right serving a collective, essentially republican, purpose emerges: a right of the people of the states and of the Union to keep and bear arms in the militia—for federal purposes when duly required under the Constitution, and for state purposes when federal demands are silent. The Amendment's introductory clause, meanwhile, leaves us with a wish, expressed in precatory words, by which our constitutional testators implored their heirs to rely, to the extent possible, on the citizen militia rather than on a corruptible standing army, and by which they defined expressly the context that gives meaning to the right the Amendment secures.

II

FROM MILITIA TO NATIONAL GUARD

4

The Decay of the Old Militia, 1789–1840

Things change. And sometimes the changes in the externalities affect the meaning of words and the applicability of once binding precepts. We have argued that the text of the Second Amendment hinged on the concept of a militia as understood in eighteenth-century usage. To the ratifiers, the right to keep and bear arms was inextricably and exclusively bound to the maintenance of a militia, and the militia was, ideally, a people's army, well-trained, commanded by local authority, self-armed, and responsive to the call of duty as necessary to protect common security. We now turn to the question of whether changes in the historical context in which that text was articulated irretrievably undermine the predicate of the right to arms. The question is: Does the history of the American militia during the two centuries following ratification fundamentally rewrite the present-day legal significance of the constitutional provision originally designed to protect that militia from undue federal encroachment? We should emphasize that we do not say that change—change in the referents of words or in the social context of their utterance—necessarily destroys meaning or saps an expressed precept of force or effect in the altered circumstances. As we develop more fully in chapter 7, we mean to say only that when the purpose of a constitutional right is expressed directly in the Constitution, as is the purpose of the right to bear arms in the Second Amendment, there may come a point in the evolution of the social predicate where the original edict can no longer be applied without unacceptable divergence from the contemplated purpose. This assertion itself rests on an underlying axiom: that enacted text is meaningful, that it binds future generations to the extent that it can be applied according to the general purposes of its enactment. We realize that what seems axiomatic to us may seem dubious to others. We try to justify our essentially conservative credo hereafter. But at this point, our mission is to examine the institution of "the militia" to determine whether it has evolved so far that the eighteenth-century term can no longer be applied to the modern version without fatally distorting the meaning of the constitutional right to arms. Crucial to our understanding of this evolution of the militia is a comparison of the context in which the militia functioned at the framing and that in which it operates now.

FEDERALISM AND THE MILITIA: ATTEMPTS AT NATIONAL REVIVAL UNDER FEDERALISTS AND JEFFERSONIANS

In the years 1789–1791, the operational role of the militia reflected the military dualism of the Founders, who envisioned both a smallish standing army and a serviceably effective militia, each held in check by the federal structure. Writing for a unanimous Court in *Perpich v. Department of Defense*,[1] Justice Stevens aptly summarized the ideological and pragmatic bipolarity at the heart of the nation's early constitutional and statutory military law:

> Two conflicting themes, developed at the Constitutional Convention and repeated in debates over military policy during the next century, led to a compromise in the text of the Constitution and in later statutory enactments. On the one hand, there was a widespread fear that a national standing Army posed an intolerable threat to individual liberty and to the sovereignty of the separate States, while, on the other hand, there was a recognition of the danger of relying on inadequately trained soldiers as the primary means of providing for the common defense.[2]

The constitutional compromise described by Justice Stevens authorized a federal army under executive command, but dependent on Congress for biannual appropriations, and simultaneously established federal authority to prescribe militia training and equipment and to call the militia into federal service for limited purposes.[3] Two years later, the Second Amendment reflected its Framers' aspirations that the nation rely primarily on militia for the national defense, and made clear that the federal government lacked the power to disarm the state militia.[4] In deference to the passion of anti-federalists, the Second Amendment, like other elements of the Bill of Rights, prohibited the federal government from exercising a power never expressed or delegated in the original seven articles of 1787.

The dualistic military theory embodied in the Constitution proved harder to implement than to expound. As Justice Stevens noted, "Congress was authorized both to raise and support a national Army and also to organize 'the Militia' . . . [but] [i]n the early years of the Republic, Congress did neither."[5] The failure to organize either citizen or regular soldiery resulted not from inattention or dereliction, but from unbridgeable differences of principle between the administration and Congress, and from culturally entrenched antimilitarism within the public at large.

The Washington administration inherited from the Confederation a regular army of 672 officers and men.[6] With such a small permanent force available, the western frontier appeared highly vulnerable to native attack and to British incursion from forts along the Great Lakes—which remained in royal hands despite clear provisions of the Treaty of Paris demanding their prompt evacuation.[7] But even with strengthened federal powers in place under the new Constitution, the nation's Revolutionary-era republicanism lived on to speak loudly for reliance on the common militia. In a climate of pervasive suspicion toward all aspects of potential central military power, the Congress of 1789 confronted the dual tasks of providing for the standing army Washington desired (if on a much smaller scale than the chief executive thought wise) and at the same time organizing the nation's militia pursuant to the militia clauses of the Constitution and the historic expectations of the states.[8]

But the first president and the First Congress were not writing military policy on a clean slate. Throughout the Confederation period, Washington had vainly pressed the old Congress to increase the size of the army.[9] The Confederation Congress lacked the authority to impose the general's desires on the states, but it had resisted Washington's suggestions for reasons of ideology as well as jurisdiction.[10] Given the scope of anti-federal hostility to a potentially vigorous federal military establishment, Washington understood that the new Congress was not likely to legislate a substantially larger army, even if the legislature was now endowed with authority to do more than merely ask the states for troops as its predecessor had done. Beyond the new powers to establish and maintain an army directly, Congress now also had the novel authority to organize the state militia for national purposes. Here Washington hoped to encounter less congressional resistance, and he personally urged Congress to act to organize the militia in August 1789.[11]

As we have noted, Congress was preoccupied during its first session with establishing the revenue system and the basic administrative and judicial machinery.[12] When Congress did take up systematization of the militia at the opening of its second session in January 1790, members became embroiled in controversy over "selection" or "classification."[13] On behalf of the administration, War Secretary Knox presented to Congress a bill to establish a select, classified national militia. Following the outline of his General Arrangement proposed to the Confederation Congress in 1786, Knox's militia bill would have grouped the eligible population by age and required substantial service and training from the youngest cadre.[14] The administration hoped to effect benefits equivalent to those of a sizable standing army without arousing anti-federal suspicions, but Knox's proposal quickly spawned resistance focused on the very issues that had generated the standing army dispute during the ratification struggle and animated the debates over the future Second Amendment in the previous congressional session.

A select—as opposed to a common or general—militia had been a favorite notion of Washington, Knox, and Treasury Secretary Hamilton since they first addressed the permanent organization of the nation's military immediately after independence.[15] All three were dissatisfied with the performance of amateur soldiers during the war and favored the creation of a substantial professional army, but had come to realize that this goal was not politically attainable. They therefore embraced the select militia as the next best option. To create an effective militia, Washington and his cabinet urged, militia soldiers required more training and discipline than could possibly be instilled by the states mustering their entire adult male population for a single or at best a few days each year. To bring a better-trained militia into existence, the administration favored classifying the nation's male population into three age-based groups subject to differing levels of service and preparation. Under the militia plan that Knox proposed to Congress,[16] young men aged eighteen to twenty were to form an "advanced corps" and train up to thirty days a year under regular army supervision. Men from twenty-one to forty-five would form the "main corps" and train four days a year, while men from forty-six to sixty would form a "reserved corps."[17]

Knox hoped to fashion a federal defense system capable of meeting all crises, "whether arising from internal or external causes."[18] This severe federal implement was needed, according to Knox, because "convulsive events, generated by the inordinate pursuit of riches or ambition, require[d] that the government should possess a strong corrective arm."[19] Knox could not have chosen more incendiary language. If classifying men according to age and selecting only the youngest group for training and active service made sense in military and economic terms, it also entailed formation of fighting bands less firmly rooted to their communities by family and property than the historic common militia.[20] While this scheme would have mitigated the economic disruption associated with sending heads of families and proprietors of farms on extended training assignments or campaigns, it also would have vested each state's military power in the group of citizens most susceptible to demagoguery and most likely to support a Caesarist conspiracy. Thus, classification may not have implied that the nation would rely on a regular military establishment, but it did imply that the militia would be less than optimally republican.

For more than two years Congress wrestled with the Knox bill and its successors,[21] but the Militia Act that finally passed into law on May 8, 1792[22] embodied no meaningful resolution of the selection issue, lacked any mechanism for federal enforcement, and therefore relied on the states to implement a largely hortatory organizational scheme. The Act also abandoned provisions for separation of the militia-of-the-whole into age groups, for federally standardized training, and for federally supervised exercises. Instead, Congress simply laid out the organizational form of the nation's militia, dividing the force into divisions and battalions that were in turn subdivided into regiments and companies to match the structure of the regular force, and left to the states the problem of compelling citizens to fill out these units. The Act required that states carry their "able-bodied white male citizen[s]" between the ages of eighteen and forty-four on the rolls, and exempted various federal officials from duty. But Congress also implicitly left the states free to continue the practice of exempting various additional categories of citizens, such as teachers, clergymen, and conscientious objectors. Indeed, Congress seemingly also left open the question of states including additional categories of persons — principally free black males — in their state militia rosters, even though no federal service requirement attached to them by virtue of the Act. In addition, the Act limited the president's power to call forth the militia so that no one man would be called to serve for more than a maximum of three months in any one year, and no single individual would be burdened any more "than in due rotation with every other able-bodied man of the same rank."[23]

More importantly for our purposes, the 1792 Act provided that citizens from whom militia service was required furnish their own standard arms and equipment. The command that citizens appear for militia duty fully armed and equipped could scarcely have been more explicit. The Act stated

> That every citizen so enrolled and notified, shall, within six months thereafter, provide himself[24] with a good musket or firelock, a sufficient bayonet and belt, two spare flints, and a knapsack, a pouch with a box therein to contain not less than twenty-four cartridges, suited to the bore of the musket or firelock, each cartridge to contain a proper quantity of powder and ball: or with a good rifle, knapsack, shot-pouch and powder-horn, twenty balls suited to the bore of his rifle, and a quarter of a pound of powder; and shall appear, so armed, accoutred and provided, when called out to exercise, or into service, except, that when called out on company days to exercise only, he may appear without a knapsack.[25]

Similar clauses set forth standards by which officers should arm themselves.[26]

Thus, the Second Congress amplified the vision of the militia as the time-honored "constitutional army"[27] that had informed the First Congress's drafting of the Second Amendment less than three years before. The Second Amendment guaranteed the right to keep and bear arms in the militia; the Militia Act laid down a detailed description of the weapons militiamen must keep and bear when called to serve. These were pointedly and unequivocally military arms ("a sufficient bayonet and belt, . . . a pouch with a box therein to contain not less than twenty-four cartridges, . . . each cartridge to contain a proper quantity of powder and ball"). Within five years of the Act's passage, muskets held under the act were to have "bores sufficient for balls of the eighteenth part of a pound." Militia members, then, were expected to keep and bear arms necessary for meeting the security needs of the nation, arms falling within certain standards and regular limits defined by Congress. Guns of that sort did not necessarily correspond to each individual's sense of convenience or perceived need to defend himself and family independent of military obligation.[28] Moreover, under the terms of the Militia Act, enrolled citizens were not simply obligated to furnish themselves with regulation weapons, they were required to "hold [the stipulated arms] exempted from all suits, distresses, executions or sales, for debt or for the payment of taxes." The militiaman's musket was therefore not an unfettered article of personal property that he might dispense with according to his sense of whim or interest. Rather, the privately held guns of the militia were tokens of social, civic responsibility, with a legal status defined in very large measure by the legislative organ of the central state.

The Militia Act of 1792 was preceptive in form. But in operation it remained little more than a catalogue of congressional exhortations to the states. While some of the states enacted early measures seeking to bring into effect the Act's provisions, all states had abandoned any pretense of compliance long before the Civil War.[29] The Act stayed on the books until 1903.[30] For 111 years it represented not simply the cornerstone, but virtually the entire edifice of federal militia law,[31] long outlasting the military utility of the muskets, firelocks, and spare flints it called on citizens to hold ready for the service of their states and country. Throughout that long period, all efforts of presidents, secretaries of war, and congressional leaders to flesh out the federal government's regulatory oversight of the myriad state militias stalled short of legislative fruition. Ultimately, from Knox's proposed classification scheme, through Secretary John C. Calhoun's attempt at centralizing reform after the repeated debacles of the War of 1812,[32] down to the ambitious and highly controversial selection plan proposed by Secretary Joel R. Poinsett during Martin Van Buren's administration,[33] the same intractable dilemma thwarted every effort to make the historic militia into a serviceable defender of American national security: although a disorganized, undifferentiated militia that made few financial or personal demands on the people was militarily useless, anything more was unpalatable to voters.

While some voters remained committed to republican rhetoric, for many, the value of a republican militia took second place to the value of private pursuits in the increasingly individualistic nineteenth century.[34] By the time the federal government finally assumed meaningful and effective supervision of the militia in 1903,[35] the ancient War Department dream of achieving effective national security through reform or reorganization of the common militia had long been abandoned by even the most zealous critics of a robust military establishment.[36]

Notwithstanding these subsequent developments, loyalty to the ideal of the common militia behind the Second Amendment—and concomitantly aversion to the establishment of an effective military, whether professional or "selectively" amateur—remained powerful during the early national period. Militarism seemed in those early days anything but a chimerical danger. Numerous episodes between 1783 and 1798 highlight the stark reality behind classically republican-inspired fears that a military coup could be directed to the subversion of the infant republic. These incidents dramatize the republican fears of an irresponsible military branch.

Late in the winter of 1783, the war was over. But no peace had been ratified, and the Continental army had neither disbanded nor received its pay. This presented an incendiary situation all too similar to the crisis at the close of the (first) English Civil War.[37] In the American version, a group of disgruntled officers circulated the so-called Newburgh Addresses through the Continental camps, threatening that the army would take matters into its own hands if Congress did not pay the veterans. Only Washington's timely address to the officers on March 15 of that year (this was the famous "I have not only grown gray, but almost blind in the service of my country" or "spectacles" speech) diffused the situation before it flared into a march on Philadelphia.[38]

Meanwhile, many of the same unhappy officers dispatched both petitions and secret communiqués to numerous sympathizers in Congress, including Washington's former aide-de-camp, Alexander Hamilton, member from New York since 1781.[39] Hamilton in turn wrote Washington, suggesting somewhat opaquely that the army might be maintained after the expected peace settlement to pressure state governments into meeting the congressional requisitions required to fund the officers' pensions and bonuses. More ominously, Hamilton proposed that failing this, the army might seize the state assets it required by direct action.[40] Washington rejected Hamilton's proposals in no uncertain terms, although the General seems never to have appreciated how deeply his favorite lieutenant had enmeshed himself in nascent plots to orchestrate a military coup. But even after the collapse of the Newburgh conspiracy, Hamilton tested the resolve of the commander of the Continental Forces by renewing thinly veiled overtures to install a military dictatorship.[41] Hamilton's ideas were doubtless as shocking to republicans then as they are to democrats today, and in those fragile days between independence and nationhood, these designs (by no means his alone) were more than antithetical to the civilian paradigm, they posed a real threat of military rule. To the further consternation of a then ultra-whiggish polity, General von Steuben chose the same juncture to announce the founding of the Society of Cincinnati, a secretive and hereditary association of veteran officers of the Revolution. To republicans, his seemed but another conspiratorial step toward the establishment of a titled, privileged military aristocracy on the European model.[42]

A few months later, young America witnessed another incident of the army running wild. In June 1783, after news of the Treaty of Paris had reached America, recruits in Philadelphia deserted and barricaded Congress in the State House, demanding pay and bonuses. Happily, this mob simply dispersed when Congress adjourned for the night without acting on the soldiers' threats.[43] But before it disbanded, the Continental army seemed poised on the brink of intervention in civil politics. These incidents, and others, gave real substance to the determination of the newly independent Americans not to recreate a government on the corrupted model of the Old World, but to entrust their security to the less dangerous hands of the classical citizen militia.

At the same time, there was ample reason for concern regarding the capability and/or dependability of the amateur, occasional military configuration. Three years after the Continental Army finally decamped, Shays's Rebellion was put down (haltingly) by Massachusetts militia. But the progress of that insurrection was facilitated when discontented members of western county militia crossed over to the rebels and assisted in the seizure of the Continental arsenal at Springfield.[44] This evidence of the local militia's unreliability helped spark the federalist movement that led to the Constitutional Convention and ultimately to the rise of the Federalist Party.[45] But if suspicions regarding the competence and loyalty of the militia gave rise to Hamiltonian federalism in the 1780s, so too suspicions of a Caesarist federal military helped usher in Jeffersonian Republicanism in the 1790s.[46] Washington himself led the federalized militia that put down the Whiskey Rebellion in 1794, but he was visibly worn and aged, and the prospect of his lieutenant, Alexander Hamilton, marching through Pennsylvania at the head of the 13,000 strong "constitutional army"[47] alarmed even moderates.[48]

In 1798, President John Adams called on Pennsylvania militia and 500 regulars to put down another tax revolt, this time instigated by Revolutionary War veteran, John Fries, who led western Pennsylvania's resistance to revenue officers' attempts to collect a "window tax" designed to finance an enormous army to fight the Quasi War with France. Adams showed great and characteristic moderation in pardoning Fries.[49] While he is rightly celebrated as the father of the navy, the second president remained at heart a Whiggish and historicist common lawyer, distrustful of over-large standing armies and committed to constitutional rule, no matter how much he resented the principles and tactics of the opposition. We cannot say the same of his erstwhile colleague, Alexander Hamilton. The former treasury secretary had been disgraced by sex scandal and departed from government, but as the leader of the "High Federalists" he was the real moving force behind the proposed army.[50] Indeed, it was Hamilton's plans for an ideologically purged army of 60,000 to fight a nonexistent war that most agitated the republican opposition. Rumors abounded that Hamilton intended to use the army to prevent Jefferson from taking power as the election of 1800 approached,[51] and republican governors in Pennsylvania and Virginia made secret plans to countermarch their militias on Washington.[52] Happily—although fully funded by Congress—the enormous phantom army never assembled, and when Adams was defeated and the electoral college convened, Hamilton showed his better nature by endorsing the republican leader, Thomas Jefferson, as a lesser evil than the "Cataline" Aaron Burr.[53] As the historian Richard Hofstadter pointed out, this marked the first time in modern history that power passed peacefully from one elected party to another,[54] but it was perhaps a much closer call between civil war and peaceful transition than is generally acknowledged.

THE LAST YEARS OF THE MILITIA-OF-THE-WHOLE:
POPULAR DISCONTENT AND GOVERNMENT INERTIA

Notwithstanding the prominence of real and imaginary regular armies in the political crises of the 1780s and 1790s, and the related persistence of republican rhetoric focusing on the constitutional importance of the militia, and despite the hortatory intentions embodied in the Militia Act of 1792, compulsory universal militia service disintegrated during the early years of the Republic. In state after state, the militia-of-the-whole fell into disfavor and disrepute.[55] In the years after the Revolution, fewer and fewer men made muster on militia days.[56] One reason was the increasing number of exceptions to the universal service obligation enacted by various state legislatures, who by the early nineteenth century had excused from military obligation not only clergy and conscientious objectors, but such citizens as school and university teachers, students, jurors, mariners, and ferrymen.[57] While the rest of the military-aged, white male population generally remained obligated to serve, in practice, more and more people simply could not or did not wish to interrupt their everyday economic activities in an increasingly bustling, productive, and differentiated society in order to appear armed and accoutered on the appointed muster day. In general, people not entitled to an exemption who failed to show up were subject to fines on the order of $10, roughly equivalent to $1,000 today.[58] These penalties were enforced sporadically and selectively,[59] adding to the growing resentment many felt at the seemingly irrelevant and obsolete service obligation. Those better off could readily afford to pay the fine for nonattendance as a sort of tax, while for the average farmer or farmer's son, $10 remained a formidable burden.[60] Class antagonism grew stronger still as the Northeast industrialized in the first decades of the nineteenth century, and state legislatures added factory owners and foremen to the list of exempted citizens.[61]

Several developments during the War of 1812 contributed to the demise of the old militia. In the first place, many New Englanders resented war with Britain and Canada. New Englanders did not hasten to make muster with a view to invading Canada, as indeed they had hesitated to bear arms for the purpose of enforcing first Jefferson's Embargo Act and then Madison's Non-Importation Order against British trade. The unpopularity of service in "Mr. Madison's War" helped sap the vitality of the militia in its New England heartland, where the institution had remained more vigorous than in other parts of the nation.[62] Then, too, the governors of Massachusetts, Connecticut, Rhode Island, New Hampshire, and Vermont, who had been reluctant to order their militia to enforce the Embargo and Non-Importation Acts against Britain prior to the war, now refused to muster their troops for an invasion of Canada as commanded by the President.[63] To be sure, the Constitution did not contemplate the President ordering the militia to serve outside U.S. borders,[64] and the President lacked clear statutory authorization to do so.[65] But in disobeying the Commander in Chief instead of seeking judicial relief, New England's chief executives flirted with treason.[66] The constitutional crisis over gubernatorial consent to presidential call-ups was not resolved in favor of the federal executive until the Supreme Court's decision in *Martin v. Mott*[67] twelve years after the war's end, and the narrower question concerning withholding of gubernatorial consent to militia service in foreign countries was not finally settled until the *Perpich* case in 1990.[68] More generally, the issue of the constitutionality of militia service outside U.S. borders remained a thorn in the side of presidents during the Mexican, Spanish, and First World Wars as well, and continues to inform National Guard policy to this day.[69] Over the course of the nineteenth century, uncertainty regarding the President's ability to rely on the militia for extraterritorial service became yet another factor contributing to the old militia's demise.

With a few exceptions, the common militia acquitted itself dishonorably during the War of 1812. Militia serving in a mixed federal/state command under General Dearborn refused to cross the international border at Lake Champlain in preparation for an attack against Montreal, forcing abandonment of the American offensive in the first year of the war.[70] Militia ineptitude was also a key factor in the August 1814 sacking of Washington, as British Regulars marched through a patchwork army of seamen, handfuls of organized militia, and multitudes of untrained common militia arrayed across the Bladensburg Road, and straight into the capital. This spectacle, marking the low point of national humiliation, unfolded within eyesight of a hapless and helpless Commanding General of the Army and President of the United States, while Secretary of State James Monroe rode about frantically giving confusing orders.[71] Admiral Morison offers the following revealing account of the Bladensburg debacle:

For five days the British army marched along the banks of the Patuxent, approaching the capital of the United States without seeing an enemy or firing a shot. In the meantime, Washington was in a feverish state of preparation. About 7000 militia, all that turned out of 95,000 summoned, were placed under an unusually incompetent general [Brigadier John Armstrong Jr.] and hurried to a strong position behind the village of Bladensburg, athwart the road over which the invaders must advance. President Madison and some of the cabinet came out to see the fight. After the militia had suffered only 66 casualties they broke and ran, and [General Robert] Ross [commander of the British land forces], delayed a few hours by the bravery of marines and naval gunners, pressed on to Washington that evening (24 August 1814). Some officers arrived in time to eat a dinner at the White House that had been prepared for the President and Mrs. Madison.[72]

One must wonder whether Madison took this occasion to reflect on his famous comment in *The Federalist* about the invincibility of a nation boasting a militia of 500,000.[73]

While the British expeditionary force was ravaging American militia up and down the Chesapeake, American fortunes were beginning to turn in the far north. Ultimately, no development of the second war with Britain bode less well for the old militia than the emergence of the regulars. Along the Niagara Falls, Winfield Scott's heavily drilled U.S. infantry regiments fought the British to a standstill at Chippewa on July 5, and again at Lundy's Lane on July 25. With Scott's success, America finally appeared capable of defending itself on the ground, even of mounting a ground-based offensive. "By God, those are Regulars!" an astounded British Commander Riall reportedly exclaimed of Scott's stalwarts at Chippewa.[74] According to Henry Adams, "[t]he battle of Chippewa was the only occasion during the war when equal bodies of regular troops met face to face, in

"The Nation's Bulwark. A Well Disciplined Militia." Hand-colored engraving by Clay. Published by R. H. Hobson, Philadelphia, 1829.

"A Militia Muster." Color lithograph by D. Claypole Johnston. Published by Johnston, Boston, 1835.

These two illustrations appear courtesy of the Anne S. K. Brown Military Collection at Brown University Library. They suggest the rapid decline of the common militia — and the increasing ridicule to which that militia was subjected — in Jacksonian America. The "Nation's Bulwark," writes Marcus Cunliffe of the citizens assembled in the first figure, "can contrive only a ragged muster. Still, the majority have been able to produce weapons of a sort. A decade or two later, even this much evidence of the martial spirit was lacking." Cunliffe's point is born out in the second print. By 1835, even in the militia's New England heartland, cornstalks, sticks, and umbrellas are as common among the soldiers as muskets and bayonets, and fighting and drinking appear to command more attention than the ridiculous captain in his overblown hat.

extended lines on an open plain in broad daylight, without advantage of position; and never again after that combat was an Army of American regulars beaten by British troops.[75] Crucially for our purposes, the regular infantry's valor in the Great Lakes campaigns of 1814 "contributed . . . much to the prestige of the Regular Army and its acceptance as the necessary axis of American defense."[76] Thereafter, no prominent statesman would argue seriously, as Jefferson and Knox had once done, that a classified militia could wholly replace the U.S. Army. Throughout the nineteenth century, the regular army remained small, numbering between 6,000 and 27,000 in peacetime, slightly more during war.[77] But it, and not the militia, was thenceforth acknowledged as the backbone of the nation's security.

As enthusiasm for militia service continued to decline after the War of 1812, so too did the ability of the average citizen to appear armed in compliance with the Militia Act of 1792 or applicable state regulations. In the early years of the nineteenth century, it was commonplace for militia captains to complain that more and more members of their companies appeared with no weapon at all, or with such poor makeshifts for guns as umbrellas, broomsticks, farm tools, and garden implements.[78] And as citizens came to lack the desire and equipment needed for militia service, so too they began to ridicule and burlesque the very concept of the citizen army. Two northern cartoons depicting typical musters of the 1820s and 1830s are illustrative (see figures opposite).

Further illustrative are Abraham Lincoln's recollections of his youthful experiences of "militia trainings" in the West, where the militia lacked even that fading status that its deep historical roots and the nostalgic memories of aging Revolutionary-era veterans preserved to the eastward:

> We remember one of these parades ourselves here, at the head of which, on horse-back, figured our old friend Gordon Adams, with a pine wood sword, about nine feet long, and a paste-board cocked hat, from front to rear about the length of an ox yoke, and very much the shape of one turned bottom upwards; and with spurs having rowels as large as the bottom of a teacup, and shanks a foot and a half long. That was the last militia muster here. Among the rules and regulations, no man is to wear more that five pounds of cod-fish for epaulets, or more than thirty yards of bologna sau-

sages for a sash; and no two men are to dress alike, and if any two should dress alike the one that dresses most alike is to be fined, (I forget how much). Flags they had too, with devices and mottoes, one of which latter is, "We'll fight till we run, and we'll run till we die."[79]

5

The Era of the Volunteers, 1840–1903

THE RISE OF THE VOLUNTEER GUARDS

In Jacksonian America, citizens retained little interest in compelled service in the old universal militia codified by the Militia Act of 1792 and extolled in the Second Amendment. Neither was service with the small regular army widely esteemed by citizenry or Congress, and the regulars continued to bear the brunt of all the familiar republican critiques, notwithstanding the grudging acceptance accorded the army by the nation and the legislature following its vindication during the War of 1812. But even as an increasingly democratic and individualistic people turned away from the common militia, and even as antimilitarism burgeoned into standard fare of the democratic press during the 1830s and 1840s, a new generation of citizen-soldiers embraced the part-time martial ideal by joining volunteer militia companies. These volunteer companies differed fundamentally from the common militia. As the name implies, the units comprised willing volunteers, not the reluctantly qualified members of the public at large. The volunteer units were selective and even elite in their membership, and consciously distanced themselves from the contemptible militia-of-the-whole. Volunteers trained more frequently and more regularly than the common militia had done, and many units took pride in staging target shoots, military displays, and parades. They wore showy, ornate uniforms fashioned after famous European units of the day. And while volunteer units were increasingly licensed and recognized by the states in which they were based, and incorporated into their states' military organizations,[1] the units were not typically (at least in peacetime) formed under state auspices, but through private initiative.

As the cities grew and the economy boomed, busted, and boomed again in the Jacksonian years, volunteer militia companies became commonplace on the urban landscapes. Typically, these new militias served as social clubs as well as military organizations, putting on balls and exhibitions in addition to engaging in military exercises.[2] Many of the companies were affiliated with, or even coextensive with, volunteer urban fire brigades. Rivalries between companies in the same cities were not uncommon, and brawling between native Protestant and Irish Catholic militia units was common sport at mid-century.[3] While some volunteer companies specialized in socializing and preening in fine uniforms, a number of elite units aspired to a genuine measure of military skill. Jefferson Davis's own Mississippi Rifles distinguished themselves in the Mexican War and, generally, the organized volunteer units fought far better in Mexico than the bands of unorganized Southwestern militia who hastened across the border notwithstanding the constitutional prohibition against foreign service. When the Civil War came, it was the presence of established volunteer companies — often fantastically uniformed like Elmer Ellsworth's New York Zouaves — that enabled Winfield Scott to put an army in the field to defend Washington while the government organized recruitment and gathered the regulars.[4]

Before the Civil War, volunteers usually acquired their arms, equipment, and elaborate uniforms wholly by their own means.[5] In this respect, too, they differed from the common militia. The Militia Act required that citizens enrolled in their states' militia provide themselves with standard arms and equipment, but soon after the Act's passage, states not already budgeting for militia arms typically set aside money for muskets for citizens unable to afford their own arms, or even contracted to purchase muskets directly.[6] In 1798, Congress provided for the purchase of 30,000 stands of arms to be requisitioned by the state militia.[7] A decade later, in hopes of counteracting the increasingly lax approach of many states to military affairs, Congress established regular federal appropriations for militia armaments, passing legislation to set aside $200,000 annually for states to claim to purchase arms.[8] Thus, Congress took its first steps down a long road leading, in the early twentieth century, to the federal government's full-scale assumption of the responsibility for arming the militia that the Militia Act of 1792 had lodged with the individual, able-bodied man.[9] For many years, most of the money set aside annually under the 1808 law went unclaimed, attesting to the growing apathy with which state governments and citizens alike viewed service in the "constitutional army."[10] Not until bloodletting in Kansas and the Dred Scott decision heightened sectional tensions in 1857 did some of the Southern states begin to tap the federal well for militia moneys with a view to replenishing armories, which, like those of their sister states throughout the country, had been neglected for many years.[11]

A NATION OF VOLUNTEERS:
THE GRAND ARMY OF THE REPUBLIC

Secession brought an end to Southern claims for federal funds, and Congress did not raise the militia appropriation during the Civil War. Instead, the War Department quickly assumed the task of arming directly the vastly expanded forces required to suppress the Southern insurrection.[12] The War of Secession marked the first time the nation confronted the need for mass mobilization under the Constitution, and the war was fought largely by citizen-soldiers, but not by the common militia. Rather, the Union army was made up overwhelmingly of Volunteers (capitalized in Civil War parlance) who rallied to the federal flag. They arrived chiefly in units raised by the states in response to calls by Congress or the President, and enlisted directly into the service of the United States before embarkation to the front.[13] And after considerable initial confusion regarding the bounds of state and federal authority, all arms used by the 2,666,999 soldiers who served in the Union armies[14] were procured and issued by the federal government.[15]

Over ninety percent of the Union Army was made up of Volunteers. These citizen-soldiers assumed a role more closely akin to that of federalized National Guard units in the twentieth-century world wars than that of early-nineteenth-century, part-time volunteer regiments. They served under federal command, wore standard-issue federal uniforms, and received federal pay (supplemented by state and federal enlistment bounties). Civil War recruitment amounted to a Napoleonic levée en masse, and while the overwhelming majority of

Union soldiers were enlistees rather than draftees, the Grand Army of the Republic partook of the universality of the old common militia, even as it acquired the training and professionalism characteristic of the regulars.

A detailed look at the gradual, piecemeal construction of the Union Army highlights a crucial, intermediate phase of the transition from the militia norm envisioned by the Second Amendment's framers to the standing army model accepted nearly universally by Americans today. The constitutional consensus on the eve of War reflected the plain meaning and historic understanding of army and militia clauses ratified in 1788: Congress had the power to raise and support armies, but what this meant is that Congress could recruit volunteer soldiers into the regular army by offering pay, bonuses, and other incentives. The sovereign power to compel military service rested exclusively with the states. The states, however, were debarred from keeping up regular troops in time of peace without congressional consent by Article 1, Section 10, Clause 3. The only military duty they could compel was service in the militia. Congress, meanwhile, was authorized to call up the state militia into national service "to execute the laws of the Union, suppress insurrections, and repel invasions" as specified in Article 1, Section 8, Clause 15, and this power was partially delegated to the President by the Calling Forth Act of 1795.[16]

When Lincoln took office on March 4, 1861, he inherited intact the Regular Army of some 15,000 men from James Buchanan, who had done virtually nothing to counter the rising rebellion of the South during the lame duck phase of his administration. Although thirty percent of the army's officers defected to the Confederacy during the winter of secession, Lincoln later boasted that not one enlisted man abandoned his post.[17] The new Commander in Chief proceeded initially with caution.[18] But on April 12, shore batteries fired on the federal garrison at Fort Sumter, in Charleston Harbor, South Carolina, and three days later Lincoln called on the states to summon 75,000 volunteers for three months' service under the Militia Acts of 1792 and 1795 for the purpose of putting down rebellious combinations in the seven states that had left the Union and proclaimed a separate Confederacy at Montgomery. 91, 816 men answered the call. A few weeks later, following the secession of Virginia and with further departure of slave-holding states deemed imminent, Lincoln, acting without congressional authorization, increased the size of the regular army by some 22,000, and called on the states to supply 40,000 three-year Volunteers. Within two months, over 200,000 had enlisted.

The Thirty-seventh Congress convened two months early on July 4, 1861, and immediately voted to raise 1,000,000 Volunteers, half to serve as three-year men, and half for the duration of the war. (The latter ended up serving three-year terms as well). By December 3, a federal recruiting service replaced the separate state recruiters, and, with one extended interruption in early 1862, it handled all recruitment for the rest of the war. But on both sides, the death tolls mounted, and visions of swift, easy victory dissipated in the smoky battlefields of Second Bull Run, Antietam, Perryville, Corinth, Fredericksburg, and Stones River during the summer and fall of 1862. No longer did Volunteers hasten to the call of arms as quickly as during the war's first heady months. The South had already adopted a system of national conscription to meet its growing manpower needs in April 1862, and now the North, reluctantly and incrementally, followed suit.[19] On July 17, 1862, Congress amended the Militia Act of 1792, delegating to the President the authority to specify a period of service of up to nine months whenever he called up the state militia, and granting him plenary power to make all necessary rules and regulations for states lacking adequate laws to govern their militia. In other words, Congress (acting seemingly without direct constitutional authorization) empowered the President to step in when states failed to compel the militia service the federal government required. But states did not make haste to implement a draft prescribed by the War Department pursuant to this framework. A restless populace chaffed in the face of danger, compulsion, commutation, and substitution, and recruitment continued almost wholly according to the volunteer principle for the next year of war.[20]

For the North, the war went badly. Manpower demands continued unabated, and Congress, the War Department, and Army Command anticipated gloomily the election year of 1864, when the three-year terms of the early Volunteers—the bulk of the federal army—were scheduled to expire. Since Confederate soldiers had largely mustered in for the duration, Union collapse loomed as a real possibility—barring reform and a change of fortune on the battlefields. On March 3, 1863, Congress acted decisively to forestall this eventuality. The Enrollment Act bypassed the militia powers altogether, and, for the first time in American history, resorted to the "power to raise and support armies" to legislate a federal draft. The Act imposed military duty on all able-bodied male citizens and applicants between the ages of twenty and forty-five, and required their enrollment on two lists from which the conscripts were to be chosen.[21] Controversially, the Act retained social-class-based legacies of the old state militia systems, permitting substitution, and commutation upon payment of a fee of $300.

In preparation for the draft, federal agents spent the spring of 1863 going door to door collecting names for the enrollment register. Implementation of the actual draft, that is, selection of names and numbers from the enrollment lists, engendered resentment throughout the loyal states. In early July, tens of thousands of irate, chiefly Irish, Democratic-voting New Yorkers took to the streets, burning, looting, and lynching to protest the class aspects of the draft law. The riots were not controlled until federal troops arrived via train from the battlefields of Gettysburg.[22] Resistance and riots notwithstanding — or perhaps because of those very factors — only six percent of soldiers to serve in the Union Army were draftees. One reason the Union was able to meet its recruiting needs short of full-scale coercion was the willingness of African Americans to enlist in the U.S. Army. Nearly 200,000 black Volunteers — most of them Southerners living in Union occupied areas, or former slaves who fled to the Union lines — had signed up by war's end. With such notable exceptions as the 54th and 55th Massachusetts' Regiments commemorated in the film *Glory,* these soldiers usually bypassed state service all together, and enrolled directly in the United States Colored Volunteers (later the U.S. Colored Troops).[23]

REVITALIZATION AND PROFESSIONALISM

At the end of the Civil War, the two-million-plus wartime Volunteers were swiftly demobilized, and the regulars dispatched to police the occupied South and the Indian frontier. The few prewar volunteer companies that survived the war as fighting units decamped and went home. Prewar-style volunteer companies, old and new, remained part of the Northern social scene, but for a time, as the nation tried to heal its wounds, the volunteers' passion for martial exercises seemed to wane. However, the outpouring of patriotism that accompanied the Centennial sparked renewed interest in volunteer soldiering, and when industrial turmoil swept the nation in 1877, state governors called on organized state volunteers to put down riots. Indeed, labor unrest prompted state legislatures to renew interest in their state forces. Legislators made no pretense of reviving the long-defunct militia-of-the-whole, but did all they could to foster the respectable part of society's interest in joining organized and newly forming volunteer units, which pointedly kept their distance from the unorganized militias memorialized in the ancient laws.[24]

In part to distinguish themselves from the disreputable unorganized militia, organized volunteer companies styled themselves guards or national guards. The revitalization of state national guards coincided with a passion for reform and improvement then sweeping all the professions, and national guard officers aggressively pursued recognition and accreditation for themselves and their organizations.[25] Organized militia officers from across the country joined forces in 1878 to form the National Guard Association (NGA) with the objective of obtaining funding and recognition from state legislatures and Congress.[26] During this period, legislative and judicial organs made crucial decisions on both the state and national fronts. While state legislatures were proclaiming the organized national guard units their only lawfully established militia,[27] the Supreme Court rejected a claim to individual entitlement to arms outside the context of militia service. In *Presser v. Illinois* (a case we have already mentioned), the Supreme Court rejected Second and Fourteenth Amendment challenges to state prohibitions on private parades of armed individuals, and held that the Constitution protected carrying arms only in lawfully established, organized militia units.[28]

Formation of the NGA reflected the professional aspirations of many late-nineteenth-century militia officers to keep pace with the increasing technical complexity of officership in an industrial age. The National Rifle Association also dates from these years, and it had its origins in some of the same concerns that animated the new NGA.[29] The NRA aimed not at aspiring officers, but at young men (particularly the wholesome, rural, native-born, nonunionized type) who might be called upon to fill out the rank and file of a rapidly mobilized, mass army of citizen-soldiers. Civilian America, according to both the NGA and the NRA, would benefit from acquiring a modicum of proficiency with firearms — not simply because this fostered such Victorian values as self-improvement, sport, and outdoorsmanship—but because military preparedness was a patriotic duty.

National respectability and national security appeared to depend on the volunteer martial spirit, as America seemed less and less isolated on an increasingly imperialistic and competitive world stage. No one doubted that a war with a major power would require mobilization on a scale surpassing even the Civil War. However, compared with the millions of full-time soldiers and trained reserves assembled by the powers of continental Europe, America's tiny Indian constabulary army of some 30,000 seemed insignificant indeed.[30] But only eccentric military reformers like Emory Upton urged America to keep pace with the Europeans, and the overwhelming majority of voters remained adamantly antimilitarist in outlook. If America were to avoid humiliation in any future conflict, it must therefore depend, at least initially, on civilian soldiery. And if these prospective citizen-soldiers were to have any hope of success, they must have prior training. To this end, the NRA saw itself fulfilling a vital purpose by fostering marksmanship and firearms skill in the population eligible for military duty.[31]

While the NRA staged target shoots and formed rifle clubs, the NGA organized seminars and retreats, circulated periodicals, and lobbied state and federal officials. As the nineteenth century drew to a close, Congress began to take notice of the state guards and the NGA alike. Washington increased the annual militia appropriation for the first time in 1887, doubling funding under the 1808 law to $400,000 per annum. Congress acted again in 1900, increasing appropriations to $1,000,000 annually.[32] When Congress next increased federal militia funding in 1903, it simultaneously replaced the minimalist and hopelessly obsolete federal militia rules laid down in the Acts of 1792 and 1795 with comprehensive National Guard legislation embodied in the Militia Act of 1903 (the Dick Act). From that time onward, increases in federal funding for the guard entailed ever-greater army and War/Defense Department supervision of the constitutionally recognized militia.

6

The United States Army and the United States Army
National Guard in the Twentieth Century

At the close of the nineteenth century, mobilization of state guard
units to fight in the Spanish-American War was characterized by scandal and disorder. The disastrous preparation for war was duly recorded by the busy yellow press, who made the most of the stupidity
of politicians, brass, and high command, as well as of the misfor-
tunes experienced by regulars and civilian soldiers alike. Prior to the
invasion of Cuba, regular army and volunteers spent months awaiting transport out of Tampa, or stranded on sidings stretching back
to South Carolina hoping for passage along the single rail line leading into the west Florida port. The soldiers' equipment was neither
standardized, serviceable, appropriate, nor up-to-date. Guardsmen
in particular went into combat wearing woolen uniforms too sweaty
for the tropics, and carrying smoky, single-shot rifles far inferior to
the models borne by their Spanish adversaries. The most notorious
reports of organizational ineptitude dwelled on servicemen suffering
through spoiled canned beef and succumbing to epidemics at a time
when advances in technology had made refrigeration readily available and inoculation against typhoid fever practicable. Few observers
doubted that a more formidable adversary than Spain would have
bested the logistically challenged Americans.[1]

In 1903, following further debacles involving mobilization of state
guard units to police the newly won empire and put down the Philippine insurrection, Congress finally acted under pressure from Presi-

dent Roosevelt to subdivide the militia-of-the-whole—by then entirely fictitious—into an active militia (the National Guard) and an unorganized militia (the nonenrolled male population between eighteen and forty-five).[2] At the same time, the federal government standardized state units and equipment, and, in return for massive increases in federal funding, the states accepted vastly enhanced federal supervision of militia training.[3]

Congress acted again in 1908 to make the National Guard the country's first-line reserve, providing that as the Organized Militia, the National Guard would be called forth before the raising of new federal volunteers.[4] More fundamentally, Congress waived existing territorial limitations on National Guard call-ups, thereby attempting to bypass the issue of the constitutionality of militia service outside the United States, which had plagued the president and War Department in the wars of 1812–15, 1846–48, and 1898–1901. Within a few years, however, both the Attorney General and the Judge Advocate General of the Army had written reports finding this use of the militia to be unconstitutional,[5] presenting Congress anew with the problem of legally deploying American reservists overseas.[6]

This controversy came to a head during the preparedness movement that proceeded American entry into the First World War. With war raging in Europe, American pacifists, socialists, and isolationists opposed any military expansion at all, while states-rights-conscious Southern Democrats (and many Midwestern Republicans) typically favored no more than incremental augmentation of the National Guard (notwithstanding the constitutional problems associated with foreign deployment). Meanwhile, the newly minted general staff and many pro-British Eastern progressives pushed for conscription, establishment of a reserve component wholly independent of the states, and the aggressive expansion of the regular army.[7] The bitterly contested National Defense Act of 1916 "federalized" the Organized Militia, thenceforth known only as the National Guard, and integrated it into the command structure of the War Department and the regular army.[8] The Act specified the guard units the states were to maintain, set standards for guard officers, and made provision for federal drill pay to Guardsmen.[9] New enlistees swore an oath to obey the President and uphold the U.S. Constitution.[10] Upon congressional authorization, the President was empowered to draft Guard members into federal service for the duration of the emergency specified in the authorization bill. In the years before American entry into World War I, then, the state militias were integrated into a federally supervised U.S. Army National Guard and supplied with standardized, congressionally prescribed arms purchased with federal funds and kept in state arsenals, which were themselves increasingly financed by the national government. During the same period, the states acknowledged delegation of the provision of security against invasion to the U.S. Army and the Organized Reserves, laying the framework of state-federal relations that allowed the massive mobilization of citizens into soldiers in both world wars.[11]

CONTINUED EVOLUTION OF THE GUARD AND
RESERVES DURING THE AGE OF STATISM

Expansion of the armed forces to wartime strength during World War I departed markedly from the systems of recruitment and mobilization established during either the Civil War or the Spanish-American conflict, when militia entered federal service in response to presidential calls to the states. Spanish-American War policy allowed individual Guard members to volunteer for duty overseas and maintained intact each state unit, from which three-quarters of personnel enlisted for federal service. By 1917, organized state volunteer units had been federalized and standardized under the rubric of the National Guard, and many Guard members had been training regularly with their regiments since the beginning of the preparedness campaign during the early years of the European war. But General Pershing was convinced, perhaps rightly, that engagement against battle-hardened German veterans required not only further training of Guard members under the auspices of the U.S. Army, but breakup of the Guard units and integration of the state soldiers into components of the U.S. Army.[12] Fully sixty-seven percent of the 3.68 million Americans serving with the army by Armistice Day were drafted directly into the U.S. Army under the Selective Service Act of 1917.[13] Still, hundreds of thousands of Guard members saw active duty during the Great War. Their units, however, did not, as state components disappeared from War Department organizational charts and entered into virtual suspension as America prepared to fight the war in Europe.[14]

Guard officers resented not only the disappearance of their units, but also the time-honored hauteur regular officers displayed toward their civilian-soldier colleagues.[15] In the aftermath of demobilization, the NGA was determined to resurrect the old state units and to preserve the Guard's role as the nation's primary reserve in the face of heavy opposition from reform-minded centrists in the War Department, who favored development of a purely federal reserve component of the army.[16] The Guard's aims coincided perfectly with the popular rejection of centralization that marked postwar reaction and the return to normalcy and isolationism. The NGA had not yet built up the Capitol Hill lobbying machine that Generals John McAuley Palmer and Milton A. Reckord commanded during and after the Second World War, but thanks to the anticentrist leanings of many rural representatives, the NGA managed to stave off a War Department campaign to oust the Guard in favor of federal reserves and even secured, at least initially, an increased level of federal funding.[17]

Under the National Defense Act of 1920, the National Guard was confirmed as the nation's first-line reserve, but the President was authorized to call out the Guard only when greater troop strength than that provided by the regulars was required.[18] Still, Congress relied forthrightly on citizen-soldiers to provide the bulk of the nation's resources in the event of war and called for 435,000 Guard members to be maintained in federally funded state units.[19] At the same time, the Defense Act restored to the Guard a greater degree of control over its own affairs, with the Militia Bureau in the War Department coming under the direction of a Guard general. Training the Guard was to be part of the army's responsibility, but as more Reserve Officers Training Corps graduates became available, citizen-soldiers were expected to take a larger role in instructing their own brigades. For all of the National Guard's success on the Hill during the waning days of Wilson's presidency, during the Harding, Coolidge, and Hoover administrations the Guard suffered from the same fiscal austerity that then plagued other federally supported programs, and rarely were Guard formations recruited to their full strength during these years of retrenchment.[20]

The course toward federal integration and consolidation of America's citizen-soldiery resumed with vigor during the Hundred Days of the New Deal. But the NGA was able to ensure that rationalization and reform preserved more than merely a dignitary role for the states and the state adjutant generals' offices in the nation's federally supervised citizen reserve. Steering a compromise course between the claims of the War Department and the Guard, Congress amended the Defense Act of 1916 to ensure that state units would continue intact when mobilized for overseas wars. More fundamentally, Congress gave express recognition to the dual status of the Guard. Henceforth, Guard units were to have twinned identities, being at once the militia of the states and a permanent reserve component of the U.S. Army. As a result of the 1933 Amendments, the states accepted the dual enlistment system that continues to this day, whereby Guard members, upon initiation, take simultaneous oaths to serve in their state units and in the regular army when called up to national duty.[21] For the first time, the National Guard became part of the army structure during peacetime as well as war, and the Guard's federal administration was justified not under the Militia Clauses, but under the Army Clause of the Constitution.[22] In the process, lawmakers "eliminated the word 'Militia' from the War Department organization by changing the name of the supervisory agency to National Guard Bureau."[23]

Notwithstanding a heightened level of Army-Guard integration, regulars retained their suspicions of Guard members as America poised for entry into World War II. But the progress the Guard achieved during the interwar years of army-supervised training left the nation far better prepared in 1941 than it had been in 1917. By the time Nazi divisions swept across the Polish frontier, 200,000 American Guard members were on active-duty status under six-year enlistments, training forty nights a year and performing an additional two weeks of field exercises each summer.[24] This citizen army seemed paltry compared to the German, Japanese, Soviet, or French establishments, but the availability of semiexperienced Guard components was of vital importance in freeing up regulars for the important job of training draftees and recruits as the army expanded to wartime strength.[25]

Members of Guard units remained together under their familiar regimental designations during World War II and contributed much to the overall success of America's civilian army against the more thoroughly professional and regimented German and Japanese forces. As the War Department anticipated victory and partial demobilization, it also envisioned a continued role for the Guard. The government's commitment to allow civilian soldiers to return home was now tempered by an appreciation for the demands of America's much expanded military role abroad.[26] Doctrinaire hostility to nonprofessional soldiers was finally fading among top defense strategists, but some regular officers retained concerns over the Guard's joint state-federal loyalties,[27] concerns partially born out by Southern governors' mobilization of Guard units to resist federally mandated racial integration in the 1950s and 1960s.[28]

From the earliest days of the Republic, the preoccupation of the peacetime army brass has been the question of manpower, that is, how to muster from a historically civilian people adequate numbers of competent soldiers in the event of a major war.[29] For much of our history, good fortune and isolation rendered this an abstract question. During the two wars with Britain, the enemy lacked both the political will and a coherent strategy for bringing its superior military resources to bear effectively against what was then still a highly diffuse country.[30] In 1846, Mexico's military establishment was no larger than our own and outclassed by the professionalism, gunnery, and engineering skills of the tiny cadre of West Pointers at the head of the invading army.[31] During the Civil War, the South was—pretensions at chivalry notwithstanding—no more militaristic or war-ready than the North, and the Union's lack of military preparedness placed it at no disadvantage.[32] In 1898, Spain was an exhausted imperial power, utterly lacking in the industrial and manpower resources required to repel invasions of Cuba, Puerto Rico, and the Philippines by a top flight naval and industrial power, no matter how disorganized the attacker's military planning.[33]

More than good luck, economic might, and optimism were required to fight and win the twentieth-century world wars. Victory over the Central Powers and the Axis required mobilization of the manpower of the entire nation. In both instances, millions of American civilians were organized and trained into armies capable of standing up to the most professional soldiers from the most militaristic countries, and far more quickly than conservative strategists in the regular establishment thought prudent or possible. Success in the world wars therefore weakened the case for the old General Staff/War Department argument that American security required permanent militarization of the population on the Prussian model.[34] Yet no strategist could underestimate the value of training or preparedness, and no one failed to credit the professional officer and noncommissioned corps for their remarkable ability to impart knowledge, system, and skill to millions of their compatriots as the army set itself on a wartime footing. Thus, rejection of Continental-style militarism did not amount to a rejection of professionalism, or augur a reversion to the inchoate amateurism of the colonial militias. Quite the contrary, the wartime experience pointed to the necessity of maintaining a thoroughly professional, if not overlarge, regular army, but with sufficient links to civilian society to prevent both debilitating hostility of the general populace toward the army and dangerous contempt for the people by the soldiers. The National Guard was ideally suited to play a prominent role in this system of security.[35]

Military strategists, of course, have a pronounced tendency to plan to fight the last war rather than the next one. The vision just described was in fact a vision premised on preparedness for mass mobilization of the civilian population to fight a prolonged ground war on several foreign fronts against formidable military adversaries similarly arrayed. It was therefore premised in part on the ideal of universal military training (UMT), which was to enable the democratic/civilian societies, led by the United States, to mobilize their civilian populations with maximum speed and efficiency, while the regular army responded to the initial aggressions of a hostile, totalitarian coalition.[36] This vision was also obsolete before it was reduced to statute. On August 6, 1945, the U.S. Army Air Forces dropped an atomic bomb on Hiroshima, Japan, all but ending the Second World War and ushering in a radically different strategic age. The advent of the American nuclear monopoly changed military planning almost overnight.[37]

At the dawn of the atomic age, the Air Force, newly separated from the Army, became the glamour wing of the armed services and the favorite of strategists and planners in the Defense Department and on Capitol Hill. Army and NGA lobbyists struggled to justify continued funding for the oldest and most traditional military arm, for it was widely assumed that no potential antagonist would be possessed of sufficient folly to challenge American nuclear might. Ground forces retained a constabulary style function in the occupied Axis countries, and as the Cold War developed, forward positioning of troops provided a visible check against communist expansion. But a showdown, if it came, was expected to be quick, nuclear, and dispositive. No one seriously considered the possibility that America might ever again be compelled to mobilize the entire nation in the manner characteristic of the major wars from Napoleon's day to Hitler's. The historic role of the Guard, as the strategic, trained personnel reserve of the nation, seemed relegated to irrelevancy, and plans for UMT were left to gather dust in Pentagon archives.

As it turns out, advance notice of the Guard's impending demise was greatly exaggerated. When the Soviet Union shocked the world by testing atomic and then hydrogen bombs long years before the intelligence community thought feasible, America's first response was the doctrine of massive retaliation, or mutual assured destruction.[38] Nuclear attack against America or its allies would be met by an overwhelming nuclear counterstrike, calculated to destroy the Soviet Union and likely to bring an end to human life on earth. But the nuclear brinkmanship of the Dulles era soon wore thin, and more flexible, less apocalyptic policies were fashioned for the benefit of frazzled nerves on both sides of the Iron Curtain.

Neither of the principal regional wars of the Cold War era—the Korean nor the Vietnam War—led to nuclear confrontation or escalated into worldwide conflict. In both instances, America's global commitments—and, principally, the forward positioning of NATO troops in Germany—so burdened the regular army that military expansion proved necessary to meet the requirements of war raging in Asia.[39] At the same time, conventional preparedness strategy dictated that trained reserves be maintained to facilitate further, rapid expansion in the event open hostilities should erupt in Europe or elsewhere around the globe while substantial American strength was committed to fighting on the Pacific Rim.[40]

Vastly exaggerated reports of Soviet army strength militated in favor of a sizable, professionally trained reserve.[41] That said, fighting substantial but limited Asian wars, even in a global security context, did not require mobilization of the entire nation.[42] In addition to feeding and paying them, the army would not have known what to do with ten or twenty million soldiers. This need for one or two million more personnel than during peacetime—but no more than that—presented grave ethical and political difficulties for the Selective Service, the Defense Department, and the government.[43] Compelling wartime service of some—but not all—Americans generated bitter anger and resentment as the U.S. death tolls climbed to 50,000 and 58,000 in the respective Asian wars.[44]

All of these factors combined to redefine and solidify a mission for the National Guard in the later years of the twentieth century. The Vietnam War proved, in myriad ways, a political disaster, and neither the defense community nor the larger nation was ever quite the same after America suffered its first military defeat. Perhaps the least popular aspect of the war was the draft, and in 1972 Congress repealed the Selective Service Act in favor of the volunteer principle.[45] The army's reversion to the recruitment system redoubled its reliance on the Guard and, by now, a substantial separate army reserve arm to meet future requirements for expansion and mobilization. This had the effect of cementing the mutual dependency and linkage between Army and Guard. With mutual assured destruction and the draft both discredited, the Guard's future in the closing decades of the twentieth century seemed far more certain than in the immediate postwar years. But the ever more federal, wholly army-trained, all volunteer National Guard of the Reagan years bore no familial resemblance to the old, independent, universal state militia.[46]

As far removed as the Cold War National Guard was from the militia described in the Second Amendment and the Militia Act of 1792, twentieth-century America never completely forgot the civic republican fears that once animated anti-federalist advocates of a constitutional right to keep and bear arms. In his farewell broadcast of January 17, 1961, President Eisenhower warned of the growing power of the military-industrial complex.[47] The bloated defense budgets, procurement scandals, and defense industry lobbyists that left the former Commanding General of the Army so uneasy were modern echoes of the suspicions concerning standing (i.e., inactive and useless) armies, salaried placemen, and overburdened exchequers of Elbridge Gerry's or James Harrington's day.[48] True, by Eisenhower's time, few Americans feared a military coup. But there had always been more to the republican antiarmy ideology than the worry that janissaries might seize the palace or oust legislators from their seats. Much more insidious was the threat that the imperial army would burden the body politic with enervating debt and burden policymakers with improper dependencies and obligations. In this respect, republican misgivings hardly seem dry relics of a bygone era.

Happily, however, the republicans' most gothic fears of a polity corrupted by an army have not materialized in the democratic Republic they helped to found. Civilian control of the military has never been challenged — itself a remarkable fact in a constitutional system now over two hundred years old. Virtually all our great generals who became presidents — Washington, Taylor, Grant, Eisenhower —

proved decidedly anti-Caesarist in the executive mansion (perhaps this is somewhat less true of Jackson, and as for poor Harrison, he did not serve long enough to admit of judgment). Indeed, throughout our history, professional military officers have demonstrated a notable commitment to civic values and respect for the democratic process. Our present Secretary of State and former top general, Colin Powell, is only the most recent example of the military leader who turned in his martial bearing with his uniform.

The antiarmy prejudices of the nineteenth century have steadily faded, and today the army is truly perceived as an instrument of the people, and not as a threatening alien organ. Localism endures in and on behalf of the National Guard, but as a species of provincial politicking and state-level patronage rather than as a genuine military counterweight to federal power. Away from the peripheral fringe, even the nation's most ardent anticentrists are now devotees of the army. More often than not, the military is the only aspect of federal power for which our modern anti-federalists have any affection at all.

Quite apart from reflecting on the contemporary relevance or irrelevance (or persistence or disappearance) of the ancient republican paradigm, our thesis ultimately turns on the evolution of the militia. And by the late twentieth century, that institution had developed into a creature all but unrecognizable from the perspective of the Second Amendment. In the years since World War II, the role of a mass reserve in assuring national security has seriously diminished in consideration of the technical complexity of equipment and tasks required of a thoroughly professional modern army, and because nuclear deterrence has made a mass war drawing all the personnel reserve of the country unlikely. The need for a whole nation in arms has — in all likelihood, permanently — disappeared. At the same time, conscription has become so unpopular as to border on being politically unfeasible.[49] In this climate, the volunteer principle has again supplanted the draft as the recruiting mechanism for fighting the limited wars that characterize the nuclear age, leaving no shadow of the old militia's compulsory universality about today's National Guard.[50]

It is not only the volunteer recruitment principle that distinguishes the early-twenty-first-century organized militia from the common militia of 1789. The issue of the militia's necessity to the security of the states and the nation has been fundamentally recast. In 1789, the regular army numbered 681 men; the common militia, Madison boasted, numbered nearly half a million. Today, the regular United States military establishment numbers some 1.4 million soldiers, sailors, air personnel, and officers, while the U.S. Army National Guard (i.e., the statutorily defined organized militia) accounts for less than 361,000.[51] With the help of lobbying by the NGA, Congress has judged and continues to judge the National Guard necessary to the nation's security and funds it handsomely in every federal budget ($6.4 billion in fiscal year 1999—10 percent of the army budget and 2.4 percent of the defense budget). In the most recent budget, Congress adjudged the Guard worthy of 2.3 percent of the total of $282 billion it deemed necessary to secure the defense of the United States.[52] The states, too, fund their Guards—or at least some of them do—albeit very much less generously than the federal government. In fact, according to Justice Stevens, "[t]he Federal Government provides virtually all of the funding, the materiel, and the leadership for the State Guard units."[53] In contrast to the National Guard, the unorganized militia—the shadow of the common militia so extolled by the framers of the Second Amendment—has not been funded by Congress since at least 1903. It is unclear that any state appropriated any of the funds Congress set aside for the common militia after Reconstruction, or that any state provided funds for the unorganized militia after 1877, or even after 1850. And by walking away from the muster points and parade grounds *en masse* during the first half of the nineteenth century, the American people themselves voted with their feet that their security, whether national or state, had nothing to do with the common militia. The old militia had died a natural death long before anyone now living was born. Indeed, it would be difficult to conceive of any institution less necessary to the security of the fifty free states at the beginning of the new millennium than the vanished common militia.

One more vital difference remains between the organized militia of today and the militia of 1789–91. It is the most striking of all. The Militia Act of 1792 required citizens to acquire specified arms and keep them in their homes, ready to bear on muster day and when called up in emergencies. No matter that noncompliance was (or soon became) the rule, or that many households actually contained no functioning regulation firearms at all.[54] The Militia Act embodied the norms envisioned in the Second Amendment. And those were that militiamen keep their required, regulation arms in their own homes. This was then the most practical approach. Armories contained some small arms as well as field pieces and powder, but the delays and in-efficiencies occasioned by first reporting to a state armory, perhaps many miles distant, and then rallying to meet one's fellows where public danger loomed, would have been intolerable given the limits of eighteenth-century transportation and communication. Moreover, arms of that period required constant oiling and repair, meaning they could be better maintained in the home, assuming householders were diligent in their charge.[55] Perhaps more fundamentally still, balls, cartridges, and shot did not begin to be standardized until Eli Whitney, after long delays, delivered on his 1798 contract to furnish the War Department with ten thousand mass-production muskets assembled on the interchangeable parts principle.[56] Prior to the rise of standard-issue arms, each gun was an individual tool, almost a piece of art, cartridges for which were best assembled by the hands of the proprietor rather than in a factory under government contract.

Today, standard, mass-produced U.S. Army automatic rifles are issued to the National Guard by the army and kept safe in armories. The very same pieces are used by both the army and the Guard, maintained according to the same manuals, and sometimes returned to the same armories, where they are stored under lock and guard until next issued to reservists, regulars, or Guard members for exercise or duty. If repairs are necessary, army specialists perform them. Ammunition and firing pins are the subjects of meticulous recordkeeping and are issued separately from the weapon at the beginning of exercises.[57] Congress, the Department of Defense, the secretary of the army, and the state adjutants general have decided national and state security is best served by this system, under which identical, interchangeable equipment centrally stored can be issued to Guard members and soldiers as training and military necessity demand.

For reasons of efficiency and public safety, it is implausible that any member of Congress or official in the Department of Defense, army, or state adjutant general's office should advocate a return to the policy of keeping the arms used by the organized militia in Guard members' homes. Most fundamentally of all, the arms once purchased by the militiamen themselves[58] are now government property and require the safekeeping accorded any other U.S. property—and especially dangerous property at that. In the year 2002, the militia world contemplated by the Second Amendment no longer exists, and no plausible analogy to that nexus can be reconstructed.

III

THE MEANING OF MEANING

7

Text and Context

The main clause of the Second Amendment recognizes—perhaps even grants—a right of access to arms. The question before the house is: how does one derive the meaning of that right? Whenever an authoritative but incomplete or ambiguous text is examined for meaning, difficult questions arise concerning the appropriate sources for elucidation. And when centuries have passed since its inscription, the complexity of those questions takes on a new dimension. We have no intention of entering the lists in the ancient and ongoing scholarly joust on the superiority of unreconstructed textualism, any of the varieties of intent-flavored originalism, or unashamed, policy-activated noninterpretivism.[1] We do feel obliged to declare (if it is not already blatant) that we position ourselves among those who believe that text counts, and that the words of the text are inflected with the common understandings and usages of the times. We do think that altered social or linguistic context can alter the meaning of text or render the sense of a provision meaningless. However, we depart from those who would revise an ancient, authoritative text on no better pretext than the promotion of present-day social preference.[2] We do not believe the meaning of such a text is "fluid," perpetually rewriting itself to keep up with the changing times.[3] In our interpretive scheme, the statements of contemporaries—"Framers" or others—may be useful primarily as a source for inferring the common understanding of the day.

We are definitely not enthusiastic about allowing the surviving comment of one or two people who were involved in the enactment process to serve as the authoritative key to the meaning (or "intent") of the diverse assortment of authors, enactors, or ratifiers.

Controversy over the relevance of the testimony of contemporaries on the scene is, apparently, not a latter-day phenomenon. Professor H. Jefferson Powell informs us that such disputation was well underway at least as early as 1796. Congress was debating the constitutionality of a resolution calling on President Washington to transmit to the House the files of John Jay's negotiation of his treaty with Great Britain. Congressman William Vans Murray of Maryland rose to express surprise that James Madison and others present at the Constitutional Convention in Philadelphia had not shared with the House their recollections of the intentions of the draftsmen. Murray's reference to actual original understanding met with a rebuke the following day from Albert Gallatin of Pennsylvania. As Professor Powell recounts it, Gallatin maintained that "[e]ven if it were proper to use the views expressed in the debates of a legislative body in interpreting that body's acts—a proposition Gallatin doubted—the opinions of the Philadelphia framers were as irrelevant as those of the legislative clerk who penned a statute."[4]

In addition, we recognize, as Professor Boris Bittker has ably demonstrated,[5] that none of the conventional sources of illumination of the Founders' "true" intentions casts better than a weak and flickering beam. "Original meaning," as he explains, is a false construct, skewed by the ineradicable sensibilities of the contemporary retrospectors. And it is virtually impossible to compensate for the distortion of the modern lens that seeks to scope the minds of generations past. Notwithstanding these formidable obstacles to understanding, however, we do insist that the text of the Constitution has meaning for us today. And if the document is worthy of respect, the message embedded in the text must be sought as conscientiously as a modern string quartet seeks to know what Beethoven had in mind as he wrote the great Opus 130.

So, in searching for today's meaning of the Second Amendment, we find ourselves among those who take account of the original understanding of the phraseology in the context of the contemporary uses and assumptions of eighteenth-century society.[6] It seems obvious to us that the meaning of the words employed in the text of the Second Amendment reflects a complex set of understandings, conventions, and assumptions peculiar to the times and shared among like-minded prisoners of the culture in which the text was created.

It is for the sake of textual integrity that we insist that the drastic change in the position of the militia in the array of protections against the overreaching of the central government does not entitle us simply to cut adrift the first phrase of the Second Amendment and enforce the remaining clause to the hilt. The Framers thought the right to arms to be closely associated with the military security of the free state, they wrote it thus in the Charter, the ratifiers so understood it, and the bond endures.

It might be worthwhile to unpack this bundle of shared assumptions and extrinsic referents to sort out those that are so critical to the interpretation of the text that, upon a change of context, the significance of the text changes. Or evaporates entirely.

LINGUISTIC CONTEXT

In the instance of the Second Amendment, the unadorned linguistics are themselves informative. The right to arms is declared by the verbs, "keep and bear," a phrase carefully selected in preference to alternatives such as "have," "own," "carry," or "possess." Scholars have informed us that, as a term of legal art, the chosen locution has a distinctly military connotation, especially the verb "to bear," which would not have been used in the eighteenth century—as it would not commonly be today—to connote purely private use of arms.[7] You do not bear a shotgun to go duck hunting. As we more fully note below however, the Court of Appeals for the Fifth Circuit has recently chosen a different construction of these words.

But we need not rely entirely on that language in the announcement of the right in the main clause. We have, as we have emphasized throughout these pages, a clear and unequivocal expression of the linguistic context of the primary right in the introductory phrase that accompanies it. The mere presence of the militia phrase sharing a single sentence with the arms clause has, as we have argued persistently, inescapable significance.

In addition, the way the two parts of the provision are expressed amplifies the significance of their conjunction. The critical introductory language does not aver the relationship of the militia to a free state in a simple declarative clause—a form that might have established two severable propositions—the importance of a militia and the right to arms. It does not say: "a well-regulated militia is necessary to the security of a free state, and the right of the people to keep and bear arms shall not be infringed."[8] Had this form been chosen, we might have argued over whether the implication is that the two propositions are linked. Indeed, we might have wondered why the two thoughts share a single sentence.[9]

But it wasn't written that way. Rather, in the first part, the verbal vehicle elected for the verb "to be" is a participle, yielding a phrase known to grammarians as an "ablative absolute construction."[10] This construction characterizes a phrase modifying the substance of the main clause as an adjective would modify a noun, often expressing the condition or circumstances of the assertion of the main clause. It creates an indissoluble link between the two parts of the sentence, and grammatically subjects the right to arms to the rule of the militia modifier. As a simple matter of grammar, the participial modifier is essential for the declarative clause to occur. Had the two statements — regarding the importance of a militia and the right to arms—not been joined in this manner, it might have been possible to argue that even if the first declaration ceases to be true, the second is undiminished. And it seems to us significant that the Framers chose the structure they did.

The linguistics certainly were understood to the framing generation (who were more likely to know the niceties of Latin grammar than we are). Taken together then — as they must be — these two components of the provision grant the people such right to arms as will preserve or empower the militia to assure the security of the community. The linguistically correct reading of this unique construction, we submit, is as though it said: *Congress shall not limit the right of the people (that is, the potential members of the state militia) to acquire and keep the sort of arms appropriate to their military duty, so long as the following statement remains true: "an armed, trained, and controlled militia is the best—if not the only—way to protect the state government and the liberties of its people against uprisings from within and incursions or oppression from without."*

The question then becomes: Has the term "militia" been so eroded by history that in today's social context the concept behind the right expressed retains none of its original meaning? Whether there ever was a time when the amateur local militia was a more effective weapon than a professional army for repelling a foreign invasion of trained and disciplined troops is, as we have shown, highly dubious. But there was a time in the early days of the Republic when states might, with good reason, fear encroachment into local authority by armed federal forces. During the uncertain months of the Paris peace negotiations in 1783, Alexander Hamilton (among others) favored the use of national troops to coerce state governments to pay their dues, and scarcely more than a decade after the adoption of the Constitution in 1788, Pennsylvania and Virginia were planning to mobilize their stand-by military units in case Hamilton attempted to rally federal troops to prevent Jefferson from taking office in 1801. Thus, it is not altogether far-fetched to postulate a generally perceived need among the founding generation for local militia to repel federal threats to the liberty of the people and the autonomy of the states.

It is, however, little short of absurd to imagine that today, apart from isolated bands of irrational libertarians, people fear the armed incursion of federal troops on local autonomy. Still, the persistence of an institution is not wholly dependent on the need that gave it birth. And it would be wrong to suppose that in modern times there is no role for locally commanded troops in the enforcement of law or the maintenance of order.

Of course, this conflict does not always play out with the states wearing the white hats as some of the Founders supposed. In one of the most memorable confrontations in recent years, Governor Orville Faubus of Arkansas called up the state militia (which was by then called the "Arkansas National Guard") to resist federal school integration orders by physically blocking African American children trying to enter the school. President Eisenhower then ordered the same units into national service, and they escorted the "Little Rock Nine" to school,[11] providing a scene for unforgettable news photographs that came to symbolize the civil rights victories in the South (as well as providing the basis for a memorable painting by Norman Rockwell).

Given the continued vitality of the social role of armed troops, has the institution of the militia evolved into a viable military force in America today? Medieval monks might enjoy the question: is a military force that developed out of an ancient construct known as "the militia" still a militia though it boasts none of the defining characteristics of that form of military organization, and is, actually, in character the contradiction of many of them? It's a little like the parable of Aristotle's knife: if I break the blade of my knife and replace it, and then put a new handle on it, is it still the same knife?

An argument might well be made (indeed, one of the present authors makes it) that if, today, Congress were to provide that the National Guard should not accept women, any person rejected on such grounds would have a cause of action, independent of any other, on grounds of a denial of Second Amendment rights. The theory would be that the right to keep and bear arms in the militia implies a right to serve in the militia, and, to the extent that the present National Guard is the evolved successor to the militia of the constitutional period, denial of the right to serve in the present National Guard amounts to denial of the right to keep and bear arms in the militia. It is not a proposition that we are likely to see tested in the courts anytime soon. But it puts the issue nicely: is the Guard the constitutional equivalent of a "militia" for any purpose? And if so, does the right to bear arms imply a right to serve?

While the other author is dubious of both propositions, he does believe that the Second Amendment, dormant though it be, has the potential of revival. Should the legislature of some state constitute an armed force, comprising all the eligible citizens of the state, self-armed and subject to training and command by state authority, and should Congress, worried by this development, enact a law punishing any group of five or more persons congregating together while armed, the law would violate the Second Amendment. So both of us, however unrealistically, can imagine situations in which, one way or another, the constitutional precept would spring to life even in today's world, so far distant from any conception of the Framers.

Returning to the real world, we have not, in recent years, seen armed troops called up to suppress insurrections or to repel invasions (two of the three purposes specifically enumerated by the Constitution for Congress to "provide for calling forth the militia"). But, it might be asserted, the security of a free state requires more than military force directed at rebels and invaders. Maintaining order, discouraging lawlessness, and reassuring the citizens in times of crisis or emergency are functions vital to security. And perhaps that is what Article I Section 8, has in mind when it speaks of mobilizing the militia to "execute the laws of the Union" (the third enumerated purpose). And the Congress retains the power to provide for the mobilization of the militia in its contemporary guise as the National Guard to "execute the laws," meaning, we suppose, to enforce federal law. State units of the Guard may also be called up by the chief executive officer of the state government. While a far cry from the security against armed incursions envisioned by the architects of the colonial militia construct, state units of the Guard on state duty also contribute to the security of the free states by enhancing domestic tranquility. Thus, it might be thought that, since the Guard today serves as the militia might have in time gone by, it is for all practical purposes its successor.

The argument from functional overlap is, however, flawed. Local police and several federal law enforcement agencies also perform security functions on a regular basis, but we would not call them the modern incarnation of the militia of old. In this complicated world of parallel functions and simultaneous responsibilities, lineage is more reliably traced by structure and composition than by function. In structure, as we have shown, the National Guard is a component of the national armed forces, and no guardsman can avoid his joint enlistment. The militia, of course, was designed and supported as an alternative to the professional standing army of the central government. The modern National Guard, then, is not just different from the militia referred to in the Constitution, it is, in many ways, its antithesis. In composition, the troops of the National Guard are a select group of volunteers in contrast to the militia-of-the-whole, composed of all able-bodied men within the prescribed age range. These are not just incidental distinctions, these are differences vital to the definition of the military units in question. In announcing the right to arms, the Second Amendment did not say *self-selected federal soldiers, trained and armed by the government as long-term, standby, defensive, peacekeeping, and law-enforcement units (clad in camouflaged fatigues or other uniforms), being vital to the security of a free state, the right of the people to keep and bear arms shall not be infringed.* It wouldn't make a lot of sense if it did. Indeed, these are the very troops the anti-federalist militia advocates most feared as threats to the security of free states.

In the final analysis, one must be wary of identifying institutions by the similarity in their functions. A saddled horse is different from an automobile, gassed up with its sunroof open. An autocratic despot cannot be equated with a democratic legislature by their respective law-making powers. The word, "militia," as used in the Constitution, we contend, must be understood by the defining characteristics of its nature to those who wrote and approved the written document. And military organizations of a later time cannot claim that designation by the fact that they are available to perform at least some of the tasks thought by the founding generation to be appropriate for a militia. The sensible conclusion, it seems to us, is that the term "militia" in anything approaching its original sense has therefore simply outlived its application. While not gone from the constitutional landscape, it is an empty shell, devoid of meaning of effect in the real world of today.

Moreover, from a pragmatic standpoint, it is simply no longer true that an independent militia, however well regulated, is necessary to the security of a free state. The legislatures in all fifty states over the course of the past two centuries have confirmed it. State assemblies first declined to fund or organize their militia, and then later accepted National Guard funding of their militia from the federal government, with all of the strings attached thereto. These incremental decisions amounted in the long term to a deliberate relinquishment of the militia function (in the first instance, no other agency picked up the slack, but later, militia functions were delegated to volunteers, then to the federal army, to the federalized Guard, and to state Guards as components of a federally controlled system, as well as to state police, local police, federal law enforcement agencies, etc.). Moreover, these transfers were not beyond legislative prerogative. Rather, they were legitimate actions by democratically accountable organs acting within their constitutionally vested authorities.

Thus, the expiration of the condition that a local militia is the best security of a free state deprives the succeeding clause of its voice. And it is once again our conclusion that the Second Amendment, with its express purpose dry, is silent on the question of free access to arms. The Constitution neither guarantees personal access for all purposes (it never did), nor does it restrict possession of arms to those destined for use for the common security.

SOCIAL CONTEXT

We are aware that interpretation—particularly interpretation in the light of changed social circumstances—is a problematic undertaking. As Professor Jefferson Powell has reminded us, interpretation of any sort was once thought anathema by the literalist Protestants and republicans who feared that legislative or judicial reconstruction of text would lead to despotism.[12] Over the many years of our long-lived Constitution, however, many terms of the original text have been reconstructed to accommodate changes in the social context of the document, adjustments that most of us have come to accept as crucial to the endurance of the constitutional regime.

To Madison and the other Founders, the term "papers and effects" meant handwritten documents and other personal possessions. It did not mean spoken words or body fluids (though both were known to the founding generation)—much less electronically stored data (which, of course, they never dreamed of). Security against unreasonable acquisition of conversations or body chemistry was not included in the Fourth Amendment because contemporary technology had not presented the citizen with the danger of such intrusions. When private conversations could be audited with no human eavesdropper lurking nearby, when blood and urine became the source of incriminating evidence, the social context shifted materially. Faithful to the concept of "security," faithful to the interpretive delineation of privacy that the term "security" implied, we were able to construe the language of the Fourth Amendment to apply to oral communication, body chemistry, and electronic data.

Even interpretations that narrow rights granted by the Bill of Rights have survived the critical test of acceptability. The word "witness" in the Fifth Amendment, for example, meant at common law (as well as in ordinary usage) a source of evidence—evidence of all sorts, but in particular documents prepared by the accused himself.[13] Yet when the Supreme Court addressed the issue, they held that the Fifth Amendment does not preclude the compelled production of adverse evidence, including prerecorded, self-incriminatory declarations.[14] The Court's first go at the issue involved the compelled surrender of body fluids for chemical analysis (blood on a driving-while-intoxicated charge).[15] But the idea eventually expanded to include documents bearing self-inculpatory statements.[16] In any event, the new technology fitted comfortably within the concept of being compelled to be a witness against oneself. And, controversial as some of these rulings may be,[17] few today believe that the art of construction to accommodate changed circumstances and new understandings has paved the way to tyranny.

These comfortable accommodations to alterations of context cannot be made in every instance where linguistic or social development has changed the meaning or reference of the original text. In some instances, the reinterpretation of the provision simply departs too far from the original concept, faithful only on the most attenuated level of abstraction. To grant women suffrage on the strength of the Fifteenth Amendment on the theory that it would otherwise be denied "on account of . . . previous condition of servitude" goes too far.[18] Women and former slaves shared a similar condition of "servitude" only on the most abstract level of that concept. As Professor Henry Monaghan has explained, the crux of the matter is the level of abstraction that the language of the Constitution can bear. While a certain amount of generality is inevitable—and tolerable—in the modern application of any ancient precept, generalization can dilute meaning to the point that the pretense of fidelity becomes illusory.[19] Faithful reading of authoritative text requires both the distillation of the essence of the provision and sensitivity to the hazards of over-accommodation of the changed circumstances of its application.

The concept of the militia embedded in the Second Amendment has so radically changed over the centuries since its adoption that the right to arms, constructed to serve it, has become deactivated, shorn of its reason for being. Changes in the concept expressed by the word "militia" have been gradual, and their impact on the meaning of the arms clause has been progressive, as we have shown. Certainly, the word continues to connote a trained and organized military force. At the same time, it is difficult for twenty-first-century ears to discern the echoes of the overtones that were characteristic of the term more than two centuries before. To the extent that the term "militia" today calls to mind some form of state quasi-military unit, it undeniably retains some meaning to our modern ears. But to confuse the term as it is used today with the very different concept of a militia as known to the Americans of 1789 is to miss the meaning of the constitutional provision. To the citizens of the new nation, the militia meant an organization comprising all eligible men, armed, and obeying a universal, statutory duty to serve and to stand ready to serve under elected officers. The new Americans, moreover, thought of the militia as the alternative to the dangerous standing army of professional soldiers, the civilian protection against the threat of military oppression. It is impossible to read in the modern use of the word militia even the faintest trace of these essential characteristics of the militia as that concept was known to the founding generation. Consequently, as used in the Second Amendment, the word simply has no application in the world we live in.

As we have recounted—and as all scholars agree—the founding generation of Americans conceived of a militia as a group composed of all free white males between eighteen and forty-five[20] (except for the conscientious objectors and others entitled to an exemption), responding willingly, as needed, for the common defense, at the call of local authority, and above all, as a viable alternative to the feared standing army. This renaissance republican conception was soon recognized as the romance of revived classicism, and the militia gradually lost its characteristic charisma. By the early twentieth century, they were trained by (1903), commanded by (1916), armed by (1903), called by (Act of 1795, as contemplated in Militia Clauses), and deployed by (always shared by state and U.S. command) federal authority. Losing virtually all distinction from the regular army (1933), they were, by the middle of the twentieth century, nothing but a shadow of the Founders' dream. Even their image as the personification of civic virtue, already clouded by weak performance before ratification, has declined since. Fouled by disgraceful episodes and disastrous campaigns, the heroic republican mantle barely preserved the dignity of the organization as it was increasingly absorbed into the very military establishment it was designed to replace.

This history of the militia seems to us to write such a drastic change in the context of the conception of a militia that we are led to conclude that there is no contemporary, evolved, descendant of the eighteenth-century "militia" on today's landscape. Although the present-day National Guard units (successors to the militia) still receive a sizable chunk of the federal defense budget and, for the most part, take their training and patriotism seriously, they are hardly of the same genus as the militia as that military organization was understood in the eighteenth century. To cite only the most glaring distinction, they are part of the standing army rather than an alternative to it. And if today's National Guard fails to fit the concept of a militia, the notion is little short of ludicrous that the constitutional term applies to the scattered, small, unregulated bands of fatigue-clad, gun-loving, self-appointed libertarians taking secret target practice in the woods while underwriting one another's bigotry.

In modern usage, then, the word "militia" —insofar as it is heard at all— describes no organization genetically related to the ennobled assembly identified by the term as originally written in the Constitution. As far as state-enforced security goes, we have today a sort of "standing army" of armed and trained police forces. For any realistically conceived threat to local interests, these people are surely adequate to the job. While one would hardly call the armed and armored legions of police a "militia" as they confront the angry mob, they do stand effectively in the place the colonials imagined their militia would serve. Thus, rather than being the modern incarnation of the ancient militia, modern police obviate any lingering necessity for a militia. Indeed, rather than believing that ad hoc assemblies of armed men are necessary —actually a necessity— for the maintenance of freedom in the states, the overwhelming majority of Americans today probably think of them as themselves a threat to the peace. Moreover, this public judgment has been confirmed by the democratic organs in whom the Constitution vested authority to define the militia. Legislatures have unanimously decided that the universal militia contemplated at the framing should be abolished, and that the role it once served should be exercised by other bodies. Therefore, the introductory clause of the Second Amendment is today devoid of meaning, an empty vessel from which time and history have sucked every trace of the considerable substance it once had. And the right standing upon it —as the right memorialized in the second clause does— collapses for lack of footing.

GENERIC FIDELITY

The key to the distinction between those provisions that can and cannot accommodate contextual shifts is *generic fidelity*. The test question is whether the text in issue refers to a generic classification that survives the contextual modification such that the provision of text can be applied in the altered context without loss of fidelity to the original conception. To us, this means that the critical term of text has a core meaning that is readily applicable to new things or events that fall within the clearly defined genus of the original term. Thus, technological evolution produces changes in applications but not of generic meaning. "Arms," for example, means exactly what it did, generically, in the eighteenth century, though the actual weapons are very different. However, social changes can be so drastic and fundamental that the original term simply has no meaning in the new world. To put it another way, to apply the original term in the new world would depart from the fundamental intent of the Framers expressed in the generic quality of that term. So, to apply the word militia from anywhere in the Constitution to any twenty-first-century military unit would be to break faith with those who bequeathed the document to our safekeeping.

Had our military establishment evolved into a complex organization that included well-organized local contingents resembling the Israeli or Swiss model of universal military service by citizens for whom soldiering is not their primary vocation, the lineal descendant of the militia might be alive today. The supposition is rather far-fetched, especially if we include the factor of personal responsibility for providing the weaponry. But, speculation aside, the right to arms acknowledged by the Second Amendment has lost meaning today because it does not have a generic application. We do not wish to abuse the Darwinian metaphor, but our militia has not evolved within its original genus; it has, rather, become extinct. And the right associated with it cannot be reinterpreted to mean a right to arms for sport or personal defense without abandoning the imperative of fidelity. Such uses of weapons are simply not of the same class or character as support for a well-organized military corps that the Framers envisioned. Hence, the change of social context that saw the disappearance of the genus militia deprived the right associated with it of meaning.

THE SECOND AMENDMENT TODAY

Proponents of a viable and vigorous Second Amendment like to affiliate the rights expressed therein with the eternally youthful First, Fourth, Fifth, Sixth, and Eighth.[21] This energetic subset have survived all sorts of changes — linguistic, social, and technological — indeed, many have been reborn and came into their prime in the latter half of the twentieth century. Of the lot, however, only one might someday qualify as a parallel to the Second: the Eighth Amendment right not to be locked up in default of "excessive" bail. One can imagine an era when every defendant (save those truly dangerous people held in custody under a pretrial preventive detention law like the federal Bail Reform Act of 1984)[22] will be automatically released for the pretrial wait with some sort of electronic monitoring device to deter flight. This sort of arrangement would make a lot of sense and, let us suppose, it totally replaces financial incentive as the means for securing future attendance in court. It would thereby instantly render the excessive bail provision of the Eighth Amendment obsolete. Monetary bail as conceived by the Founders would itself be anachronistic. And the constitutional right not to be held awaiting trial on bail that is too high would become a meaningless entitlement and would join the Second Amendment in a graceful (and indolent) retirement.

All the other rights embodied in the Bill of Rights, as we read them, are distinguishable from the right granted by the Second Amendment. To demonstrate this difference, a minor distinction might first be drawn between rights granted as assurances against experienced or imagined government abuses on the one hand (call them "proscriptive"), and, on the other, rights granted as enabling entitlements ("prescriptive"). The right not to be forced to bear witness against oneself might be thought of as a proscriptive right adopted in response to a prevalent abuse. The right to jury trial in civil suits is prescriptive. The disappearance of an abuse that motivated the adoption of a proscriptive right does not render inactive the right proclaimed. If we were fortunate enough to live in a time when confessions were no longer coerced (even constructively coerced per *Miranda*[23]), the right not to be compelled to be a witness against oneself would not lapse. The right is the living guardian against return of the faded abuse. So too we might say that, even without threat of unwelcome soldiers claiming beds in our houses, we all still enjoy the right accorded by the Third Amendment to be free of the visit.

The Second Amendment is not in this category of abuse-corrective provisions where the granted right must stand eternally vigilant. No abuse, real or potential, motivated the adoption of that provision—unless you count the perceived (though not firmly rejected) threat of a standing army. The right granted by the Second Amendment was an *enabling* provision, prescribing the means for the maintenance of an effective militia. The change in social context is not the removal of the threat, real or imagined, but rather the disappearance of the enabled institution.

A proscriptive right—ascending to the abstract, perhaps—remains viable so long as the threatened activity may recur. It is a negative entitlement: the right not to have an abuse imposed upon you. A negative entitlement is, by nature, somewhat abstract. The affirmative right to guns, by contrast, is active only insofar as it serves the social purpose for which it was awarded. Because it is meaningless to enable a defunct institution, the right decays with the decay of the institution it serves. If someday the judicial structure on the civil side is dismantled as an inefficient way to resolve private disputes (replaced with some form of mandatory arbitration, let us imagine), the Seventh Amendment right to jury trial in civil actions would disappear.

The primary distinction between the Second Amendment and its companions can be traced to a subtle shift in the intellectual framework of American "rights talk" over the last half of the eighteenth century. Few if any new abstract rights were discovered by the Anglo-Americans during the years surrounding or following the Revolution. Indeed, most of the rights enumerated in the first ten Amendments would have been familiar to Locke or even Cromwell as aspects of the common law tradition which formed the backbone of the English Constitution. (This is not to say—we hasten to insert—that all the rights in the American Bill of Rights had enforceable antecedents in actual English practice.) What had changed so markedly by 1791, on this side of the Atlantic, was not so much the content of Whig rights and liberties, but the context in which those long familiar rights were articulated, and the theoretical foundations upon which they were reconstructed on American soil.

For most of the seventeenth century, English liberties were explained, invoked, and grounded by reference to the ancient, mixed, balanced assortment of statutes and conventions known as the English Constitution.[24] "Constitutional" liberties were considered important because they preserved order and balance in a structured society. The English Constitution (often called ancient or gothic) balanced the interests of three social and political orders, the one (monarch), the few (lords), and the many (commons). When the King, or the judiciary acting at his bidding, disregarded ancient constituted liberties of subjects, by imprisoning them without charge or indictment, for example, or by refusing the writ of habeas corpus, or by denying trial by jury, the magistracy endangered the political equilibrium among the orders of society, and hence imperiled the mixed Constitution.[25]

Under the old way of thinking, liberties served to protect the Constitution. Rights were deemed just because they were (or were claimed to be) old and established, that is to say: constituted. When Charles I arrested the parliamentary leader John Pym and imprisoned him without sufficient legally cognizable cause or adequate procedure, parliamentarians were concerned not so much because Pym's individual freedoms had been violated, but because his privileges as a subject and parliamentarian were constituted safeguards against an overreaching monarch, and the Crown's disregard for these safeguards threatened imbalance. Pym's champions asserted his rights from a structural perspective. They looked to preservation of the political equilibrium among the social orders; their ultimate goal was preservation of the balanced Constitution by enforcing constituted liberties.[26]

Nearly half a century later, John Locke was perfectly at home in the political universe just described. As a 1680s Whig, he remained a 1640s Commonwealthsman at heart. But he was also a great figure of the Enlightenment, and he reinforced his Commonwealth understanding of rights and liberties with a radical new set of arguments.[27] In addition to being ancient, provident, constituted — and therefore just and reasonable — the familiar catalogue of rights became in Locke's mind *rational*. They were respected on the grounds that it was just and progressive to do so. Rights became to Locke not only cherished instrumental heirlooms, but fundamental logical postulates of the just political society.

Locke's *political* influence on pre-Revolutionary America was exerted more as a representative old Whig than as an apostle of reason, and in this capacity his status fell short of Cato's or the Whig martyr, Algernon Sidney's.[28] But Locke had an enormous impact on American *philosophical* sensibilities as the author of the Letter on Toleration, as an epistemologist, as a moralist, and as a vision theorist. And this enlightened philosophy, so pervasive in the eighteenth century, gradually reshaped the world in which the old Whiggish rights existed. When twenty-two-year-old James Madison returned from Princeton and saw Baptist preachers imprisoned in Orange County, Virginia, he was troubled not only for the instrumental reason that it was politically and constitutionally destabilizing for the state to presume to exclude or punish discourse or belief, but also because this imprisonment lacked a rational basis, and therefore was unjust.[29]

Thomas Jefferson, like Locke, was as Whiggish as any Commonwealthsman. But as the youthful Virginian contemplated mounting political differences between his colony and the mother country, the Whig foundations for the rights of Englishman were supplemented in his mind by thoroughly enlightened, rationalistic, and theoretical justifications. In the *Summary View of the Rights of British North America* (1774),[30] Jefferson supported colonial rights of resistance against parliamentary abuse by masterfully blending the Whiggish and the rational philosophies. By 1776, in the Declaration of Independence, he postulated American and universal rights on wholly rational grounds, and in so doing created the Enlightenment's quintessential political manifesto based on natural rights theory.

Or perhaps we should say, based principally on natural rights theory. For the Declaration also famously invoked the "Creator" as the well-spring of the most fundamental rights with which all people are endowed prior even to the formation of a social contract. While this aspect of the Declaration may strike some early twenty-first century skeptics as an appeal to authority beyond the ambit of pure reason, it did not appear thus to even the most anticlerical devotees of the eighteenth-century Enlightenment, who assumed that the basic laws governing both natural and social science had their origins in omniscient (or at least epistemologically impregnable) creation, whether by the God of Nature, the God of Christianity, or some as yet unfathomed force. For present purposes, the important insight is that the Declaration of Independence, for the first time in Anglo-American political discourse, sought the legitimizing origins of government and law in abstract philosophical principles wholly outside the framework of preceding Anglo-American history, real or imagined.

Thirteen years after Jefferson's immortal proclamation of a new nation's independence, the American Bill of Rights marked a departure in "rights-talk" every bit as fundamental as the much-discussed departure from British traditions in the creative structuralism established by the Constitution.[31] In 1789, all of the elements of the Bill of Rights were in a sense "bi-lingual," partaking of both the new natural rights learning of the Enlightenment and their older English Whig heritage. But the new discourse was clearly ascendant — except in one (or perhaps two) instances: the right to keep and bear arms (and maybe the right against quartering). The right to keep and bear arms was too wedded to the ancient, mixed, and balanced Constitution, too steeped in English political history to make an easy transition into a universal "rights" framework. It did not readily lend itself to Locke's rational and enlightened discourse about the nature of man and the entitlements appurtenant thereto. Despite latter-day efforts to tie the right to arms to human nature, to entitlements of individualism like freedom of speech and worship,[32] and governmental restraint in the criminal process, despite the earnest attempt to associate the Second Amendment right with the postulates of the liberal, enlightened philosophy of the eighteenth century,[33] the Second Amendment right to arms remains firmly fixed in its seventeenth-century English heritage. It never evolved from the particular to the general, never grew from one of the historically conditioned rights of Englishmen into one of the unconditional and universal rights of humankind.[34]

We do not deny that other elements of the Bill of Rights still resonated in 1789 with echoes and overtones of their familiar English constitutional heritage. But while the procedural rights that once served to check the monarchy and preserve the political balance among the orders of society could easily develop into bulwarks of individual liberty in a post-Renaissance world, the right not to bear arms in the militia could not.

Over the course of the nineteenth century, individualists like John Stuart Mill cultivated a notion of rights essentially linked to the desire to be left alone by the state. In this context, the right not to be charged without grand jury indictment, so useful in preventing Charles I from establishing an absolutist state that would have undone the balance among the social orders and the branches of government, became just as useful for an individual asserting his purely autonomous and personal right to be immune from criminal prosecution unless first duly indicted by his peers. However, the "right" not to be prevented by the Crown from doing militia duty could not easily be recast as the exercise of a private entitlement to be free of government oppression. The concepts are diametrically opposed, one premised on civic duty, the other on radical individualism and isolationism.

The right to arms differs from its now individualistic companions also because it never escaped its heritage as a corporate entitlement belonging to individuals only because they were members of a group.

Thus, unlike the other provisions of the Bill of Rights, the right to bear arms derives from the individual's membership in a group that requires that arms be borne. Moreover, the cohabitation of obligation and entitlement on the same patch of ideological turf is not inherently contradictory. It seems unusual today, but it made perfect sense in the seventeenth century when the Anglo-American right to arms was born.

As Professor David Williams and others have noted,[35] the Second Amendment, more than the Constitution as a whole, is descended from a republican system of beliefs that featured a strong streak of communitarian responsibility.[36] But while, as Williams suggests, the Second Amendment must be understood as a republican provision, the rest of the Bill of Rights reflects more closely a rational, enlightened, even liberal conception of individual rights, a conception shaped by James Madison's tutelage in the classic writings of the Scottish, English, and French Enlightenment under the eminent Scottish theologian and philosopher James Witherspoon at Princeton,[37] and sharpened and refined fifteen years later by his correspondence with Jefferson and immersion in the crates of eighteenth-century texts on political theory his friend sent from Paris.[38] These other rights announced in 1789—understood later as entitlements even against the majority of the people or the communal interest—are in a sense antithetical to the ideals of selfless service for the public weal that characterize the republican model and the Second Amendment. While it is possible to view the freedom of speech and press (and even of religion) as serving communitarian objectives,[39] it seems much more comfortable today to think of them as personal entitlements. The founding generation, while still beholden to an older conception, was the first to conceive of rights broadly according to this new paradigm. Jefferson and Madison could readily offer historical, instrumental, and collective justifications for the intellectual and procedural liberties they cherished, but the nonmilitary rights ratified in 1791 no longer required the old Whiggish props. They could stand, naturally, on their own footing.

It is largely in this individualistic guise—novel in its time—that the majority of the rights secured in 1791 have been transmitted to us today. Examining the Fourth and Fifth Amendments, for instance, there seems little social purpose in prohibiting the search of private spaces for inculpatory evidence, or even proscribing the enlistment of an unwilling defendant in his own prosecution. These rights strike a chord not because they serve the collective welfare, but because they protect individuals (and all of us as individuals) against abuse. Like the rights of the Fourth and Fifth Amendments, the basic trial rights detailed in the Sixth Amendment might be said to enhance the social fabric by establishing a "fair" system of criminal justice. But it's a stretch, even if we could come to a universal understanding of "fair." The trial rights of the Sixth and the guarantees of fair bail and punishment expressed in the Eighth Amendment are, in essence, personal rights of a liberal democracy.

The Second Amendment right to bear arms in the militia is typologically different. It does not speak to individual liberty, and it is neither procedural nor intellectual in character. It isn't even, ahistorically speaking at least, political. It is social and instrumental. Perhaps the Founders linked it to a stated collective purpose because it seemed intuitively unable to stand on its own as an unqualified assertion of an individual's sovereign immunity against state interference. In fact, to have meaning, the Second Amendment right required state activation, or even, according to its own terms, "regulation." Though baldly stated as a right, the bearing of arms was in a true sense an obligation of republican virtue. To recall once more Justice Story's conclusion about the Second Amendment, it is indeed "difficult to see" "[h]ow it is practicable to keep the people duly armed, without some organization."[40] And in this dependence on a government-activated militia and the people's willingness to continue to participate in that organization, the Second Amendment right to keep and bear arms was and remains quite a different creature from its fellows in the famous catalogue of 1789.

Thus, we conclude as we began: The personal right to possess arms constitutionalized in the Second Amendment must be understood in the context in which it was written, as a grant to the individual constituents of a communal military organization the means of making the militia effective. The Amendment established an individual right serving a collective, republican purpose — "to provide for the common defense," as the Constitution's Preamble promised. It was a grant of instrumental, enabling power to individuals. No more. And for such an enabling right, responsive to no threat of abuse of personal freedom, a change in the underlying social assumptions so radically alters the context of the enactment that the meaning must be rediscovered in the new context. History has clearly written the conclusion: today, no remnant of the original context of the Second Amendment language survives. Without those referents, linguistic and social, the meaning of the provision has been lost and the right must be deemed to be in suspension.

This conclusion, we recognize, will be unpalatable to those who claim that the threat of enforced disarmament posed today by comprehensive gun control is just the sort of threatened abuse of personal liberties that all the rights in the 1791 Bill were designed to preclude. It is no solace to them that the Framers perceived no threat of abuse of liberties in the restriction of weapons owned for purely private ends. It is enough for them that they perceive such a threat today. We reply: well it may be, but if such is your concern your resort must be to the democratic institutions for remedy. The Constitution offers only that protection articulated in its text, understood in the light of prevailing context, and applied in new circumstances only to the extent consistent with generic meaning. And all the historical evidence points to a right heavily dependent on public purpose. Legislation — or amendment — must do the rest.

8

Other Theories of Meaning Considered

In the ten years since Professor Sanford Levinson bemoaned the scant attention the Second Amendment had received from courts and scholars,[1] a fair number of law professors, historians, and other commentators have contributed their thoughts. While some, to a greater or lesser degree, have seen the picture as we do, a substantial number see it very differently. In this chapter, we have selected a few for rather extensive comment. This does not purport to be a random or representative sampling of what has become an extensive literature on the subject. Rather, we have taken people whose contributions have particularly interested us, with emphasis on those scholars who differ with us in whole or in part.

SANFORD LEVINSON: CITIZEN GUERILLAS BEING NECESSARY TO THE SECURITY OF A FREE STATE . . .

In a sense, the scholarly debate on the configuration of the Second Amendment begins with an influential article published in 1991 by the highly respected scholar Professor Sanford Levinson of the University of Texas Law School.[2] He was not, of course, the first to take to print on the issue. Several advocates for and against gun control[3] and at least two historians[4] had evinced an interest in the constitutional question. But, at least among legal scholars, they had failed to stir up much serious interest. Thus, partly because of his eminence in other fields, Levinson remains the progenitor of the debate, still cited and referred to wherever the issue is aired—including in a recent declaration of policy by the current Attorney General of the United States.[5]

In his short, oddly casual comment, Levinson's only purpose appears to have been to rouse interest in what he believed to be an unjustly ignored provision of the Bill of Rights. Courts and scholars, he complained, had failed to give the Second Amendment the attention that the peoples' interest demanded. Levinson insists that it is not his "style to offer 'correct' or 'incorrect' interpretations of the Constitution," and that his only aim is to introduce "skepticism" regarding the "elite, liberal" views, epitomized by Professor Laurence Tribe's then offhand treatment.[6]

However, Levinson's somewhat rambling tour of the subject is susceptible of the reading that it has been commonly accorded: support for those who contend that the provision prohibits any interference by Congress with the private possession of guns. Thus, he writes: "[I]t seems tendentious [presumably in the sense of partisan] to reject out of hand the argument that one purpose of the Amendment was to recognize the individual's right to engage in armed self-defense against criminal conduct."[7] Further departing from his ostensible neutrality, Levinson notes that he, for one, has been persuaded that the term "militia" does not have the "limited reference" to a "communitarian right," but instead refers to "all of the people, or at least those treated as full citizens of the community."[8]

Levinson, regrettably, is far from forthright about the point of his conversion to the individualist interpretation and his adoption of the dubious equation of militia = people. But it is quite clear that Levinson takes a position different from our belief that the Second Amendment slumbers alongside its dormant companion, the Third. He vehemently protests any suggestion of obsolescence shared with letters of marque and reprisal, and the granting of titles of nobility.[9] "The Second Amendment," he writes, "is radically different from these other pieces of constitutional text."[10] Support for this assertion, however, is not summoned from history or doctrinal analysis. Rather, Levinson cites the frequent appearance of letters to the editor, congressional campaigns, and the deep concern of members of both the American Civil Liberties Union and the National Rifle Association. He thus casts his contribution to the debate in distinctly political terms.

He abandons, somewhat reluctantly, the notion (today associated with Professor Lott)[11] that private firearms curtail crime. Thus, he writes: "Circumstances may well have changed in regard to individual defense, although we ignore at our political peril the good-faith belief of many Americans that they cannot rely on the police for protection against a variety of criminals."[12] Levinson then comes to what may be the crux of this odd—almost coy—argument. While disclaiming anarchy, and withholding the claim that the state is "necessarily tyrannical," he cites the suppression of the people on Tiananmen Square to demonstrate that "it seems foolish to assume that the armed state will necessarily be benevolent."[13] This leads to what he terms "the principal point, that a state facing a totally disarmed population is in a far better position, for good or for ill, to suppress popular demonstrations and uprisings than one that must calculate the possibilities of its soldiers and officials being injured or killed."[14] So Levinson arrives ultimately at the neo-Lockean assertion that, in the final analysis, the right of armed resistance or insurrection is a necessary safeguard against a tyrannical state.

Yet to the extent—circumlocutions and disavowals notwithstanding—that Professor Levinson's sketchy but influential paper comes down to a reading of the Second Amendment as assurance that the people, as individuals, will have the means to resist the oppression of the state, it is highly suspect even under the republican banner that Levinson unfurls. Although Levinson does not pursue the point to its theoretical foundations, the Second Amendment is based on Whig ideology and political heritage that postulated constitutional justifications for armed resistance to illegitimate governance and tyranny in seventeenth-century Stuart England. These doctrines in turn played a prominent role in legitimizing the American Revolution. The crucial point for present purposes, we insist, is that this aspect of radical Whiggery was forsaken with the adoption of the first seven Articles of the Constitution.

The question of how to remedy tyrannical rule was hardly one of first impression for the seventeenth-century Whigs or Revolutionary Americans. Resistance to tyranny is one of the oldest problems of political thought, forming a central theme in the historical and philosophical writings of the Greeks and Romans. More precisely, the question was not so much how to bring about the end of illegitimate or impolitic rule—banishment and indeed tyrannicide were direct and obvious solutions—but how to justify those ultimate remedies, and when to invoke them.[15] In seventeenth-century England, particularly after the execution of Charles I, the answer to this question assumed a distinctly republican cast that foreshadowed the drift toward American independence in the second half of the next century. To most post-Restoration Whigs, the remedy against tyranny involved in the last instance coerced substitution of one king for another rather than abolition of the monarchy. But this violent substitution had now become enmeshed in layers of legitimizing nuance and constitutional doctrine that specified limits on kingly government and defined tests by which to establish whether those limits had been transgressed. John Locke's *Second Treatise of Government,* a quasi-official manifesto for the failed revolutions of 1683[16] and 1685[17] and the successful one of 1688–89, epitomizes the Whigs' canonical approach to resistance theory.

To Locke, the right of resistance was premised on the "dissolution of government," for nothing could have been further from his Whiggish purpose than the forceful overthrow of a just, legitimate government. Although Locke developed the people's right to resist arbitrary power as a fundamental, timeless right, his immediate objective in the *Second Treatise* was to justify resistance against the specific abuses of Charles II, and in so doing firm up the resolve of conspirators planning a general insurrection and an attempt on the King's life outside the "Rye House" as he made his way back to the capital from races at Newmarket.[18] Locke argued, much as Jefferson later would in the Declaration of Independence, that the King had violated the peoples' trust in the magistracy, effectively "unkinging" himself, and so dissolving the civic compact. To this end, Locke considered two fundamental conditions under which "governments are dissolved from within," namely (1) "alteration" of the legislature,[19] and (2) violation of the public trust.[20] These amounted, in more modern parlance, to means whereby the executive might assume or subvert the law-making function of the legislature or the law-finding function of the judiciary. The first condition arose whenever power to make laws was usurped in contravention of the law, and popularly delegated authority thereby excluded from power. The second obtained wherever corruption became so endemic as to preclude the processes of legitimate governance in any branch.

Locke took pains to argue that removal of Charles II would not constitute treason. He defined rebellion narrowly as opposition to just authority "founded only in the constitutions and laws of the government." By this definition, whenever princes, ministers, or legislators violated the constitution and thereby brought about the dissolution of government, it was they who were guilty of rebellion. In the literal Latin sense of *rebello,* they returned to a state of war by dissolving the laws preserving "society and civil-government." To Locke and the radical Whigs he spoke for, there remained no doubt but that Charles had breached his trust by invading the "lives, liberties, and estates of the people."[21] In so doing, he dissolved the government. The people and the monarch, then, were placed in opposition, but there remained no earthly court to hear their dispute. The King's refusal to rule under law and abide by the law caused a return to the prepolitical state of perpetual war, and left the people no appeal but to Heaven for vindication of their abridged rights and liberties.

Lockean overtones are unmistakable in the Declaration of Independence. Jefferson's list of grievances against George III mirrors Locke's indictment of Charles II for dissolving the government from within, both by altering the legislature and by breach of trust. Jefferson, of course, did not simply derive his grievances from Locke. Not only do the Declaration's grievances correspond to particular acts of the Westminster Parliament in the 1760s and 1770s, they largely rehearse a list established by the Continental Congress in its Bill of Rights and List of Grievances and Declaration of Causes.

Nonetheless, a comparison of the *Second Treatise* and the Declaration of Independence reveals a remarkable continuity in Whig ideology and in Whig resistance theory. The Revolution of 1688–89 provided more than a historical lens through which Americans understood their own Revolution. It established the typology of revolutionary politics that Americans applied to their experiences. And it proved particularly apt in that the ministry of George III possessed an uncanny capacity to repeat the failed measures of the past century as it confronted increasingly intractable colonial legislatures, growing ever more adamant in their insistence that the guarantees settled in the last Revolution applied in America as in England.

More even than their hostility to arbitrary power, Locke and Jefferson shared a suspicion of ministerial conspiracy against liberty and a conviction that such conspiracy justified resistance. In this respect, some have argued that Jefferson was so compelled by Locke's language that he chose to incorporate it into the Declaration.[22] In the *Second Treatise,* Locke warned:

> [b]ut if a long train of abuses, prevarications and artifices, all tend-
> ing the same way, make the design visible to the people, and they
> cannot but feel what they be under, and see wither they are going;
> it is not to be wondered, that they should then rouze themselves,
> and endeavour to put the rule into such hands which may secure
> to them the ends for which government was first erected.[23]

Ninety-seven years later, in the Declaration, Jefferson wrote:

> [b]ut when a long train of abuses and usurpations, begun at a dis-
> tinguished period and pursuing invariably the same object, evinces
> a design to reduce the [people] under absolute despotism, it is their
> right, it is their duty to throw off such government, and to provide
> new guards for their future security.

Thus, Jefferson's Declaration of 1776, although developed independently and adapted to different political purposes — abolishing
the monarchy rather than exchanging the monarch — resounds un-
mistakably in the language of Lockean resistance theory. Indeed, if
the Second Amendment were an appendage to the Declaration of Independence, one might plausibly argue that its context (though not its
text) suggested a purpose of preserving a right to insurrection, if only
in cases where the government of the day was guilty of a long series
of illegal and extra-constitutional transgressions of the class meticu-
lously described in the Declaration and in Locke's *Second Treatise.* But
the Second Amendment, of course, is not appended to the Declaration, but to the Constitution of 1787. And how different Madison's
constitutional universe of 1787 was from Jefferson's of 1776![24] After
1787, with remedies against usurpation defined in the constitutional
instrument itself, recourse to external bodies of law or theory was no
longer required to right the ship of state if the government became
corrupted. For purposes of American constitutionalism, Lockean resistance theory was therefore relegated into irrelevancy.

The Madisonian specification of instrumental remedies against
tyranny affected the most profound transformation in American constitutional history.[25] By spelling out precisely what remedies were
available to specified bodies of the peoples' magistrates or representatives in the event of unconstitutional governmental action, Madison

bypassed two unanswerable questions that had forever vexed whig-gish constitutionalism, namely (1) who constituted the people entitled to determine when the sovereign had unkinged himself, and (2) what means other than the sword might arbitrate between rival factions claiming to embody the vox populi in the event of constitutional crises.

Circumventing these old conundrums worked two fundamental consequences. First, civil war ceased to be the court of last resort for troublesome constitutional questions (excepting, ultimately, only the question of federal territorial jurisdiction over slavery, and even this question required resolution by war only because secession dictated forceful recovery of the South as a precondition for the reestablishment of federal authority). Second, the impossible demands that the old constitutional paradigm had placed on popular civic virtue now fell silent. No longer was constitutional legitimacy linked to the sainthood of the voting and office-holding classes. No longer was the incessant conspiracy watch a linchpin of legitimacy. Institutional avenues for redressing balance replaced the fateful heroes who once stood guard against corruption. In short order, these institutional systems acquired legitimacy in the popular eye. Constitutional disputation (at least constitutional disputation unrelated to slavery) lost its martial edge.

In his *Embarrassing Second Amendment,* Professor Levinson endeavors an extratextual resurrection of the old heroic doctrine of violent resistance two-hundred-odd years after its abandonment by the ratifiers. This effort is ill-advised. It is imprudent, in that the Madisonian structural model has worked better than the old "system" of constitutional arbitration since its installation in 1788. And it is dangerous because the self-anointed vigilantes of today are far removed in outlook, virtue, perspective, education, experience, and public-spiritedness from the Lockeans of yesteryear. The Earl of Shaftesbury, John Locke, and Algernon Sidney in the 1680s, like John Adams, Benjamin Franklin, and Thomas Jefferson in the 1770s, were the most educated and forward looking public servants of their times. They spoke for substantial bodies of thoughtful, public-spirited people committed to the rule of law, who nevertheless believed that a right of resistance against extreme forms of extralegal rule represented a rational, principled, and positive alternative to a hopeless subordination to unchecked, arbitrary absolutism. In their hands, the public weal was truly safer than in those of royal placemen and salaried fools who flattered themselves unanswerable to the law. The old Whigs nobly laid the foundations of American republicanism. Their refusal to accept the Stuarts' asserted civic duty of nonresistance, like their hostility to military establishment, helped prevent the English-speaking world from falling under the absolutism that reigned in seventeenth- and eighteenth-century Europe.

But in 1788, their doctrine of entitlement to resist arbitrary authority was supplanted by the new constitutionalism and the fixation of a nonarbitrary system of government in America. And no matter how low our opinion of twenty-first-century American politicians or civil servants, today's bigoted, gun-hoarding insurrectionists' claim to have better title to determine policy (or annul policy) for the nation than the constitutionally established and constitutionally answerable government cannot be justified by implausible analogy to historical principles long since forsaken. Perhaps Levinson can picture today's American "militia" safeguarding our independence by raising their beloved assault weapons against government tanks on some future Tiananmen Square. Alas, we cannot.

The insurmountable problem with the insurrectionism Levinson endorses is its hopeless vagueness, and the fundamental insolubility of any political question submitted to its arbitrage. The "principle" of insurrectionism, particularly in the modern, postdeferential society we live in, is no principle at all unless it comes to grips with the question of who is justified to undertake armed resistance in the face of tyranny, usurpation, or difference of opinion on constitutional issues. One of the old answers to this ancient question was the army. This was the Cromwellian solution,[26] and it is also the solution of the modern Turkish constitution, which provides that the army has the duty to intervene in civil affairs to protect the constitutional system and maintain constitutional rule.[27] Army intervention, however, becomes decidedly unrepublican if the army does not represent the virtuous nation in arms, but instead serves the heavy hand of a corrupted magistracy or a tyrannical usurper.

Another historically favored solution, to which this work has devoted considerable attention, is of course the common militia composed of virtuous citizens under the command of their elected natural leaders. In that guise, the militia embodied the people or acted as agent for the people. The conventional Whig view of the militia as the "constitutional army" or as even the "army of the constitution" thus required only slight reformulation along less martial and more political lines to yield Locke's solution of 1683, John and Samuel Adams's of 1774–75, and Jefferson's of 1776, that the "people" were entitled to determine if and when the government had breached its trust, and in the event that it had, to intervene forcefully to institute new government.

But this principle of popular intervention as a last resort for reestablishment of constitutional rule brings us all the way back to the original dilemma of determining who defines "the people" entitled to intervene—all the more so because pivotal constitutional questions by their very nature foster differences of opinion and passionate factionalism. Locke himself wrestled elsewhere (in the *Letter Concerning Toleration*)[28] with the unknowability of complete truth and inevitable prevalence of error in human society. The appeal to arms or to Heaven represented the invocation of a higher authority to arbitrate between rival claimants to the truth. The results of such appeal in constitutional cases could be very bloody. In 1688 they were not, because the anti-Stuart consensus was so strong that once the Dutch Army took the field, the English militia joined them and the English Army melted away. In 1775, things were very different. One-third of the population favored the patriot cause, one-fifth were loyal to the Crown, and the rest tried to stay neutral. By 1783, perhaps 20,000 had been killed on the battlefields, and tens of thousands of loyalists were dispossessed and exiled.[29]

The Philadelphia Convention of 1787 devised a third way to adjudge constitutional disputes, one involving appeals to Heaven by neither the army nor the people under arms. This was the Madisonian solution of constitutionally defined civic mechanisms to resolve impasses and rectify abuses.[30] Except for the fratricidal conflict of 1861, it has been considerably less sanguinary. Under the system ratified in 1788, frequent, regular elections were fixed permanently on foundations more solid than those underlying the Parliamentary Septennial Act, and the old Whig doctrine that legislators must periodically be reduced to civilian status was placed beyond the reach of Congress. After ratification, whenever the executive claimed to be above the law, he could be forced to comply by means of the constitutionally specified remedy of appeal to the law courts for a writ of mandamus (affirmed in *United States v. Nixon* perhaps more paradigmatically than in *Marbury v. Madison*). When the President refuses to assent to salubrious laws or to execute existing laws, Congress might now resort to the override or to impeachment (both illustrated by the showdown with Andrew Johnson by the Thirty-ninth Congress). When states overstep their bounds and judge or legislate in derogation of the Constitution, federal judicial review now provided a corrective (asserted in *Martin v. Hunter's Lessee, Cohens v. Virginia,* and *McCulloch v. Maryland*).

The case for the radical nature of Madison's innovations, and the related case for ratification's overthrow of the old Whig right of insurrection are buttressed by Professor Rakove's convincing argument that the Convention intended federal judicial review to extend also to congressional lawmaking.[31] In fact, Representative Egbert Benson's comments (referred to in chapter 3) during the debates on the Second Amendment[32] afford strong evidence that judicial review of federal law was integrated by the Framers into the constitutional design, and ratified in 1788, rather than spun from whole cloth by Chief Justice John Marshall with the Marbury decision in 1803 (as the conventional myth would have it). And finally, the Constitution established the process of amendment in case the constitutional system itself should prove insufficient to meet unforeseen crises (consider the Twelfth Amendment as a response to the near theft of the presidency by Aaron Burr), or inadequate to cope with fundamentally altered circumstances (addressed by Amendments XIII, XIV, and XV). The variety and diversity of remedies provide additional assurance that no usurper could nullify them all. Thus, so long as these constitutionally guaranteed mechanisms endure, constitutional government continues capable of unseating a tyrant and of resisting an abusive office holder. The moment of Lockean reversion to first principles need never, and (from the perspective of constitutional legitimacy) can never, come.

With ratification in 1788, Madisonian structuralism supplanted the old panoply of Whiggish constitutional doctrines, including the much contested radical Whig principle of justified resistance to illegal rule famously memorialized in Locke's *Second Treatise*.[33] And while the American Bill of Rights can be understood as a series of limited if meaningful reassurances and concessions to anti-federalists still deeply wedded to the old Whig theory of the English constitution, no radical right to insurrection can be read into the textually specified guarantees ratified by the Americans in 1791. Indeed, the Senate, while debating the Bill of Rights, chose to reject a proposed amendment condemning the "slavish doctrine of non-resistance"[34] once espoused by the Vatican, Archbishop Laud, and the Stuarts, and in so doing turned its back on perhaps the most favored mantra in the whole Lockean discourse of resistance.

In sum, the arrival of Madisonian constitutionalism deprived seventeenth-century Whiggish radicalism of any claim on the interpretation of the right to arms embodied in the Second Amendment. Despite its apparent influence on Jefferson's thinking in 1776, after ratification in 1788, Locke's remedy for tyranny was obsolete. And insofar as Professor Levinson has sounded the ancient trumpet for armed resistance, he is living in a preconstitutional era.

Though we find the source of its considerable influence elusive, Professor Levinson's famous paper has surely accomplished its ostensible purpose of raising interest—and controversy—in the Amendment that, as he charges, has been all but ignored by the Supreme Court. Beyond that, we think it regrettable that his unpersuasive thesis has lent respectability to the outlaw libertarians who claim to be the legitimate guardians of American freedom.

CARL BOGUS: AN ARMED MILITIA BEING NECESSARY
TO THE SECURITY OF A SLAVE STATE

One scholar who has proposed an alternative to our republican interpretation of the Second Amendment is Professor Carl Bogus of Roger Williams University. In his thoughtful and challenging *Hidden History of the Second Amendment*,[35] Professor Bogus advances two fundamental propositions. The first is that the Second Amendment was designed to secure a collective right rather than a personal liberty.[36] The second holds that an unwritten understanding among the Framers committed the young nation to the Second Amendment right to arms for an essentially oppressive purpose. Southern slave owners, Bogus reminds us, feared slave insurrection, and therefore, he insists, they demanded sureties that Northern abolitionists would never use newly established federal powers to disarm Southern militia (i.e., slave patrols) and thereby pave the way to revolt. Those very guarantees, Bogus concludes, form the tacit underpinnings of our constitutional right to arms. We agree with Professor Bogus that the

Second Amendment does not protect a wholly individualistic right, but we cannot join him in the contention that the constitutional right to arms belongs to the states rather than to natural persons. Nor can we endorse the intriguing thesis that the Framers' purpose of preserving a collective right to arms responded directly to strong Southern fears that Congress might disarm the Southern state militias and thereby undermine social control over the slave population. To state the thesis in his words: "The Second Amendment . . . was written to assure the Southern states that Congress would not undermine the slave system by using its newly acquired constitutional authority over the militia to disarm the state militia and thereby destroy the South's principal instrument of slave control. In effect, the Second Amendment supplemented the slavery compromise made at the Constitutional Convention in Philadelphia and obliquely codified in other constitutional provisions."[37]

This reading is, we think, misguided. While provocative, it is not only inconsistent with the historical record of the factors impelling adoption, but in several important respects, contradicted by the known facts. Of course, Bogus knows that his thesis is novel, and recognizes that explicit documentary evidence to support it is scarce. In this fix, Professor Bogus is forced to build his argument on a series of inferences, some of which, we feel, are seriously mistaken. For example, Bogus relies heavily on the Stono, South Carolina, rebellion of 1739. But major slave uprisings on the North American continent were rare and getting rarer in the eighteenth century; they were even less common in the 1700s than they were in the sixty years preceeding secession.[38] In fact, the Stono rebellion, along with a Long Island/New York City conspiracy of similarly ancient vintage, were the only two notable domestic slave revolts (or threatened revolts) to have occurred before 1789 when the First Congress took the Second Amendment under consideration.[39] Thus, when the militia Amendment was drafted, slaveowners were likely less obsessed with potential revolts than Bogus supposes.

To give Professor Bogus his due, it is quite true that Southerners were aware of the latent potential for violent resistance in the late eighteenth century,[40] and that Southern militia took prominent and leading roles in putting down the major slave disturbances of the nineteenth century. Southern state militias suppressed Nat Turner's rebellion in Virginia in 1831, the Denmark Vessey conspiracy in South

Carolina in 1822, and the Gabriel plot in Virginia in 1800.[41] But these attempts at insurrection occurred 9, 30, and 41 years after the Second Amendment was ratified. When the Virginia Ratifying Convention, on whose deliberations and motivations Professor Bogus's thesis turns, called for assurance of the rights of local militiamen to bear arms, no one could have foreseen the nineteenth century insurrections, and the Stono story was more legend than recollection, nearly fifty years having passed since that bloody Sunday.

Of more immediate impact on the Virginia ratifiers of the Second Amendment were recent events that Professor Bogus oddly fails to mention.[42] On August 22, 1791, the largest slave revolt in western history erupted on the island of Haiti, when the 200,000 slaves in the French colony of Saint Domingue rose against the island's 20,000 *gens du coleur* and 20,000 whites.[43] Most of the colony's whites were killed or forced out by 1793. Several hundred refugees safely escaped to Virginia and a smaller number sought refuge in other Southern states.

The arrival of the Haitian refugees in Virginia touched off an obsessive and soul-searching debate on slavery, security, and manumission in the local newspapers, running many columns of print in the Commonwealth's numerous weeklies and semiweeklies. This debate began before Virginia became the ninth state to ratify the Bill of Rights and the Second Amendment to the United States Constitution passed into law, and certainly influenced the minds of the state senators who sat down to consider the Second Amendment in the fall of 1791.[44]

Moreover, it was in 1792, at the height of the violence in Haiti, that the national government made its first concerted effort to regulate and standardize the state militia under the militia powers. If Bogus were right about the legislative intent behind the Second Amendment, and the adamancy of Southern insistence on local control of the militia *qua* slave patrol, then one would expect that the same men who championed a Second Amendment focused on slave control would have made themselves heard regarding the Uniform Militia Act of 1792. That statute was far more explicit on federal control of the militia than the constitutional provision. But no member of the House, Southern or otherwise, voiced slavery-related opposition to the federal control over the militia established in the Act, even though the impending militia legislation was hotly debated for many months.[45] The absence of such statements cast considerable doubt on the proposition that Southern members feared a Northern plot to use the federal militia powers to disarm the Southerners with a view to unleashing a second Haiti on the mainland. If Southern members had no such fears in 1792, with the political climate sensitized by the much reported slaughter of their fellow planters, it seems even less likely that, during the relatively tranquil summer of 1789, they were burdened by fears of federal disarmament and their vulnerability to slave rebellion.

In the absence of explicit documentation, Bogus relies on the Second Amendment's "hidden" history to make his case that white fear of black violence generated constitutional protection for the collective right to keep and bear arms in the militia. He points out that it is not altogether surprising that expressions of the true purpose of the Second Amendment are lacking since slavery—and certainly the repression of slaves—was seldom mentioned by name in the state papers and public manifestos of the revolutionary years.[46] And true enough, of the twelve members to speak while the proposed Amendment was under consideration, not one mentioned slavery.[47] "A decent respect to the opinions of mankind," to use the Jeffersonian locution, dictated that the issue, if broached at all, be broached delicately.

It is, however, significant that when questions bearing directly on local control over slaves and slavery were raised in the Constitutional Convention[48]—and they were raised—slavery was defended by name in the debates (although references were made by euphemism in the constitutional instrument itself).[49] South Carolina was then and always in the vanguard of proslavery militancy, and when the vital interests of slavery were at issue—however remotely—South Carolinians were the first to speak. But they were not heard on slavery during the debate on the Bill of Rights. South Carolina was clearly not as animated in 1789 by concerns that Congress or the President might disarm the militia as it was in 1787 by concerns that the Northeast might carry disproportionate weight in the federal Congress, or unduly burden the South with debt under the proposed Constitution. In 1789, unlike 1787,[50] 1819–20,[51] 1832–33,[52] 1844–46,[53] 1848–50,[54] 1857,[55] or 1860–61,[56] no threats of disunion were issued, no secessionist stock phrases were uttered, and no fighting honor was invoked.[57]

South Carolina did not, along with whatever support could be rallied among Southern kindred, threaten to walk out of the Union if slavery was not vouchsafed for the ages.[58] The Bill of Rights debate, and more particularly the House debate on the proposed Second Amendment, simply lack this telltale sign, and all told, do not bear the hallmarks of a slavery-focused constitutional crisis. Rather, the debate sounds in terms of civic humanism and other values that did not divide along latitudinal lines.[59]

Ample and readily accessible evidence attests to the anxiety of Southern whites over social control and safety in the plantation districts,[60] but this local concern hardly proves that Southern drafters of the Second Amendment feared an abolitionist cabal to disarm the patrols. Occasionally, Bogus hedges his bets, and appears to say no more than that the preservation of an armed local military force was of paramount importance in the states where slavery was most widespread and firmly rooted, and this much is little more than a truism. More frequently, however, Bogus asserts forthrightly that the Southern imperative for slave control created the need for, determined the content of, and ultimately led to the adoption of the Second Amendment. He says, for example, "As a Virginian, Madison knew that the militia's prime function in his state, and throughout the South, was slave control. His use of the word 'security' is consistent with his writing the amendment for the specific purpose of assuring the Southern states, and particularly his constituents in Virginia, that the federal government would not undermine their security against slave insurrections by disarming the militia." Bogus also says: "Madison's colleagues in the House and Senate almost certainly considered the Second Amendment to be part of the slavery compromise"; and further:

> The Constitution had given Congress the power to organize and arm the militia. Focusing on this provision, the anti-Federalists sent a chill down the spine of the South: would Congress, deliberately or through indifference, destabilize the slave system by "disarming" the state militia. . . . [T]he Second Amendment was written to assure the South that the militia—the very same militia described in the main body of the Constitution—could be armed even if Congress elected not to arm them or otherwise attempted to "disarm" them.[61]

But Professor Bogus's argument fails to take account of cross-sectional support for the Second Amendment. The anti-federalist movement that gave impetus to the adoption of the Bill of Rights drew support broadly in the new states. While, as Bogus reminds us,

Virginia was a crucial state in the process of securing constitutional protection for the right to keep and bear arms,[62] republican misgivings concerning a standing army, and hence popular emphasis on the importance of the citizen's militia, came as strongly from the North as from the South.[63] And given the pacifistic, nonconfrontational character of the late-eighteenth-century antislavery movement, we think it highly unlikely that Virginia and other plantation states could have feared that northern abolitionists would so dominate the federal government that they might deprive their Southern brothers of arms in order to encourage slave revolt.[64]

Perhaps the most serious quarrel we have with the Bogus slave suppression thesis is that it ignores the linkage between maintenance of a militia and the prevalent repugnance for a professional standing army. This association of ideas seems to us to be so open, strong, and pervasive that it easily overcomes the marginal energy the movement might have acquired from sectional anxiety. In the face of what seems to us manifest, Bogus disparages the importance of the founding generation's support for the militia as an alternative to the feared standing army. Thus, he says: "While some anti-federalists continued to talk about the evils of a standing army, they had lost this argument in Philadelphia."[65] Presumably, he means that the Constitutional Convention itself had resolved the issue: Congress was granted the power to establish a peacetime army. From this resolution, Professor Bogus suggests that there could have been no residual concern with the dangers of a professional army to motivate the adoption of measures protecting the armament of the civilian alternative. Hence, he argues, in effect, the reason for the formulation and adoption of the Second Amendment must have been some other concern, and the most likely, although covert, candidate is slave control.

It is certainly true that the troubling issue of the power of the central government to raise, train, and maintain a regular army was settled by the time the draft constitution was ratified in 1789. The standing army was to be supported financially only in two-year intervals, at the will of Congress, and was subject to civilian command, but the regular army was indeed a federal fact. To that extent, Bogus is right: the federalists had had their way. But the issue was far from resolved against republican apprehensions. The First Congress authorized a standing army of only 2,000 men. It was clear—and still a matter of high priority on the anti-federalist agenda—that the professional army was to be only part of the military story. The same instrument that established the army recognized an independent militia, albeit a militia that was largely under the control of Congress and the President. Contrary to Professor Bogus's thesis, we see the Second Amendment as a response to the anti-federalists' urgent concern that the new fledged regular army not be allowed to overwhelm and obviate the citizen brigades.

Professor Bogus stresses the importance of the Virginia Declaration of Rights, the score of proposed amendments and second score of hortatory provisions that became the model for the Bill of Rights. In particular, he relies on the seventeenth provision which contains language very much like the Second Amendment. As quoted in chapter 1, this provision provides

> That the people have a right to keep and bear arms; that a well-regulated militia, composed of the body of the people trained to arms, is the proper, natural, and safe defense of a free state; that standing armies, in time of peace, are dangerous to liberty and therefore ought to be avoided, as far as the circumstances and protection of the community will admit; and that, in all cases, the military should be under the strict subordination to, and governed by, the civil power.

Bogus's reliance on this document is somewhat puzzling. In one breath, he disparages the proclaimed right to arms as "a cathartic exercise for the defeated anti-federalists,"[66] consisting of nothing but "rhetoric recycled from newspaper articles and from speeches made and rejected at the Constitutional Convention in Philadelphia."[67] In the next, he regards the Declaration as a significant departure from the Virginia Bill of Rights of 1776, which contained no provision for a right to bear arms. Between 1776 and 1788, Bogus contends, "Mason and Henry had raised the specter of the national government undermining the slave system by disarming the state militia."[68] Thus, he would have us believe, the model for the Second Amendment included the provision of an armed militia in direct response to Virginians' fears about slave revolt (hardly an exercise in empty rhetoric).

We are not persuaded. It seems to us highly unlikely that this Declaration consciously departed from the 1776 Bill of Rights to send a secret message for perpetuation of an ad hoc system of slave repression. We do not stress the irony that such a proposal should be made to defend a slave state by reciting the importance of defending a free state.

Other language in the Virginia Declaration more clearly asserts a purpose different from saving the militia from the abolitionists. Most obviously, the text expresses support for the armed militia as the preferred alternative to a standing army. The face of the provision could hardly be more explicit, the safe defense by a militia being immediately juxtaposed to the dangerous standing army. This cannot be fairly dismissed as rhetoric recycled from newspapers; rather, the army-militia dichotomy goes to the heart of military-related rights set out in the Virginia Declaration.

Moreover, no covert hint can be discerned in the language of the Declaration that the people of Virginia sought domestic tranquility by the exercise of police power. The document might have been drawn otherwise if, as Bogus suggests, Virginians conceived of their militia primarily as a patrol force rather than a hedge against a standing army. There were, of course, no domestic police units in the eighteenth century; the concept of a local peacekeeping and law enforcement body wholly independent of the military did not really arrive on the American scene until the middle of the nineteenth century.[69] But Virginians could, if such was their thinking, express the value of the armed militia as domestic peacekeepers without ever mentioning the forbidden word. Rather than calling for a well-regulated and armed militia as an alternative to a standing army, they might have appealed to the need to protect the lives and property of law-abiding citizens from the depredations of outlaws or savages, as was done in the passages of the Declaration of Independence indicting Britain for inciting slave revolt,[70] or to the importance of bringing criminals to justice, as was done in the Fugitive Slave Clause of the Constitution.[71] It is, we submit, significant that the Framers of the Virginia Declaration of Rights chose not to do so.

More fundamentally still, as even Bogus acknowledges, the right to bear arms did not originate in Richmond. Several states, including Massachusetts, which abolished slavery by judicial decision in 1783,[72] had already incorporated the right to bear arms in their constitutions before the federal Constitution was ratified in 1789.[73]

Professor Bogus also turns to the Declaration of Rights to search for clues to the mind of James Madison, reluctant champion of the Bill of Rights and draftsman of the Second Amendment.[74] Bogus thinks there is little doubt that item 17 of Virginia's Declaration became the template for the Second Amendment. He therefore skillfully employs the textualist's literary device and examines for significance the words dropped or changed. He is not surprised to find that the architect of federalism substituted the word "country" for "state" in the Declaration.[75] He discusses the syntactical change from a right granted, as expressed by the Virginia draft, to a restraint on infringement of a presumably inherent right in the Madisonian style that we know today.[76] He suggests that Madison dropped the language defining the militia as "composed of a body of the people trained to arms" because it appeared to undercut the provision in Article 1, Section 8, granting to Congress the authority to "provide for organizing" the militia. The exegesis then arrives at Madison's editorial alteration critical for Bogus's thesis.

Where the Virginia model stipulated that the militia is "the proper, natural, and safe defense of a free state," Madison wrote, "the best security of a free country." Passing the substitution of "best" for "proper, natural, and safe," Bogus emphasizes that the myth of a militia as a *defense* against foreign invasion had been long discredited,[77] but Madison knew that *security* — in the South, at least — meant protection against slave revolt. The implication of Professor Bogus's point is unmistakable: Madison, a Southern slave owner, crafted the Second Amendment to serve the purposes of slave control.[78] The argument, we think, is mistaken.

Security, we concede, suggests a broader purpose than *defense.* But *security* itself implies a broader concept than violence control on the plantations. Either *security* or *defense* might be employed to express several potential uses of a well-regulated militia in the new Nation, including provision of protection against frontier Indian tribes or incursion by foreign troops. But beyond these basic military purposes, *security* could apply to a variety of functions less aptly labeled defensive, such as suppression of antitax or debt-relief mobs like the Shaysites. And while *security* better describes the function of stamping out domestic insurrection than does *defense,* it also captures aptly the state of being politically *secure* against the dangers of expensive and corrupting standing armies, a function *defense* entirely fails to address. Moreover, there was still — among the die-hard anti-federalists, at least — substantial concern that the autonomy and integrity of the individual states would be transgressed by the central government, and *security* against such a threat better expressed the object of anti-federal militia enthusiasts than *defense*. Indeed, the word *secure,* used in its other location in the Bill of Rights, the Fourth Amendment, refers quite pointedly to protection against federal governmental incursion. So, in sum, it seems to us the choice of the word *security* in preference to *defense* has several plausible explanations other than the one favored by Bogus.

While *defense* implies making resistance to a real or potential physical attack, *security* suggests additionally and much more broadly maintaining a state of safety. Financial instruments and insurance policies afforded in the eighteenth century afford in the twenty-first a sense of security (and can even be traded as securities), but they were not then and are not now called defensive weapons. When Jefferson informed Madison that the people were entitled to "a bill of rights providing . . . for . . . protection against standing armies,"[79] he did not mean military protection against a huge marching army so much as political security that such an army would not be assembled in the first place, and financial security that such an army would not be funded by taxation or debt. Both *defense* and *security* imply protection. But *security* has a wider reference, and the safety that comes with security can be of a type several levels removed from confrontation with real or potential physical aggression. The Defense Department assures one type of safety, the Social Security Administration another. The National Security Administration, if it really exists, presumably provides for both military and political security. From a classical republican perspective, the militia provided both security in the form of military defense, and security in the form of political stability.

In arguing for his thesis, Professor Bogus recites the comments, the speeches, and the subjective consciousness of the Virginia delegates to the ratifying convention in Richmond in 1788 as though this band of patriots had devised, promoted, and by themselves enacted the Second Amendment.[80] Meanwhile, Bogus ignores the commentary of congressmen during the floor debates in the U.S. House of Representatives relating directly to the pending Amendment itself. During the debates in the House, Elbridge Gerry of Massachusetts was the Amendment's most devoted and long-winded advocate, notwithstanding the many changes he favored to the version reported from committee.[81] Nearly as vocal was Congressman Benson of New York.[82] While six of the twelve members to join the debate in favor of the Second Amendment were Southerners (expansively defined),[83] an equal number of Northerners (restrictively defined) spoke in favor of the Amendment.[84]

More telling, however, is the breakdown of states whose ratifying conventions appended suggested amendments: Georgia recommended none, and South Carolina recommended only mechanical changes to the federal system unrelated to the militia (but very likely related to the security of slavery). The states to recommend an amendment protecting the right to bear arms in the militia were Pennsylvania, New Hampshire, Virginia, and North Carolina.[85] In 1789, these states were widely regarded as the heartland of republicanism and, accordingly, would have been expected—on those grounds—to favor the well-armed militia over a standing army. At the same time, they were not united in their interest in the perpetuation of slavery or the repression of slaves. New Hampshire, with few slaves, and Pennsylvania, with a strong abolitionist sentiment, were in fact more ardent advocates of the Second Amendment than South Carolina, with the strongest interest in enforcing slavery. The only logical conclusion must be that the push for the Second Amendment came more vigorously from the republican coalition than from the proslavery group.

In a larger sense, Bogus is right, of course. Passage of the Second Amendment, combined with the undoubted role of the militia in maintaining social peace, was not irrelevant to the future of slavery. But slave repression was also not an issue that pitted Northern interests against Southern or even Deep Southern ones. At the time of the Constitutional Convention, most delegates, North and South, assumed, perhaps mistakenly, the existence of a broad, moderate nationwide antislavery consensus, at least among the educated classes.[86] To the north of Georgia and South Carolina at least, the enlightened elite generally agreed that slavery was unjust and that it should one day be abolished. What, if anything, to do to bring about its abolition was generally a different—and much harder—question.[87] But among a smaller subset of thinkers with evangelical or philosophical inclinations (again, and more emphatically here, north of South Carolina) it seemed increasingly certain that termination of the trans-Atlantic slave trade was a liberal, enlightened, and Christian short-term objective in its own right, and perhaps a necessary or even sufficient step toward emancipation as well.[88] A canvass of delegates at the Constitutional Convention would have revealed that, as one moved further south, the abstract antislavery commitment waned by degrees, becoming tempered in the major slave-holding regions by a sense that—evil or not—slavery remained necessary for the sake of social stability until African deportation could be effected.[89] Only in the extreme South—in South Carolina and Georgia—was slavery justified openly for the sake of economic utility, for without coerced labor the fertile rice marshes of South Carolina and Georgia would revert to wasteland.[90] But even South Carolinians hesitated to speak openly of slavery's unmitigated virtues in the Revolutionary years. And with fire eating not yet ascendant, Northern antislavery men remained quiescent, sharing with most of their enlightened countrymen in the North, and even the upper South, the belief that slavery, left to its own devices, and the munificent course of progress and unforced policy, would continue quietly along a course toward ultimate extinction.[91]

In these optimistic, forward-thinking revolutionary years, Southerners had little reason to fear the abolitionist zeal of the Northern states. The North was still in the process of effecting gradual emancipation on its own turf, and before 1800, the lower tier of northern states hardly seemed farther down the road to freedom than the upper tier of southern ones.[92] No Northerners articulated a desire to interfere actively with Southern slavery in the constitutional period. No Northern antislavery man of that day would have dreamed of disarming any Southern militia to facilitate slave insurrections. This was simply not the style of late-eighteenth-century antislavery thought. Benjamin Franklin was no John Brown.[93]

The consensus among antislavery leaders in the 1780s and 1790s hardly favored slave rebellion, let alone slave rebellion instigated by Northern intervention in the South.[94] Franklin and the other American Revolutionaries had long been desperate to proclaim that their own rebellion was no rebellion at all, but a legitimate exercise of authority to preserve the British Constitution from perversion.[95] Stirring up an actual social rebellion such as the one unfolding in France was anathema in the eyes of the staid, enlightened, gradualists who first spoke out against slavery during the late eighteenth century. Antislavery was a respectable, not heretical, cause.[96] In the Revolutionary era, antislavery leaders pursued abolition of the slave trade, freedom suits on behalf on individual slaves, state-level gradual emancipation laws, and improvement of the condition of freedpeople.[97] Thus, their programs could take much the same form on either side of the Mason-Dixon Line. In the 1780s and 1790s, the overwhelmingly Quaker—and hence pacifist—American Convention (of state level abolition societies) did not seek to set the plantations aflame with righteous liberty, and its devotees did not pray the Lord to wash away the sins of the nation in a sea of blood.[98] When the Second Amendment was ratified, South Carolinians, ever slavery's sentinels, had no activists to fear among the philosophically inclined antislavery salons of Philadelphia, and they had not yet conjured millennialists like Nat Turner or John Brown out of the American social fabric.[99]

In sum, in 1789—and surely by the fall of 1791 (when news of Haiti was pouring in)—some Southern slave owners may have seen in the promise of the Second Amendment assurance that their local armed militia troops would be free to continue patrols to discourage major slave uprisings and to suppress occasional lawlessness. But any such sentiment was scattered and incidental, and hardly the motivating and actuating force that generated the drafting and adoption of the Second Amendment. Professor Bogus can come up with no historical evidence that Southern champions feared Northern abolitionists would deprive them of arms, leaving them helpless in the face of a slave rebellion. Nor does his thesis pass the plausibility test in the light of what we know of the moderate character and gradualist inclinations of the influential political figures of the day.

The inescapable historical fact that torpedoes Professor Bogus's theory is that the anti-federalist call for limitations on the militia powers granted by Article I, Section 8, of the Constitution came from Northern as well as Southern states. Conversely, his root premise that Southerners from 1787 to 1791 feared Northern-instigated federal intervention to facilitate slave violence in the plantation districts cannot accommodate the Article 4, Section 4, guarantee that the "United States . . . protect each of the [states] . . . on Application of the Legislature, or of the Executive (when the Legislature cannot be convened) against domestic Violence," or the broad support that provision garnered from Northern and Southern delegates alike. And so we return to what seems to us obvious on the face of the historical record: the guarantee of an armed militia was sought and enacted to counterbalance the federal army and to assure states that they would remain securely free of federal military oppression.

While we disagree with Professor Bogus's thesis that the Second Amendment was designed to secure the South against potential abolitionist-inspired disarmament of the militia, we hasten to add that his supposition of a threat by abolitionist-minded Northern politicians to weaken slavery in the South through aggressive use of federal powers is not historically misguided, only chronologically misplaced. Some seventy years after the adoption of the Bill of Rights, commitment to use powers constitutionally vested in the federal government to attack slavery became a mainstay of Republican Party ideology. By the late 1850s the commitment was evident, and it was incorporated in the Platform of 1860.[100] Thus, by the time Lincoln first sought the presidency, at least the radical wing of his party favored using the Commerce Power to restrict or terminate the interstate slave trade and congressional action to bypass Dred Scott, banish slavery from the territories, and declare every federal enclave — including the District of Columbia — free soil. No doubt Sumner and Chase would have favored disarming the militia patrols as well, if that were within the federal power. The Second Amendment, however, assured that such action could not withstand constitutional scrutiny. So, finally, the Amendment did the work Bogus had in mind for it, though it could hardly have been contemplated at the time of its adoption. And, of course, the threat Bogus envisioned materialized only on the eve of the cataclysmic use of federal military force that ended slavery altogether.

WILLIAM VAN ALSTYNE: THE PEOPLE HAVING A RIGHT TO ARMS, THE SECURITY OF A WELL-REGULATED MILITIA AND A FREE STATE ARE ASSURED

Like Professor Levinson, Professor William Van Alstyne of Duke Law School professes confusion at the wording of the Second Amendment.[101] It is, of course, what he considers an ill-matched introductory proviso that makes him stumble. Without it, the provision would make sense in the same natural, "unforced" way as the "right of the people" is understood in the neighboring Fourth Amendment. Also echoing Levinson, Van Alstyne, writing in 1994, bemoans the paucity of Supreme Court exegesis on the Second Amendment. He then calls upon the judicial and scholarly community to commence the development of a jurisprudence of the Second Amendment by considering the possibility that the interpretation favored by the NRA is not wrong after all. Consideration of this possibility brings him to the point that, notwithstanding its regrettable discontinuity, the language of the Second Amendment can be read as simply as that of the Fourth Amendment—or the First— plainly to create a personal right to the possession of firearms.

While not labeling himself a textualist or using the term "plain meaning," Van Alstyne appears to favor that mode of analysis. Thus, he writes (in his characteristic locution): "The stance of those inclined to take the Second Amendment seriously reverts to the place we ourselves thought to be somewhat worthwhile to consult—namely, the express provisions of the Second Amendment."[102] And looking to the language of the main clause, he finds that "[t]he very assumption of the clause, moreover, is that ordinary citizens (rather than merely soldiers, or merely the police) may themselves possess arms, for it is from these ordinary citizens who as citizens have a right to keep and bear arms (as the second clause provides) that such well regulated militia as a state may provide for, is itself to be drawn."[103] Van Alstyne argues that one of the propositions accepted by "those inclined to take the Second Amendment seriously"[104] is that, under it, Congress simply may not restrict the people's right to keep and bear arms even though the restriction is not inconsistent with the maintenance of some kind of militia which is necessary to the security of a free state. We think this is what he says though the meaning of his text is not always plain. What he actually writes is: "Nor is there any basis so to read the Second Amendment as though it said anything like the following: 'Congress may, if it thinks it proper, forbid the people to keep and bear arms if, notwithstanding that these restrictions it may thus enact are inconsistent with the right of the people to keep and bear arms, they are not inconsistent with the right of each state to maintain some kind of militia as it may deem necessary to its security as a free state.'"[105]

We count ourselves among those who take the Amendment seriously, but we dispute that proposition. We contend that the Amendment does not prohibit congressional restriction of the possession of guns that are not part of the armament of a well-regulated militia. No individual right to arms is created that does not serve the community interest in the security offered by an armed militia. Van Alstyne then asserts (on his own authority, it seems) that the guarantee to the people to have arms is "the predicate" for the militia, in that "it looks to an ultimate reliance on the common citizen . . . as an essential source of security of a free state."[106] Thus, despite his initial confession of confusion, he intuits the meaning of the Amendment to be that a free state and well-regulated militia depend on the guarantee of private armament.[107] On this point, we should note, we have no quarrel, though it seems a fair distance from the position of the NRA that Van Alstyne initially commended. The NRA has steadfastly maintained that the constitutional right to arms is independent of any communitarian reliance on the local militia.

Van Alstyne's argument from plain meaning depends ultimately on deference to ratified language on the grounds that this language embodies the voice of the people at the sovereign, constitutional moment. Yet throughout "The Second Amendment and the Personal Right to Arms," Van Alstyne reads the words of the Second Amendment as though they were parcels of late-twentieth-century common parlance instead of late-eighteenth-century terms of legal art. This unwillingness to heed his own injunction to take seriously the words of the Amendment—in their own wrappings, preferring the intuitive plain meaning of language perceived through the lens of modern usage, seriously undermines Van Alstyne's argument.

He begins by asserting that "[t]he reference to a 'well regulated Militia' is in the first as well as the last instance a reference to the ordinary citizenry."[108] But in truth, first or last, the militia was never coextensive with the "ordinary" population, nor even with the special segment of citizens afforded civil or political rights. Nor was it a self-generating or self-defining organization. The militia had always been a creature of provincial or state law, which sprang into being at the command of the legislature.[109] Throughout colonial and early national times, colony and state legislatures determined the size and composition of the militia, defined precisely who was to bear arms in such militia, and prohibited other classes of people not only from serving in the militia, but from owning weapons for military or other purposes.[110] Thus, Van Alstyne's central assumption is contradicted by the historical reality that the late-eighteenth-century militia was nowhere coextensive with "the people," and that its membership was everywhere subject to statutory definition and control. The text of the Amendment itself so provides, using the words "well regulated" to remind us that the "militia" the Framers had in mind is a creature of statute, defined and governed by laws and regulations, rather than an informal collection of armed citizens — "the people."

Despite his insistence that he is only reading the clear language of the text itself, Van Alstyne ignores not only the implications of the modifier, "well-regulated," but the fact that the critical phrase, "right . . . to keep and bear arms" does not have a timeless and universal meaning. Nor do the words mean what a twentieth-century scholar wants them to mean. Rather, in eighteenth-century usage, the terms had clearly recognized meaning quite apart from "own and carry." As Gary Wills has demonstrated with scholarly depth and precision — as well as humor (and as we have noted heretofore) — bearing arms had, from its earliest recorded employment and through the late eighteenth century, an exclusively military connotation. "One does not bear arms against a rabbit," Wills points out. He elaborates:

> By legal and other channels, the Latin "*arma ferre*" entered deeply into the European language of war. Bearing arms is such a synonym for waging war that Shakespeare can call a just war " 'just-borne arms" and a civil war "self-borne arms." Even outside the special phrase "bear arms," much of the noun's use echoes Latin phrases: to be under arms (*sub armis*), the call to arms (*ad arma*), to follow arms (*arma sequi*), to take arms (*arma capere*), to lay down arms (*arma poenere*). "Arms" is a profession that one brother chooses the way another chooses law or the church. An issue undergoes the arbitrament of arms.[111]

Wills might have added the most famous use of all, the opening stanza of Virgil's *Aeneid, arma virumque cano,* wherein the poet sings of arms and a man, recounting an epic tale of wars and a hero.[112] These uses recurred countless times in the literature and legal writing with which the Framers were fully familiar. To the ratifiers, bearing arms unequivocally meant rendering military service. In his perception of meaning from the surface of the text, Van Alstyne accords the words "bearing arms" a connotation entirely different from that which it conveyed to the ratifiers.

When Van Alstyne finally lays aside his own intuitions and inferences and comes at last to a reference to the Framers, he cites James Madison to make the point that the United States was distinct from European nations in its trust in the citizenry to bear arms. Van Alstyne's reference to constitutional history is confined, pretty much, to a single sentence in which he writes: "And the quick resolve to add the Second Amendment, so to confirm that right [the right to keep and bear arms] more expressly, as not subject to infringement by Congress, is not difficult to understand."[113] The sentence itself is not easy to understand. It appears to postulate a preexisting right to bear arms, and attributes to the Amendment nothing more than express—if quick—confirmation.[114]

It would surely come as a surprise to the vehement anti-federalists to learn that their prized Amendment was nothing but a restatement of law already established under the new Constitution. To be sure, there was a firmly rooted, preexisting Whig tradition that a militia was the natural defense of a free people, and that the right to bear arms in the militia should not be infringed by just government. But the sweeping powers expressly delegated to the federal government under the written Constitution—powers including the authority to raise and maintain armies, organize, arm, and "call forth" the militia—threatened to overwhelm any unwritten traditions of the common law or the "ancient constitution."

Van Alstyne also joins an array of others who argue that the Second Amendment was designed to ensure personal access to weapons for all purposes by citing Blackstone, the great eighteenth century commentator on the laws of England. As we noted in chapter 2, those who seek the support of Blackstone typically misread his views on the point. But quite apart from the ignored feature of Blackstone's thesis—that the citizens' right to arms served the limited purpose of checking monarchical usurpation in moments of ultimate constitutional crisis—it should be emphasized that Blackstone is hardly considered the last word on the meaning of the American Constitution. In spite of the prominent place his Commentaries occupied in the libraries of self-trained, provincial practitioners in the early years of the nineteenth century, many of the socially elite whiggish lawyers who figured so prominently among the Framers viewed Blackstone as a Tory apostate rather than a revered authority on the deeper principles of constitutionalism. Shortly before his death in 1826, Thomas Jefferson lamented that young lawyers were embracing "the honeyed Mansfieldianism of Blackstone" and forsaking the Whiggish principles of the Revolution of 1776.[115] Jefferson's views on Blackstone were unusual by 1826, but his negative assessment of Blackstone would have seemed commonplace a generation before.

However far "the law" of the newly independent republic embodied the common law of its former motherland (a matter of some dispute), the Bill of Rights is not understood to have enshrined Blackstone's understanding of British law and custom. Rather, the great document of the new government constitutionalized exactly those rights that it expressly articulates. Thus, Blackstone remains a useful and constructive advisor insofar as he elucidates terms of art appearing in the Bill of Rights, but when looking to Blackstone for guidance as to meaning, we should take care not to graft his assertions of legal principle onto the ratified Bill of Rights, or to look to his Commentaries for the meaning of the textually articulated precepts of the written document.

Rather than rely upon historical context or examine linguistics, Van Alstyne is fond of reasoning by analogy and favors in particular the comparison with the First Amendment. Thus, he says that the proper interpretation of the Second Amendment, as it is of the First, is that while a person may be held accountable for an abuse of the entitlement granted, those who use it responsibly must be left alone.[116] Van Alstyne repeats the point in his concluding section where he concedes that "restrictions generally consistent merely with safe usage . . . are not all per se precluded."[117] Again associating the Second Amendment with the First, he says there is "a rule of reason" which may limit, for example, the type of arms one is permitted to keep or the location in which one is permitted to carry them. We regard the analogy as dubious because of the unique first clause of the Second Amendment specifying its scope and purpose. But apart from the significance of that dissimilarity, we cannot help but wonder how far the implicit qualifications conceded by Van Alstyne undermine the asserted free access to arms. Those who "abuse" their entitlement may be punished, he says. So, too, restrictions on gun possession are tolerable so long as they are dictated by a "rule of reason." Notwithstanding analogies in the First Amendment area (where limitations of time and place, for example, may be employed to curtail public speech), these are very uncertain demarcations, inviting litigation over every restriction and regulation of private gun use. And, owing to their elasticity, Van Alstyne's allowances may yield a regime of handgun control not much to the liking of the NRA.

In the final rinse, Professor Van Alstyne's reliance on common sense and plain meaning is stunning. Recovering fully from any stumble on the first reading of the Amendment, he announces that the provision is neither mysterious, equivocal, nor opaque.[118] It is only unwelcome to those who would limit arms to the police: "It is for them to seek a repeal of this amendment (and so the repeal of its guarantee) in order to have their way. Or so the Constitution itself assuredly appears to require, if that is the way things are to be."[119] Reliance on assured appearances may satisfy those who believe all should be free of any government control of arms, but it hardly satisfies the requirements of rhetorical sufficiency for those not already convinced.

Moving to the applicability of the Second Amendment to the states following the Civil War, Professor Van Alstyne contents himself with (mis)quoting Senator Howard of Michigan delivering the report of the Senate Committee on Reconstruction, who informed the body that the Privileges and Immunities Clause of the Fourteenth Amendment restrains the states from interfering with the "right to keep and bear arms," along with the other rights protected by the first eight Amendments. Not only the remarks of Senator Howard, but also the comments of John A. Bingham, who led the fight for adoption of the Fourteenth Amendment in the House, support the idea that at least some members of the Congress intended to bind the states to the first eight Amendments wholesale by the guarantee of federal "privileges and immunities."[120] Indeed, there is reason to believe that a minority of members thought it necessary to put beyond state infringement the personal right to possession of firearms, even divorced from its original service to the organized militia, in order to vouchsafe to the emancipated slaves the means to protect themselves against the Ku Klux Klan and other Reconstruction thugs.[121]

Notwithstanding these sentiments, the case for incorporating into the Fourteenth Amendment a right to keep arms for private purposes is not so straightforward as Professor Van Alstyne supposes. Let us assume that radical Republicans, including the House manager Bingham and Senate manager Howard, intended the Fourteenth Amendment's privileges and immunities clause to incorporate the Bill of Rights, and that some radical Republicans even intended this incorporation to extend the Second Amendment right to include a personal right to arms unlike anything envisioned by its Framers in 1789. This assumption does not prove Professor Van Alstyne's case; it only illustrates the old problem with interpretation by "legislative intent." Regardless of the intentions — even the clearly expressed intentions —

of individual Framers, it is the text as ratified that counts, and the text of the Fourteenth Amendment (of course) does not reflect any such purpose. Even if the text might be considered cloudy on the point, the expressed understanding of some Framers is only one of several factors that must be consulted for clarification. Most obvious among the competing considerations in this instance is the fact that passage of the Fourteenth Amendment required support not just from radical Republicans, but from at least some moderate Republicans, conservative Republicans, and moderate Democrats. And it is quite apparent from the debates of the Thirty-ninth Congress, and from newspaper accounts from across the nation, that moderates and conservatives did not intend the Privileges and Immunities Clause of the Fourteenth Amendment to incorporate the whole of the Bill of Rights.[122]

Instead, moderates and conservatives agreed to join radicals in reaching a compromise on less sweeping and more ambiguous language. Thus, the Fourteenth Amendment does not proclaim, "The Bill of Rights, including a personal right to arms for private purposes such as self-defense, shall apply against the states." The support for ratification required by Article V—adoption by two-thirds of both Houses of Congress and by three-fourths of the states—could not have been mustered for such language and for such dramatic alteration of the federal balance. Rather, the Fourteenth Amendment as ratified says, "No state shall make or enforce any law which shall abridge the privileges and immunities of citizens of the United States; nor shall any state deprive any person of life, liberty, or property, without due process of law; nor deny to any person within its jurisdiction the equal protection of the laws."

In addition to consideration of the composition of the voting majority, ambiguities in enacted provisions may be resolved by judicial construction—a resource that appears to interest Van Alstyne far less than it interests us. When the Supreme Court got around to the piecemeal incorporation of all but four of the provisions in the first eight amendments into the Fourteenth, and by means of that device bound state governments to their observance, it was not the attractive language of privileges and immunities, or even the equal protection clause, but rather due process that was selected as the vehicle. In the several decisions over the years in which the Supreme Court considered the constitutional entitlements one by one, they did not ask whether the particular provision of the Bill of Rights established a "privilege" or "immunity" of United States citizenship. Nor did they inquire whether equal protection of the laws required that citizens of the states receive the same protection against state encroachments as citizens of the United States enjoyed against the federal government.

Rather, the Court choose to examine whether a given provision of the Bill of Rights established so fundamental an attribute of citizenship that its denial by a state government would amount to a denial of due process of law. This choice puts deeper into the dubious category Van Alstyne's reliance on the preferences of the senator from Michigan as the authoritative guide to the applicability of the Second Amendment to the states. Even a devoted originalist, not to say textualist, would scruple to rely on the expressed purpose of a senator or two that has been repeatedly rejected by an unbroken line of Supreme Court cases to the contrary. Although he may think that the Court erroneously selected the Due Process Clause of the Fourteenth Amendment as the rubric for application of federal injunctions to state governments, surely *stare decisis,* the doctrine that decided cases control recurring issues, counts for something even with Van Alstyne.

We should acknowledge here that Professor Van Alstyne's suggestion that the Second Amendment's guarantee of personal access to weaponry became secure against infringement by the states following the Civil War has been supported by others. Some scholars—notably Professor Akhil Amar, whom we discuss at greater length in the following section—hold that the Second Amendment was wholly rewritten by the Fourteenth, that the right to arms was transformed, *sub silentio,* by the urgent concerns of the Reconstruction agenda. In this view, the social circumstances of 1789 that dictated assurance that the states could continue to muster their militias, bearing the arms of individual members, was replaced by the political imperative that recently emancipated slaves and their supporters be assured that their state governments would not attempt to disarm them, leaving them helpless before their armed and aggressive tormenters. As reborn, these commentators would assert, the introductory clause of the eighteenth-century provision has simply withered away, giving the rights clause unconditional sway. Attractive as the notion may be to those who favor a flexible Constitution, we are not persuaded. In our conservative view, amendment of the Constitution is not accomplished *sub silentio,* nor does the wish — or even express intention — of some contemporaries implicitly rewrite a standing text.

It might also be argued that the Second Amendment was not rewritten, but simply applied — its militia clause intact — against state governments. This argument would run thus: by disarming its citizens (or to be more realistic, its formerly enslaved citizens) a state might prevent them from serving in its militia (assuming the militiamen were required to furnish their own arms). And by denying African Americans membership in the militia, that body might more easily be put to their suppression. By this reasoning, the states were commanded by the Fourteenth Amendment not to pervert the universalist character of the local militia by selective disarmament of its people. Put thus, the application to the states of the Second Amendment harmonizes with the general program of promoting equality of the newly liberated Americans while assuring their physical safety.

While this approach has the commendable virtue that it does not suppose a tacit rewrite of the Second Amendment, it still suffers major impediments to acceptance. First, of course, there is still no reason to think that the majority of ratifiers of the Fourteenth Amendment deemed the right to bear arms in a militia a privilege or immunity of United States citizenship. Indeed, Professor Raoul Berger reminds us that the derivation of the phrase "privileges and immunities" strongly suggests that it referred only to rights of trade and commerce.[123] Nor can we ignore the unbroken line of authority in all courts that have considered the question to the effect that the Second Amendment entitlement was not applicable to the states through the Due Process Clause of the Fourteenth Amendment. Probably the final refutation of the theory, which neither Van Alstyne nor its other proponents recognize, is its historical improbability.

If the Framers were concerned about the exclusion of former slaves from the militias of the Southern states, the best and most likely way they would have selected to provide assurances was the enlargement of Amendment XV to include an express guarantee of an inclusive militia. The Fifteenth Amendment, adopted two years after the Fourteenth, expressed the *political* right of suffrage, a recognized extension of the *civil* rights guaranteed by the Fourteenth. The right/obligation of qualified citizens to serve in the common militia is a political right closely analogous to the right/obligation to vote. It would have been a simple and natural response to the postwar efforts of some Southern states to purge their police and militia units of liberated slaves to add to the 1870 amendment a clause expressly guaranteeing that, in addition to the right to vote, the right to serve in the local militia shall not be abridged by any state "on account of race, color, or previous condition of servitude." No such language was enacted—or even proposed.

To sum it up, we do not believe that the Reconstruction Amendments made the Second Amendment—truncated or as written—applicable against state governments for four reasons: first, there was no indication that the phrase "privileges or immunities of citizens of the United States"—or any other clause of the Fourteenth Amendment—was generally thought to include the right to bear arms; second, no court has since read the Fourteenth Amendment as binding the states to the Second Amendment; and third, regardless of the urgent need to assure emancipated African Americans that they would not be deprived by the states of the weapons of self-protection, the Second Amendment, as adopted by the Founders cannot be surgically reconstituted as a purely personal right, the "militia" as referred to therein cannot be redefined as bands of private citizens. Finally, the notion that the original Second Amendment was or should be applied against the state governments because of its salubrious effect on selective disarmament by former confederate states is pure fantasy. It is indeed quite possible that the failure of Reconstruction was due in large measure to the failure to maintain racially integrated police and militia forces in the Southern states. If so, it was because Congress failed to include the political right—or civic obligation—of militia service in the Fifteenth Amendment, not because of any erroneous understanding of the nature of the civil rights embraced by the Fourteenth.

Nor do we find compelling Professor Van Alstyne's argument by analogy to the First Amendment. As we see it, the fundamental weakness in the link he seeks to construct between the First and Second Amendments is simply that the two provisions are designed to protect against altogether different evils, one of which is readily applicable as a restraint against state government while the other is not. The First announces a prohibition against government interference with peoples' rights of expression, worship, assembly, and protest. It is obviously a prohibition that can (and should) be readily applied against all government, national or local. In contrast, the Second is not about private liberties, but the federal balance of powers, and the inability of the central government to disarm the citizen militia. If the right of the people to keep and bear arms were, as Van Alstyne would have it, like the right of free expression or worship, one could argue that neither state nor federal government should be allowed to curtail it. But, as we have sought to demonstrate throughout, that is not a fair way to describe the import of the Second Amendment. Neither the ratifying generation nor courts that have subsequently touched upon the issue have seen it thus. Hence the analogy fails.

So the Van Alstyne paper concludes, with little more analysis or authority than what appears to the author self-evident, that the "essential claim" of the NRA is "extremely strong."[124] Not to disparage Professor Van Alstyne's educated intuition, nor the importance of plain meaning in the interpretation of texts, we must protest that in this instance, there is more to it than that. As we have attempted to show, agitation for, debate about, and ultimately the adoption of the constitutional provision on arms and the militia were embedded in historically significant events and attitudes. These conditions of enactment not only inform the reading of the text as written, but are essential to understanding the meaning of the document as transmitted through the centuries to us today.

AKHIL REED AMAR AND DAVID YASSKY:
TRANSFORMATION BY INCORPORATION

We turn, then, to the prolific and controversial Professor Akhil Reed Amar of the Yale Law School. He offers a provocative thesis that, if true, would pull the rug out from under our firm stance that the Second Amendment is a unitary provision that must be read as a whole. The idea is based on the Ackermanian notion that the Constitution of 1789–1791 was rewritten by the Reconstruction Amendments.[125] The notion was hinted at earlier in a footnote by Professor Van Alstyne and previously articulated by others, including the team of Cottrol and Diamond and the energetic gun rights advocate Stephen P. Halbrook.[126] Amar is of much the same mind as we are concerning the meaning of the Second Amendment in 1791, and the close conjunction of the right to arms and the importance of the militia. But, he says the lowercase-r republicans of 1789–1791 had a very different vision from that of the capital-R Republicans of 1866–1868. Three years after the War of Secession, the great concern was not collective security nor the prospect of a professional standing army. Rather, the architects of the new, postwar society viewed with dismay the brutal attacks on newly freed slaves in the South, and responded to their vital interests in having at hand the means of self-protection. State efforts to deprive vulnerable new citizens of personal arms required constitutional attention.

Amar collects historical material supporting his view that the Fourteenth Amendment not only applied the Second Amendment to the states, but, in the process, rewrote it in a material respect. The right to arms was subtly disengaged from the military implications of the word "bear," and uncoupled altogether from the now-obsolete militia preamble. It was, Amar contends, the clear and express purpose of those who redesigned the United States government by the Reconstruction Amendments to assure the newly free citizens the protection of personal firearms against the thugs who threatened their personal security. "Once we remember," he writes, "that, strictly speaking, 1860s Republicans sought not to incorporate clauses but to apply (refined) rights against states, it seems rather natural textually that Reconstructors . . . invoked the operative rights clause of the Second Amendment while utterly ignoring its preambulatory ode to the militia." [127]

It is an appealing argument. There is good reason to believe that many Americans, including a number in Congress, were in fact justly concerned with the growth of the Ku Klux Klan and the prevalent violence against recently liberated Americans, together with the complicity of governments that recently fought to preserve the slave system. Truly, security of person and family had replaced communal concerns with local military sovereignty and the importance of an amateur army. And perhaps a number (whom Amar quotes) did in fact "invoke" the rights clause of the Second Amendment alone. But invocation is not enactment.

Professor Amar, vivid in his description of the new vision of the importance of guns to security, is somewhat less clear on how this new vision found its way into the Constitution, how it reconfigured the old Second Amendment while applying it to the states. He deftly highlights the several ways in which the original Second Amendment with its republican aura spoke of *political* rights, the rights of "the people" like voting and serving on juries, whereas those he likes to call the Reconstructors had *civil* rights in mind, rights that belonged to women and children and protected individual persons against the state, rights more liberal than republican in flavor. Thus, the Reconstructors, in a nineteenth-century frame of mind, intended to grant to all citizens as individuals the civil right to armed self-protection. This dichotomy sets up a certain tension between the generally collective Bill of Rights (as Amar sees them), together with the republican Second Amendment, on the one hand and, on the other, the liberal Fourteenth Amendment.

Undaunted by the admittedly poor fit of the eighteenth-century devices into the mid-nineteenth-century mentality, Professor Amar offers what he calls a new model of incorporation: "refined incorporation." The refinement he proposes is intended to make the privileges and immunities clause of the Fourteenth Amendment work. For despite the universal concordance of the courts to the contrary, Amar insists that it is the privileges and immunities clause that carries the provisions of the Bill of Rights to the states. Calling John Bingham, the author of the first clause of the Fourteenth Amendment, as his star witness,[128] Amar argues that the intent of Congress in proposing the great Reconstruction Amendment was to bind the states to honor the privileges and immunities of United States citizenship as expressed in the Bill of Rights and elsewhere. This wholesale approach, Amar recognizes, has its problems; not all national entitlements are appropriately invoked against the state. Asking then which privileges and immunities of American citizenship must be respected by the states, Amar comes up with the solution: those which express personal right—as contrasted with state or public rights—become obligatory on the states. Amar's reasoning then appears to run like this: transformed by the concerns of many political figures of the late 1860s, the principle of access to arms originally embodied in the republican Second Amendment became a personal, civil right of individual citizens, and as such, was binding on the states by virtue of the privileges and immunities clause of the Fourteenth Amendment, according to the doctrine of refined incorporation.

Undeniably, the argument has a certain ring to it. We would like it to be so—to believe that in the wake of the great war, the victorious Northerners were so concerned with southern violence against the new black citizens that they wrote the right to personal firearms into the new Constitution. The National Rifle Association would like it to be so today, long after lynch mobs faded into history. Their supporters may be heard to argue that today crime has replaced racial violence, and the need for constitutionally assured private firepower to repel it remains as strong as ever. Since the opening of Ackerman's third constitutional era, the New Deal, did nothing to undo the work of the Reconstruction Amendments, the self-defensive character of the refined Second Amendment presumably persists into modern times. His thesis has installed Akhil Amar, along with Levinson and Van Alstyne, in the pantheon of heroes not only of the NRA but of Attorney General John Ashcroft (who cites all three in his letter endorsing the personal rights interpretation of the Second Amendment) and all others of like persuasion.

Whatever its appeal might be, Professor Amar's thesis suffers from a fatal flaw. It confuses what should have been done with what was done. It's a little like poor old Ronald Reagan who, according to one account, so deeply believed that we should have an impenetrable missile shield in place that he convinced Gorbachev that we did have it in place—and thereby hastened the end of the cold war. Amar follows those in the Reconstruction era who assumed that their concerns with personal access to arms were expressed in the Privileges and Immunities Clause of the Fourteenth Amendment. But the sort of privilege (or right, as we would more likely term it today) expressed by the Second Amendment as an entitlement of the citizens of the United States was not precisely the right Amar's reconstructionists wished to grant the citizens of the states. It was not the privilege of United States citizens to bear arms in an organized militia that the citizens of the several states required in 1866. So it is not a simple transfer by means of the Privileges and Immunities Clause that satisfies Amar's postulate.

The eminent legal historian, Professor Raoul Berger, has termed Amar's transformation of eighteenth-century rights by the process of absorption into the Fourteenth Amendment as "a wondrous feat indeed."[129] He criticizes Amar for his analogy to the notable adaptability of the common law; the Constitution is not as readily reconstructed as legal precedent.[130] The Article V amendment process remains the only way to "remould" or "reshape" the Constitution, Berger asserts. Amar, he notes, "leaps like a mountain goat over such obstacles." Berger assembles evidence that even among northern Republicans, there was serious concern that the Reconstruction Amendment might cut too deeply into state sovereignty. He quotes Judge Richard Posner to the effect: "[A]pply the Bill of Rights to the States through the due process clause and you weaken the states tremendously by handing over control of large areas of public policy to federal judges . . . It is hard to believe that this was intended by all the state legislators whose votes were necessary to ratify the [fourteenth] amendment."

In addition, Amar's faith in the privileges and immunities clause as his vehicle for incorporation runs up against some severe historical and judicial impediments. As Professor Berger points out, the first use of the term—in the Articles of Confederation—made it pretty plain that the privileges referred to were privileges of trade and commerce. The phrase made its way into Section 2 of Article IV of the body of the Constitution where, judicial decisions assure us, it reflected the same meaning: rights associated with trade and commerce. The phrase entered the Fourteenth Amendment by way of the Civil Rights Act of 1866 where some read it to include the rights to sue and be sued, to acquire real property, and to travel. There is little support in contemporary records for so expansive a reading as Amar would give it in his "refined incorporation."

So the major problem with Professor Amar's attractive thesis is that, however much they might have wanted to, however loud the imperative, however we might wish they had done so, the framers and ratifiers of the Fourteenth Amendment simply did not include the required gun provision in the text. Section 1 (the only one having any bearing on the question) provides:

> All persons born or naturalized in the United States, and subject to the jurisdiction thereof, are citizens of the United States and of the state wherein they reside. No State shall make or enforce any law which shall abridge the privileges or immunities of citizens of the United States; nor shall any State deprive any person of life, liberty, or property, without due process of law; nor deny to any person within its jurisdiction the equal protection of the laws.

It's really hard to find in those words any suggestion that personal access to arms for self-protection is assured against state encroachment.[131] Had the amendment been intended as a civil rather than political right, it would have been easy to add at the end: "or the means to protect himself (which in the nineteenth century implied herself as well) against unlawful violence."

It is one thing to expand the reach of several of the original amendments so that the state may make no laws abridging speech, the state may not invade secure spaces without warrant, etc. It is quite another to remake the right in the process of binding the state to its provisions. And all without a word of text indicating what was going on. One needn't be an ardent textualist to look askance at *sub silentio* amendment of constitutional text. To more fully appreciate the anomaly of such implicit amendment, consider the incorporation and application to state proceedings of the right against compelled self-incrimination of the Fifth Amendment.[132] It reads, "No person . . . shall be compelled in any criminal case to be a witness against himself . . ." At the time of incorporation, 1964 (and at all times before and since), the word "witness" meant only the source of evidence induced by coercion from the mind of the suspect. The Fifth Amendment, in federal courts, meant no coercive interrogation. Would Amar—or anyone—argue that, because of some abuse that troubled us in the 1960s, as applied to the states, the word "witness" in the constitutional clause included the sources of evidence from written records? Would they claim that the same words in the same provision could be expanded to mean something altogether different when read in a state setting? The scope of the constitutional protection could be rewritten, of course; the Fifth Amendment is itself subject to amendment. But the new form of the old amendment would have to be set forth in words, debated, and then ratified according to the very specific provisions of Article V of the Constitution itself. Although Professor Amar is well known for proposing a radical alternative to this process,[133] we assume that even he would not approve the implicit detachment and burial of half the provision, along with the express limitation it conveys, leaving the newly expansive entitlement to serve the needs of the contemporary community. And we hope that he would agree that, however compelling those social needs might have been, no matter how many people spoke in recognition of the grim reality, the Constitution and its amendments do not spontaneously morph into a suitable instrument for dealing with the problem. To some, perhaps, Amar presents a compelling argument that the Reconstruction Amendment should have rewritten the Second Amendment to fit the needs of the time. But he fails to offer convincing evidence that it did.

It probably should be added, by way of postscript (and explanation of Judge Posner's choice of operative clause that may have slipped by a few paragraphs back), that when incorporation proceeded, piecemeal and selectively, through the courts, the Privileges and Immunities Clause was shunned by the courts as the vehicle in favor of the Due Process Clause. Amar pays no heed to the judicial contribution to the question of the binding effect on states of the Second Amendment when viewed through the medium of the Fourteenth Amendment. It is difficult to imagine an argument fashioned on the "refined incorporation" model that would fit the prevailing judicial theory of incorporation through the Due Process Clause. As Justice Cardozo, speaking for the Supreme Court, made clear at the start,[134] and as the Court has reiterated ever since, the due process test of incorporation is neither original intention nor the personal quality of the right in question. Rather, those of the specific provisions of the Bill of Rights that are deemed "implicit in the concept of ordered liberty" bind the states. The right to bear arms in the militia, critical as it might have been to the framing generation, can hardly be deemed fundamental to the functioning of our democracy for all time. It is, therefore, not surprising that during the mid-twentieth century — the years of piecemeal, selective incorporation — courts have not found the Second Amendment embedded in due process as implicit to the concept of ordered liberty.

We realize that it may not be a wholly satisfying answer to a scholar who chooses to deviate from a deeply etched, seventy-five-year-old[135] path of doctrine to remind him that such titans as Brandeis, Harlan Fiske Stone, and the second John Marshall Harlan — without complaint — trod the route Cardozo had blazed for them, nor to assert that application of the concept of due process has, over the years, yielded a fairly just and inclusive selection of the Bill of Rights to be respected by the states. We cannot discredit his effort by pointing out that, as far as we can see, the only purpose of revisiting the line of authority holding that the Second Amendment (whatever it may mean today) does not apply to the states is to outlaw state gun control measures (at least insofar as they transgress Van Alstyne's rule of reason). What Amar is after, he will protest, is a more perfect understanding. Reverting to the vehicle of privileges and immunities and inventing a standard of "refined incorporation" that would allow the right to guns to be included among the constitutional rights to be asserted against states are the true path to understanding, he might say.

The thesis invites refutation on its own terms. But, other than the arguments from history, from text, and from practice and common acceptance, it is very hard to contradict someone who says: ideally, this is the true way. Nor does it advance the argument to point out that since few Framers or ratifiers — or anyone else for that matter — regarded the right to carry arms in a local militia as a privilege or immunity of national citizenship, Amar might just as profitably try to fit the right to guns into the fundamental freedoms guaranteed by due process. The essential ingredient of the effective refutation is still missing: support for our confident belief that the "wondrous feat" of transforming a constitutional text to excise a vital component in the process of applying it to a state government simply cannot be performed in an world of good legal order. Ultimately, the question of whether Professor Amar has detected the hidden trail to true understanding of the Second Amendment in the state forum may depend upon one's credo concerning the uses to which authoritative text may be put.

Another who regards the Fourteenth Amendment as critical to understanding the Second is Professor David Yassky of Brooklyn Law School, a formidable young scholar and recent entrant in the Second Amendment forum.[136] While Yassky praises Amar's book as a "tour de force," advancing a "thorough and powerful argument," he takes issue with Amar's theory of "refined incorporation," and advances a sharply different view of the effect of the Reconstruction Amendments on Amendment II. In essence, Yassky sees the Fourteenth Amendment as constitutionalizing federal conscription, thereby rejecting the Founders' fundamental faith in a decentralized amateur army. Madison had proposed the draft of soldiers for the War of 1812, Lincoln had gotten a draft law for the Civil War. Yassky believes both were unconstitutional as altering the fundamental balance worked out by the Constitution to keep the strength of the professional army low. But just as the Thirteenth Amendment constitutionalized the Emancipation Proclamation, the Fourteenth constitutionalized a large, conscripted federal army at the expense of state-controlled militia. Yassky puts it this way: "After the military defeat of States' Rights proponents at the hands of Unionists, the Founders' notion of militia as protection against national despotism was no longer tenable. From the perspective of the Unionists who wrote the Fourteenth Amendment, the Southern states' militia were an instrument of, not a remedy for, tyranny. To the Founding Federalists, the states' militia had symbolized freedom; to the Reconstruction Republicans, the states' militia symbolized slavery and rebellion." From this fundamental repudiation of the ideal of the militia as our primary military instrument, Yassky draws the conclusion that the Second Amendment itself is crippled and, though not totally disabled, in search of a new identity.

There is much in Professor Yassky's treatment that we applaud. There is much that echoes our own understanding. But we cannot buy his construction of the Fourteenth Amendment. As he is frank to acknowledge, it is a bold stab of imagination. There is nothing in the historical record to suggest that the Framers or ratifiers intended that the new amendment validate military conscription. Indeed, had they intended anything like Yassky supposes, one could hardly imagine a more uncomfortable home for that purpose than the language of the amendment as written. The words themselves enjoin the states to respect the rights of national citizenship and observe the commands of fair treatment and nondiscrimination. No more. To read into this provision anything regarding involuntary military service, or the replacement of reliance on the eighteenth-century militia with faith in the large standing army requires acuity of vision that, alas, we lack. Which is not to say that we are far from Professor Yassky's view that, by the late 1860s the meaning of the Second Amendment had fundamentally changed. We simply do not base that conclusion on any invisible, subliminal constitutional revision of the old amendment. Rather, we respect the slow and gradual erosion of the institution of the militia until, by the end of the War of Secession, the militia—in anything approaching the eighteenth-century meaning of the term— had virtually disappeared from the apparatus of government. Further, as we follow the evolution of military forces to the present time, we find no trace of that once noble conception and, as Yassky does, we conclude that the right to arms that was founded upon it has lost its significance. With or without a draft, the regular army is our trusted military fist today, but the right to arms under private control has nothing whatever to do with such security as it provides.

9

The Emerson Case

As these words are being written, a curious little case is ticking its way slowly through the courts. It may be that, ultimately, this case does not turn out to be the vehicle for a modern, definitive, authoritative interpretation of the meaning of the Second Amendment, but at the moment all eyes of the ardent coterie of Second Amendment watchers are trained upon it. In the Fifth Circuit Court of Appeals, where it is currently in residence, it garnered no fewer than twenty briefs from interested nonparties.[1] As the maverick that it is, as the bait it offers for the Supreme Court to chew on, this little case probably warrants a few paragraphs of description here.

It all began in the late summer of 1998 in Tom Green County, Texas, when Sacha Emerson filed a petition for divorce from her husband, Dr. Timothy Joe Emerson. During a hearing on a routine order restraining financial transactions during the pendency of the divorce action, Mrs. Emerson informed the judge that her husband had threatened to kill her lover. The judge then issued an order that, among other things, restrained Dr. Emerson from subjecting his wife to threats to injure her, their young child, or any other person. Two months later, at Dr. Emerson's office where his wife had gone with her daughter to pick up a payment, the Emersons got into a quarrel. Dr. Emerson pulled a Baretta pistol from his desk drawer and pointed it at his wife and their child demanding that she leave at once. Two weeks later, police responding to an ill-founded complaint by Dr. Emerson had a little conversation with him. He told them that he had an AK-47 as well as a 9mm handgun in his office. He said something about shooting his wife and her new boyfriend, and stated that if any of his wife's friends set foot on his property, they would "be found dead in the parking lot . . ."[2] This apparently aroused the interest of the visiting officers and, eight days later, a federal grand jury indicted Timothy Joe Emerson for the unlawful possession of the Baretta pistol that he had brandished before his wife and child.

The Government's theory was that Emerson illegally possessed the weapon under a federal law (Section 922[g][8] of Title 18 of the United States Code] that provides that it is unlawful for a person to possess a firearm if that person is subject to a court order that restrains him or her from threatening or intimidating an "intimate partner." The Baretta in question had been purchased a little less than a year before the divorce action was filed, so there was no outstanding order of restraint at that time. But in connection with the purchase, Emerson signed a form notifying him of the provisions of section 922(g)(8). Thus, the Government contended, he was on notice that when he became subject to the restraining order, his possession of the Baretta automatically became unlawful. The fairness of this springing criminality is a secondary issue in the case.

Principally, Judge Cummings of the federal court of first impression, the United States District Court for the Northern District of Texas, evaluated the statute, 18 U.S.C. 922(g)(8), under the Second Amendment to the Constitution. Correctly observing at the outset that the petitioner's motion to dismiss the indictment on this basis can succeed "only if the Second Amendment guarantees Emerson a personal right to bear arms," the judge noted that the government stoutly argued that "it is 'well settled' that the Second Amendment creates a right held by the states and does not protect an individual right to bear arms." We don't know what the prosecutor argued orally, but the government's brief does not make the foolish claim that the Second Amendment right is held by states. In its brief, the government clearly contends that the right is granted to the people, but is closely linked to the Militia Clause. They correctly cite *United States v. Miller* for that proposition, and note that all the federal Circuits that have passed upon the issue have agreed on the importance of the Militia Clause.

Recognizing the competing schools of thought on the Second Amendment, Judge Cummings finds that "textual analysis" supports the individual rights interpretation. The word "people" in the main clause, he believes, demonstrates that "the right exists independent of the existence of the militia." Moreover, "people" means people, not states, the same people as take protection from the First, Fourth, Fifth, and Ninth Amendments. Moving on to a rather long section of "historical analysis," Judge Cummings offers a summary of events and quotations spanning the period from the middle of the first millennium through the adoption of the American Constitution. For this recitation, Judge Cummings relies almost entirely on the authority of Joyce Lee Malcolm (twenty-two citations in thirteen columns of text) with occasional references to Stephen Halbrook, Don B. Kates, and Sanford Levinson. With the latter's help, Judge Cummings also disposes neatly of any contention that the Second Amendment was intended to assure the right of states to maintain a militia; the Bill of Rights (with the exception of the Tenth Amendment) was not designed as a catalogue of states' rights.

Coming to the matter of prior constructions by other courts, Judge Cummings acknowledges that other circuits have concluded that the Second Amendment confers no absolute right to arms on individuals. However, he reads the most recent decision in the United States Supreme Court, *United States v. Miller,* as ambiguous on the individual-collective rights issue. Moreover, he refers to a recent concurrence by Justice Clarence Thomas in which, with the help of Joyce Lee Malcolm, Stephen Halbrook, William Van Alstyne, Akhil Amar, Sanford Levinson, Don Kates, among others, he opines that there is "a colorable argument" that the federal government's entire regulatory scheme regarding the possession of firearms "runs afoul" of the Second Amendment.[3]

The District Court goes on to find the statute under which Dr. Emerson was charged, 18 U.S.C. 922(g)(8), unconstitutional because "it is absurd that a boilerplate state court divorce order can collaterally and automatically extinguish a law-abiding citizen's Second Amendment rights . . ." Since Emerson had a "liberty interest" in gun possession "imbedded in the Second Amendment," it was a violation of due process under the Fifth Amendment to convict him of it when he had no reason to believe that that order rendered his continued possession felonious.

What do we make of the Emerson decision at the District Court level? We should probably begin by saying that we are not unsympathetic to the court's view that the statute in question, as applied to Dr. Emerson, was unconstitutional as a violation of due process under the Fifth Amendment. For an act—the purchase and possession of a handgun—lawful in its inception under Texas law to be silently and automatically converted into a federal crime by the seemingly unrelated event of the issuance of a routine order of restraint does seem like a violation of ordinary principles of legality. There was little or less in the document that Emerson signed at purchase or in the advice issued along with the court's order to alert him to the fact that he was obliged instantly on the issuance of the order to surrender all firearms on pain of criminal sanction. Of course, that is not to say Emerson was entitled to pull the gun and menace his wife and child. And the mystery of the case is why he was not simply prosecuted for that unlawful display of the weapon, and why he was not hauled into court and charged with contempt for his violation of the no-threat provisions of the court's order. Such response would implicate no constitutional concerns.

The Court of Appeals for the Fifth Circuit—and the Supreme Court, if it comes to that—could dispose of this appeal on the due process claim alone if they are of the same mind as we are and inclined to strike down the statute as applied in the circumstances of Emerson's case. That would leave Judge Cummings' idiosyncratic view of the Second Amendment out there as a judicial sport, a peculiar construction of no particular jurisprudential significance. However much it might warm the hearts of the small band of like-minded authorities on whom the judge chose to rely, the opinion of this single district court judge has virtually no impact beyond his own corner of Texas, and indeed not much outside of Judge Cummings' own courtroom.

Despite what we regard as good, solid reasoning behind a disposition on fairness grounds, it would be disappointing. Second Amendment scholars, we suspect, would be happier if this due process/Fifth Amendment argument would just go away and leave us with the unencumbered Second Amendment issue, ripe for decision on a high level. Why, oh why, were the players not far-sighted enough to set up the case at the beginning? It could have been easily done by informing Dr. Emerson at the time the restraining order was issued that he was required by federal law to surrender any weapons in his possession and have him refuse on Second Amendment grounds to do so. Ah, well. . . .

In the interest of full disclosure, we must note that there is another ground on which the Emerson case might be ultimately resolved which would also leave us utterly in the dark concerning the true shape of the Second Amendment. This attractive route to decision involves the Commerce Clause of the Constitution. Among its powers enumerated in Section 8 of Article I of the Constitution, Congress has authority to regulate (or penalize) activity the only federal impact of which is its direct bearing on "commerce" among the states. Indeed, it was pursuant to this power that Congress enacted the penal provision under which Emerson was charged. The Supreme Court, of late, has read this authorization more strictly than previously, and struck down as beyond federal interests such efforts by Congress as penalizing the possession of a gun in close proximity to a school.[4] Along the same lines, it might be argued that gun possession by a person subject to a nonintimidation order of a local court goes beyond the regulation of matters in interstate commerce. And, indeed Dr. Emerson so argued. However, the District Court noted that the constitutionality of 18 U.S.C. 922(g)(8) under the Commerce Clause was upheld in a recent, prior case in the Fifth Circuit.[5] Thus, however tempting Judge Cummings found it, that issue was inaccessible to him, a lower court judge within the Fifth Circuit. But the Court of Appeals for the Fifth Circuit could change its mind and rescind their own prior ruling (unlikely). Or the Supreme Court, if and when it gets the case, could correct the Circuit Court's misunderstanding of the scope of the Commerce Clause. Without going too deeply into the point, let us simply note that the possibility of such a disposition does not strain the bounds of likelihood. The Supreme Court would only be following its own recently expressed inclinations. Thus, they might well disappoint the doctrinal warriors on the battlefield of Amendment II, and simply strike down section 922(g)(8) as exceeding the powers of Congress to pass laws affecting interstate commerce.

Assuming for the moment, however, that one way or another the Court of Appeals for the Fifth Circuit, and eventually the United States Supreme Court review Judge Cummings' decision on Second Amendment grounds, what can we hope for, what can we expect? For one thing, we can certainly hope that the judges who ponder the issue will be exposed to a better version of the history of the Second Amendment, or at least to a more diverse historiography. Without wider and deeper reading, including the work of a variety of broad-gauge historians, it is difficult for a judge to recognize the flaws in the "standard model." As we have attempted to demonstrate throughout these pages, the historical record is rich and, objectively read, over-whelming on the basic premises behind the Second Amendment, the fair import of its language, and the scant surviving meaning of the animating premise to the individual right announced. With a better understanding of the history of the provision, we expect, a review-ing court will recognize that Judge Cummings' notion that the Con-stitution guarantees an individual's right to have a gun for private use, regardless of its instrumental link to the militia, simply does not hold up. No seventeenth-century English antecedents, no few and scattered comments of members of our founding generation, no occasional proposals of ratifying conventions—carefully culled by the standard modelers—can overcome the solid record of the pur-poses of the Second Amendment.

Second, we might hope and expect that, despite the obvious inter-ests of most of the amici, the appellate courts deciding the case will understand that the issue before them is not gun control. Whether pri-vate citizens should be forbidden or encouraged to possess firearms, how and to what extent the state (or national government) should limit access to all or certain weapons—these are questions of policy on which well-meaning citizens might differ. They are questions that the democratic branch, the legislature, is designed to grapple with, and to resolve, without any advice from the Constitution—and the undemocratic courts that tell us what it says. The issue that we hope the little Emerson case will bring to the high court's attention is simply: does the Second Amendment today have any voice on the issue of gun regulation? Is there any way to read that single sentence to restrain federal—or state—governments in their efforts to make policy on the access of their citizens to aggressive or defensive weap-onry? On this issue, we hope, of course, that the courts will finally and definitively hold that the provision cannot be rewritten to reflect today's realities, and that as originally written, it has no application in today's world. We would like to think that the final word will come down endorsing our position that the militia as known to the found-ing generation has evaporated from our political landscape, and there are no recognizable descendants to which the right to keep and bear arms might be reattached. Let them boldly tell us that without that essential linkage, the right to keep and bear arms is meaningless.

Finally, and in the context of the Emerson appeal, we must express some concern about the position of our government on the issue. On May 17, 2001, only a few weeks before these words are written, John Ashcroft, Attorney General of the United States, wrote to James Jay Baker, executive director of the National Rifle Association, rejecting the "collective" interpretation. He put it emphatically: "Let me state unequivocally my view that the text and the original intent of the Second Amendment clearly protect the right of individuals to keep and bear firearms." Nor does he use "keep and bear" in a purely military context. He concludes, "I believe it is clear that the Constitution protects the private ownership of firearms for lawful purposes." He drops a footnote to the effect that "of course, . . . the Second Amendment does not prohibit Congress from enacting laws restricting firearm ownership for compelling state interests, such as . . . ownership by convicted felons, just as the First Amendment does not prohibit shouting fire in a crowded movie theatre." Apart from the fact that any attempt to align the Second Amendment with the first reflects a serious misunderstanding of both, it is difficult to understand how an unequivocal position that the Second Amendment guarantees individuals their access to arms for any purpose "will not be infringed" can tolerate the silent proviso: "except sometimes." When Congress finds a "compelling state interest," Ashcroft sees lawful restriction on the personal right to arms.

Citing several of the Federalist Papers, the Attorney General assures the NRA that his view "comports with the all but unanimous understanding of the Founding Fathers." Further, he explains, his position reflects the "routine" early decisions of the Supreme Court.[6] The Attorney General's assertion that the Supreme Court at any time in its history "routinely" construed the right to arms as an individual entitlement is startling. He cites four cases to support his claim, one of which, *Miller v. Texas*, does come from the pathetically thin canon of Supreme Court expressions on the subject. But, as we explained in chapter 1, this 1894 decision says nothing whatever about the scope of the Second Amendment, and what minimal hint it contains runs counter to the Attorney General's thesis. This was a murder conviction decided almost wholly on technical grounds about the writ of error by which it was challenged and the record supporting it. At one point—in the only passage remotely approaching the constitutional claim—the Court does say that they examined the record in vain for support for the defendant's claim that the gun law of Texas violated his Second and Fourth Amendment rights, and even had they found such support, it would avail the defendant naught since "it is well settled that the restrictions of these amendments operate only upon the federal power and have no reference whatever to proceedings in state courts."

Of the other cases cited by the Attorney General, one—*Robertson v. Baldwin*[7]—makes no mention of the Second Amendment, while another—*Logan v. United States*[8]—says only this: "It was held that the second amendment of the constitution, declaring that 'the right of the people to keep and bear arms shall not be infringed,' was equally limited in scope." Meaning, like the First Amendment, it offered protection only against the federal government. Finally, Ashcroft cites *Maxwell v. Dow*,[9] which mentions the Second Amendment only in a reference to *Presser v. Illinois* (one of the standard canon discussed earlier), which, while holding that Amendment II applies only to Congress, did slip in a rather odd extension that would bind the states not to undermine the military resources of the United States. That the lawyer-in-chief of the United States could read those cases as a pattern of authority supporting his view of the meaning and scope of a constitutional principle is disheartening, to say the least.

The Attorney General also calls upon the scholarly community, finding that the "preponderance of legal scholarship" supports him. He cites only four—the heavily cited four whom we discuss at length elsewhere: William Van Alstyne, Akhil Reed Amar, Sanford Levinson, and Don Kates. We can only hope that his reading will be broadened.

Although differing in several respects, our Attorney General has allied himself with Judge Cummings on the basic issue of individual entitlement. Perhaps that is where his politics take him. But he no longer speaks as a senator but with the tongue of the government. John Ashcroft assured us at his confirmation hearings that, as Attorney General, he would put personal beliefs to one side and exert himself to enforce the laws as enacted. Presumably, that pledge includes 18 U.S.C. 922(g)(8). But he is also pledged to uphold the Constitution. Does that mean that he has the authority to superimpose his unequivocal understanding of the demands of the Constitution upon the statutes he is called upon to defend?

The government, however, has already filed briefs appealing from Judge Cummings holdings, and on June 13, 2000, argued orally before the Court of Appeals for reversal. Will the Justice Department continue with a vigorous argument against the decision which the Attorney General has indirectly informed us he unequivocally supports? If not, will the government seek reargument, withdraw its briefs, and switch sides? They have not yet done so, but will they maintain their position to make or oppose an application for certiorari to the Supreme Court (depending on how the case comes out in the Circuit)? Will they argue contrary to the Attorney General's unequivocal position if certiorari is granted? Or will the government switch sides to support the District Court's peculiar view of the Second Amendment? And if the Justice Department switches, will the Supreme Court have to swear in a private lawyer to argue what should be the government's position (as they did recently in *Dickerson v. United States* regarding Congress' effort to repeal *Miranda*)?

In short, we look to *United States v. Emerson* as the long-awaited opportunity for the high court to revisit the controversial Second Amendment issues, to give us a clear, modern, picture of an inert constitutional element, and—with the help of an unflinching, uninflected reading of the historical record—to help the Constitution to step aside and leave the troubled question of gun regulation to the democratic processes. As ever, however, there are more than a few obstacles to the realization of this jurisprudential dream.

POSTSCRIPT

A few months after the foregoing was written and some fifteen months after the case was argued to the Court of Appeals for the Fifth Circuit, the court decided the appeal. Obviously aware of the attention the district court decision had attracted, Judge Garwood (for the court) wrote an opinion of some eight-one pages in length, including sixty-seven footnotes, a hefty bundle for a judicial opinion. It is, of course, not the opinion we would have liked, and not the decision that invites review by the United States Supreme Court. Hence, from this case, Americans do not have, and likely will not have, the modern, authoritative, national construction of the Second Amendment with respect to the right to private ownership of weapons for private purposes.

Still, we do feel it incumbent upon us to describe the Circuit Court opinion, if only to share our disappointment that the issues we described above were not salubriously resolved. Actually, the opinion produces an odd sensation for us. We find that we are in agreement with the court—up to a point. Then suddenly the reasoning of the court seems to slip off the chain of logic to an unwarranted conclusion, only to return to our way of thinking until it wanders off again.

Earlier in this chapter, we expressed some sympathy for Emerson in his claim that his right to due process was lost when his possession of the gun, perfectly lawful, suddenly and automatically became criminal with the issuance of an order of protection against him. The Court of Appeals made short work of the point. Relying on some pretty well established doctrine, the court held that the only culpable knowledge required was the understanding that the weapon was a gun of the sort that was prohibited by the statute, not knowledge that the entry of the order automatically made possession of the gun unlawful. Ignorance of the law, after all, is no excuse. In addition, the court found that Emerson had adequate notice of the conversion of lawful to unlawful possession when he signed the form at the time he bought the Baretta.

The Court of Appeals gave even shorter shrift to the argument that the statute in question, penalizing possession of a weapon after a local court issues the order of protection, exceeds the power of the United States Congress. Citing their own prior decision, the court reaffirmed that the statute penalizes only the possession of firearms that have been shipped in interstate commerce, and is therefore within the power of Congress to enact legislation "affecting commerce."

The court gives a considerably more extensive treatment to the arguments predicated on the Second Amendment. The main thesis of the court with regard to the argument from judicial precedent is to disagree with the government's construction of *Miller v. United States.* That was the case involving the sawed-off shotgun where the Supreme Court held that the National Firearms Act, prohibiting interstate transportation of such weapons, did not offend the Second Amendment inasmuch as such weapons were not used by the militia. Closely studying the decision, the Court of Appeal for the Fifth Circuit concluded that the *Miller* decision does not support the Government's argument for a collective rights interpretation of the Second Amendment. However, they do not, on that account, assume that *Miller* propounded the individual rights construction. Rather, they turn to the text of the Second Amendment for enlightenment on the issue.

Examining first the term "the People," the court finds that it was used, consistently with its use in other parts of the Constitution, to mean the individual citizens, not the states, nor the citizens assembled as a militia. So far so good. We agree with this reading of the term. The court then goes on to consider the term, "bear arms." Contrary to many commentators and to our own interpretation, the court finds "numerous instances" where the words were employed to connote private carrying for private purposes. Accordingly, they conclude that the term refers to carrying or wearing arms generally.

It is when the court turns to an interpretation of what they call "the preamble," the introductory clause of the Amendment, that reasoning falters. In fact the discontinuity is apparent in a single paragraph. The paragraph begins with this sentence: "Certainly the preamble implies that the substantive guarantee is one which tends to enable, promote or further the existence, continuation or effectiveness [of] that 'well-regulated militia' which is 'necessary to the security of a free state.'" This and the sentences that follow seem to be wholly in accord with our own position that the meaning of the substantive clause is inescapably modified by the language of the introductory clause. Mid-paragraph, however, the court states, "Accordingly," the preamble does not support those who argue for an interpretation that the recognition of a right to arms serves the collective security of the state. "Accordingly"? The court, rather, appears to have written a classic non sequitur. The court then returns to a line of argument fully compatible with our own. "The militia," they wrote, "consisted of the people bearing their own arms when called to active service, arms which they kept and knew how to use. If the people were disarmed there could be no militia (well-regulated or otherwise) as it was then understood. That expresses the proper understanding of the relationship between the Second Amendment's preamble and its substantive guarantee." We could not have put it better ourselves.

With that, the court undertakes a long essay on history. This learned discussion concludes that the history of the adoption of the Second Amendment confirms its plain meaning: it was intended as a guarantee of individual access to arms to ensure that the citizens' militia would be armed. From this conclusion—sound, to our way of thinking—the court glides effortlessly into the present tense and finds that the Second Amendment "protects individual Americans in their right to keep and bear arms whether or not they are a member [sic] of a select militia or performing active military service or training."

In applying that holding to the case at hand, the Court of Appeals hastily notes that protection of individual rights does not mean absolute protection. Specific, reasonable, and narrow exceptions, the court finds, are not inconsistent with the historical right of Americans to keep and bear their private arms. Dr. Emerson, the court notes, does not claim that he had an absolute Second Amendment right to keep his Baretta, but only that his constitutional right required the local district court to make a showing that, armed, he posed a "credible threat" to the safety of his wife or child. The Court of Appeals was not persuaded. They preferred to assume that state law would require a showing of a real threat of injury before an order is issued that has consequences under the federal law. However, they decline to review the validity of the initial order that converted Emerson's possession of his gun into a criminal offense under federal law.

So the Court of Appeals for the Fifth Circuit (1) endorses the district court ruling on the Commerce Clause point; (2) reverses the district court on the Fifth Amendment due process point; and (3) agrees with the district court that "the Second Amendment protects the right of individuals privately to keep and bear their own firearms that are suitable as individual personal weapons. . . ." However, the predicate order in Emerson's case is sufficient to support the deprivation of those Second Amendment rights. So the reversal on Second Amendment grounds is reversed and the case remanded for further proceedings.

The upshot, then, of this exceptionally long and thoroughly developed decision is that although the court below is deemed right about the application of the Second Amendment to private weapons held for private purposes, that entitlement can be easily abrogated—even without a particular determination or express finding of threat. Thus, the Circuit Court manages to craft a decision that is disappointing to both sides and all of the legions of "friends of the court" who filed unsolicited briefs. One side got a circuit level court to say what they have been so long and so eagerly waiting to hear: Yes, the Second Amendment is a personal entitlement to all sorts of arms for all sorts of purposes. At the same time, gun control people heard the court say that all kinds of reasonable social purposes allow the government to restrict or suspend the exercise of that right of keeping and bearing. And, for them, the punchline was the reinstatement of the criminal charge despite the challenge to it on Second Amendment grounds.

For us the case is also a disappointment, but for somewhat different reasons. We wish the court had been somewhat more coherent in its logic, somewhat more comprehensive in its scholarship, but mainly we wish the court had understood the history of the militia since the founding as a factor bearing on the modern meaning of the Second Amendment. We are sorry that, with the eyes of the nation upon them, Judge Garwood and the Court of Appeals did not recognize that this provision of the Constitution, once designed for maintaining individual access to arms, lost its meaning when radical social change deprived it of its predicate purpose.

POST POSTSCRIPT

As this book goes to press, we steal a few lines to note that, as expected, the Supreme Court, without comment, declined the opportunity to review the Emerson case (along with another). And we report that the Attorney General, while opposing the petition for certiorari to review these cases, dropped a footnote in the Government's brief informing the Court that the United States had reversed its longstanding position on the construction of the Second Amendment. As John Ashcroft had promised the NRA a few months earlier, the Department of Justice now believes that the Second Amendment "broadly protects the rights of individuals, including persons who are not members of any militia or engaged in active military service or training, to possess and bear their own firearms." The constitutional right, however, was subject to "reasonable restrictions."[10] Gun control, in other words, is not inimical to the broadly stated (and uninfringable) right to arms. Presumably, then, this sudden and dramatic reversal of American policy on the meaning of the Second

Amendment will have little effect on such laws as the federal statute under which Dr. Emerson was charged, or on state licensing laws that take care that guns will not be "criminally misused" or fall into hands of "unfit persons," both recognized by the Attorney General as legitimate restrictions.

Inspired by the classical republican model — reinvented in the Renaissance, expounded by Machiavelli, and transmitted to the Founders' mind frame by English and colonial pamphleteers — the Second Amendment guaranteed the individual right to all (all free, white, adult men, anyway) to own and carry firearms. That individual right is, however, limited by both text and context to the service of communal security by provision for a well-regulated military force known as a militia. By *militia* is meant a trained, organized, and armed collection of qualified citizens, save only those of conscientious scruple and others exempted from service by their states, called together from their normal pursuits to respond to occasional and particular threats, internal or external, to community peace. Thus conceived, the eighteenth-century militia stood in contrast to — and for many, in preference to — the professional standing army. To the consternation of the anti-federalists, however, the professional national army — which Washington knew deserved most credit for winning the War of Independence — was also tolerated by the Constitution.

By the dawn of the twentieth century, the standing army had replaced the long-defunct local militia as America's primary fighting force. Long before the Mexican War, moreover, private arms had ceased to supply the ordnance of such state militia units as still lingered. By the time of the Civil War, the old state militia had vanished, losing all corporeal existence beyond the ghostly whisper of a name, a faded banner, and, in some instances, a proud — if ill-defined —

history. Elite Volunteer Companies had taken their place, but their members' weapons, the *Presser* Court made clear in 1885, were constitutionally protected only insofar as they were held pursuant to statute, official authorization, or license from the state government that chartered the company.

The Regular Army and existing volunteer companies could not meet the enormous manpower demands of the Civil War, but the newly formed state units that answered "Father Abraham's" call[1] were sworn into federal service as soon as they made muster, and promptly issued U.S. government arms purchased pursuant to act of Congress and War Department orders. With America's rise to world power in the twentieth century, the U.S. Army ballooned to levels previously unthinkable during peacetime. But in order to facilitate further rapid wartime expansion, Congress realized the nation needed a more reliable reserve than the nineteenth-century style volunteer state "National Guards." Starting in 1903, Congress passed legislation to create a modern, professional, federal National Guard, and over the course of the century, the U.S. Army and the War/Defense Departments assumed larger and larger roles in administration of the Guard. By mid-century, all guardsmen took a federal oath upon enlistment, Guard units were trained and supervised by the army, and the Guard was issued U.S. Army weapons and equipment kept in state arsenals built to federal specifications with federal dollars.

This drastic change in the nature, status, and even vitality of the militia has utterly drained the Second Amendment right to arms of meaning in modern America. To conceive of a constitutionally enshrined personal right to weaponry independent of communal, republican obligations is to distort beyond recognition the constitutional design. And with no contemporary descendent to inherit the Framers' concept of a republican militia, the incidental right of citizens to bear and to keep the arms necessary to the life of such a militia has atrophied; it has simply fallen silent in the midst of the tumultuous debate on the issue in today's world.

What this means is that on the pressing question of gun control, the Constitution is neutral. The Second Amendment would take no notice if the Congress, appalled by the prevalence of gun-assisted crimes, outlawed all handguns and assault rifles in private hands. By the same token, the Congress could vacate the field, and with a similar retreat by the states, the National Rifle Association would realize its fondest wish, and every clean, competent adult would be allowed free purchase and proud ownership of firepower of every description. So, we conclude: let the great debate continue to rage — in the democratic branch where it belongs. But let us understand at last that the Second Amendment has no voice in the matter.

INTRODUCTION

1 John R. Lott, Jr., *More Guns, Less Crime* (University of Chicago Press, 1998).

2 See, e.g., "Do Guns Mean Crime," *The Economist,* Jan. 13, 2001.

3 We had considerable difficulty selecting the word "null" in this sentence. We want to make it clear that we use the word in the sense of "inoperative," "without present binding force or effect," in accord with the first two definitions of the *Oxford English Dictionary* but not as "nil," "non-existent," or "dead." (OED's third definition). In fact, both of us believe that in certain conceivable — though highly unlikely — circumstances, the Second Amendment would revive and become controlling authority. We mention these circumstances in chapter 8.

4 In 1989, gun control advocates Dennis Henigan and Keith Ehrman mapped out an argument not dissimilar to our own: see Keith A. Ehrman and Dennis A. Henigan, "The Second Amendment in the Twentieth Century: Have You Seen Your Militia Lately?" 15 *University of Dayton Law Review* 5 (1989), suggesting that developments including "the split between an organized and unorganized militia; the passage of the militias from state authority to largely federal authority; and the rise of the army as the main defense force of the country" help explain why *United States v. Miller* was correctly decided, and why, in modern times, curbs on purely private possession of guns cannot be said to interfere meaningfully with the Second Amendment right to arms (at page 39). Ehrman and Henigan, however, lacked a thorough grounding in history, and numerous errors and problematic glosses undermine their generally well-aimed account. Their analysis suffers additionally from its failure to articulate a theoretical basis for reconciling fidelity to original intent and changed historical circumstance. Most significantly, however, while Ehrman and Henigan focused on

refuting individualist readings of the right to arms, they ignored entirely the obvious republican roots of the Second Amendment, and therefore did not address the most serious problem involved in the individualists' efforts to read a private liberty into an essentially communitarian political theory.

CHAPTER ONE: THE GUN IN
THE AMERICAN SELF-PORTRAIT

1   Bernard Bailyn, *The Ideological Origins of the American Revolution,* 1–19 (1967); *Pamphlets of the American Revolution* (Bernard Bailyn, ed., 1965) passim; J. G. A. Pocock, *The Machiavellian Moment: Florentine Political Thought and the Atlantic Republican Tradition,* esp. 506–509 and passim (1975).

2   But see Daniel J. Boorstin, *The Americans: The National Experience* 52–57 (1966), making the point that settlers adopted communal, even regimented ways to protect themselves against native tribes. See also Leo Marx, *The Machine in the Garden: Technology and the Pastoral Ideal in America* (1964) on the colonial and early national, and Frederick Jackson Turner, *The Frontier in American History* (Dover Publications 1996) (1920) on the far west frontiers as shapers of the national character.

3   "No Soldier shall, in time of peace be quartered in any house, without the consent of the Owner, nor in time of war, but in a manner to be prescribed by law." U.S. Const. Amend. III.

4   Residents and visitors to northern Virginia may have noted that, as recently as 1999, the NRA Headquarters building, visible from Interstate 66, proudly displayed the motto "The Right to Keep and Bear Arms Shall Not Be Infringed," but failed to quote the Amendment's introductory language. The sign has since been removed.

5   Stephen P. Halbrook, *That Every Man Be Armed: The Evolution of a Constitutional Right* (1984); Joyce Lee Malcolm, *To Keep and Bear Arms: The Origins of an Anglo-American Right* 130 (1994) ("Blackstone emphatically endorsed the view that keeping arms was necessary both for self-defense, the natural right of resistance and self-preservation, and to restrain the violence of oppressions. Blackstone's comments on this subject are of the utmost importance, since his work immediately became the great authority on English common law in both England and America.") (internal quotation marks omitted); Stephen P. Halbrook, "Congress Interprets the Second Amendment: Declarations by a Co-Equal Branch of the Individual Right to Keep and Bear Arms," 62 *Tenn. L. Rev.* 597, 641 (1995) ("[T]he right to keep and bear arms is a fundamental, individual right, and . . . statutes regulating this right should be narrowly construed against the government and in favor of the people."); Don B. Kates Jr., "Handgun Prohibition and the Original Meaning of the Second Amendment," 82 *Mich. L. Rev.* 204, 205–26 (1983) ("The unanimity with which Federalists and Anti-Federalists supported an individual right to arms is a reflection of their shared philosophical and historical heritage. Examinations of contemporary materials reveals that the founders ardently endorsed firearms possession as a

personal right and that the concept of an exclusively state's right was wholly unknown to them.") (footnotes omitted); Sanford Levinson, "The Embarrassing Second Amendment," 99 *Yale L. J.* 637, 658 (1991) ("For too long, most members of the legal academy have treated the Second Amendment as the equivalent of an embarrassing relative, whose mention brings a quick change of subject to other, more respectable, family members. That will no longer do. It is time for the Second Amendment to enter full-scale into the consciousness of the legal academy."); Harry Summers, "Gun Collecting and Lithuania," *Washington Times,* March 29, 1990, at F4.

6   Laurence H. Tribe, *American Constitutional Law* 299 note 6 (2d ed. 1988). In the recently published third edition, however, Professor Tribe appears to have had a change of heart. In his much expanded treatment on the subject, Tribe now expresses greater sympathy for those who read the Second Amendment to accord a right to individuals to own guns for private purposes. 1 Laurence H. Tribe, *American Constitutional Law* 901–902 note 221 (3d ed. 2000). Tribe's seeming conversion to the "individualist" camp, as well as his new take on the Second Amendment, are analyzed in detail by Professor Carl Bogus. Carl T. Bogus, "The History and Politics of Second Amendment Scholarship: A Primer," 76 *Chicago-Kent L. Rev.* 3, 19–21 (2000).

With a few prominent exceptions (Akhil Reed Amar, "The Bill of Rights As a Constitution," 100 *Yale L. J.* 1131, 1162–73 (1991); Sanford Levinson, "The Embarrassing Second Amendment," 99 *Yale L. J.* 637, 658 (1991); William Van Alstyne, "The Second Amendment and the Personal Right to Arms," 43 *Duke L. J.* 1236, 1255 (1994)), Tribe's summary articulated in his second edition continues to epitomize the position of academic professionals in law schools and on history faculties who have entered the Second Amendment debate.

Similarly, until a recent abrupt shift on the part of the current Attorney General, John Ashcroft (discussed in detail in chapter 9), the U.S. government was firmly on record interpreting the Second Amendment to establish the constitutional validity of state militias rather than a purely private right to arms. In 1912, for example, the attorney general issued an opinion adopting findings contained in a War Department report leveling the Militia Reform Act of 1908 (*Statutes at Large* XXXV, 399–403) unconstitutional, and finding that the militia drew its essential constitutional legitimacy from the Second Amendment. "Authority of President to Second Militia into a Foreign Country," 29 Op. Atty Gen. 322 (1912). For a discussion of the attorney general's opinion and the report of the War department, see Russell F. Weigley, *History of the United States Army* 324–25, 340 (Indiana University Press 1984) (1967) (hereinafter, Weigley, *United States Army*); Alan R. Millet, "The Constitution and the Citizen-Soldier," 69 *Revue Internationale D'Histoire Militaire* 97, 109 (1990). But see also the recent letter, dated May 17, 2002, from John Ashcroft, on offical letterhead of the Attorney General, to James Jay Baker, Executive Director of the National Rifle Association, www.cbsnews.com/htdocs/pdf/ag.pdf, and the discussion in chapter 9.

7   Adams v. Williams, 407 U.S. 143, 150 (1972) (Douglas, J., dissenting).

8   *MacNeil/Lehrer NewsHour:* Interview by Charlayne Hunter-Gault with Warren
    Burger (PBS television broadcast, Dec. 16, 1991) (Monday transcript # 4226),
    available in LEXIS, News Library, NewsHour with Jim Lehrer File. See also,
    Warren Burger, "The Right to Keep and Bear Arms," *Parade Magazine,* Jan. 14,
    1990, at 4.

9   Printz v. United States, 571 U.S. 898 (1997) (Thomas, J., concurring). The Court
    held a portion of the Brady Act (a federal gun control law) unconstitutional as
    a congressional directive to state officials exceeding constitutional authority;
    the majority opinion did not involve the Second Amendment in any way. In
    addition to Justice Thomas, Justice Scalia has expressed approval of the indi-
    vidual right construction of the Second Amendment, but he has never done
    so in an opinion. Antonin Scalia, *A Matter of Interpretation: Federal Courts and the
    Law* 136–37 note 13 (1990).

10 United States v. Miller, 307 U.S. 174 (1939); Miller v. Texas, 153 U.S. 535 (1894);
    Presser v. Illinois, 116 U.S. 252 (1886); United States v. Cruikshank, 92 U.S. 542
    (1876). See also Perpich v. Department of Defense, 496 U.S. 334, 110 S. Ct. 2418
    (1990), in which the Court considered claims by the governor of Minnesota that
    a federal statute violated the Militia Clauses of the Constitution by preventing
    a governor from withholding consent to the federal call-up of National Guard
    units for overseas service on account of the governor's objection to the purpose
    of the guard's mission. The opinion by Justice Stevens reviewed the history
    of American military policy and ascribed to the drafters of the Constitution's
    Militia Clauses an intent consonant with a collective purpose to the Second
    Amendment, but Justice Stevens did not address the Second Amendment or
    reach any Second Amendment issues in his holding. See also United States v.
    Cardoza, 129 F.3d 6 (First Cir.) (Mass) (1997) in which the First Circuit upheld
    the Youth Handgun Safety Act in the face of a *Lopez*-based challenge because
    the act, unlike the statute in *Lopez,* was expressly directed at economic activity
    and hence well within the Commerce Power; United States v. Michael R., 90
    F.3d 340, 359 (9th Cir. 1996).

11 In United States v. Emerson, 86 F. Supp. 2d 598 (N.D. Tex. April 7, 1999),
    the United States District Court for the Northern District of Texas became
    the first and only court to decline to follow *United States v. Miller* in a Second
    Amendment case, upholding a Second Amendment challenge to 18 U.S.C.
    § 922 (g)(8). The decision was reversed on appeal. The Court of Appeals agreed
    that the Second Amendment protects a purely private right to arms, but held
    that the application of the statute in Emerson's case was not unconstitutional.
    See chapter 9.

12 Cases v. United States, 131 F.2d 916 (1st Cir. 1942); United States v. Scanio,
    No. 97–1584, 1998 U.S. App. LEXIS 29415 (2d Cir. Nov. 12, 1998); United States
    v. Rybar, 103 F.3d 273 (3d Cir. 1996), cert. denied, 522 U.S. 807 (1997); Love v.
    Pepersack, 47 F.3d 120 (4th Cir.), cert. denied, 516 U.S. 813 (1995); United States
    v. Warin, 530 F.3d 103 (6th Cir.), cert. denied, 426 U.S. 948 (1976); Quilici v.
    Morton Grove, 695 F.2d 261 (7th Cir. 1982); United States v. Synnes, 438 F.2d

764 (8th Cir. 1971); Hickman v. Block, 81 F.3d 98 (9th Cir. 1996); United States
v. Oakes, 564 F.2d 384 (10th Cir. 1997); United States v. Wright, 117 F.3d 1265
(11th Cir. 1997); Fraternal Order of Police v. United States, 173 F.3d 898 (D.C.
Cir. 1999); United States v. Henson, Criminal No. 2:99–00068, 1999 U.S. Dist.
LEXIS 8987 (S.D.W. Va. June 14, 1999) (rejecting Second Amendment challenge to 18 U.S.C. 922 [g][8]) and Lewis v. United States, 445 U.S. 55, 65–66 n.8
(1980)(reaffirming *United States v. Miller*) ("These legislative restrictions [18 U.S.C.
§ 922 (h)(1), making it unlawful for convicted felons to receive firearms trans-
ported in interstate commerce] are neither based upon constitutionally suspect
criteria, nor do they trench upon any constitutionally protected liberties." See
United States v. Miller, 307 U.S. 174, 178 [1939]) (the Second Amendment guarantees no right to keep and bear a firearm that does not have "some reasonable relation to the preservation or efficiency of a well regulated militia"). No
reported decisions question the Second Amendment holdings of *Cruikshank,
Presser,* or *Miller v. Texas.*

13   92 U.S. at 553.

14   On the distinction between civil and political rights, see Raoul Berger, *Government by Judiciary: The Transformation of the Fourteenth Amendment* 38–48 (2d ed. 1997).

15   Section 1 of Amendment XV provides: "The right of citizens of the United
States to vote shall not be denied or abridged by the United States or by any
State on account of race, color, or previous condition of servitude." Incidentally, in view of this language, it comes as a surprise to learn that it required
another fifty years and the passage of the Nineteenth Amendment before the
"right of the citizens . . . to vote" included women.

16   153 U.S. at 538 (1894).

17   The Supreme Court has not passed on the Second Amendment since the
wave of incorporation decisions during the Warren era, see inter alia Mapp v.
Ohio, 367 U.S. 643 (1961) (guaranteeing against the states the Fourth Amendment right to be free from unreasonable searches and seizures and to have
excluded from criminal trials any evidence illegally seized), Gideon v. Wain-
wright, 372 U.S. 325 (1963) (enforcing against the states the Sixth Amendment
right to counsel), Malloy v. Hogan, 378 U.S. 1 (1964) (enforcing against the
states the right guaranteed by the Fifth Amendment to be free of compelled
self-incrimination), Pointer v. Texas, 380 U.S. 400 (1965) (enforcing against the
states the Sixth Amendment right to confront opposing witnesses), Klopfer
v. North Carolina, 386 U.S. 213 (1967) (enforcing against the states the right to
a speedy trial), and Washington v. Texas, 388 U.S. 14 (1967) (enforcing against
the states the Sixth Amendment right to compulsory process for obtaining
witnesses).

18   32 U.S. (7 Pet.) 243 (1833).

19   83 U.S. (16 Wall.) 36 (1873).

20   Nearly all the guaranties of individual rights against the federal government
set out in the first eight Amendments have been applied, one by one, against
the states through the Due Process Clause of the Fourteenth Amendment, on

the grounds that they are fundamental to the principles of fairness and ordered liberty inherent in due process. This development is known as selective as opposed to total incorporation. See Palko v. Connecticut, 302 U.S. 319, 323–26 (1937), in which Justice Cardozo rejects total incorporation, but articulates the rationale that procedural principles fundamental to the sense of ordered liberty inherent in due process can be enforced against the states, and Adamson v. California, 322 U.S. 46, 71–72 (1947) (Black, J., dissenting) in which Justice Black sets forth the classic — and losing — argument for total incorporation.

21 Fresno Rifle and Pistol Club, Inc. v. Van De Kamp, 965 F.2d 723, 729–30 (9th Cir. Cal. 1992).

22 The others are the right against quartering of troops (Third Amendment), the right to grand jury indictment (Fifth Amendment), and the right to jury trials in civil controversies where more than twenty dollars is in dispute (Seventh Amendment, in its entirety).

23 Freedom from religious establishment, free exercise of religion, freedom of speech, freedom of the press, freedom of assembly, freedom to petition the government for redress of grievances. U.S. Const. amend. I.

24 Security against unreasonable searches and seizures of persons, houses, papers, and effects; security against general warrants (description of elements of a valid warrant). U.S. Const. amend. IV.

25 Rights of criminally accused to presentment or grand jury indictment; security against double jeopardy, self-incrimination, deprivation of life, liberty, or property without due process of law; and against takings except for public use with just compensation. U.S. Const. amend. V.

26 Right to speedy and public trial by jury of the state and district, to be informed of nature and cause of criminal accusation, to confront witnesses, compulsory process, and to counsel. U.S. Const. amend. VI.

27 Freedom from excessive bail, excessive fines, and cruel and unusual punishments. U.S. Const. amend. VIII.

28 Right to jury trial in civil suits where value in controversy exceeds twenty dollars, freedom from reexamination of fact tried by jury except under the rules of the common law. U.S. Const. amend. VII. These rights have not been incorporated against the states.

29 And, as we have noted, we do not read the Fourteenth Amendment as a silent amendment of the language of the Second Amendment.

30 Technically, *Cruikshank* held that the constitutional rights of two black citizens, Levi Nelson and Alexander Tillman, had not been criminally violated when they were prevented by armed Klansmen from voting in a Louisiana election (the decision does not make clear whether this was a state or federal or combined election, because the indictment failed to set forth the answer to this question with sufficient particularity and detail). The Court held that the statute enforcing the Fourteenth Amendment applied only to incidents of national citizenship, and that while the right not to be prevented from voting

on account of race was an incident of national citizenship, the right to vote itself remained purely an incident of state citizenship, and that because the indictment merely stated that black voters had been prevented from exercising their suffrage and did not specify that they had been denied this right *on account of race,* the actions alleged in the indictment did not fall within the statute. Writing for a unanimous Court, Chief Justice Waite thus took a very narrow reading of the scope of federal constitutional rights protected by the Enforcement Act and contemplated within the Fourteenth Amendment. To this day, the Privileges and Immunities Clause is burdened by a similarly restrictive reading, while jurisprudence under the Equal Protection and Due Process Clauses has grown far more expansive in its protection of individual rights. Gerald Gunther, *Constitutional Law* 408–11, 601–608 (12th ed. 1991). See also the excellent discussion in Doe v. Daily News, 173 Misc.2d 321, 330–31, 660 N.Y.S.2d 604 (N.Y. Sup. Ct., N.Y. County, 1997) regarding the supersedure of *Cruikshank* on the scope of the Fourteenth Amendment Due Process and Equal Protection Clauses. The *Cruikshank* Court reached the Second Amendment question because Nelson and Tillman had endeavored to protect themselves against the Klansmen with weapons of their own and held that there was no constitutional right against disarmament by private actors. The opinion implies that the only right of national citizenship contained in the Second Amendment is that of keeping and bearing arms for service in the militia free of unwarranted molestation by the federal Congress. Cruikshank, 92 U.S. at 592–93. Interestingly, it is by no means clear from the record that Nelson and Tillman were not in fact disarmed while serving in the militia, because Louisiana's legitimately elected Republican governor had called out heavily black loyalist militia units to police the polling stations and resist the insurrectionist forces of the "White League." Of further interest is the fact that the White League operated under the authority of Louisiana's rival self-proclaimed Democratic governor, which raises the question of whether Nelson and Tillman might be said to have been disarmed "under color of state law" while serving dutifully in the militia, circumstances that would, even under Justice Waite's absurdly reductionist reading of the Fourteenth Amendment and the Enforcement Act, constitute a civil rights violation. On Louisiana during the later stages of Reconstruction, see generally Eric Foner, *Reconstruction: America's Unfinished Revolution* 1863–1877 at 529–31, 550 (1988) (hereinafter, Foner, *Reconstruction*).

31 On the Colfax massacre, see generally Foner, *Reconstruction* 529–31, 550 (1988).

32 United States v. Dixon, 595 F.2d 178, 180 (7th Cir. Wis. 1979).

33 See generally Foner, *Reconstruction* at 529–34, 569, 587, on the Supreme Court's flaunting the purposes of the Reconstruction Amendments. Doe v. New York Times, 173 Misc. 2d at 321 ("The radical plan to protect the Negro by subjection of the states was thus 'demolished' by Waite and his associates [referring to the decisions in *Cruikshank* and the *Slaughter-House Cases*]. . . . This marked the overthrow of the congressional plan of reconstruction within seven years

after the adoption of the Fourteenth Amendment.") (quoting Trimble, Chief Justice Waite, Defender of the Public Interest [1938]), which lauds Waite for nullifying reconstruction; Slaughter-House Cases, 16 Wall. (83 U.S.) 36, 89–98 (Field, J., dissenting).

34   United States v. Miller, 307 U.S. at 178.

35   Caplan, "Restoring the Balance: The Second Amendment Revisited," 5 *Fordham Urban L. J.* 31, 44–48 (1976); Gardiner, "To Preserve Liberty: A Look at the Right to Keep and Bear Arms," 10 *Northern Kentucky L. Rev.* 63, 88; Black, "From Trenches to Squad Cars," *American Rifleman,* June 1982, at 30, 72–73.

36   United States v. Scanio, No. 97–1584, 1998 U.S. App. LEXIS 29415 (2d Cir. Nov. 12, 1998); United States v. Rybar, 103 F.3d 273, 285–86 (3d Cir. 1996), cert. denied, 522 U.S. 807 (1997); Love v. Pepersack, 47 F.3d 120 (4th Cir.), cert. denied, 516 U.S. 813 (1995); United States v. Warin, 530 F.2d 103 (6th Cir.), cert. denied, 426 U.S. 948 (1976); Quilici v. Village of Morton Grove, 695 F.2d 261 (7th Cir. 1982); United States v. Synnes, 438 F.2d 764 (8th Cir. 1981); Hickman v. Block, 81 F.3d 98 (9th Cir. 1996); United States v. Oakes, 564 F.2d 384 (10th Cir. 1977); United States v. Wright, 117 F.3d 1265 (11th Cir. 1997); Fraternal Order of Police v. United States, 173 F.3d 898 (D.C. Cir. 1999); see also United States v. Henson, 55 F.Supp.2d 528 (S.D. W.Va. 1999); Lewis v. United States, 445 U.S. 55, 65–66 n.8 (1980). But see United States v. Emerson, 270 F.3d 203 (5th Cir. 2001), finding that the Second Amendment protects a purely private right to arms even outside the context of service in the organized militia.

37   United States v. Rybar, 103 F.3d 273, 285–86 (3d Cir. 1996)

38   Throughout, we use the word "clause" not in its strictly grammatical sense but as lawyers use it: to mean a portion of a provision. In chapter 7, we have something to say about the grammatical structure of the Second Amendment.

39   307 U.S. at 178.

40   116 U.S. 252 (1886).

41   Roy G. Weatherup (1975), "Standing Armies and Armed Citizens: An Historical Analysis of The Second Amendment," 2 *Hastings Constitutional Law Quarterly* 185, 220 ("[U]ndoubtedly the most important Second Amendment case was *Presser v. Illinois.*").

42   Military Code of Illinois, Act of May 28, 1879, ch. 192, § 5 (current version as amended at 20 Ill. Comp. Stat. 1805/94 [2000]).

43   This translates as the "Teach and Defend Club," which helps round out what is indeed a rather alarming image of Presser's spiked-helmeted, rifle-bearing Germans on unlicensed marches through Chicago in celebration of ostensibly worthy and civic values.

44   116 U.S. at 264–65.

45   On Trumbull's constitutional politics, see Foner, *Reconstruction* 226, 243–47, 250, 272, 336, 453–56, 507 (1988).

46   Supplemental Brief for Plaintiff in Error at 116 U.S. at 256–57.

47   Supplemental Brief for Plaintiff in Error at 116 U.S. at 259.

48   116 U.S. at 263. "We have not found it necessary to consider or decide the ques-

tion thus raised, as to the validity of the entire Military Code of Illinois, for, in our opinion, the sections under which the plaintiff in error was convicted may be valid, even if the other sections of the act were invalid. For it is a settled rule 'that statutes that are constitutional in part only will be upheld so far as they are not in conflict with the Constitution, provided the allowed and prohibited parts are separable.'" Packet Co. v. Keokuk, 95 U.S. 80; Penniman's Case, 103 U.S. 714, 717; Unity v. Burrage, 103 U.S. 459. Trade Mark Cases, 100 U.S. 82 (citations thus in original).

49 116 U.S. at 265.

50 The so-called Supremacy Clause is found in the second clause of Article 6, which provides, in part: "This Constitution, and all the Laws of the United States which shall be made in Pursuance thereof; and all Treaties made, or which shall be made, under the Authority of the United States, shall be the supreme law of the Land . . ."

51 U.S. Const. art. I § 8." The Congress shall have Power . . . To provide for calling forth the Militia to execute the Laws of the Union, suppress Insurrections and repeal Invasions; To provide for organizing, arming, and disciplining, the Militia, and for governing such Part of them as may be employed in the Service of the United States."

52 Presser, 116 U.S. at 264–65 and 267. "To right voluntarily to associate together as a military company or organization, or to drill or parade with arms, without, and independent of, an act of Congress or law of the State authorizing the same, is not an attribute of national citizenship. Military organization and military drill and parade under arms are subjects especially under the control of the government of every country. They cannot be claimed as a right independent of law. Under our political system they are subject to the regulation and control of the State and Federal governments, acting in due regard to their respective prerogatives and powers. The Constitution and laws of the United States will be searched in vain for any support to the view that these rights are privileges and immunities of citizens of the United States independent of some specific legislation on the subject."

53 In Trumbull's words "[t]he citizen of the United States has secured to him the right to keep and bear arms as part of the militia which Congress has the right to organize, and arm, and to drill in companies." Supplemental Brief for Plaintiff in Error, 116 U.S. at 257–58. The Supreme Court clearly understood Trumbull's argument for a right to arms as premised on the militia's desirability as an alternative to a standing army. Thus, the Court reported "[i]t is said [by counsel for plaintiff in error] that the object of the act of Congress is to provide for organizing, arming, and disciplining all the able bodied male citizens of the States, respectively, between certain ages, that they may be ready at all times to respond to the call of the nation to enforce its laws, suppress insurrection, and repel invasion, and thereby avoid the necessity for maintaining a large standing army, with which liberty can never be safe." Presser, 116 U.S. at 261–62.

54 153 U.S. 535 (1894).

55 153 U.S. at 538 (citing, inter alia, *Cruikshank, Baron v. Baltimore,* and the *Slaughter-House Cases*).

56 United States v. Lopez, 514 U.S. 549 (1995). See also United States v. Cardoza, 129 F.3d 6 (1st Cir. 1997) in which the First Circuit upheld the Youth Handgun Safety Act in the face of a *Lopez*-based challenge because the act, unlike the statute in *Lopez,* was expressly directed at economic activity and hence well within the Commerce Power. United States v. Michael R., 90 F.3d 340, 359 (9th Cir. 1996).

57 514 U.S. at 602–603 (Stevens, J., dissenting).

58 The powers not delegated to the United States by the Constitution, nor prohibited by it to the States, are reserved to the States respectively, or to the people. U.S. Const. amend. X.

59 We realize that grammatically the first half of the Second Amendment is not a clause at all, but throughout we occasionally use the word in the legal sense of a particular verbal provision of legal significance in a larger document.

60 Had they done so, the doctrine of self-incrimination might have developed in accord with the interpretation expounded by Professor Albert Alshuler, who argues that "as embodied in the United States Constitution, the privilege against self-incrimination was not intended to afford defendants a right to remain silent or to refuse to respond to incriminating questions. Its purpose was to outlaw torture and other improper methods of interrogation." Albert W. Alschuler, "A Peculiar Privilege in Historical Perspective: the Right to Remain Silent," 94 *Michigan L. Rev.* 2625, 2631 (1996).

61 See Eugene Volokh, "The Commonplace Second Amendment," 73 *N.Y.U. L. Rev.* 793 (1998).

62 Letter from Thomas Jefferson to Peter Carr (Aug. 19, 1785), in 8 *The Papers of Thomas Jefferson* 405, 407 (Julian P. Boyd ed., Princeton University Press 1953) [hereinafter Boyd, *Papers of Jefferson*].

63 Rhys Isaac, *The Transformation of Virginia,* 1740–1790 at 98–104 (1980) on the nature and cultural importance of sport in late colonial Virginia. Edward Hotaling, *The Great Black Jockeys: The Lives and Times of the Men Who Dominated America's First National Sport* 9–37 (1999) for an interesting and insightful description of the sociology of horseracing in the colonial South.

64 William V. Wells, *The Life and Public Services of Samuel Adams,* 267 (1865). We discuss Adams' effort to append to the recommendations that the Massachusetts Ratifying Convention submitted to Congress a draft amendment securing a private right to arms at page 82.

65 Third Draft Constitution, 1 Boyd, *Papers of Jefferson* 356. Boyd's notation indicates that the words "within his own lands or tenements" were not entirely legible in the best preserved text, but that this represents a probable reading.

66 First Draft Constitution, 1 Boyd, *Papers of Jefferson* 329.

67 Third Draft Constitution, 1 Boyd, *Papers of Jefferson* 356, 362. ("Every person of full age neither owning nor having owned [50] acres of land, shall be entitled to an appropriation of [50] acres or to so much as shall make up what he owns

or has owned to [50] acres in full and absolute dominion, and no other person shall be capable of taking an appropriation.")

68 Incidentally, one of the most intriguing, radical aspects of Jefferson's land grant proposal is that it lacked any express racial exclusion. This notable omission adds yet another fragment to the insoluble puzzle of Jefferson's attitude toward slavery, and his perception of the fitness of African Americans for political and social equality. On Jefferson's tortured relationship with slavery, see generally, Winthrop D. Jordan, *White on Black: American Attitudes Towards the Negro, 1550–1812* (1969); David Brian Davis, *The Problem of Slavery in the Age of Revolution, 1770–1823* (1975); Jack P. Greene, *All Men Created Equal: Some Reflections on the Character of the American Revolution: An Inaugural Lecture Delivered Before the University of Oxford on 10 February 1976* (1976); Fawn M. Brodie, *Jefferson: An Intimate History* (1974); William G. Merkel, *Liberty, Racism, and Anti-Slavery: A Re-Evaluation of Thomas Jefferson* (unpublished D.Phil. dissertation, on file with author), and, for a more hostile analysis, Paul Finkelman, *Slavery and the Founders: Race and Liberty in the Age of Jefferson* (1996).

69 In 1776, Jefferson drafted a gradual emancipation plan for Virginia to be included as an amendment to Bill 51 on slavery in the proposed laws eventually submitted to the state legislature by the Committee of Revisors (Jefferson, Pendleton, Whythe) in 1784. 2 Boyd, *Papers of Jefferson* 470–72. This is the same project that produced the Virginia Statute for Religious Freedom, but the emancipation proposal was never introduced in the assembly, and no record of it survives.

70 Letter from Thomas Jefferson to James Madison (Dec. 20, 1787), in 12 Boyd, *Papers of Jefferson* 438, 440.

71 William V. Wells, *The Life and Public Services of Samuel Adams,* 267 (1865). We acknowledge also the Fifth Circuit's diligence in cataloguing every known instance of endorsements of a right to arms for purely private purposes. See Emerson, 270 F.3d 203 (2001). The key point, however, is that these endorsements almost invariably issue from the pens of marginal, radical figures who did not represent the mainstream of either federal or antifederal thought. It is worth considering—as we discuss below—that every comment concerning the Second Amendment made on the house floor when that measure was pending reflected clearly the right to arms' military linkage. See discussion at 98–103 above, and note 74 for this chapter below. On the marginality of demands for a purely private right to arms see Saul Cornell, "Commonplace or Anachronism: The Standard Model, The Second Amendment, and the Problem of History in Contemporary Constitutional Theory," 16 *Constitutional Commentary* 221, 231–34 (1999).

72 Uniform Militia Act of 1792, ch. 33, § 1, 1 Stat. 271, 271, *repealed by* Dick Act, ch. 196, 32 Stat. 775 (1903).

73 Garry Wills, "Why We Have No Right To Keep and Bear Arms," *The New York Review of Books,* September 21, 1995, at 62, 64–65 (hereinafter, Wills, "To Keep and Bear Arms"), containing a scholarly exposition of the etymology and tech-

nical meaning of *bearing arms*. In this sense, even Jefferson's constitutional proposal of 1776 (although not his original draft thereof) admits quite plausibly of a less expansive, exclusively military reading.

74 *A Century of Lawmaking for a New Nation: U.S. Congressional Documents and Debates,* http://memory.loc.gov/ammen/amlaw/lawhome.html_ (2001) (cited in David Yassky, "The Second Amendment: Structure, History, and Constitutional Change," 99 *Michigan L. Rev.* 588, 618 [2000]). It is interesting to note that the Fifth Circuit's Emerson opinion wholly ignores this fact. See United States v. Emerson, 270 F.3d 203 (2001) .

75 Aymette v. State, 21 Tenn. 154, 158 (1840).

76 Wills, "To Keep and Bear Arms" at 62, 64. Williams, "Civic Republicanism and the Citizen Militia: The Terrifying Second Amendment," 101 *Yale L. J.* 551, 554 (hereinafter, Williams, "The Terrifying Second Amendment") ("The militia must be the people acting together, not isolated persons acting individually.").

77 Bliss v. Commonwealth, 12 Ky. 90, 2 Litt. 90 (1822).

78 Second Constitution of Kentucky (1799) Article 10 Section 23.

79 For example, see David B. Kopel, "The Second Amendment in the Nineteenth Century," 1998 *B.Y.U. L. Rev.* 1359, 1399.

80 Article 10, Section 23, of the Second Constitution of Kentucky, adopted in 1799, provides "[t]hat the rights of the citizens to bear arms in defense of themselves and the State shall not be questioned." Article 13, Section 25, of the Third Constitution of Kentucky (1850) sets forth "[t]hat the rights of the citizens to bear arms in defense of themselves and the State shall not be questioned; but the General Assembly may pass laws to prevent persons from carrying concealed weapons." See Poore, The Federal and State Consistutions, Colonial Charters and Organic Laws, Part I, pp. 667, 685 (2d ed. 1972).

81 Nunn v. Georgia, 1 Ga. (1 Kelly) 243 (1846).

82 Central to the reasoning of the court was a series of rhetorical questions:

"Questions under some of these amendments, it is true, can only arise under the laws and Constitution of the United States. But there are other provisions in them, which were never intended to be thus restricted, but were designed for the benefit of every citizen of the Union in all courts and in all places; and the people of the several States, in ratifying them in their respective State conventions, have virtually adopted them as beacon-lights to guide and control the action of their own legislatures, as well as that of Congress. If a well-regulated militia is *necessary* to the *security* of the State of Georgia and of the United States, is it competent for the General Assembly to take away this security, by disarming the people? What advantage would it be to tie up the hands of the national legislature, if it were in the power of the *States* to destroy this bulwark of defence? In solemnly affirming that a well-regulated militia is necessary to the *security* of a *free State,* and that, in order to train properly that militia, the unlimited right of the *people* to *keep* and *bear* arms shall not be impaired, are not the sovereign people of the State committed by this pledge to preserve this right inviolate? Would they not be recreant to themselves, to free government, and false to their own vow, thus voluntarily taken, to suffer this right to be questioned? If they hesitate or falter, is it not to concede (themselves being judges) that the safety of the States is a matter of indifference?

"Such, I apprehend, was never the meaning of the venerated statesman who recommended, nor of the people who adopted, this amendment."

83 Barron v. Baltimore, 32 U.S. (7 Peters) 243 (1833).

84 Joseph Story, *Commentaries on the Constitution of the United States,* § 1896 at 607–608 (2d ed. 1851) (1833).

85 Randy E. Barnett and Don B. Kates, "Under Fire: The New Consensus on the Second Amendment," 45 *Emory L. J.* 1139 (1996).

86 Joseph Story, *Commentaries on the Constitution of the United States* § 1896, at 607–608 (2d ed. 1851).

87 Marcus Cunliffe, *Soldiers and Civilians: The Martial Spirit in America,* 1775–1865 at 202–12 (1968) (hereinafter, Cunliffe, *Soldiers and Civilians*).

88 Act of Apr. 23, 1808, ch. 55, § 1, 2 stat. 490, 490. For an analysis of the law, see Cunliffe, *Soldiers and Civilians* at 193.

89 Uniform Militia Act of 1792, ch. 33, § 1, 1 Stat. 271, 271, *repealed by* Dick Act, ch. 196, 32 Stat. 775 (1903). For an analysis of the Uniform Militia Act of 1792, see Cunliffe, *Soldiers and Civilians* at 184; Weigley, *United States Army* at 93–94.

90 Weigley, *United States Army* at 204; Frederick Bernays Wiener, "The Militia Clause of the Constitution," 54 *Harvard L. Rev.* 181, 191 (1940).

91 Weigley, *United States Army* at 216–18.

92 Weigley, *United States Army* at 203–204.

93 The Dick Act, ch. 196, 32 Stat. 775 (1903); analyzed in Perpich, 496 U.S. at 342; Martha Derthick, *The National Guard in Politics,* 26–27 (1965); Frederick Bernays Wiener, "The Militia Clause of the Constitution," 54 *Harvard L. Rev.* 181, 193–96 (1940).

94 29 Op. Atty. Gen. 322 (1912).

95 Weigley, *United States Army* at 324–25.

96 The National Defense Act of June 3, 1916, 39 Stat. 166.

97 Weigley, *United States Army* at 344–50.

98 Act of June 15, 1933, 48 Stat. 153.

99 Frederick Bernays Wiener, "The Militia Clause of the Constitution," 54 *Harvard L. Rev.* 181, 209 (1940). Wiener comments "the 1933 Act proved conclusively that a well-regulated militia is impossible of attainment under the militia clause, and can be organized only by resort to the plenary and untrammeled powers under the army clause."

100 The dual enlistment system continues in force to this day. In the words of Justice Stevens, "[s]ince 1933 all persons who have enlisted in a State National Guard unit have simultaneously enlisted in the National Guard of the United States. . . . [U]nder the 'dual enlistment' provisions of the statute that have been in effect since 1933, a member of the Guard who is ordered to active duty in the federal service is thereby relieved of his or her status in the State Guard for the entire period of federal service." Perpich, 496 U.S. at 345–46.

101 Perpich, 496 U.S. at 346.

102 Ibid.

103 Weigley, *United States Army* at 505–506.

104 Consider, for example, Wills, "To Keep and Bear Arms" at 73 (citing Sanford Levinson, "The Embarrassing Second Amendment," 99 *Yale L. J.* 637, 657–59 (1991) and William Van Alstyne, "The Second Amendment and the Personal Right to Arms," 43 *Duke L. J.* 1236, 1255 (1994).

105 In other words, if Judge Bork is right on *Roe v. Wade,* then the NRA has no Second Amendment argument against the Brady law. Cf. Robert H. Bork, *The Tempting of America: The Political Seduction of the Law* 110 and passim (1990).

106 198 U.S. 45, 74–75 (1905).

107 For the new, pragmatic thesis, see Richard A. Posner, "Against Constitutional Theory," 73 *N.Y.U. L. Rev.* 1 (1998); Richard A. Posner, "The Problematics of Moral and Legal Theory," 111 *Harvard L. Rev.* 1637, 1640–42 (1998).

108 See County of Riverside v. McLaughlin, 500 U.S. 44, 60 (1991) (Scalia, J., dissenting), see also the thoughtful discussion in Lawrence Lessig, "Understanding Changed Readings: Fidelity and Theory," 47 *Stanford L. Rev.* 395, 397–98.

CHAPTER TWO: THE MILITIA IDEAL IN
THE AMERICAN REVOLUTIONARY ERA

1 One commentator, Eugene Volokh, argues that the structure of the Second Amendment is really not unusual after all. While no other provision in the Federal Bill of Rights features a "justification clause" [we prefer to label the Amendment's initial phrase a "purpose clause"], Volokh points out that such constructions were not uncommon in state bills of rights of the founding period. Eugene Volokh, "The Commonplace Second Amendment," 73 *N.Y.U. L. Rev.* 793 (1998). Those who profess at least initial confusion on account of the Amendment's seemingly unusual juxtaposition of clauses include Sanford Levinson and William Van Alstyne, whose views we analyze in detail in chapter 8.

2 Keith A. Ehrman and Denis A. Henigan, "The Second Amendment in the Twentieth Century: Have You Seen Your Militia Lately?" 15 *University of Dayton L. Rev.* 5 (1989); Andrew D. Herz, "Gun Crazy: Constitutional False Consciousness and Dereliction of Dialogic Responsibility," 75 *Boston University L. Rev.* 57 (1995); see also articles by Paul Finkelman, Steven J. Heyman, Michael C. Dorf, and Robert J. Spitzer, writing in the "Symposium on the Second Amendment: Fresh Looks," published in 76 *Chicago-Kent L. Rev.* at pages 195, 237, 291, and 349 (2000).

3 One of the most forceful expositors of this viewpoint is Eugene Volokh, "The Commonplace Second Amendment," 73 *N.Y.U. L. Rev.* 793 (1998).

4 Glenn Harlan Reynolds, "A Critical Guide to the Second Amendment," 62 *Tennessee L. Rev.* 461, 466–67 (1995), Randy Barnett and Don B. Kates, "Under Fire: The New Consensus on the Second Amendment," 45 *Emory L. J.* 1139 (1996), Stephen P. Halbrook, "Congress Interprets the Second Amendment:

Declarations by a Co-Equal Branch on the Individual Right to Keep and Bear Arms," 62 *Tennessee L. Rev.* 597, 598 (1995), and Joyce Lee Malcolm, "The Right of the People to Keep and Bear Arms: The Common Law Tradition," 10 *Hastings Constitutional Law Quarterly* 285, 314 (1983). By stating that individual rights interpreters of the Second Amendment view gun possession as "an entitlement immune from government curtailment," we do not mean to imply that all adherents of the individual rights view necessarily rule out reasonable government regulation of what they see as a protected activity. Preeminently, three of the most respected members of the orthodox legal academy to embrace an individual rights reading of the Second Amendment emphasize that this right—like the other individual rights protected in the first eight amendments—should be subject to reasonable regulation. Laurence H. Tribe and Akhil Reed Amar, "Well-Regulated Militias, and More," *N.Y. Times,* March 27, 2000, at A27; William Van Alstyne, "The Second Amendment and the Personal Right to Arms," 43 *Duke L. J.* 1236, 1253–54 (1994).

5   There were, of course, exceptions to this general consensus, chiefly among radicals at either end of the political spectrum. As discussed in chapter 3, some anti-federalists on the libertarian, anti-state margins favored a purely private right to arms even outside the context of militia service. And more influentially, some arch-federalists, including many veterans of the Revolutionary officer cadre did not consider the militia necessary (or even useful to) the preservation of national security. Weigley, *United States Army* at 80–81, 88 and see our discussion at 65–71. Alexander Hamilton went further; he did not believe the militia useful to the preservation of political liberty. Hamilton's view of the militia's utility to the conservation of liberty has much to do with his conception of the type of liberty sound government was designed to secure. To Hamilton, liberty meant no more than the ability of the financial and commercial classes to rely on a strong executive's ability to check the mobocracy, and to this end, the militia was hardly a useful tool at all, but rather a foil. But see Lance Banning, *The Jeffersonian Persuasion: Evolution of a Party Ideology* (1978) on the republican (Republican) conception of Hamilton's politics; and see generally Williams, "The Terrifying Second Amendment," on the importance of republicanism to the framers of the Second Amendment.

6   W. & M., Sess. 2, ch. 2 (1689) ("That the Subjects which are Protestants may have Arms for their Defence suitable to their Conditions, and as allowed by Law.") and U.S. Const. amend. II.

7   On the individualists' misuse and misunderstanding of historical source material, see Jack N. Rakove, "The Second Amendment: The Highest State of Originalism," 76 *Chicago-Kent L. Rev.* 103 (2000), and Saul Cornell, "Commonplace or Anachronism: The Standard Model, The Second Amendment, and the Problem of History in Contemporary Constitutional Theory," 16 *Const. Commentary* 221 (1999). Specifically, on the individualists' misunderstanding of the English Bill of Rights of 1689, see our discussion at 52–56 and Lois Schwoerer, "To Hold and Bear Arms: The English Perspective," 76 *Chicago-Kent L. Rev.*

27 (2000); on the individualists' misreading of Blackstone's Commentaries see Steven J. Heyman, *Natural Rights and the Second Amendment* 237, 252–60 (2000) and on the dubious relevance of Blackstone's constitutional theory to the American Bill of Rights see our discussion at 195–96, on the individualists' misreading of the floor debates in the First Congress concerning the future Second Amendment see our discussion infra 102–103, and on William Van Alsytne and Akhil Amar's historically problematic assertion of a Fourteenth Amendment right to arms see our discussion at 197–209.

8   The "standard model" label was first attached to the individualists' analysis of the Second Amendment by Professor Glenn Harlan Reynolds of the University of Tennessee School of Law. Glenn Harlan Reynolds, "A Critical Guide to the Second Amendment," 62 *Tennessee L. Rev.* 461, 463 (1995).

9   The "standard model," appears to have the endorsement of only one practicing academic historian, Joyce Lee Malcolm of Bentley College, an undergraduate business school in Massachusetts. Robert Shalhope of the University of Oklahoma, who was once cited with admiration by standard modelers, has recently subjected standard model history to stinging criticism. Apart from the controversial Michael Bellesiles, other noted eighteenth-century specialists to reject the standard model include Jack N. Rakove of Stanford University, Saul Cornell of Ohio State University, Don Higginbotham of the University of North Carolina, Paul Finkelman of the University of Tulsa College of Law, and Lois Schwoerer of George Washington University. Joyce Lee Malcolm, *To Keep and Bear Arms: The Origins of an Anglo-American Right* (1994); Robert E. Shalhope, "The Ideological Origins of the Second Amendment," 69 *Journal of American History* 599 (1982) (cited favorably by standard modelers); Shalhope, "To Keep and Bear Arms in the Early Republic," 16 *Constitutional Commentary* 269 (1999) (critical of the standard model); Michael Bellesiles, "Suicide Pact: New Readings of the Second Amendment," 16 *Constitutional Commentary* 247 (1999); Bellesiles, "The Second Amendment in Action," 76 *Chicago-Kent L. Rev.* 61 (2000); Jack N. Rakove, "The Second Amendment: The Highest State of Originalism," 76 *Chicago-Kent L. Rev.* 103 (2000); Saul Cornell, "Commonplace or Anachronism: The Standard Model, the Second Amendment, and the Problem of History in Contemporary Constitutional Theory," 16 *Constitutional Commentary* 221 (1999); Don Higginbotham, "The Second Amendment in Historical Context," 16 *Constitutional Commentary* 263 (1999); Paul Finkelman, "'A Well Regulated Militia': The Second Amendment in Historical Perspective," 76 *Chicago-Kent L. Rev.* 195 (2000); Lois Schwoerer, "To Hold and Bear Arms: The English Perspective," 76 *Chicago-Kent L. Rev.* 27 (2000). See also Lawrence Delbert Cress, "An Armed Community: The Origins and Meaning of the Right to Bear Arms," 71 *Journal of American History* 22 (1984) for an analysis incompatible with the standard model developed before the standard model had taken form. This is not to deny that a great many articles support the standard model. The point is that while some of these are written by reputable law professors, most are written by advocates, and (excepting only Malcolm's work and Shalhope's

earlier contributions) none are by historians, let alone specialists in eighteenth-century political thought.

10 The New Hampshire Ratifying Convention proposed amendments that appear to endorse a purely private as well as a militia-based right to arms. See our discussion in chapter 3.

11 We review and analyze other scattered expressions often cited in favor of a private rights reading of the Second Amendment in chapter 3.

12 James Madison, *The Debate in the Federal Convention of 1787 Which Framed the Constitution of the United States of America* 663–64 (Gaillard Hunt and James Brown Scott, eds., int'1 ed. 1920).

13 Robert E. Shalhope, "The Ideological Origins of the Second Amendment," 69 *Journal of American History* 599, 611 (1982). Shalhope, however, does not share our position that the right to keep and bear had no meaning outside the militia context.

14 Wills, "To Keep and Bear Arms" at 62, 64.

15 Joseph Story, *Commentaries on the Constitution of the United States* (1833) at 677. See also Cunliffe, *Soldiers and Civilians* at 177–212.

16 Joseph Story, *Commentaries on the Constitution of the United States* (2d ed. 1851) at 608.

17 See our discussion of Madison's conversion to the cause of a Bill of Rights and his role in drafting the Second Amendment at 90–95.

18 For an excellent summary of some the most influential approaches to originalism, see Jack Rakove's insightful introduction to his compendium, Jack Rakove, *Interpreting the Constitution: The Debate over Original Intent* 3–10 (1990). For a classic exposition of the viewpoint that we are expressly bound by the original meaning of constitutional and statutory text, see Antonin Scalia, *A Matter of Interpretation: Federal Courts and the Law* (1990) and the intelligent retorts of Gordon S. Wood, Laurence Tribe, Mary Ann Glendon, and Ronald Dworkin reprinted therein.

19 Gordon S. Wood, *The Creation of the American Republic, 1776–1787,* 4–10 (1969) (hereinafter, Wood, *Creation of the American Republic*).

20 Reflecting upon the momentous events of his youth, John Adams wrote to Jefferson in 1815, "[w]hat do we mean by the Revolution? The war? That was no part of the Revolution; it was only an effect and consequence of it. The Revolution was in the minds of the people, and this was effected, from 1760 to 1775, in the course of fifteen years before a drop of blood was shed at Lexington. The records of the thirteen legislatures, the pamphlets, the newspapers in all the colonies, ought to be consulted during that period to ascertain the steps by which the public opinion was enlightened and informed concerning the authority of Parliament over the colonies." (Cited in Bernard Bailyn, *The Ideological Origins of the American Revolution* 1 [1967] [hereinafter, Bailyn, *Ideological Origins*]).

21 Wood, *Creation of the American Republic* at viii–ix, 83–90, 593–615.

22 The terms *civic humanism* and *republicanism* connote different historical phases of what is essentially a single political ideology. They will be described in text to

follow. We use the first term, civic humanism, to refer to the political ideology of the Florentine Renaissance, as described particularly by J. G. A. Pocock in J. G. A. Pocock, *The Machiavellian Moment: Florentine Political Thought and the Atlantic Republican Tradition* 183–218. James Harrington expanded upon these Florentine principles during the English Commonwealth, and his political thought became known as classical republicanism. Ibid. at 381–422. By itself, the term *republican* has been used to refer to the entire system of thought from Machiavelli onward, but the term also refers more narrowly to the eighteenth-century American variant, which is described best in the first part of Gordon Wood's *Creation of the American Republic* 3–90.

23 On republicanism as the ideology that drove the American Revolution, see generally Douglas Adair, *Fame and the Founding Fathers* (1974); Bernard Bailyn, *Pamphlets of the American Revolution* (1965); Bernard Bailyn, *Ideological Origins;* H. Trevor Colbourne, *The Lamp of Experience, Whig History and the Intellectual Origins of the American Revolution* (1965); J. G. A Pocock, *Politics, Language, and Time: Essays on Political Thought and History* (1972) (hereinafter, Pocock, *Politics*); J. G. A. Pocock, *Machiavellian Moment,* and J. G. A. Pocock, *Three British Revolutions: 1644, 1688, 1776* (1980); Wood; and Caroline Robbins, "Men of Little Faith: The Anti-Federalists on the Nature of Representative Government," 8 *William and Mary Quarterly* 3d ser. 3. For historiographical reviews of scholarship on the American Revolution emphasizing the republican perspective, see Robert E. Shalhope, "Toward a Republican Synthesis: The Emergence of an Understanding of Republicanism in American Historiography," 29 *William and Mary Quarterly* 3d ser. 49 (1972) and Robert E. Shalhope, "Republicanism and Early American Historiography," 39 *William and Mary Quarterly* 3d ser. 334 (1982). For a countervailing perspective, arguing that overestimation of republicanism's role in late-eighteenth-century America has obscured a protocapitalist animus at the root of Jeffersonian democracy, see Joyce Appleby, *Capitalism and a New Social Order: The Republican Vision of the 1790s* (1984) (Appleby's title refers to Jefferson's party, not to the classically derived ideology); but see also John Ashworth, "The Jeffersonians: Classical Republicans or Liberal Capitalists?" 12 *Journal of American Studies* 425 (1984) for a trenchant critique of Appleby.

Apart from Appleby (see *Capitalism* [mentioned above] and Appleby, *Liberalism and Republicanism in the Historical Imagination* [1992]), most postrepublican revisionists still concede the centrality of republican ideology during the emotionally charged years before the Revolutionary War, but argue that republicanism loses its analytical incisiveness and even its meaning by being too widely applied as an explanation for every phenomenon of the Revolutionary period or, in extreme cases, for all of American history. See Daniel T. Rogers, "Republicanism: The Career of a Concept," 79 *Journal of American History* 11 (1992). Some commentators simply point out that liberal and republican modes of discourse co-mingled freely in Revolutionary America. See e.g. Isaac Kramnick, "The Great National Discussion: The Discourse of Politics in 1787," 45 *William and Mary Quarterly* 3d ser. 3 (1988) and James T. Kloppenberg, "The Virtues of

Liberalism: Christianity, Republicanism, and Ethics in Early American Political Discourse," 74 *Journal of American History* 9 (1987). Professor Timothy Breen, who once emphasized the republican Weltanschauung of Virginia planters during the 1760s, see Breen, *Tobacco Culture: The Mentality of the Great Tidewater Planters on the Eve of Revolution* (1985), goes further than most postrepublicans, and now argues that the New England boys of '75 were animated by "Lockean" conceptions of rights when they mustered outside Boston to fight the King's Army. See Breen, "The Lockean Moment: The Languages of Rights on the Eve of the American Revolution" (2001). Paul Rahe, in his monumental *Republics Ancient and Modern* (1994), argues that Pocock and company have seriously overstated the similarities between Greco-Roman political ideology and early modern republican discourse in England. On the whole, however, republicanism still stands as the dominant paradigm of Revolutionary era interpretation among historians. See Linda K. Kerber, "The Revolutionary Generation: Ideology, Politics, and Culture in the Early Republic," 34–37 in Eric Foner, ed., *The New American History* (1997). In the decade since Professor Rodgers announced the end of the concept's career, republican historical writing of the highest order has continued to flourish, and historians continue to build on the essential republican insights of Wood, Bailyn, and Pocock as they reshape and deepen our appreciation of the constitutional period. See e.g. Rakove, *Original Meanings: Politics and Ideas in the Making of the Constitution* (1996) at ix–x, 22, 35, and passim, Herbert E. Sloan, *Principle and Interest: Thomas Jefferson and the Problem of Debt,* 5–10 (1995); David N. Mayer, *The Constitutional Thought of Thomas Jefferson* (1995).

While we would not deny that liberalism figured alongside republicanism in American political discourse by the time of the ratification struggle, see our argument in chapter 7 at 162–66, or that liberalism colored Americans' understanding of most elements of the Bill of Rights in 1789–91, as we stress in chapter 7, the right to arms formed a peculiar exception, see 164–66. See also Cornell, "Commonplace or Anachronism," 230 and passim for the argument that "standard modellers" wrongly read libertarian principles of our own day into essentially civic and corporatists utterances of the late eighteenth century. The right was invoked almost exclusively in a republican idiom. Among antifederalists and federalists alike, the right to arms was discussed preeminently as a facet of the Whig/republican antiarmy paradigm. The few radical anti-federalists who discussed the right to arms as a private, libertarian entitlement failed to strike a chord, see our discussion at 81–85 (chapter 3) and Cornell, id., and their voices did not resonate with the ratifying public. Liberal analysis of the text and context of the Second Amendment fails not only the test of historical probability, but that of logic as well. See our discussion in chapter 7 at 162–66. Even if one were to accept Appleby's views of Jeffersonian economic theory, see Appleby, *Capitalism and a New Social Order: The Republican Vision of the 1790s* (1984)—and in fact, we find Drew McCoy's description of Jeffersonian political economy far more persuasive, see McCoy, *The Elusive*

Republic: Political Economy in Jeffersonian America (1980)—Applebyian liberalism simply cannot account for the collectivist, corporate terminology to which the right to arms was generally linked by the ratifying generation. Indeed, as Justice Story's *Commentaries* make clear, a republican understanding of the Second Amendment continued to hold sway in the antebellum years, long after Charles Sellers' market revolution was well underway, cf. Joseph Story, *Commentaries on the Constitution of the United States*, § 1897 at 608 (2d ed. 1851) (1833) and Sellers, *The Market Revolution: Jacksonian America*, 1815–46 (1991). Beginning in the 1980s, republicanism embarked upon a second career in the law schools, see e.g. Cass Sunstein, "Beyond the Republican Revival," 99 *Yale L. J.* 1539 (1989) (part of a special issue of the *Yale Law Journal* devoted to republicanism) and Wendy Brown, "Guns, Cowboys, Philadelphia Mayors, and Civic Republicanism," 99 *Yale L. J.* 661 (1989). Robert Shalhope, an eminent historian with a strong interest in constitutional theory, had written on the republican roots of the Second Amendment as early as 1982, see *The Ideological Origins of the Second Amendment*, but, by his own admission, he originally failed to stress sufficiently the Amendment's collective focus. Shalhope has recently refined his analysis. See Shalhope, *To Keep and Bear Arms in the Early Republic*, 16 *Constitutional Commentary* 221 (1999). Shalhope was the first established academic to address in detail the Second Amendment's republican foundations, but the legalist who has undertaken the most thoughtful analysis of the republican background of the right to arms is Professor David C. Williams of the University of Indiana School of Law. Williams has written several significant pieces on the Second Amendment. See Williams, "The Terrifying Second Amendment"; "The Militia Movement and the Second Amendment: Conjuring with the People," 81 *Cornell L. Rev.* 879 (1996); and "The Unitary Second Amendment," 73 *N.Y.U. L. Rev.* 822 (1998).

Like the team of Uviller and Merkel, Williams emphasizes the Amendment's deep roots in classical republican ideology. He stresses that under republican theory, the militia-of-the-whole both fostered and reflected the civic virtue of citizen soldiers drawn from (what was then at least ideally) an egalitarian, undifferentiated republic. Williams points out that this republican premise of social and economic homogeneity has been thoroughly repudiated by the subsequent American experience, and the growth of a multivalent polity reflective of numerous and varied interests. Similarly for Williams, the concept of civic virtue so central to republican thought is difficult to reconcile with the intensely individualistic and pluralistic political cultures of contemporary America. Having in significant measure rejected both civic virtue and a concomitant readiness to bind themselves to a sometimes onerous species of communal obligation, Americans are, according to Williams, ill-equipped to give meaning to the right to serve in the militia that the framers enshrined. This right then, unmoored from the political philosophy that leant it meaning when it was written into the constitutional charter, cannot be applied coherently today. Contemporary efforts to ground a universal right to arms in republican theory fail, because the partial "militias" of today—be they the National Guard, self-proclaimed libertarian units, or a putative unorganized body of all American gun owners—do not embody or represent the entire people, but only selective, specially interested, and not necessarily virtuous subparts of the nation. Despite the insurmountable problems associated with any effort to revive a universal militia or link a right to arms to a universal "unorganized" militia, Williams concludes (with a nod to the republican revivalists of the 1990s) that creative application of civic humanist values to other American constitutional questions (such as presidential war-making) is an approach worthy of serious consideration.

Clearly, Williams' perspective is not entirely dissimilar to our own. We join Williams in emphasizing the Amendment's unmistakable republican allusions; indeed, we go one step farther by stressing the Amendment's classical grammar and style as well as its neoclassical politics. And like Williams, it strikes us as incongruous—even unfaithful—to read into the Amendment's manifest collectivist purposes a private, post-Enlightenment, atavistic ideal. But we part company from Williams in that we root our constitutionalism of republican fidelity in the express terms of the Constitution and its Amendments. No doubt Williams is right that the Second Amendment is premised on concepts of virtue, and that their decay in modern America helps explain the Amendment's conceptual irrelevance to problems of gun control in contemporary society. Still, we prefer to base our argument for the Second Amendment's irrelevance to the issue of a universal, private entitlement to gun ownership on the language of the Amendment itself—language, that when ratified, was clearly intended (according to the overwhelming weight of evidence, contextually read and understood) to convey a militia-dependent right. The question for us is therefore not what happened to the right to arms when civic virtue (nowhere mentioned in the Constitution or Bill or Rights) perished from the face of the Earth, but what happened to the right to arms when the militia, on which that right depended, went out of business. Our conclusion, of course, is that the right to arms closed up shop as well.

In addition to—or, more frequently, in pointed opposition to—the Whig/republican heritage, many commentators invoke the name of John Locke. But in American historiography, the long-standing assumption that Locke was the dominant figure in eighteenth-century political thought, and the determinative influence behind the ideology of the Revolution, see Carl Becker, *The Declaration of Independence* (1940), did not survive focused, detailed probing of the pamphlets and papers of the Revolutionary period during the 1950s and 1960s which ushered in the republican historical revision. Pocock, *Politics* 107 ("the textbook account of Augustan political thought as Locke et praeterea nihil badly needs revision"). Locke's chief political influence, it emerged, flowed from his status as a representative Restoration era opposition thinker, not from any protoindividualism inherent in his political writings. See Bailyn, *Ideological Origins* 54. Moreover, Locke was known to the colonists not so much as a political theorist, but as the epistemologist behind the *Essay Concerning Human Understanding* (1690) and the pragmatist behind *The Thoughts Concerning Education* (1693). See Garry Wills, *Inventing America: Jefferson's Declaration of Independence 167–74* (1978) (hereinafter, Wills, *Inventing America*). Finally, it emerged during the 1980s that Locke was hardly a conservative individualist at all, that he had not written his *Treatises on Government* after the fact in the 1690s to provide the post-Settlement government with theoretical underpinnings, but instead had penned the *Second Treatise* as a revolutionary manifesto in support of the Rye House Plot of 1682–83, an abortive regicidal and communitarian combination spearheaded by Locke's patron, the radical Whig leader Earl Shaftsbury. See Richard Ashcraft, *Revolutionary Politics and Locke's Two Treatises of Government* 327 and passim (1986). We have a great deal more to say about Locke and his manifest (but not determinative) influence on the Revolutionary and Constitutional periods in chapters 7 and 8.

24 Banning, "Republican Ideology and the Triumph of the Constitution, 1789 to 1793," 31 *William and Mary Quarterly* 3d ser. 167, 178–79 (1974).

25 Wood, *Creation of the American Republic* at 65–70.

26 Ibid. at 28–36; Pocock, *Politics* at 93–94.

27 Pocock, *Politics* at 92–93.

28 Wood, *Creation of the American Republic* at 18–36; Pocock, *Politics* at 88.

29 Bailyn, *Ideological Origins* at 61–63.

30 Pocock, *Politics* at 126 (quoting *A Letter From a Parliament Man to His Friend* [1675], reprinted in 2 *State Tracts: Being a Collection of Several Treatises Relating to the Government, Privately Printed in the Reign of K. Charles II* 68 [London 1693]).

31 On the centrality of the possession of independent arms to the thought of James Harrington in the middle of the seventeenth century, see Pocock, *Politics* at 110.

32 Wood coins this phrase to refer to the political system of the Constitution, which he sees as Madison's innovative structural and federal resolution of the fatalistic and pessimistic aspect of the republican paradigm. Blending, checks and balances, phased and filtered elections, judicial review, and enumerated powers rendered possible a survivable polity composed of less than virtuous citizens. Wood, *American Republic* at 593–618.

33 Pocock, *Machiavellian Moment* at 156–218. Richard B. Morris likewise notes the debt to Machiavelli and the classical republican ideal of civic virtue in a short but rich essay. Richard B. Morris, "The Origin and Framing of the American Constitution," 9 *Revue Internationale D'Histoire Militaire* 41 (1990).

34 Pocock, *Politics* at 81–90.

35 Ibid. at 85–86.

36 Pocock, *Machiavellian Moment* at 156–218, and Pocock, *Politics* at 88.

37 Pocock, *Machiavellian Moment* at 201–203, 386.

38 In the next century, Francis Bacon echoed Machiavelli's views, commenting that a prince who depends upon professional soldiers "may spread his feathers for a time, but he will mew them soon after," quoted in Lois G. Schwoerer,

"No Standing Armies!" The Antiarmy Ideology in Seventeenth-Century England 10 (1974) (hereinafter "Schwoerer, *No Standing Armies*") from Francis Bacon, *Of the True Greatness of Kingdoms and Estates*, reprinted in 6 James Spedding, ed, et al. *The Works of Sir Francis Bacon* 446 (1858).

39 Pocock, *Machiavellian Moment* at 413–15.

40 Pocock, *Politics* at 90–93, and especially 112–14 on the importance of independently furnished arms; Garry Wills, *Cincinnatus: George Washington and the Enlightenment* 225–30 (1984) on the image of Cincinnatus.

41 Pocock, *Machiavellian Moment* at 210–11.

42 See Schwoerer, *No Standing Armies*, for a detailed study of antiarmy and pro-militia ideals in English political thought from the sixteenth through eighteenth centuries (theme of book). Schwoerer discusses evidence of Machiavelli's influence on English early modern antiarmy thought, ibid. at 17–18. But one underestimates Machiavelli's influence in the English-speaking world by dwelling on his reception into English political thought during his own lifetime. He became much more familiar to readers on both sides of the Atlantic through translations by the arch-republican Henry Neville titled *The Works of the Famous Nicholas Machiavel, Citizen and Secretary of Florence, including The Discourses, The Florentine History and The Arte of Warre*, published in 1680, 1694, and 1695, and reprinted throughout the eighteenth century in England, Scotland, and America. Schwoerer, *No Standing Armies* at 114–15.

43 This phrase gained currency with the publication of Professor Michael Roberts Inaugural Lecture The Military Revolution, 1560–1660, delivered at Queens University, Belfast in January 1955. Geoffrey Parker expands on Roberts' ideas in *The Military Revolution: Military Innovation and the Rise of the West, 1550–1800* (1984) (hereinafter, Parker, *The Military Revolution*). Parker summarizes Roberts' historiographical influence at 1–5.

44 Parker, *The Military Revolution* at 14–28, discussing professionalization and expansion of armies in the context of technological changes, in particular, the advent of commercial credit, the coming of siege artillery, the rise of "horizontally" designed siege-resistant fortification, and the triumph of archers and gunners over cavalry on the battlefield.

45 Schwoerer, *No Standing Armies* at 16–18 regarding England's reception of neo-classical and Renaissance attitudes toward soldiers, and ibid. at 12 regarding English isolation from the military revolution. Parker points out that England made limited experiments implementing progressive fortification design under the Tudors (Parker, *The Military Revolution* at 26–28) and thus dates the arrival of the military revolution in England to the sixteenth century. Parker, *The Military Revolution* at xiv. But for present purposes, the important consideration is that large, professional armies were not introduced into the British Isles until Cromwell's time. Schwoerer, *No Standing Armies* at 52.

46 Schwoerer, *No Standing Armies* at 10–12.

47 Ibid. at 14; 6 *New English Dictionary* 438 (Sir James A. H. Murray, ed. 1908).

48 Schwoerer, *No Standing Armies* at 14.

49   Ibid.

50   Ibid. at 12.

51   For the divine right theory expounded by the first two Stuarts, see James VI of Scotland (James I of England in 1601), *The True Law of Free Monarchies* (1598) and *Basilikon Doron* (1599), and Charles I, *Eikon Basilikon* (1649) (possibly ghost-written by Dr. John Gauden), three classic (and self-interested) early tracts on absolutism.

52   On the contemporary and subsequent celebration of an Elizabethan "golden age," see Frances A. Yates, *Astraea: The Imperial Theme in the Sixteenth Century* 29–87 (1975) and Roy Strong, *The Cult of Elisabeth I: Elisabethan Portraiture and Pagentry* passim (1977). The golden image was designed in part to flatter and persuade while Elisabeth yet reigned. Later, invocation of an Elisabethan golden age became implicitly a critique of James I. William Camden's enormously influential *Annales . . . Regnante Elisabetha . . . ad Annum 1589* (2 parts 1615 and 1627), was hugely popular at the time also in English translation. A modern translation was published as William Camden, *The History of Princess Elisabeth, Selected Chapters* (Wallace McCaffrey, ed. 1970).

53   G. M. Trevelyan, *England under the Stuarts* (1904), still the classic history of seventeenth-century England, and J. P. Sommerville, *Politics And Ideology in England, 1603–1640* (1986). Schwoerer, *No Standing Armies,* presents a good specialized study of military politics in seventeenth-century England.

54   Lacey Baldwin Smith, *The Realm of England,* 1399–1688 at 206–15 (1983) (hereinafter, Smith, *The Realm of England*); Schwoerer, *No Standing Armies* at 3–4.

55   Schwoerer, *No Standing Armies* at 20.

56   Smith, *The Realm of England* at 217–25.

57   Ibid. at 222–25.

58   Ibid. at 225–29.

59   Ibid. at 229–33.

60   Garry Wills, *Cincinnatus: George Washington and the Enlightenment* 133–37 (1984); Bailyn, *Ideological Origins* at 34.

61   Pocock, *Machiavellian Moment* at 410.

62   Bailyn, *Ideological Origins* at 34.

63   Wood, *Creation of the American Republic* at 15–17, 20, 41–43.

64   The description of the postwar years of Confederation government as a critical period, during which fundamental questions of union, order, and liberty hung in the balance, gained currency through the publication of John Fiske, *The Critical Period of American History, 1783–1789* (1896). This image was famously reassessed in Merril Jensen, *The New Nation, A History of the United States During the Confederation, 1781–1789* (1950).

65   Wood, *Creation of the American Republic* at 404–405, 410–411 on the emerging federalist conception that unchecked populism imperiled established rights and liberties and 537–40 on the anti-federalist reliance on traditional Whig theory to attack the proposed Constitution and urge a bill of rights.

66   Pocock, *Machiavellian Moment* at 372–76. On the ideological ambiguities at the

heart of the New Model Army's changing sense of mission, see generally Schwoerer, *No Standing Armies* at 51–71.

67 Christopher Hill, *God's Englishman: Oliver Cromwell and the English Revolution* 76–77 (1970); Schwoerer, *No Standing Armies* at 51–52.

68 This phrase, referring to nostalgia for the Commonwealth among Civil War veterans unhappy with subsequent counter-republican developments, occurs commonly in the academic literature, for example, A. H. Woolrych, "The Good Old Cause and the Fall of the Protectorate," 13 *Cambridge History Journal* 133 (1957); J. G. A. Pocock, "James Harrington and the Good Old Cause: A Study of the Ideological Context of his Writings," 10 *Journal of British Studies* 30 (1970). It has its origins in the influential Humble Petition of Several Colonels of the Army of 1654 that referred to the "good cause . . . that old cause mentioned in our publicke Declarations and Engagements," see J. G. A. Pocock, "James Harrington and the Good Old Cause: A Study of the Ideological Context of his Writings," 10 *Journal of British Studies* 30, 33 (1970).

69 In Cromwell's famous words "I had rather have a plain russet-coated captain that knows what he fights for and loves what he knows than what you call a gentleman and is nothing else. I honour a gentleman that is so indeed . . . If you chose godly honest men to be captains of horse, honest men will follow them. . . . A few honest men are better than numbers." Quoted in Christopher Hill, *God's Englishman: Oliver Cromwell and the English Revolution* 74 (1970).

70 G. E. Aylmer, *Rebellion or Revolution: England from Civil War to Restoration* 94–102 (1986); Schwoerer, *No Standing Armies* at 71. But see also the following from an anonymous radical pamphleteer: "It is our conquest, not the Army's: the Army being considered as the people's power, chosen by the people, paid by the people, entrusted with the people's welfare and defence, acting all–hitherto they have done and we hope shall–for the good, liberty and freedom of the people. By 'people' is meant the sound, well-affected part, the rest are the conquered subdued part, who can challenge no right in the free election, which is the fruit of conquest." Anon., *The Extent of the Sword* (1653–54), quoted in Christopher Hill, *God's Englishman: Oliver Cromwell and the English Revolution* 79 (1970).

71 Pocock, *Machiavellian Moment* at 413.

72 Schwoerer, *No Standing Armies* at 196 on American opposition to standing armies in the run up to the Revolution, and at 189 on that opposition's roots in the antiarmy reaction during the interregnum.

73 David Underdown, "Settlement in the Counties 1653–1658," in *The Interregnum: The Quest for Settlement 1646–1660,* 165–82 (G. E. Aylmer ed.1990); Schwoerer, *No Standing Armies* at 62–63.

74 John Milton, *The Ready and Easy Way to Establish a Free Commonwealth (1660),* according to the *Oxford Companion to English Literature* (5th ed. 1985), "a last minute attempt to defend the 'Good old Cause' of Republicanism and to halt the growing tide of royalism and the defection of 'the misguided and abused multitude.'" The extent to which Milton's great later works *Paradise Lost (1667), Para-*

dise Regained (1671), and *Samson Agonistes (1671)* served as allegories of the vanished Commonwealth is, of course, the subject of varied interpretations. For an excellent recent discussion of the political implications of Milton's writings, see David Norbrooke, *Writing the English Republic: Poetry, Rhetoric and Politics 1627–60* at 109–39 and 433–98 (1999).

75   Pocock, *Machiavellian Moment* at 361–422, and Pocock, *Politics* at 104–47.

76   Bailyn, *Ideological Origins* at 38–44.

77   Parker, *The Military Revolution* at 62.

78   Smith, *The Realm of England* at 266–71.

79   Schwoerer, *No Standing Armies* at 136–47.

80   Lois G. Schwoerer, *The Declaration of Rights, 1689* at 289–90 (1981) (hereinafter, Schwoerer, *Declaration*).

81   *Convention Parliament, The Declaration of the Lords Spiritual and Temporal, and Commons, Assembled at Westminster* (12 Feb. 1688), reprinted in Jack N. Rakove, *Declaring Rights, A Brief History with Documents* 41–45 (1998) and William III, *His Majesties gracious Answer, to the Declaration of Both Houses* (15 Feb. 1688), reprinted in Jack N. Rakove, *Declaring Rights, A Brief History with Documents* 45 (1998); and see generally Smith at 303–306. The Declaration of Rights, with some modifications, became statute with the passing of the Bill of Rights on December 16, 1689, Schwoerer, *Declaration* at 3.

82   Schwoerer, *No Standing Armies* at 136–46.

83   *Convention Parliament, The Declaration of the Lords Spiritual and Temporal, and Commons, Assembled at Westminster* (12 Feb. 1688), reprinted in Jack N. Rakove, *Declaring Rights, A Brief History with Documents* 41 (1998).

84   Schwoerer, *Declaration* at 7, 291 and passim.

85   Ibid. at 267.

86   Ibid. at 126–27, 25–26.

87   Ibid. at 267–80.

88   Ibid. at 28.

89   Joyce Lee Malcolm, "The Right of the People to Keep and Bear Arms: The Common Law Tradition," 10 *Hastings Constitutional Law Quarterly* 285 (1983) notes that the right to arms remains part of the British constitutional edifice to this day. But she does not remark that this right has not interfered with any subsequent parliament's ability to place stringent curbs on ownership and use of firearms, most recently with the Firearms (Amendment) Act, 1997, ch. 5 (U.K.), outlawing ownership of handguns in the wake of the Dunblane Primary School massacre.

90   *The Heads of Grievances, Art. 5,* reprinted as Appendix 2 in Schwoerer, *Declaration* at 299. This article refers to the restoration militia acts, which confirmed royal command of the militia, royal appointment of officers in the militia, and royal use of martial law to compel the militia to engage in objectionable and allegedly illegal acts, such as confiscation of arms held by subjects deemed opposed to the king or his military and religious policies. Ibid. at 76. Shifting

command of the militia (and indeed, command of the Army and the power to make war) from king to Parliament were among the radical Whig objectives left unfulfilled by the Glorious Revolution. Ibid. at 289.

91　*The Heads of Grievances, Art. 7,* reprinted as Appendix 2 in Schwoerer, *Declaration* at 299.

92　Joyce Lee Malcolm, "The Right of the People to Keep and Bear Arms: The Common Law Tradition," 10 *Hastings Constitutional Law Quarterly* 285, 307–312 (1983).

93　Schwoerer, *Declaration* at 23.

94　Ibid. 23–25 (1981).

95　Ibid. at 284–85 (1981).

96　Ibid. at 284–87 (1981).

97　An Act Declaring the Rights and Liberties of the Subject and Settling the Succession of the Crown (English Bill of Rights), 1689, 1 W. & M., Sess. 2, ch. 2, 7 (Eng.).

98　Henry Horwitz, *The Parliamentary Diary of Narcissus Luttrell, 1691–1693* at 444 (1972), cited in Lois Schwoerer, "To Hold and Bear Arms: The English Perspective," 76 *Chicago-Kent L. Rev.* 27, 51 (2000).

99　Lois Schwoerer, "To Hold and Bear Arms: The English Perspective," 76 *Chicago-Kent L. Rev.* 27, 50–51 (2000).

100　An Acte Corcerninge Crossbowes and Handguns, 33 Hen. VII Ch. 6, reprinted in *The Statutes of the Realm,* 832–33 (London, 1817), and, for game acts and other statutes controlling gun possession subsequent to the Bill of Rights see 4 William Blackstone, *Commentaries on the Laws of England,* 175 (Chicago, 1979), P. B. Munsche, *Gentlemen and Poachers: The English Game Laws* 1671–1831, 8–27 (1981).

101　Weeks after passage of the Bill of Rights, Parliament voted to disarm Catholics, and in 1693, the Commons voted 169 to 65 to reject an amendment to pending game legislation that would have annulled existing class-based gun ownership restrictions and allowed all Protestants to keep guns. It is in this context that Sir John Lowther, M.P., commented that the proposal would "arm the mob, which I think is not very safe for any government." Lois Schwoerer, "To Hold and Bear Arms: The English Perspective," 76 *Chicago-Kent L. Rev.* 27, 50–51 (2000).

102　Thomas J. Curry, *The First Freedoms: Church and State in America to the Passage of the First Amendment* 142–48 (1986). Curry describes Madison's efforts to defeat a proposed assessment giving state government support to clergy of denominations specified by taxpayers and Madison's subsequent stewardship of Jefferson's Virginia Statute for Religious Freedom through the Assembly. In Madison's Virginia, antipopery was still a recognizable and forceful paradigm, but as Curry explains, the Virginia gentry of Madison's youth were confident enough to take toleration for granted. Madison himself moved one step further and led the vanguard of reformers in advocating complete disestablishment.

103 The suspicion that Catholics were beholden to subversive, alien authority was founded on more than paranoia and prejudice. In 1689, the Bill of Rights expressly required office holders and oath takers to abjure the papal doctrine immunizing assassins of Protestant heads of state and commanding Catholics residing in Protestant-governed lands to rise in resistance to local authority. An Act Declaring the Rights and Liberties of the Subject and Settling the Succession of the Crown (English Bill of Rights), 1689, 1 W. & M., Sess. 2, ch. 2, 15 (Eng.).

104 For a detailed but impressionistic account of anti-Catholicism in early America, see William Lee Miller, *The First Liberty: Religion and the American Republic* 280–82, passim (1986). As Miller makes clear, American anti-Catholicism flourished as a subspecies of nativism from the 1830s onward. Ibid. at 275–77, 283–84. But this anti-Catholic ideology differed fundamentally from the historically rooted Anglo-American anti-Catholicism nurtured in the English Civil War and hardened by the Popish Plot and Exclusion crisis. It is this earlier incarnation of anti-Catholicism, with all of its overtones of whiggish constitutionalism, that was on the wane by 1775 as whiggery blended into Enlightenment rights theory. But see J. C. E. Clark, *The Language of Liberty, 1660–1832: Political Discourse and Social Dynamics in the Anglo-American World* 296–381 (1994). Clark argues that anti-Catholicism played a determining role in the decision to separate from Britain, with particular reference to, among other issues, the opposition of the Virginia gentry to the proposed establishment of an Anglican bishopric in the 1770s, ibid. at 344, and the opposition of New Englanders and Presbyterians throughout the colonies to the Quebec Act of 1774 making Catholicism the official religion of that province, ibid. at 360, both of which resistance movements cast British policy toward the colonies in the light of popish plots. On the New England response to the Quebec Act, see William Lee Miller, *The First Liberty: Religion and the American Republic* 280–82 (1986). For the purposes of the Quebec Act, the territories in which British authorities recognized the establishment of the Roman religion extended far beyond Quebec proper southward past St. Louis to present-day Cairo and westward some miles further than Duluth, thus encompassing over half the habitable surface of British North America. Lawrence Henry Gipson, *The Coming of the Revolution, 1763–1775* at 130–31 (1954) (hereinafter, Gipson, *Coming of the Revolution*).

105 Wood, *Creation of the American Republic* at 506–10. Wood makes this point with reference to social and political leadership; his insights are especially applicable in the case of the military.

106 Ibid. at 602–15 and our discussion at notes 318–26 and accompanying text. Again, Wood's discussion is cast in terms of the polity as a whole, but it is particularly relevant to the military situation.

107 These points are developed in chapter 3 at 78–81.

108 William B. Willcox and Walter L. Arnstein, *The Age of Aristocracy, 1688 to 1830* at 62–64 (4th ed. 1983).

109 Bailyn, *Ideological Origins* at 35–36.

110 The Real Whigs, or Old Whigs, disassociated themselves from the Court Whigs in the 1690s and clung to the principles of 1689. As Lois Schwoerer explains, after coming to power with the accession of William and Mary:

> Court Whigs . . . became increasingly conservative. They resisted the efforts of Tories to link them with republican notions, deism, and popular rights and to tar them with the charge of "deposing" James II. . . . Old Whigs joined with Country Tories to form a "New Country Party," which generally reiterated the arguments of the right of resistance, the contractual basis of government, and the sovereignty of the people (however "people" was defined) that had appeared in debates and tracts at the time of the revolution. [By 1710, when Court Whigs forsook the Dissenters in favor of Court Tories to form a majority,] the bankruptcy of Court Whiggism was laid bare. Debate on "revolution principles" was no longer the focus. Passive obedience to Parliament and parliamentary sovereignty became official Whig doctrine with the success of the Septennial Act of 1716 and the ascendancy of Sir Robert Walpole. For their part Country Whigs and Country Tories denounced "corruption" and oligarchy.

Schwoerer, *No Standing Armies* at 290. Real Whiggery survived as an extra-parliamentary opposition movement in Hanoverian England, long after Toryism became dormant.

111 Lance Banning, *The Jeffersonian Persuasion: Evolution of a Party Ideology* 71–72 (1978).

112 Bernard Bailyn, *Pamphlets of the American Revolution, 1750–1776* (1965). See especially Bailyn, *Ideological Origins* at 22–54, where Bailyn consolidates and summarizes the ideology of the hundreds of pamphlets he had studied. See also Lance Banning, *The Jeffersonian Persuasion: Evolution of a Party Ideology* 72–73, 75 (1978).

113 Bailyn, *Ideological Origins* at 35–36, 61–63, 112–19.

114 Ibid. at 36; Schwoerer, *No Standing Armies* at 195–96.

115 Bailyn, *Ideological Origins* at 62.

116 John Trenchard, *Argument, Shewing, that a Standing Army Is Inconsistent with a Free Government, and Absolutely Destructive to the Constitution of the English Monarchy* (London 1697). The significance of this pamphlet in its original context is described in Schwoerer, *No Standing Armies* at 174–75. In 1697, in the aftermath of the War of the Grand Alliance, Trenchard and his Real Whig allies campaigned successfully to reduce drastically the scale of King William's wartime army.

117 Bailyn, *Ideological Origins* at 62 (quoting John Trenchard, *Argument, Shewing, that a Standing Army Is Inconsistent with a Free Government, and Absolutely Destructive to the Constitution of the English Monarchy* [London 1697]).

118 Bailyn, *Ideological Origins* at 64–65; Wood, *Creation of the American Republic* at 30. Wood writes:

> In the course of a single year both Sweden and Poland had been enslaved, leaving on the continent only the Swiss cantons and the Dutch provinces

free; and their liberty appeared short lived. "Where is the kingdom," devout Whigs asked, "that does not groan under the calamities of military tyranny?"

Ibid. (quoting Jonathan W. Austin, *An Oration Delivered March 5th, 1778* [Boston 1778]). But the military overthrow of the Danish republic in 1660, as described in Robert Molesworth's An Account of Denmark (reprinted ten times in British North America during the eighteenth century), was the colonists' favorite example of the dangers inherent in maintenance of large standing armies. Schwoerer, *No Standing Armies* at 190.

119 Bailyn, *Ideological Origins* at 63.

120 John Allen, *An Oration, upon the Beauties of Liberty, or the Essential Rights of the Americans* at xiii–xiv (Boston 1773) (quoted in Robert E. Shalhope, "The Ideological Origins of the Second Amendment," 69 Journal of American History 599, 606 [1982]).

121 Richard Price, *Observations on the Importance of the American Revolution, and the Means of Making It a Benefit to the Rest of the World*, 16, 69 (London, 1784) quoted in Robert E. Shalhope, "The Ideological Origins of the Second Amendment," 69 *Journal of American History* 599, 605 (1982).

122 Josiah Quincy Jr., *Observations on the Act of Parliament, Commonly Called the Boston Port Bill; with thoughts on Civil Society and Standing Armies* (Boston 1774) (quoted in Bailyn, *Ideological Origins* at 61).

123 Bailyn, *Ideological Origins* at 61 (quoting Thomas Jefferson, *A Summary View of the Rights of British America* [1774], reprinted in 1 *The Papers of Thomas Jefferson* 121, 134).

124 Schwoerer, *No Standing Armies* at 191.

125 Bailyn, *Ideological Origins* at 63–64.

126 Lawrence Delbert Cress, *Citizens in Arms: The Army and the Militia in American Society to the War of 1812*, at 3–8 (1982); Pocock, *Politics* at 506–11.

127 Daniel J. Boorstin, *The Americans: The Colonial Experience* 345–69 (1958), for a fascinating impressionistic account of the tension between centrifugal individualism and the metropolitan and provincial governments' quests for organization that characterized the colonial militias. Boorstin reports that only in the immediate frontier environment of the earliest settlements was the organizational impulse readily accepted by the population.

128 For ample evidence that militia attendance was rarely, if ever, enforced in the decades before the Revolution, and of growing popular indifference to militia service (at least away from the frontier), see Michael A. McDonnell, *The Politics of War: Popular Mobilization and Political Culture in Revolutionary Virginia* (forthcoming, University of North Carolina Press for the Omohundru Institute of Early American History and Culture).

129 Lawrence Delbert Cress, *Citizens in Arms: The Army and the Militia in American Society to the War of 1812* at 3 (1982).

130 Michael A. Bellesiles, "Gun Laws in Early America: The Regulation of Firearms Ownership, 1607–1794," 16 *Law and History Review* 566, 577 (1998).

131 See our discussion below at note 78 for chapter 4, and note 54 for chapter 6.

132 Michael A. Bellesiles, "Gun Laws in Early America: The Regulation of Fire-arms Ownership, 1607–1794," 16 *Law and History Review* 566, 580, 582–83 (1998).

133 Weigley, *United States Army* at 14–16.

134 Ibid. at 16; Daniel J. Boorstin, *The Americans: The Colonial Experience* 358–60 (1958).

135 Lawrence Delbert Cress, *Citizens in Arms: The Army and the Militia in American Society to the War of 1812* at 3 (1982).

136 Weigley, *United States Army* at 16.

137 Letter from George Washington to Colonel John Stanwix (July 15, 1757), in 2 *The Writings of George Washington* 96, 97 (John C. Fitzpatrick ed. 1931–44).

138 George Washington, *General Instructions to all the Captains of Companies* (July 29, 1757), in 2 *The Writings of George Washington* at 109, 114.

139 Daniel J. Boorstin, *The Americans: The Colonial Experience* 361 (1958); J. G. A. Pocock, "Political Thought in the English-Speaking Atlantic, 1760–1790: The Imperial Crises," in *The Varieties of British Political Thought, 1500–1800* at 246, 259 (J. G. A. Pocock et al. eds. 1996).

140 Don Higginbotham, *The War of American Independence, Military Attitudes, Policies, and Practice 1763–1789* at 21 (1983).

141 Gipson, *Coming of the Revolution* at 55 (1954).

142 Ibid. at 34 (1954).

143 Ibid. at 33 (1954).

144 Ibid. at 57–59 (1954).

145 Edmund S. Morgan, *Birth of the Republic, 1763–1789* at 36 (3d. ed. 1992).

146 Don Higginbotham, *The War of American Independence, Military Attitudes, Policies, and Practice 1763–1789* at 14 (1983).

147 Robert Middlekauf, *The Glorious Cause: The American Revolution, 1763–1789* at 132 (1982).

148 Lawrence Delbert Cress, *Citizens in Arms: The Army and the Militia in American Society to the War of 1812* at 34–35 (1982).

149 Ibid.; Bailyn, *Ideological Origins* at 43–46.

150 For a succinct summary, see Edmund S. Morgan, *Birth of the Republic, 1763–1789* at 54 (3d. ed. 1992).

151 Robert Middlekauf, *The Glorious Cause: The American Revolution, 1763–1789* at 151 (1982).

152 Gipson, *Coming of the Revolution* at 189–90 (1954).

153 Don Higginbotham, *The War of American Independence, Military Attitudes, Policies, and Practice 1763–1789* at 16–17 (1983).

154 On the special situation in Florida, Georgia, and South Carolina, see Lawrence Delbert Cress, *Citizens in Arms: The Army and the Militia in American Society to the War of 1812* at 47 (1982).

155 Ibid. at 3–4, 8–11 (1982).

156 Ibid. at 13 (1982); on New York, see Robert Middlekauf, *The Glorious Cause: The American Revolution, 1763–1789* at 144–45 (1982), and on Massachusetts, see Don

Higginbotham, *The War of American Independence, Military Attitudes, Policies, and Practice 1763–1789* at 39–44 (1983).

157 *Sixteenth Report of the Boston Record Commissioners* 263 (1768) (quoted in Bailyn, *Ideological Origins* at 113).

158 Letter from Rev. Andrew Eliot to Thomas Hollis (Sept. 27, 1768), in 4 *Massachusetts Historical Society Collections* 428 (4th ser.) (quoted in Bailyn, *Ideological Origins* at 114).

159 Bailyn, *Ideological Origins* at 43–46.

160 Richard Ashcraft, *Revolutionary Politics and Locke's Two Treatises of Government* 291–333 (1986), and on the Americans' application of this history to the late imperial constitutional crisis, Lawrence Delbert Cress, *Citizens in Arms: The Army and the Militia in American Society to the War of 1812* at 35–36 (1982).

161 Bailyn, *Ideological Origins* at 112–19.

162 Ibid. at 114.

163 Robert Middlekauf, *The Glorious Cause: The American Revolution, 1763–1789* at 232–33 (1982).

164 Ibid. at 200–203 (1982).

165 Edmund S. Morgan, *Birth of the Republic, 1763–1789* at 43, 46, 50–51 (3d. ed. 1992); and Gipson, *Coming of the Revolution* at 190–91, 200, 205, 208 (1954).

166 Bailyn, *Ideological Origins* at 117–18.

167 Ibid. at 118–19.

168 Robert W. Tucker and David C. Hendrickson, *The Fall of the First British Empire: Origins of the War of American Independence* 327–28 (1982).

169 Don Higginbotham, *The War of American Independence, Military Attitudes, Policies, and Practice 1763–1789* at 50 (1983).

170 Ibid. at 10, 45 (1983); on Massachusetts, see Robert Middlekauf, *The Glorious Cause: The American Revolution, 1763–1789* at 256 (1982); on Virginia, Robert Middlekauf, *The Glorious Cause: The American Revolution, 1763–1789* at 259 (1982).

171 Don Higginbotham, *The War of American Independence, Military Attitudes, Policies, and Practice 1763–1789* at 46 (1983).

172 Robert Middlekauf, *The Glorious Cause: The American Revolution, 1763–1789* (1982).

173 For a rather bloody and macabre account, see Robert Middlekauf, *The Glorious Cause: The American Revolution, 1763–1789* at 269–70 (1982).

174 *The Toll of Independence: Engagements and Battle Casualties in the American Revolution* (Howard Peckham ed., 3d ed. 1974).

175 Letter from George Washington to the President of Congress (Dec. 16, 1776), in 6 *The Writings of George Washington* 379–80 (John C. Fitzpatrick ed., 1931–44).

176 Weigley, *United States Army* at 31–36.

177 Letter from George Washington to the President of Congress (Sept. 24, 1776), in 6 *The Writings of George Washington* 110, 112 (John C. Fitzpatrick ed., 1931–44).

178 Letter from George Washington to the President of Congress (Sept. 15, 1780), in 20 *The Writings of George Washington* 49–50 (John C. Fitzpatrick ed., 1931–44).

179 *The Federalist No. 25* at 195 (Alexander Hamilton) (Isaac Kramnick ed., 1987).

180 Weigley, *United States Army* at 33.

181   Ibid. at 35.

182   Ibid. at 39–42, 67–68.

183   Wood, *American Republic* at 398–403.

184   Letter from George Washington to the President of Congress (Sept. 24, 1776), in 6 *The Writings of George Washington* 112 (John C. Fitzpatrick ed., 1931–44).

185   Weigley, *United States Army* at 75.

CHAPTER THREE: MADISONIAN STRUCTURALISM:
THE PLACE OF THE MILITIA IN THE NEW
AMERICAN SCIENCE OF GOVERNMENT

1   U.S. Const., art. 1, sec. 8.

2   Although the constitutional formulation may not have satisfied anti-federalists, actually it reserved greater powers to the states than appears at first glance. The states retained authority to (1) organize their militia as they saw fit should Congress fail to act to establish uniform rules, (2) arm their militia when Congress failed to do so, and (3) deploy their militia however they wanted whenever it was not called up into federal service. As things turned out, these contingent powers were substantial, because the federal government never did much (except spend money) under its militia powers in the early national period. So despite the Constitution's delegation of militia powers to Congress, to the extent that it had any life at all, the militia continued to be principally a creature of the states' control. The principal military authority the states lost with the transition from Confederation to constitutional government was their effective veto over federal requisitions of manpower and money. Under the old regime, Congress could command military contributions in terms of men and manpower from the states, and these requisitions were mandatory in theory, but they took effect only when and if state legislatures severally voted to conscript and tax. This they almost never did, which was why Hamilton was suggesting military intervention to collect army funds in 1781.

3   Cunliffe, *Soldiers and Civilians* at 180.

4   This document is set out in John McAuley Palmer, *Three War Statesmen: Washington, Lincoln, Wilson* 375–96 (1930).

5   Ibid. 393; Cunliffe, *Soldiers and Civilians* at 81.

6   For commentary on today's self-styled "militia," see Garry Wills, "The Militias: The New Revolutionaries," *N.Y. Review of Books,* August 10, 1995, which features an arresting photograph of the South Michigan Regional Militia Wolverines 14th Brigade, 4th Division, on a training exercise with dangerous dogs. Justice Scalia has also had occasion to take note of the Michigan militia. While discussing the insurrectionist favorite, Joyce Lee Malcolm's *To Keep and Bear Arms: An Anglo-Saxon Right* (1994)—which he labeled an "excellent study"— Justice Scalia made the interesting observation that the author was not even "a member of the Michigan Militia, but an Englishwoman." (Malcolm is in fact American.) Antonin Scalia, *A Matter of Interpretation: Federal Courts and the Law* 136–137 n.13 (1997).

7 *Observations Leading to a Fair Examination of the System of Government Proposed by the Late Convention; And to Several Essential and Necessary Alternations in It. In a Number of Letters from the Federal Farmer to the Republican* (hereinafter, *Letters from the Federal Farmer*) (letter of Oct. 10, 1787), in 2 *The Complete Anti-federalist* 214, 342 (Herbert J. Storing ed., 1981). For many years, the *Federal Farmer* was widely attributed to Richard Henry Lee, but more recently, scholars such as Herbert Storing and Gordon Wood have raised doubts about Lee's authorship of the *Farmer*. Many experts now ascribe the *Letters from the Federal Farmer* to Melancton Smith of New York. Jack N. Rakove, "The Second Amendment: The Highest Stage of Originalism," 76 *Chicago-Kent L. Rev.* 103, 105, 144 (2000).

8 During the 1783–84 sessions, Congress was compelled to change its situs on three occasions, owing to the pressure of anti-Continental mobs demanding debt relief and back pay to veterans. Dumas Malone, 1 *Jefferson and His Time: Jefferson the Virginian* 403–404 (1948).

9 Articles of Confederation, Article 5.

10 2 Irving Brant, *Life of Madison "James Madison: The Nationalist, 1780–87"* at 305 (1948).

11 Friederich von Steuben, *A Letter on the Subject of an Established Militia, and Military Arrangements, Addressed to the Inhabitants of the United States* (1784), discussed in Cunliffe, *Soldiers and Civilians* at 182.

12 Henry Knox, *A Plan for the General Arrangement of the Militia of the United States* (1786), described with commentary in John McAuley Palmer, *Three War Statesmen: Washington, Lincoln, Wilson* 84–94 (1930).

13 Cunliffe, *Soldiers and Civilians* at 182.

14 Weigley, *United States Army* at 89. The Act of Sept. 29, 1789, ch. 25 § 1, 1 Stat. 95, 95–96, legalizing the army inherited from the Confederation government, confirmed an earlier act authorizing a force of 840, but only 672 were actually in service at this time. Ibid.

15 Wood, *Creation of the American Republic* at 395–96.

16 Ibid. at 416–17.

17 Ibid. at 399.

18 Ibid. at 412 and Weigley, *United States Army* at 84–85.

19 Jack N. Rakove, *Original Meanings: Politics and Ideas in the Making of the Constitution* 33–34 (hereinafter, Rakove, *Original Meanings*).

20 Weigley, *United States Army* at 84.

21 Wood, *Creation of the American Republic* at 471–75 (quoting John Dickinson, "The Letter of Fabius in 1788, on the Federal Constitution; And in 1797 on the Present Situation of Public Affairs: With Additional Notes" [1797], in *Pamphlets on the Constitution of the United States* 188 [Paul L. Ford ed., 1888]).

22 Jack N. Rakove, *Original Meanings: Politics and Ideas in the Making of the Constitution* 33–34 (1994).

23 Wood, *Creation of the American Republic* at 44–45.

24 Ibid. at 18–19.

25 Ibid. at 226–37.

26 Ibid. at 471–75, 560–61, and, from a more paradigmatic perspective, Pocock, *Machiavellian Moment* at 530–31.

27 Wood, *Creation of the American Republic* at 593–615.

28 Ibid. at 474–75.

29 Ibid. at 506–19; Jack N. Rakove, *Original Meanings* 29–34, and Garry Wills, *A Necessary Evil: A History of American Distrust of Government* 70–82 (1999).

30 Weigley, *United States Army* at 84.

31 Wood, *Creation of the American Republic* at 406–407; Letter from James Madison to Thomas Jefferson (Oct. 24, 1787), in 12 *The Papers of Thomas Jefferson* 270, 276 (Julian P. Boyd ed., 1953).

32 Wood, *Creation of the American Republic* at 493–99.

33 *U.S. Const.* art. 1, sec. 8, cls. 12 (Army), 13 (Navy), 14 (Military Rules), 15 (Calling Forth), 16 (Militia); art. 2, sec. 8, cl. 1 (Commander in Chief). For an analysis, see Perpich v. Department of Defense, 496 U.S. 334, 340 (1990).

34 Rep. 118a (C.P. 1610), ("the common law will controul acts of Parliament, [and] adjudge them to be utterly void . . . [when] against common right and reason.") (Lord Coke). Of course Coke is really asserting principles of judicial review as opposed to judicial independence from the magistracy, which would come only with tenure on good behavior. But James I realized that in the context of resistance to his assertions of royal prerogative, this amounted to much the same thing — a challenge to his putatively absolute powers. "If the Judges interprete the lawes themselves and suffer none else to interprete, then they may easily make of the laws shipmens hose," the King quipped. Quoted in J. P. Sommerville, *Politics and Ideology in England 1603–1640* at 96 (1986) ("Shipmens hose" were one-size-fits-all sailor pants). Bonham's case was not respected precedent by the age of Mansfield, but it remained an icon of whiggish sentiment.

35 Schwoerer, *No Standing Armies* at 289. The Heads of Grievances of 1689 also proposed to secure judicial tenure on good behavior, but this was one of the radical Whig measures requiring the creation of new law that was struck at the Lords' insistence before passage of the Declaration of Rights.

36 Smith, *The Realm of England* at 305–306.

37 Charles-Louis De Secondàt Baron de Montesquieu, *De L'Espirit des Lois [The Spirit of the Laws]* bk. 11, ch. 6 (1748), translated in 1 *the Founders' Constitution* 624 (Philip B. Kurkland and Ralph Lerner eds., 1987).

38 Wood, *Creation of the American Republic* at 550–52; and Letter from James Madison to Thomas Jefferson (Oct. 24, 1787), in 12 *The Papers of Thomas Jefferson* 275 (Julian P. Boyd ed., 1953).

39 Letter from James Madison to Thomas Jefferson (Oct. 24, 1787), in 12 *The Papers of Thomas Jefferson* 271 (Julian P. Boyd ed., 1953).

40 Weigley, *United States Army* at 86–87.

41 Wood, *Creation of the American Republic* at 507–508.

42 Ibid. at 610–14.

43 Cecelia Kenyon, "Men of Little Faith: The Anti-Federalists on the Nature of Representative Government," 12 *William and Mary Quarterly* 3 (1955).

44 Letter from James Madison to Thomas Jefferson (Dec. 9, 1787), in 12 *The Papers of Thomas Jefferson* 408–409, 411 (Julian P. Boyd ed., 1953) ("The Constitution proposed by the late Convention engrosses almost the whole political attention of America."). See also Letter from James Madison to Thomas Jefferson (Feb. 19, 1788), in 12 *The Papers of Thomas Jefferson* 607–608 (Julian P. Boyd ed., 1953) ("The public here continues to be much agitated by the proposed federal Constitution and to be attentive to little else.").

45 Robert J. Spitzer, "Door No. 1: Muskets? Or Door No. 2: Free Speech?" *Christian Science Monitor*, Sept. 19, 1997, at 19.

46 Robert Allen Rutland, *The Birth of the Bill of Rights, 1776–1791* at 82, 127, 204 (1983) (hereinafter, Rutland, *Birth of the Bill of Rights*); and Bernard Schwartz, *The Great Rights of Mankind: A History of the American Bill of Rights* 157–58 (1992) (hereinafter, Schwartz, *Great Rights of Mankind*). In several states, the largest anti-federalist constituency comprised Presbyterians, Baptists, and other sectarians who feared federal establishment, or taxes for religious purposes. But not only sectarians lobbied for what we know as First Amendment freedoms. Madison himself, "Father of the Constitution," leader of the proratification movement in Virginia, and eventually architect of the Bill of Rights, had made his reputation opposing the Virginia General Assessment and securing passage of Jefferson's Virginia Statute for Religious Freedom; Thomas J. Curry, *The First Freedoms: Church and State in America to the Passage of the First Amendment* 142–48 (1986), and William Lee Miller, *The First Liberty: Religion and the Early Republic* 42–43 (1986) (hereinafter, Miller, *First Liberty*). Professor Banning, for one, has implied that Madison's sensitivity to the checking role of factions in a constitutional system derived from his experience in Virginia politics, where the countervailing claims of Anglicans, Presbyterians, and Baptists prevented dictation of a strong state policy on religion, and ultimately facilitated separation of church and state, Lance Banning, *The Sacred Flame of Liberty: James Madion and the Founding of the Federal Republic* (1995) 84–97, esp. 89–91. Madison's sympathies on issues of religion made him receptive to anti-federalist calls for a Bill of Rights, notwithstanding his deep personal commitment to ratification of the Constitution as initially written. Letters from his mentor Jefferson, arguing that "a bill of rights is what the people are entitled to against every government on earth, general or particular, and what no just government should refuse, or rest on inference," helped convince Madison that the Constitution should be fortified with guarantees of specific rights, see Letter from James Madison to Thomas Jefferson (Dec. 20, 1787), in 12 *The Papers of Thomas Jefferson* 438, 440 (Julian P. Boyd ed., 1953), and our discussion at 91–96. More than any other principles, it was devotion to disestablishment and free exercise that brought Madison round to Jefferson's view in favor of a bill of rights. According to one Madison specialist, the future drafter of the Bill of Rights considered "First Amendment freedoms" and the right to jury trial as the most important liberties embodied in the Virginia Bill of Rights (Rutland, *Birth of the Bill of Rights* at 208) while another commentator, author of a classic Madison biogra-

phy, calls freedom of religion "Madison's first concern," Irving Brant, *James Madison: Father of the Constitution* 268 (1950). Charlton Heston labels the right to bear arms the most important political freedom, because in his mind only that right can guarantee the security of all rights. But to James Madison, spiritual and intellectual freedoms rated at the apex of American liberties, because only freedom of the mind rendered liberty meaningful and enduring.

47 George Mason, "Objections to this Constitution Government," published in 2 *Records of the Federal Convention* 637–40 (Max Farrand ed. 1974); Letter from James Madison to Thomas Jefferson (Oct. 24, 1787), in 12 *The Papers of Thomas Jefferson* 280 (Julian P. Boyd ed., 1953).

48 Rutland, *Birth of the Bill of Rights* at 121.

49 Don B. Kates Jr., "Handgun Prohibition and the Original Meaning of the Second Amendment," 82 *Michigan L. Rev.* 204, 222 (1983).

50 Rutland, *Birth of the Bill of Rights* at 82–91. Rutland rates freedom of religion the most important issue in the eyes of the votaries of the day. Freedom of religion has thirty-eight entries in his table of contents, as opposed to two entries for the right to keep and bear arms.

51 Schwartz, *Great Rights of Mankind* at 105–11, 115–18, 156–59. Schwartz stressed the emphatic demand for an express reservation to the states of powers not expressly delegated to the federal government, and for the erection of limitations about the seemingly plenary federal authority to legislate within its delegated mandate.

52 Jack N. Rakove, "The Second Amendment: The Highest State of Originalism," 76 *Chicago-Kent L. Rev.* 103, 112 (2000).

53 *Records of the Federal Convention* 208–09.

54 *The Complete Bill of Rights: The Drafts, Debates, Sources and Origins* 181–83 (Neil H. Cogan ed., 1997). A militia-linked right to arms was endorsed by a Minority of the Official Maryland Committee, by the conventions of New York, Rhode Island, Virginia, and North Carolina, and by the so-called Pennsylvania minority, which also (perhaps schizophrenically) endorsed a private individual right to arms, which right was also recommended by New Hampshire and a Massachusetts minority.

55 Ibid. at 215.

56 Ibid. at 181.

57 William V. Wells, *The Life and Public Services of Samuel Adams* 267 (1865).

58 Robert E. Shalhope, "To Keep and Bear Arms in the Early Republic," 16 *Constitutional Commentary* 269, 277–78 (1999).

59 Kermit L. Hall, *Major Problems in American Constitutional History* 64 (1992).

60 The heyday of the Carolina Regulators was the immediate prewar period. Richard Middleton, *Colonial America: A History 1585–1776* at 460–62 (2d ed.) (1996). Yet in western parts of the Carolinas and other states, groups calling themselves Regulators continued to assert popular sovereignty in the face of seaboard governance up to and beyond the establishment of federal authority. The Massachusetts "Shaysites" consciously styled themselves Regulators to

suggest an affinity with the western Carolina populists. Wood, *Creation of the American Republic* at 320–21, 325.

61 In the very words employed by Virginia, North Carolina proposed "[t]hat the people have a right to keep and bear arms; that a well regulated Militia composed of the body of the people trained to arms is the proper, natural and safe defence of a free State. That standing armies in time of peace are dangerous to liberty, and therefore ought to be avoided, as far as the circumstances and protection of the Community will admit; and that in all cases the military should be under strict subordination to and governed by the Civil power." 2 Schwartz, *Documentary History of the Bill of Rights* 966, 968.

62 Schwartz, *Great Rights of Mankind* at 154–56.

63 Robert Dowlut, "Federal and State Constitutional Guarantees to Arms," *University of Dayton L. Rev.* 62–63 (1989); Col. Charles J. Dunlap Jr., "Revolt of the Masses: Armed Civilians and the Insurrectionary Theory of the Second Amendment," *Tennessee L. Rev.* 650, n.35 (1995); and Robert E. Shalhope, "The Ideological Origins of the Second Amendment," 69 *Journal of American History* 599, 609 (1982).

64 *The Address and reasons of Dissent of the Minority of the Convention of Pennsylvania to Their Constituents* (Dec. 12, 1787), in 3 *The Complete Anti-Federalist* 145, 151 (Herbert J. Storing, ed., 1981) (originally published in *Pa. Packet & Daily Advertiser,* Dec. 18, 1787). The Address provided in part

> That the people have a right to bear arms for the defence of themselves and their own State, or the United States, or for the purpose of killing game; and no law shall be passed for disarming the people or any of them, unless for crimes committed, or real danger of public injury from individuals. . . .

Ibid.; Edward Dumbauld, *The Bill of Rights and What it Means Today* 174 (1957).

65 Wills, "To Keep and Bear Arms" 62, 65–66 citing "The Dissent of the Minority of the Convention" (Sept. 18, 1787), in 2 *The Documentary History of the Ratification of the Constitution* 617–649 (Merril Jenson ed.).

66 Saul Cornell, "Commonplace or Anachronism: The Standard Model, The Second Amendment, and the Problem of History in Contemporary Constitutional Theory," 16 *Constitutional Commentary* 221, 232–33, and fn. 44 (1999) (hereinafter, Cornell, "Commonplace or Anachronism").

67 Cornell, "Commonplace or Anachronism" at 221, 238–41.

68 Penn. Const. of 1776, Declaration of Rights, art. 13, reprinted in 1 Kermit L. Hall, *Major Problems in American Constitutional History* 79, 81 (1992).

69 Cornell, "Commonplace or Anachronism" at 221, 228–29; Michael Bellesiles, *Arming America: The Origins of a National Gun Culture* 72–80 (2000).

70 Cornell, "Commonplace or Anachronism" at 221, 237–41.

71 Letter from James Madison to Thomas Jefferson (Dec. 9, 1787), in 12 *The Papers of Thomas Jefferson* 409–10 (Julian P. Boyd ed., 1953).

72 Rutland, *Birth of the Bill of Rights* at 162–74.

73 Jonathan Elliot, *The Debates in the Several State Conventions of the Adoption of the Fed-*

eral *Constitution, as Recommended by the General Convention at Philadelphia in 1787* at 379 (1836).

74 Ibid. at 386 (1836).

75 Ibid. at 382–83, 421 (1836).

76 James Madison, *The Debates in the Federal Convention of 1787* at 662 (G. Hunt and J. B. Scott ed. 1920).

77 Ibid.

78 The Nineth and Tenth Principles of the Virginia Convention, in James Madison, *The Debates in the Federal Convention of 1787* at 660.

79 Duncan MacLeod, *Slavery, Race, and the American Revolution* 65–69 (1974), discussing this question with reference to the philosophy of Jeffersonian theorist John Taylor of Caroline.

80 "Essays of Philadelphiensis IX," in 3 *The Complete Anti-Federalist* 127–128 (Herbert J. Storing ed., 1981) (originally published in the *Independent Gazetteer,* Feb. 7, 1788).

81 The Centinel essays have been attributed to Samuel Bryan, the hasty compiler of Pennsylvania's "minority report," discussed in notes 64–68 and accompanying text. See 2 *The Complete Anti-Federalist* 130, 135 n.3 (Herbert J. Storing ed., 1981).

82 Letter from Centinel to the People of Pennsylvania (Nov. 5, 1787), in 2 *The Complete Anti-Federalist* 154, 159–60 (Herbert J. Storing ed., 1981) (originally published in the *Independent Gazetteer,* Nov. 8, 1787).

83 Letter from John DeWitt to the Free Citizens of the Commonwealth of Massachusetts (Dec. 3, 1787), in 4 *The Complete Anti-Federalist* 34, 36 (Herbert J. Storing ed., 1981).

84 Federalist Nos. 25, 27, 28, 29 (Alexander Hamilton) at 192–96, 201–16 (Kramnick, ed. Penguin Classics 1987) (1788).

85 Federalist No. 25 (Alexander Hamilton) at 193 (Kramnick, ed. Penguin Classics 1987) (1788).

86 Federalist No. 46 (James Madison) at 301 (Kramnick, ed. Penguin Classics 1987) (1788).

87 Federalist No. 84 (Alexander Hamilton) at 475 (Kramnick, ed. Penguin Classics 1987) (1788).

88 Schwartz, *Great Rights of Mankind* at 134–42.

89 Rutland, *Birth of the Bill of Rights* at 28–29 (discussing the relative importance Americans attached to various historical, political, and natural rights during the critical period). Rutland labels the five "fundamental tenet[s] of civil liberty" as government according to laws approved by the people, jury trial, the writ of habeas corpus, freedom of the press, and freedom of religion.

90 Schwartz, *Great Rights of Mankind* at 157–58 features a table listing the references to various future provisions of the Bill of Rights occurring in the recommendations of state ratifying conventions. In all, six state conventions (Mass., S.C., N.H., N.Y., Va., N.C.) submitted official recommendations. Of these, the reports of Massachusetts and South Carolina were concerned chiefly with feder-

alism, and took only limited account of individual liberties. Schwartz's table also includes references to the so-called report of the Pennsylvania minority, and the recommendations of both the majority and minority of the committee charged by the Maryland convention with suggesting amendments. None of these last three sets of recommendations were adopted by their respective states. In Schwartz's table, reserved powers appear the maximum eight times, jury trial in civil cases seven times, and religious freedom six times. Next follow the right to bear arms, a free press, the right against quartering of soldiers, the right against unreasonable searches and seizures, and jury trial in criminal cases, with five mentions each. However, only the New Hampshire report and the so-called report of the Pennsylvania minority contemplated a right to arms outside the militia context. If, as Garry Wills suggests, in "To Keep and Bear Arms" at 65, we discount the report of the Pennsylvania minority as the rambling catch-all compendium of one man bent on scuttling ratification, we are left with a solitary endorsement of a right to arms for private purposes. That renders the putative private right to arms the least popular of the twenty-three rights suggested by the conventions, just behind the right against double jeopardy, with two mentions — an official endorsement by New York, and an unofficial endorsement by the majority of the Maryland committee.

91 Lawrence Delbert Cress, *Citizens in Arms: The Army and the Militia in American Society to the War of 1812* at 101 (1982) contains an insightful discussion of the federalists attitude toward the military and the militia, focusing on their hostility to centralization of military power, and their increasingly ambivalent and indeed accepting view of professionalism.

92 Adrienne Koch, *Jefferson and Madison: The Great Collaboration* (1950).

93 Thomas J. Curry, *The First Freedoms: Church and State in America to the Passage of the First Amendment* 141–48 (1986), and Miller, *First Liberty* at 32–36, 74–75, 85–86.

94 Joseph J. Ellis, *American Sphinx: The Character of Thomas Jefferson* 277 (1997).

95 Letter from James Madison to Thomas Jefferson (Aug. 31, 1783), in 6 *The Papers of Thomas Jefferson* 335–36 (Julian P. Boyd ed., 1953), and discussion in Fawn Brodie, *Jefferson An Intimate Biography* 174 (1974) (hereinafter, Brodie, *Intimate Biography*). Madison's infatuation with Kitty Floyd, daughter of New York Representative William Floyd, with whom Madison shared a Philadelphia rooming house, is discussed in greater detail in 2 Irving Brant, *James Madison (James Madison: The Nationalist 1780–1787* at 283–287. Madison began spending inordinately at the barbers as soon as he took up lodgings with the Floyds at Mrs. House's famous establishment.

96 3 Dumas Malone, *Jefferson and His Time: Jefferson and the Ordeal of Liberty* 187 (1962) (discussing Jefferson's reaction to Madison's betrothal to Dolley Todd). Madison did not marry until 1794, the year he turned forty-three.

97 Between August 1784 and October 1789, when Jefferson was in Europe, he received at least forty-six letters from Madison and sent Madison at least thirty-five in return. 7–15 *The Papers of Thomas Jefferson* (Julian P. Boyd ed., 1953).

98 Miller, *First Liberty* at 32, 34–35; and Brodie, *Intimate Biography* at 177–78.

99 Letter from Thomas Jefferson to James Madison (Dec. 20, 1787), in 12 *The Papers of Thomas Jefferson* 438, 440 (Julian P. Boyd ed., 1953).

100 Letter from Thomas Jefferson to James Madison (Feb. 6, 1788), in 12 *The Papers of Thomas Jefferson* 568, 569–70 (Julian P. Boyd ed., 1953).

101 Letter from Thomas Jefferson to Edward Rutledge (July 18, 1788), in 13 *The Papers of Thomas Jefferson* 371, 378 (Julian P. Boyd ed., 1953).

102 Letter from Thomas Jefferson to James Madison (July 31, 1788), in 13 *The Papers of Thomas Jefferson* 440 (Julian P. Boyd ed., 1953).

103 Jefferson served consecutive one-year terms as Governor of Virginia, holding office from June 1, 1779, through June 2, 1781. His administration came to a chaotic close, with Banastre Tarleton's British Regulars chasing the government from Richmond and then hounding Jefferson out of Monticello into sylvan seclusion. Many faulted Jefferson for not summoning the militia more quickly to defend the capitol, but, given the militia's demonstrated ineffectiveness, it is perhaps difficult to see what the irregulars might have accomplished had they been rallied more quickly. Thirty-three years later Madison summoned 100,000 militia to the defense of Washington in ample time, but a British Army no larger than Tarleton's marched right through those militia who mustered straight into the national city, see our discussion in chapter 4 at 120–212. For Jefferson's correspondence and official communiqués during his wartime governorship, as well as documents relating to subsequent politically motivated inquires into his handling of the British invasion (Jefferson was exonerated of any wrongdoing), see *The Papers of Thomas Jefferson* (Julian P. Boyd ed., 1953) from volume 2 at 277 through volume 6 at 114.

104 On Jefferson's challenging experiences as wartime governor of Virginia, see Dumas Malone, *Jefferson the Virginian*, 301–69, and *The Papers of Thomas Jefferson* (Julian P. Boyd ed., 1953) from Volume 2 at 277 through Volume 6 at 114.

105 Letter from Thomas Jefferson to James Madison (July 31, 1788), in 13 *The Papers of Thomas Jefferson* 440, 442 (Julian P. Boyd ed., 1953); Letter from Thomas Jefferson to James Madison (Feb. 6, 1788), in 12 *The Papers of Thomas Jefferson* 568, 569–70 (Julian P. Boyd ed., 1953); Letter from Thomas Jefferson to James Madison (Dec. 20, 1787), in 12 *The Papers of Thomas Jefferson* 438, 440 (Julian P. Boyd ed., 1953).

106 Rakove, *Original Meanings* at 153.

107 Schwartz, *Great Rights of Mankind* at 134–59.

108 Ibid. at 161.

109 Speech of James Madison in House of Representatives June 8, 1789, in I *Annals of Congress* at 440–41 (Joseph Gales and William Seaton eds., 1834) (hereinafter, I *Annals of Congress*).

110 Letter from Thomas Jefferson to James Madison (Dec. 20, 1787), in 12 *The Papers of Thomas Jefferson* 438, 440 (Julian P. Boyd ed., 1953).

111 Schwartz, *Great Rights of Mankind* at 163.

112 I *Annals of Congress* at 257.

113 Ibid. at 258–60, 282.

114 Ibid. at 442; comments of Congressman Vining during debates of June 8, 1789, in Ibid. at 446.

115 Ibid. at 441.

116 Quoted in Schwartz, *Great Rights of Mankind* at 162.

117 I *Annals of Congress* at 448.

118 Ibid. at 448.

119 Ibid. at 449.

120 Ibid. at 450–53.

121 Letter from James Madison to Thomas Jefferson (Oct. 17, 1788), in 14 *The Papers of Thomas Jefferson* 16, 18 (Julian P. Boyd ed., 1953) (enclosing the pamphlet).

122 Schwartz, *Great Rights of Mankind* at 165.

123 Schwartz, *Great Rights of Mankind* at 173.

124 I *Annals of Congress* at 451.

125 Ibid. at 467–68.

126 Ibid. at 685.

127 Ibid. at 690.

128 Ibid. at 699.

129 Schwartz, *Great Rights of Mankind* at app. B. at 235–36.

130 I *Annals of Congress* at 730–44.

131 Schwartz, *Great Rights of Mankind* at 185–86. The first of the proposed amendments, requiring periodic congressional reapportionment to ensure small constituencies, failed to gain the approval of three-fourths of the existing states. The second proposed amendment, preventing congressional pay rises from taking effect during the life of a sitting Congress, also fell short originally. But after lying dormant until the 1980s, the proposed amendment was revived and finally ratified in 1992, becoming the Twenty-seventh Amendment 203 years after submission to the states. Ratification of the Twenty-seventh Amendment owed much to the efforts of Gregory Watson, a Texas college student who embarked upon a letter-writing campaign on behalf of the proposed amendment in 1981, and in due course persuaded enough governors and state legislators of the amendment's merits to secure its passage. Jack N. Rakove, *Declaring Rights: A Brief History With Documents* 192, n. 12 (1998).

132 The familiar Second Amendment was the fifth of seventeen amendments submitted by the House to the Senate and the fourth of the twelve amendments proposed by Congress for ratification. It appeared second among the catalogue of ten amendments ratified in 1791 because the two proposals atop the list submitted to the states in 1789 failed to attain ratification along with the rest of the Bill of Rights, see note 131. For the sake of convenience, we refer to the proposed amendment as the draft of the Second Amendment throughout the book.

133 Schwartz, *Great Rights of Mankind* at 176, 183.

134 I *Annals of Congress* at 778.

135 Ibid. at 778.

136 Ibid.

137 Ibid. at 779. Gerry's specter of selective disarmament under the guise of co-erced conscientious objection remained plausible in late-eighteenth-century America, in part because religious tests for office excluding Catholics (and in some instances certain sectarians) from government posts persisted in various states and in England. Miller, *First Liberty* at 108.

138 I *Annals of Congress* at 779.

139 Ibid. at 780.

140 For constitutional scholars, it is interesting to note that fourteen years before Marbury v. Madison, 5 U.S. (1 Cranch) 137 (1803), Benson takes for granted judi-cial review, and the judicial invalidation of "regulations" (i.e., statutes) that violate the proposed amendment. The case that judicial review of state and fed-eral legislation was envisioned by the framers in 1787, and that Justice Marshall did not therefore create the mechanism from whole cloth in 1803, is argued in detail in Jack N. Rakove, "The Origins of Judicial Review: A Plea For New Contexts," 49 *Stanford L. Rev.* 1031, 1038, and especially 1040–41, 1047–48, 1050 (1997).

141 I *Annals of Congress* at 780. It must be emphasized that Benson, like Gerry, was not hostile to conscientious objectors, but rather believed their rights ill-suited to constitutional protection. Thus, Benson continued on from the pas-sage quoted above to inform the House "I have no reason to believe but the Legislature will always possess humanity enough to indulge this class of citi-zens in a matter they are so desirous of; but they ought to be left to their dis-cretion." Ibid.

142 As discussed previously, a private right to possess weapons for purposes broader than military service numbered among the amendments proposed by the New Hampshire Ratification Convention. Edward Dumbauld, *The Bill of Rights and What It Means Today* 182 (1957), and a "minority" of the Pennsylva-nia Ratification Convention, Wills, "To Keep and Bear Arms" at 65–66, citing "The Dissent of the Minority of the Convention" (Sept. 18, 1787), in 2 *The Docu-mentary History of the Ratification of the Constitution* 617–49 (Merril Jenson ed.). Samuel Adams moved the Massachusetts Ratifying Committee to propose a broadly based, private right to arms amendment to Congress, but Adams' mo-tion was rejected, 3 William V. Wells, *Life and Public Services of Samuel Adams, Being a Narrative of His Acts and Opinions and of His Agency in Producing and Forwarding the American Revolution* 267 (1865).

143 I *Annals of Congress* at 780.

144 In full, the provision is: "No State shall, without the Consent of Congress, lay any Duty of Tonnage, keep Troops, or Ships of War in time of Peace, enter into any Agreement or Compact with another State, or with a foreign Power, or engage in War, unless actually invaded, or in such immanent Danger as will not admit of delay." *U.S. Const.* art. 1, sec. 10, cl. 3. It is interesting that "troops" so evidently referred to standing armies only and not to militia, that anti-federalists made no effort to seize on the just-quoted constitutional lan-guage as evidence of a conspiracy to disarm the states and set up a national army

of dangerous proportions. That "troops" implied standing, kept, paid soldiers as opposed to civilian militia can be seen in Hamilton's usage in federalist 25 at 195 and passim (Krammick ed.). "The Bill of Rights of that State [Pennsylvania] declares that standing armies are dangerous to liberty, and ought not to be kept up in time of peace. Pennsylvania, nevertheless, in a time of profound peace, from the existence of partial disorders in one or two of her counties, has resolved to raise a body of troops; and in all probability will keep them up as long as there is an appearance of danger to the public peace."

145   I *Annals of Congress* at 780.

146   Ibid. at 781.

147   Ibid. at 751–52. The draft sent by the House to the Senate on August 24, 1789, reads in full "ARTICLE THE FIFTH: A well regulated militia, composed of the body of the People, being the best security of a free State, the right of the People to keep and bear arms shall not be infringed, but no one religiously scrupulous of bearing arms, shall be compelled to render military service in person," reprinted in Rakove, *Declaring Rights* at 184. The phrase "composed by the body of the People," like the Conscientious Objector Clause, was pruned by the Senate. Generally, the upper house tightened and consolidated the text of the Amendments, and it may have considered the "body of the people" clause a redundant reference to the militia. Alternatively, the Senate may not have wished to trample on the power of the states to determine who would be born on the militia rolls, although Congress ultimately took steps in that direction by specifying age requirements for service in the Militia Act of 1792, acting, presumably, under its power to organize the militia provided in art. 1, sec. 8, cl. 16. It seems worth noting that the plainest meaning, and the most neglected, of the rights entitlement under the Second Amendment may well go directly to the issue of who may be born, or to put it more clearly, who may be excluded, from the militia rolls. In other words, the right to keep and bear arms, taken seriously, to use Professor Van Alstyne's phrase, could well have much more to do with whether gays are constitutionally entitled to serve in the National Guard or even the Reserves without fear of status-based federal disqualification than with whether good ole boys may stockpile AK47s in the barn without interference by the ATF. This dimension of the Second Amendment, for all its amenability to the "rights talk" and rights-based jurisprudence more typical of the other Amendments comprising the Bill of Rights, is not discussed by other commentators, and to our knowledge has never been raised in court.

148   I *Annals of Congress* at 796.

149   Ibid.

150   For a classic statement of the argument that legislative intent is generally unascertainable, see Antonin Scalia, *A Matter of Interpretation: Federal Courts and the Law* 32 and passim (1997).

151   Robert E. Shalhope, "The Ideological Origins of the Second Amendment," 69 *Journal of American History* 599, 611 (1982).

152   I *Annals of Congress* at 796.

153   Elbridge Gerry of Massachusetts; Roger Sherman of Connecticut; Egbert Benson of New York; Thomas Hartley and Thomas Scott of Pennsylvania; Elias Boudinot of New Jersey; John Vining of Delaware; Joshua Seney and Michael Jenifer Stone of Maryland; William Smith and Erasmus Burke of South Carolina; and James Jackson of Georgia; cf. I *Annals of Congress* 778–80.

154   *The Diary of William MacLay,* reprinted in 9 *Documentary History of the First Federal Congress of the United States* 143–55.

155   The Senate Journal covering proceedings related to the Bill of Rights is reprinted in 2 Bernard Schwartz, *The Bill of Rights: A Documentary History* 1147–57 (1971).

156   Ibid. at 1146 (1971).

157   Ibid. at 1122, 1149 (1971). The deletion of the "body of the people" clause is discussed supra at 00000.

158   Ibid. at 1154 (1971).

159   Ibid. at 1153–54 (1971).

160   Ibid. at 1154 (1971).

161   Wills, "To Keep and Bear Arms" at 63–64. As Wills explains:

> The Standard Modelers draw on an argument made by Stephen Halbrook, an argument often cited by the NRA: "The Senate specifically rejected a proposal to add 'for the common defense' after 'to keep and bear arms,' thereby precluding any construction that the right was restricted to militia purposes and to common defense against foreign aggression or domestic tyranny."

Ibid. (citing Stephen P. Halbrook, *That Every Man be Armed: The Evolution of a Constitutional Right* [1984]).

162   Bernard Schwartz, *The Bill of Rights: A Documentary History* 1145 (1971).

163   Ibid. at app. C at 238–41 (1971) (amendment passed by House of Representatives, Aug. 24, 1789). It must be acknowledged, however, that the Senate trimmed not merely with a view to efficiency (although this was its overriding purpose.) House-reported substantive provisions, among them the conscientious objector clause, see ibid., app. C at 239, and an amendment binding the states to respect what have become known as "First Amendment freedoms" and the right to jury trial in criminal cases, ibid., app. C at 240, were also deleted.

164   The Articles of Confederation mentions "the common defense" three times. "The said states hereby severally enter in a firm league of friendships with each other for their common defense, the security of their liberties, and their mutual and general welfare, binding themselves to assist each other, against all force offered to, or attack made upon them, or any of them, an account of religion, sovereignty, trade, or any pretense whatever." Art. 3. "When land forces are raised by any State for the common defense, all officers of or under the rank of colonel, shall be appointed by the legislature of each State respectively, by whom such forces shall be raised, or in such manner as such State shall direct,

and all vacancies shall be filled up by the State which first made the appointment." Art. 7 (implicit reservation of appointment of brigadiers and generals to Congress evincing federal purpose of the "common defense"). "All charges of war, and all other expenses that shall be incurred for the common defense or general welfare, and allowed by the United States in Congress assembled, shall be defrayed out of a common treasury, which shall be supplied by the several States in proposition to the value of all land within each State, granted or surveyed for any person, as such land and the buildings and improvements therein shall be estimated according to such mode of the United States in Congress assembled, shall from time to time direct and appoint. The taxes for paying that proportion shall be laid and levied by the authority and direction of the legislatures of the several States within the time agreed upon by the United States Congress assembled." Art. 8. See also Wills, "To Keep and Bear Arms" at 64, analyzing the Articles of Confederation.

165   See Gerry's convention-floor indictment of proposed federal militia powers: "This power in the United States as explained is making the states drill sergeants. [I] had as lief let the citizens of Massachusetts be disarmed, as to take command from the states, and subject them to the General Legislature. It would be regarded as a system of Despotism." 2 *The Records of the Federal Convention of 1787* at 74 (Max Farrand ed., 1966).

166   Rakove, *Original Meanings* at 57–70.

167   Wills, "To Keep and Bear Arms" at 65–67.

168   The "standard model" label was coined in 1995 by Professor Glenn Harlan Reynolds of the University of Tennessee School of Law, Glenn Harlan Reynolds, "A Critical Guide to the Second Amendment" 62 *Tennessee L. Rev.* 461, 463 (1925). The notion that the private right mode of Second Amendment analysis represents a scientific consensus has met with equal parts approval and ridicule. See the approving Eugene Volokh, "The Commonplace Second Amendment," 73 *N.Y.U. L. Rev.* 793 (1998), and the scathing Cornell, "Commonplace or Anachronism" at 221.

169   Joyce Lee Malcolm, "The Right of the People to Keep and Bear Arms: The Common Law Tradition," 10 *Hastings Constitutional Law Quarterly* 285, 309–13 (1983).

170   Robert J. Cottrol, "Introduction to Gun Control and the Constitution," in *Gun Control and the Constitution: Source and Explorations on the Second Amendment*, at ix, xvi (Robert J. Cottrol ed., 1993). The *Address and Reasons of Dissent of the Minority of the Convention of Pennsylvania to Their Constituents* is discussed at notes 64–68 for this chapter and accompanying text.

171   Adams proposed denying Congress the power to prevent "the people of the United States who are peaceable citizens from keeping their own arms," quoted in 3 William V. Wells, *The Life and Public Services of Samuel Adams* 267 (1865).

172   See the proposal of the New Hampshire Ratifying Convention that "Congress shall never disarm any citizen unless such as are or have been in Actual Rebel-

lion," quoted in Edward Dumbauld, *The Bill of Rights and What it Means Today* 182 (1957).

173 Nearly a hundred different substantive provisions were suggested by the eight state ratifying conventions to submit official and or unofficial, minority proposals. Schwartz, *Great Rights of Mankind* at 157. As Professor Schwartz has emphasized, "Madison's job as draftsman of the Federal Bill of Rights" was not "that of [a] mere compiler. On the contrary . . . Madison was able to play a most important creative role. He had to chose from the myriad of state proposals those which were worthy of being raised to the federal constitutional level. He also had to define their language, so that the Federal Bill of Rights would be, at the same time, both an eloquent inventory of basic rights and a legally enforceable safeguard of those rights." Schwartz, *Great Rights of Mankind* at 159. And in the case of the right arms for nonmilitary purposes proposed by New Hampshire and in the *Report of the Pennsylvania Minority,* Madison and the Congress pointedly opted against inclusion.

174 The House Select Committee reversed the order of the militia and bear arms clauses.

175 The House Select Committee deleted the qualification that the militia be "well armed," see discussion supra at page 97, while the Senate struck the conscientious objector clause, see discussion supra page 103.

176 The House Select Committee replaced "free country" with "free state," see discussion supra at page 97, while the Senate rephrased "being the best security of" as "being necessary to the security of," Schwartz, *Great Rights of Mankind* at 264.

CHAPTER FOUR: THE DECAY OF THE OLD MILITIA 1789–1840

1 496 U.S. 334, 340 (1990).

2 496 U.S. at 340 (footnotes omitted).

3 U.S. Const. art. 1, sec. 8, 12; art. 2, sec. 2; discussion supra at pages 105–106.

4 See discussion supra at pages 105–106.

5 Perpich v. Department of Defense, 496 U.S. 334, 342 (1990).

6 The Act of Sept. 29, 1789, ch. 25, § 1, 1 Stat. 95, 95–96, legalizing the army inherited from the Confederation government, confirmed an earlier act authorizing a force of 840, but only 672 were actually in service at this time. Weigley, *United States Army* at 89.

7 Samuel Eliot Morison et al., *The Growth of the American Republic* 235–36 (7th ed. 1980).

8 Cunliffe, *Soldiers and Civilians* at 43–48, 182–84 (1968); Weigley, *United States Army* at 88–91.

9 Weigley, *United States Army* at 79–80, 85–86; see also discussion supra 69–70.

10 Weigley, *United States Army* at 81–82; see also discussion supra 70–71.

11 Cunliffe, *Soldiers and Civilians* at 182–83.

12 I *Annals of Congress* 442, 446–48; see generally discussion supra 95.

13 Cunliffe, *Soldiers and Civilians* at 182–83.

14 Weigley, *United States Army* at 89.

15 Cunliffe, *Soldiers and Civilians* at 180–83; 45–48 (analyzing Alexander Hamilton, Federalist Nos. 24–26).

16 Henry Knox, "A Plan for the General Arrangement of the Militia of the United States (1790)," in 1 *American State Papers: Military Affairs* 6–13 (Walter Lowrie and Matthew Clarke eds., 1832) (hereinafter, Knox Plan). The Knox Plan can also be found in 1 *Annals of Congress* app. at 2141–61. The Knox Plan largely traced Knox's 1786 proposal to the Confederation Congress. Weigley, *United States Army* at 89; Cunliffe, *Soldiers and Civilians* at 182–84; discussion supra 71–72. Knox read his plan aloud to Congress and lobbied hard for its adoption. During Washington's first administration, cabinet officers followed the British practice of appearing in person before the legislature to advocate legislation and answer questions. This practice was abandoned after the President himself decided it would be improper to appear in person before Congress to debate the merits of pending legislation.

17 Knox Plan at 8–10.

18 Ibid. at 6.

19 Ibid. at 6.

20 A telling criticism of plans to base the nation's defense policy on a revitalized militia focused on the economic and social dislocation associated with militia members' extended absences from home and family. Consider Alexander Hamilton's reservations expressed in Federalist No. 29:

> To oblige the great body of the yeomanry and of the other classes of citizens to be under arms for the purpose of going through military exercises and evolutions, as often as might be necessary to acquire the degree of perfection which would entitle them to the character of a well-regulated militia, would be a real grievance to the people and a serious public inconvenience and loss. It would form an annual deduction from the productive labor of the country to an amount which calculating upon the present numbers of the people, would not fall far short of a million pounds. To attempt a thing which would abridge the mass of labor and industry to so considerable an extent would be unwise: and the experiment, if made, could not succeed, because it would not long be endured.

Federalist No. 29, at 209–10 (Alexander Hamilton) (Kramnick ed., 1987). Knox's classification scheme would have minimized the adverse social and economic effects of militia duty by restricting service in the "advanced corps" to young men between 18 and 20 years of age. At a time when ninety percent of the population still engaged in agricultural pursuits, men this young were unlikely to be proprietors of their own farms or bear responsibilities for providing for wives and children. Particularly in land-scarce New England, men often had to wait until their late twenties before they were in a position to purchase or inherit a farm or acquire a parcel of land as part of a marriage settlement. William

Pencak, *War, Politics and Revolution in Provincial Massachusetts* 201–203 (1981). Land shortage, large families (averaging five and six children), and long-lived parents contributed to a sense of restlessness among young New Englanders, to which circumstance several scholars have attributed Massachusetts's leading role in the Revolution. Ibid. at 201. With the frontier opened for settlement after independence in 1783, New England men streamed westward and laid out the new communities of western New York State and the Old Northwest. Other sons of the old New England went to sea in trading ships and carried the Stars and Stripes to China and the far reaches of the globe. Within a generation, as young men fled westward and took to the seas, Massachusetts was blessed with a superabundance of young women. Daniel J. Boorstin, *The Americans: The National Experience* 28–29 (1966). Leaving their parents' farms at age fourteen or fifteen, these "Lowell" girls often worked a term in the new factory towns, where life was regimented but not unwholesome by later industrial standards, and where the workers acquired attributes and skills deemed useful for later family life. See ibid. at 29.

21   Cunliffe, *Soldiers and Civilians* at 183.

22   Uniform Militia Act of 1792, ch. 33, § 1, 1 Stat. 271, 271, repealed by Dick Act, ch. 196, 32 Stat. 775 (1903).

23   Ibid.

24   It is interesting to note that Professor Michael Bellesiles misquotes this statute in his controversial *Arming America*. Arguing that lawmakers and administrators envisioned government arming of the militia from the very beginning, Bellesiles writes that the Militia Act required that "citizens so enrolled, shall be . . . constantly provided with a good musket or firelock." Michael A. Bellesiles, *Arming America: The Origins of a National Gun Culture* 230 (2000). Thus, Bellesiles would seemingly shift the onus of arming from militiamen to government. The act, however, clearly mandated that citizens arm themselves (but made no mention that they should do so "constantly"), 1 Stat. 271, quoted in main text supra. In a sense, Bellesiles is not that far off the mark, for, as he demonstrates throughout his book by references to numerous other sources such as letters from militia commanders to their superiors and censuses of gun ownership and militia enrollment, the private arming paradigm nearly always failed. In practice, government assumed the responsibility of arming the militia in perceived times of danger, or at the very least took upon itself the task of supplementing privately held arms by public requisition and procurement. In fact, in 1798, only six years after passage of the Militia Act, Congress authorized the federal government to purchase 30,000 stands of arms for use by the militia. 1 Stat. 576. It is a shame that Bellesiles overstates his case and treats recklessly with his copious evidence, for in so doing he undermines what should have been a powerful, well-presented, and insightful argument. In fairness, it should also be said that Bellesiles elsewhere acknowledges that the 1792 act mandated individual arms acquisition. *Arming America* at 231 (a mere one page after the bald assertion that the act mandated government arming).

25 Uniform Militia Act of 1792, ch. 33, § 1, 1 Stat. 271, 271, repealed by Dick Act, ch. 196, 32 Stat. 775 (1903).

26 Ibid.

27 J. G. A. Pocock, *Machiavellian Moment* 414, 416–17 (1975) (discussing the sacrosanct status of the historic English county militia under the "ancient" constitution venerated by the Real Whigs); Weigley, *United States Army* at 101 (describing the federalized militia President Washington led out against the Whiskey Rebellion as the "Army of the Constitution").

28 Uniform Militia Act of 1792, ch. 33, § 1, 1 Stat. 271, 271, repealed by Dick Act, ch. 196, 32 Stat. 775 (1903). While the rifles described in the act of 1792 were useful for private purposes as well as military ones, the muskets—less expensive to acquire and far more common than rifles among both regulars and militiamen—had less utility outside of the military context because of their relative inaccuracy. A company arrayed along a firing line two or three tiers deep became effective in the military parlance of the day because of "volume of fire." Weigley, *United States Army* at 21. In a crack eighteenth-century regiment, soldiers were expected to load and fire three times per minute. Stephen Brumwell, *Redcoats: The British Soldier and War in the Americas, 1755–1763,* 194–96 (2002). As an enemy formation closed within range, it could thus expect to meet a hail of musket balls, with one rank of a three-tiered formation firing every ten seconds. Geoffrey Parker, *The Military Revolution: Military Innovation and the Rise of the West, 1550–1800* at 147–48 (1988). Accounts differ as to whether soldiers were instructed to aim at particular targets. "Shooting at the mark" was certainly a more common part of a British soldier's regimen during North American duty than it was in Europe. Indeed, North American conditions made aimed firing more important than it was on the open battle fields of Europe, where massed ranks confronted one another at close range and under a haze of powder smoke. Brumwell 248–52. But outside the most well trained regiments, even a good shot could not consistently hit a barn door with a musket fired at sixty paces. Michael A. Bellesiles, "The Origins of Gun Culture in the United States, 1760–1865," 83 *Journal of American History* 425, 436 (1996). Thus, while militarily useful, a musket was not necessarily a practical tool in the late eighteenth century for such civilian purposes as hunting or pursuing a fleeing felon. Ibid. at 439; Weigley, *United States Army* at 21. "Fowling pieces," more accurate but unwieldy and less powerful than muskets, were better tools for shooting birds but fall outside the terms of the Militia Act. Michael A. Bellesiles, "The Origins of Gun Culture in the United States, 1760–1865," 83 *Journal of American History* 425, 431 n.13, 435 (1996). Likewise, the antiquated blunderbuss, which, if still in working order, remained a marginally suitable tool for shooting an intruder in the bedroom or a would-be highway man aside one's Conestoga wagon, if, that is, one spotted the malefactor in time to lift and fire the cumbersome trumpet-shaped relic. Ibid. at 425, 434, 441.

29 The states were required to furnish the secretary of war with an annual report on their militia. According to Marcus Cunliffe, "[e]ven from the outset the re-

ports were scrappy, in some cases nonexistent." Cunliffe, *Soldiers and Civilians* at
185. Jefferson, in his final State of the Union address delivered on November 8,
1808, remarked to Congress, "[i]t is . . . incumbent on us, at every meeting, to
revise the condition of the militia. . . . Some of the States have paid a laud-
able attention to this object; but every degree of neglect is to be found among
others." 9 *The Writings of Thomas Jefferson* 213, 223 (Paul Leicester Ford ed., 1898).
Delaware and Mississippi (following its admission in 1817) routinely failed to
file reports; by the 1830s, only Massachusetts and Connecticut were reporting
some semblance of an organized general militia. Cunliffe, *Soldiers and Civilians*
at 211. Delaware did away with fines for nonattendance at militia musters in
1814; most states that revised their constitutions during the Jacksonian period
incorporated abolition of imprisonment for nonpayment of fines for nonattendance as part of their new fundamental law. Ibid. Compulsory militia service was abolished by law in Massachusetts in 1840; in Maine, Vermont, and
Ohio in 1844; in Connecticut and New York in 1846; in Missouri in 1847; and
in New Hampshire in 1851. Ibid.

30 Dick Act, ch. 196, 32 Stat. 775 (1903).

31 The Uniform Militia Act of 1792 was supplemented by the Calling Forth Act
of 1795, which provided in part:

> That whenever the United States shall be invaded, or be in imminent danger
> of invasion from any foreign nation or Indian tribe, it shall be lawful for
> the President of the United States to call forth such number of the militia
> of the state, or states, most convenient to the place of danger, or scene of
> action, as he may judge necessary to repel such invasion, and to issue his
> orders for that purpose, to such officer or officers of the militia, as he shall
> think proper.

Act of Feb. 28, 1795, ch. 36, § 1, 1 Stat. 424, 424.

32 The uncharacteristically large regular army of the War of 1812, which swelled
to about 35,000 by 1814 and would have numbered over 60,000 if recruited to
authorized strength, was quickly demobilized following the Treaty of Ghent.
Weigley, *United States Army* at 120–21. Congress scaled back the regular force to
6,000 men by 1821. Ibid. at 139–40. Monroe's young, then ardently nationalis-
tic, Secretary of War John C. Calhoun proposed a variety of precocious reforms
to render the streamlined force effective, including a peacetime general staff
and a system of expansibility to absorb trained reserves into regular units in
the event of emergency. Ibid. at 141–43. Congress ignored the secretary's proposals. Ibid. at 142. The reforms Calhoun envisioned were not implemented
until the eve of World War I. Ibid. at 142–43.

33 Poinsett's plan would have divided the country into eight militia districts, each
with a force of 12,500 in active service and another 12,500 in ready reserve,
giving the nation an enormous organized militia of 200,000. Cunliffe, *Soldiers
and Civilians* at 197. Congress rejected it out of hand. Ibid. at 197–99. The unpopularity of Poinsett's proposal contributed substantially to Van Buren's de-

feat by William Henry Harrison in the presidential election of 1840. Ibid. at 198–99. Antimilitary rhetoric, broadsheets, and pamphlets—still classically republican in tone—took a prominent place in the first stump and whistle stop campaign. Ibid. at 198–99.

34 Ibid. at 184.

35 Dick Act, ch. 196, 32 Stat. 775 (1903); see also detailed discussion at pages 133–34 above.

36 Opponents of America's expansion overseas and emergence as a colonial/ military power during the Spanish-American War generally preferred to rely on America's geographic isolation, coastal artillery, the navy, or simply naive pacifism for security. While arguments that citizen-soldiers were better suited to defend a democracy than career professionals were commonplace at the turn of the twentieth century, no one then seriously argued that soldiers as lightly trained and disciplined as the founding-era general militia had been could serve any serious military purpose.

37 Christopher Hill, *God's Englishman: Oliver Cromwell and the English Revolution* 85–86 (Norman F. Cantor ed., 1970). As Hill explains:

> Parliament . . . resolved on 18 February [1647] to disband the Army without making any provision for payment of arrears or pensions for widows and orphans of those killed in Parliament's service, or even for indemnity for illegal actions committed under orders during the fighting. The troops might be permitted to re-enlist for service in Ireland . . . [but would receive no other compensation]. The rank and file of the Army were at once up in arms. During March . . . regiments . . . appointed Agitators or delegates to represent them.

Ibid. The consequent politicization of the English army (along with the intransigence of King and Presbyterians in Parliament and revolts in the provinces) led within a year to the second civil war. Ibid. at 88–97.

38 Weigley, *United States Army* at 77–78.

39 Regarding these affairs, see generally the classic account in Merril Jensen, *The New Nation: A History of the United States During the Confederation, 1781–1789* at 67–84 (1967) [1950].

40 Letter from Hamilton to Washington, 7 Feb. 1783, 9 *Works of Hamilton*, 310–13 (Henry Cabot Lodge ed. 1886), discussed in Merril Jensen, *The New Nation: A History of the United States During the Confederation, 1781–1789* at 71 (1967) [1950].

41 Letters from Hamilton to Washington, 25 Mar. 1783 (two separate of this date), 8 *Letters of Members of the Continental Congress* 103 (Edmund C. Burnett ed.), discussed in Merril Jensen, *The New Nation: A History of the United States During the Confederation, 1781–1789* at 78 (1967) [1950]. Hamilton wrote "As a citizen zealous for the true happiness of this country—as a soldier who feels what is due to an army which has suffered everything and done much for the safety of America . . . I cannot myself enter into the [hostile] views of coercion which some gentlemen entertain, for I confess could force avail, I should almost wish

to see it employed. I have an indifferent opinion of the honesty of this country, and ill-forebodings as to its future system."

42 Weigley, *United States Army* at 77; Daniel J. Boorstin, *The Americans: The Colonial Experience* 371 (1958).

43 Weigley, *United States Army* at 78.

44 Ibid. at 84.

45 Ibid.; Wood, *Creation of the American Republic* at 465, 498 (1969).

46 Pocock, *Machiavellian Moment* at 528.

47 On the origins of the phrase "constitutional army," see ibid. at 414, 416–17; Schwoerer, *No Standing Armies* at 13, and discussion at note 27 for this chapter.

48 Weigley, *United States Army* at 100–102.

49 William H. Rehnquist, *Grand Inquests: The Historic Impeachments of Justice Samuel Chase and President Andrew Johnson* 48–49 (1992).

50 For a detailed (if somewhat hostile) account of Hamilton's scandals, resignation, and continued influence, see generally Dumas Malone, *Jefferson and His Time: Jefferson and the Ordeal of Liberty,* 325–34 (1962).

51 Weigley, *United States Army* at 101–103.

52 4 Dumas Malone, *Jefferson and His Time: Jefferson the President, First Term, 1801–1805* at 6–7, 10–11 (1970). There is documentary evidence that 20,000 Pennsylvania militia were held ready to intervene in the winter of 1801, but only in the event that the electoral college chose someone other than Jefferson or Burr as President, thereby effectively staging a coup. Letter from Thomas McKean to Thomas Jefferson (Mar. 21, 1801), discussed in Dumas Malone, *Jefferson and His Time: Jefferson the President, First Term, 1801–1805* at 10–11 (1970).

53 Hamilton, it turns out, was prophetic. A year after fatally wounding Hamilton in a duel in Weehawken, New Jersey, former Vice President Burr did conspire to commit treason against the Republic by handing over the old Southwest to Spain and setting himself up as a sort of military Vice-Royal in New Orleans. He was acquitted of treason in a highly politicized trial presided over by Chief Justice Marshall in Richmond, in part because the scheme he orchestrated with General Wilkinson was poorly planned and ill conceived and thus not clearly documented, but there can be little doubt as to Burr's treacherous intent. For a comprehensive (if pro-Jeffersonian) account of the Burr treason affair, Dumas Malone, *Jefferson and His Time: Jefferson the President, Second Term, 1805–1809* at 215–346 (1974).

54 Richard Hofstadter, *The Idea of a Party System: The Rise of Legitimate Opposition in the United States, 1780–1840* at 128 (1969).

55 Cunliffe, *Soldiers and Civilians* at 202–12.

56 Michael A. Bellesiles, *Arming America: The Origins of a National Gun Culture* 425 (2000).

57 Cunliffe, *Soldiers and Civilians* at 206–207.

58 Ibid. at 205.

59 Ibid. at 205–206.

60 Ibid. at 205.

61   Ibid. at 207.

62   Ibid. at 202–203.

63   Weigley, *United States Army* at 125.

64   Article 2, sec. 2, cl. 1, of the Constitution provides that "The President shall be Commander in Chief of the Army and Navy of the United States, and of the militia of the several States, when called into the actual Service of the United States." But the President's powers as commander in chief of the militia remain circumscribed by the scope of Congress's power to call the militia into federal service in the first place. Article 1, sec. 8, cl. 15, provides "The Congress shall have Power . . . [t]o provide for calling forth the Militia to execute the Laws of the Union, suppress Insurrections and repel Invasions." The clearest exposition of the territorial limitations of this power is Attorney General Wickersham's in his 1912 opinion discussed infra. There, the attorney general wrote,

> The plain and certain meaning and effect of this constitutional provision is to confer upon Congress the power to call out the militia "to execute the laws of the Union" within our own borders where, and where only, they exist, have any force, or can be executed by any one. This confers no power to send the militia into a foreign country to execute our laws which have no existence or force there and can not be there executed.

29 Op. Atty. Gen. 322, 327 (1912).

65   The Calling Forth Act of 1795 (really a series of amendments to the Uniform Militia Act of 1792) authorized the president to call up the militia when the country faced "imminent danger of invasion." Act of Feb. 28, 1795, ch. 36, § 1, 1 Stat. 424, 424. According to Professor Weigley, Governor Roger Griswold of Connecticut

> asserted that militia could not lawfully be offered since the state officials knew of no declaration by the President that an invasion had taken place. Secretary (of War) Eustis replied that the President declared that an imminent danger of invasion existed. Governor Griswold in turn argued that war was not invasion and the presence of a hostile fleet off the coast represented only a "slight danger of invasion, which the Constitution could not contemplate."

Weigley, *United States Army* at 125.

66   Ibid.

67   25 U.S. (12 Wheat.) 19 (1827). Jacob E. Mott, a private in the New York militia, refused to obey President Madison's August 1814 order to make muster under federal command in New York City to fight against British forces. 25 U.S. at 21–22. At a subsequent court martial, Mott was fined $96, which he refused to pay. 25 U.S. at 36. Mott was then sentenced to one year's imprisonment, while Martin, a U.S. Marshal, executed a forfeiture of Mott's personal property to satisfy the fine. 25 U.S. at 23. A New York court allowed Mott to replevin his goods from Martin, who, after an unavailing appeal to the New York Senate,

which then sat as that state's highest court of appeals, sought relief from the U.S. Supreme Court. 25 U.S. at 28. In reversing the replevin judgment, Justice Story passed on the Calling Forth Act of 1795 and on the question of ultimate command authority over the militia. He rejected out of hand Mott's constitutional argument that the President's judgment as to whether the danger of invasion warranted calling forth the militia was subject to the review of state officers and militiamen. 25 U.S. at 32–33. Executive authority, Justice Story held, could not practically be fettered by an implied license for de novo review at each subordinate level. Presidential authority under the Calling Forth Act was supreme, and must not be checked by the second-guessing of any soldier or officer, including the governor of a state. 25 U.S. at 33. Thus, twelve years after the end of the War of 1812, it was firmly settled that the New England governors had acted unconstitutionally in refusing to follow Madison's orders to deploy their states' militia across state lines, and that supreme command of any militia called into federal service rested squarely with the President. 25 U.S. at 31–32. Story did not reach the question of whether the governors might constitutionally withhold consent for presidentially ordered militia service in foreign territory, which itself appeared facially unconstitutional.

68 Perpich v. Department of Defense, 496 U.S. 334, 354 (1990).

69 Weigley, *United States Army* at 183, 297, 324–25, 337–38, 340, 348–49, 401–402.

70 Ibid. at 120.

71 Ibid. at 122.

72 Samuel Eliot Morison et al., *The Growth of the American Republic* 377 (6th ed. 1969).

73 Federalist No. 46 (James Madison) at 301 (Krammick, ed. Penguin Classics 1987) (1788).

74 Weigley, *United States Army* at 131.

75 Henry Adams, *The War of 1812* at 179 (H. A. Deweerd ed., 1999 (1944) (excerpted from Henry Adams, *History of the United States 1801–1817,* 8 Vols. [1889–91]).

76 Weigley, *United States Army* at 131.

77 Ibid. at 597–98.

78 See generally Cunliffe, *Soldiers and Civilians* at p. 205, and consider the comments of New York's Adjutant General J. Watts de Peyester regarding his own state's commmon militia in 1855: "We always associate the term militia with the rag-tag and bob-tail assemblages armed with broomsticks, cornstalks and umbrellas," 2 *Eclaireur* 116 (March–April 1855). Broomsticks, cornstalks, and umbrellas (along with diverse other implements) figure prominently among the equipment of the New England militia unit depicted by David Claypole Johnston in 1836, see illustration above at page 122. The Federal Militia Censuses, compiled by the state adjutants general and reported to the War Department intermittently as directed by Congress, offer perhaps the strongest evidence of the common militia's decline. Beginning with partial reports for 1802, each census lists numbers of militia units, officers and men, and armaments maintained in each state force. The censuses also count muskets and rifles, and hence allow tabulation of the percentage of militia members who

were armed. The censuses are reprinted in *American State Papers, Class V, Military Affairs,* Vol. I 159–162 (returns for 1802, incomplete), Vol. I 198–203 (returns for 1806), Vol. I 210–214 (returns for 1807), Vol. I 253–262 (returns for 1810), Vol. I 297–301 (returns for 1811), Vol. II 134–137 (returns for 1820), Vol. II 320–323 (returns for 1821), Vol. IV 687–691 (returns for 1830) (Vol. I published 1832, Vol. II published 1834, Vol. IV published 1860) along with correspondence between the War Department and Congress and congressional reports that shed important light on the census data. The accompanying materials help clarify the role of the public purse in supporting the private responsibility of every militia-eligible citizen to arm himself in accordance with the Militia Act of 1792, as amended in 1803. Over the course of the period 1802–1830 covered by the militia censuses reprinted in *American State Papers,* federal grants became available to assist states whose citizens were failing to arm themselves according to the Militia Act. New England units were generally substantially armed, with compliance in Connecticut approaching, and sometimes exceeding, 100%. The fact that the number of muskets and rifles sometimes exceeded the number of infantry soldiers born on the roles has several likely causes, including counting state-owned guns maintained in armories, guns owned by officers, non-commissioned officers, artillery men, cavalry soldiers, musicians, and others born on the rolls but not expected to carry muskets or rifles into service, and multiple pieces owned by single militia soldiers. Travelling southwards and westwards, the militia became increasingly less and less well armed. Excepting Tennessee and Kentucky, newer states of the Southwest filed spotty returns, and reported very few citizens armed. Over the course of the period 1802–1830, several states, including conspicuously Delaware, appear to have abandoned compliance with the militia law, and maintenance of state forces. Some of the new states appear never to have established a militia at all. For our purposes, the most important information revealed by the censuses is that the proportion of citizen-soldiers armed with muskets or rifles in compliance with the Militia Act fell sharply from 1820 to 1830, from about 50% to approximately 32%, suggesting strongly that the common militia was beginning to collapse. More specifically, the figures reveal that by 1830, the common militia was still functioning (at least on paper) in New England, that it was still in existence (but only partly armed) in other parts of the East, and in Ohio, Kentucky, and Tennessee, but that it had collapsed or never come into being in the rest of the country. It is difficult to compute precise percentages of armed compliance based on the censuses. Non-reporting by some states, and issues such as whether or not to count officers and others not expected to carry long guns, whether to include cavalry pistols, and whether to count the obsolete "fusees" reported in some state lists for the earlier returns make exact tabulation problematic. Michael Bellesiles has reported that 44.8% of enrolled citizens were armed with muskets or rifles in 1803, 45.4% in 1810, 47.8% in 1820, and 31.8% in 1830; see Bellesiles, "Origins of Gun Culture in the United States, 1760–1865," 83 *Journal of American History* at 430. He might have noted that he elected to include officers and others unlikely to carry long guns into the field in his calculations, thereby yielding somewhat lower percentages than he would have obtained had he counted only citizens enrolled as privates in the state infantry. Still, his figures comport closely with our own independent review of the censuses. While Bellesiles's numbers regarding militia censuses seem sensible, it should be noted that his findings concerning probate inventories have been challenged in the most severe terms. See our discussion in chapter 6, note 54.

79 Speech to the Springfield Scott Club (Aug. 14, 1852), in 2 The Collected Works of Abraham Lincoln 135, 149–50 (Roy P. Basler ed., 1953).

CHAPTER FIVE: THE ERA OF THE VOLUNTEERS, 1840–1903

1 On the eve of the Civil War, many states' adjutants general listed only volunteer units in their organizational charts. Cunliffe, *Soldiers and Civilians* at 220–22.

2 Urban volunteer companies were by no means an exclusively northern phenomenon. For a fascinating sociocultural description of Richmond's volunteer regiments during the late antebellum years (including detailed treatments of the "Light Blues" and "Grays," the city's best known companies). See Gregg D. Kimball, *American City, Southern Place: A Cultural History of Antebellum Richmond* passim (2000).

3 Cunliffe, *Soldiers and Civilians* at 88–95, 227, 230.

4 Ibid. at 203 on Jefferson Davis's Mississippi Rifles; at 252–54 on the role of established, elite Volunteer units during the initial defense of Washington in 1861; at 5–7 on the Zouaves and other gaily uniformed Volunteers at First Bull Run.

5 Some companies even maintained their own armories under state license, or rented neglected arsenals from their local government. Ibid. at 219–20, 227. But see also Michael Bellesiles' treatment of the antebellum volunteers in *Arming America*. In keeping with his overall argument that the federal government played a determining role in creating an American gun culture and an armed populace, Bellesiles stresses that even the most exclusive volunteer militia units with the most expensive uniforms and accouterments not infrequently received or cajoled federally financed arms from state arsenals. Michael A. Bellesiles, Arming America: *The Origins of a National Gun Culture* (2000).

6 On the states' role in providing arms for militia members prior to 1792, see Michael A. Bellesiles, "The Origins of Gun Culture in the United States, 1760–1865" 88 *Journal of American History* 425 (1996). On federal dissatisfaction with state efforts to arm the militia to come into compliance with the 1792 Act, see ibid. at 429–35; Cunliffe, *Soldiers and Civilians* at 192–203, 209–12.

7 Act of July 6, 1798, ch. 65, § 1, 1 Stat. 576, 576.

8 Act of Apr. 23, 1808, ch. 55, § 1, 2 Stat. 490, 490, analyzed in Cunliffe, *Soldiers and Civilians* at 193. The law remained on the books until 1887, when Congress increased the annual militia appropriation to $400,000. See discussion infra page 132.

9 Uniform Militia Act of 1792, ch. 33, § 1, 1 Stat. 271, 271, repealed by Dick Act, ch. 196, 32 Stat. 775 (1903). For an analysis of the Uniform Militia Act of 1792,

see discussion supra pages 113–115; Cunliffe, *Soldiers and Civilians* at 184; Weigley, *United States Army* at 93–94.

10 Cunliffe, *Soldiers and Civilians* at 193, 209–11.

11 Weigley, *United States Army* at 195 (discussing Southern rearmament after Kansas); Cunliffe, *Soldiers and Civilians* at 209–12 (discussing prior nationwide indifference).

12 Weigley, *United States Army* at 201–204.

13 Ibid. at 204; Frederick Bernays Wiener, "The Militia Clause of the Constitution," 54 *Harvard L. Rev.* 181, 191 (1940).

14 Weigley, *United States Army* at 246.

15 Ibid. at 203–04.

16 An excellent account of the constitutional foundations of compelled military service during the Civil War can be found in David Yassky, "The Second Amendment in Context," 99 *Michigan L. Rev.* 588 (2000). Our account of the constitutional dimensions of Civil War conscription also draws heavily on Harold M. Hyman and William Wiecek, *Equal Justice Under Law: Constitutional Development 1835–1875* at 232–78 (1984), and Harold M. Hyman, *A More Perfect Union: The Impact of Civil War and Reconstruction on the Constitution* 141–224 (1973).

17 On December 31, 1860, eleven days after South Carolina's secession and just before its winter recess, the 36th Congress had authorized increasing the size of the 15,000 strong peacetime army by eleven regiments, or 11,000 men. Weigley, *United States Army* at 199–200.

18 Ibid. at 209.

19 Ibid. at 205.

20 Ibid. at 207–208.

21 The Class II List included males twenty to thirty-five and unmarried men thirty-five and over, while the Class I List comprised married men over thirty-five. The Class II list was to be exhausted before any names were selected from Class I. The only sons of widows, widowers, and infirm parents were exempted entirely. Ibid. at 208–10.

22 Foner, *Reconstruction* at 33.

23 Weigley, *United States Army* at 211–13, 215.

24 Martha Derthick, *The National Guard in Politics* 13 (1965); Scott Skowronek, *Building a New American State: The Expansion of National Administrative Capacities* 104–105 (1982).

25 Scott Skowronek, *Building a New American State: The Expansion of National Administrative Capacities* 92–95 (1982).

26 Ibid. at 93 (1982).

27 Ibid. at 104–105 (1982).

28 Presser v. Illinois, 116 U.S. 252, 267 (1886). Presser is discussed in detail supra 19–21 and notes 52–53 to chapter 1.

29 Bellesiles, "Origins of Gun Culture" at 453 (citing Russell Stanley Gilmore, *Crackshots and Patriots: The National Rifle Association and America's Military-Sporting*

Tradition, 1871–1929 [1974] (unpublished Ph.D. dissertation, University of Wisconsin; on file with the University of Wisconsin Library); *Americans and Their Guns: The National Rifle Association Story Through Nearly a Century of Service to the Nation* (James B. Trefethen compiler and James E. Serven ed., 1967).

30 Scott Skowronek, *Building a New American State: The Expansion of National Administrative Capacities* 85 (1982).

31 Bellesiles, "Origins of Gun Culture" at 435.

32 Martha Derthick, *The National Guard in Politics* 22 (1965).

CHAPTER SIX: THE UNITED STATES ARMY
AND THE UNITED STATES ARMY NATIONAL
GUARD IN THE TWENTIETH CENTURY

1 Weigley, *United States Army* at 298–305. It should perhaps be added that, thanks to America's vast naval and industrial superiority, the outcome of this war was never in doubt.

2 Dick Act, ch. 196, § 1, 32 Stat. 775, 775 (1903). For analyses of the Dick Act, see Perpich v. Department of Defense, 496 U.S. 334, 342 (1990); Martha Derthick, *The National Guard in Politics* 26–27 (1965) (hereinafter, Derthick, *National Guard*); Weigley, *United States Army* at 320–22; Frederick Bernays Wiener, "The Militia Clause of the Constitution," 54 *Harvard L. Rev.* 181, 193–96 (1940) (hereinafter, Wiener, "Militia Clause"). The act provided in relevant part:

> That the militia shall consist of every able-bodied male citizen of the respective States, Territories, and the District of Columbia, and every able-bodied male of foreign birth who has declared his intention to become a citizen, who is more than eighteen and less than forty-five years of age, and *shall be divided into two classes — the organized militia, to be known as the National Guard of the State, Territory, or District of Columbia, or by such other designations as may be given them by the laws of the respective States or Territories, and the remainder to be known as the Reserve Militia.*

Dick Act, ch. 196, § 1, 32 Stat. 775, 775 (1903) (emphasis added).

3 Dick Act, ch. 196, § 3, 32 Stat. 775, 775–76 (1903).

4 Militia Reform Act of 1908, ch. 204, § 1, 35 Stat. 399, 399.

5 29 Op. Atty. Gen. 322 (1912).

6 Weigley, *United States Army* at 324–25.

7 Ibid. at 344–47.

8 National Defense Act of 1916, ch. 134, § 1, 39 Stat. 166, 166.

9 Weigley, *United States Army* at 348.

10 Ibid. at 348.

11 Ibid. at 344–50.

12 Ibid. at 375–76.

13 Ibid. at 356–58.

14 Ibid. at 386–87.

15 Scott Skowronek, *Building a New American State: The Expansion of National Admin-istrative Capacities* 244 (1982) (hereinafter, Skowronek, *Building a New American State*); Weigley, *United States Army* at 397–400.

16 Weigley, *United States Army* at 395–400.

17 Derthick, *National Guard* at 44–47, 49, and at 93–107 (regarding the NGA's lobbying machine of the forties and fifties). On the lobbying effectiveness of Palmer, Reckord, and the NGA during the interwar years, see ibid. at 94.

18 Eventually, in 1952, Congress abandoned the requirement of an emergency and gave the President essentially discretionary authority to call up National Guard units with gubernatorial consent. Perpich v. Department of Defense, 496 U.S. 334, 346 (1990).

19 Weigley, *United States Army* at 401.

20 Ibid.

21 In the words of Justice Stevens,

> Since 1933 all persons who have enlisted in a State National Guard unit have simultaneously enlisted in the National Guard of the United States. . . . [U]nder the "dual enlistment" provisions of the statute that have been in effect since 1933, a member of the Guard who is ordered to active duty in the federal service is thereby relieved of his or her status in the State Guard for the entire period of federal service.

Perpich, 496 U.S. at 345–46.

22 Act of June 15, 1933, ch. 87, 48 Stat. 153.

23 Wiener, "Militia Clause" at 209. Wiener adds, "the 1933 Act proved conclu-sively that a well-regulated militia is impossible of attainment under the militia clause, and can be organized only by resort to the plenary and untrammeled powers under the army clause."

24 Weigley, *United States Army* at 420.

25 Ibid. at 436.

26 Ibid. at 486.

27 Ibid.

28 Prominent cases of governors ordering state militia to defy federal court orders relating to desegregation include actions by John Patterson of Alabama in 1956 (Autherine Lucy case), Orval Faubus of Arkansas in 1957 (high school integra-tion), and Ross Barnett of Mississippi in 1962 (state university integration). In each instance, the state militia was subsequently federalized by order of the President (i.e., called up into National Guard duty), and ordered to enforce federal law. The most famous case is that of Alabama Governor George Wallace in 1963. Wallace responded to a federal injunction preventing state troopers from obstructing integration by replacing the troopers with militia. President Kennedy federalized the guardsmen, who reluctantly ordered the governor to stand aside from a schoolhouse door he had ostentatiously obstructed. Dan T. Carter, *The Politics of Rage* 113, 154 (1995); Charles and Barbara Whalen, *The Longest Debate: A Legislative History of the 1964 Civil Rights Act* 33–34 (1985). Interestingly,

Wallace toyed after his election in 1962 with the idea of forming an irregular state militia apart from the National Guard, which would not have been subject to presidential command and thus could have conscientiously followed the governor's orders to enforce segregation. Dan T. Carter, *The Politics of Rage* 113 (1995).

29 Weigley, *United States Army* at 497.

30 Robert Middlekauff, *The Glorious Cause: The American Revolution, 1763–1789* at 575–81 (1982) (regarding the Revolutionary War); 1 Samuel Eliot Morison et al., *The Growth of the American Republic* 384–85 (7th ed. 1980) (regarding the War of 1812).

31 Weigley, *United States Army* at 184–85.

32 On the similarity of Northern and Southern militia and military cultures in the antebellum years and the insubstantiality of the Southern chivalric myth, see Cunliffe, *Soldiers and Civilians* at 337–84.

33 Weigley, *United States Army* at 305, 307, 309.

34 Ibid. at 497.

35 Ibid. at 486–87, 497.

36 Ibid. at 498.

37 Ibid. at 500.

38 Ibid. at 525–26, 535–36.

39 Ibid. at 533–34.

40 Ibid. at 533–34.

41 Ibid. at 508.

42 Ibid. at 508.

43 Ibid. at 508.

44 Ibid. at 509–10, 534–35.

45 Ibid. at 558.

46 Ibid. at 578–92.

47 In Eisenhower's words:

> This conjunction of an immense military establishment and a large arms industry is new in the American experience. . . . We recognize the imperative need for this development. Yet we must not fail to comprehend its grave implications. . . . In the councils of government, we must guard against the acquisition of unwarranted influence, whether sought or unsought, by the military-industrial complex. The potential for the disastrous rise of misplaced power exists and will persist.

> *The Oxford Dictionary of Modern Quotations* 73 (Tony Augarde ed., 1991).

48 On Harrington's antiarmy thought, see supra 49; on Gerry's fear of armies, see supra 98–100.

49 Weigley, *United States Army* at 509–10, 534–35, 558.

50 Ibid. at 505–06.

51 In addition to the 357,000 National Guard personnel, our citizen defense force includes 1,064,912 army reserves, of whom 395,038 are ready reserves, 684 standby reserves, and 669,190 retired reserves. Situation Report (visited

Nov. 11, 2000), www.dtic.mil/soldiers/ jan2000/pdfs/sitrep1.pdf; U.S. Army
Reserve: End Strength (visited Nov. 11, 2000), www.army.mil/usar/briefings/
civilian/sld005.htm. The regular establishment comprises 491,707 active duty
army; 381,203 active duty navy; 363,479 active duty air force; and 172,632 active
duty marine personnel. *The World Almanac and Book of Facts 1999* at 204 (Robert
Famighetti et al. eds.).

52   Situation Report (visited Nov. 11, 2000), www.dtic.mil/soldiers/jan2000/
pdfs/sitrep1.pdf; Situation Report (visited Nov. 11, 2000), www.dtic.mil/
soldiers/jan2000/pdfs/ sitrep3.pdf; Budget of the United States Government:
Fiscal Year 2000 at 158 (visited Nov. 11, 2000), w3.access.gpo.gov/usbudget/
fy2000/pdf/budget.pdf.

53   Perpich v. Department of Defense, 496 U.S. 334, 351 (1990).

54   In his Bancroft Prize book *Arming America* and elsewhere, Michael A. Bellesiles has argued that early American probate records suggest gun ownership
was not at all widespread before 1850, and that as few as ten to fifteen percent
of households contained functioning firearms in the early Republic (Bellesiles,
Arming America: The Origins of a National Gun Culture, 445 [2000], Bellesiles, "Gun
Laws in Early America: The Regulation of Firearms Ownership," 1607–1794,
16 *Law and Hist. Rev.,* 567 [1998], Bellesiles, "The Origins of Gun Culture in the
United States," 1760–1865, 83. *J. Am. Hist.* 425 [1996]). Bellesiles's use of the probate data has come under severe scrutiny, and his findings and methods have
been sharply criticized. Northwestern law professor and social scientist James
Lindgren has been Bellesiles's most vocal critic. Lindgren and coauthor Justin
Lee Heather have recently published a systematic rebuttal of Bellesiles's findings in the *William and Mary Law Review,* see "Counting Guns in Early America,"
43 *William and Mary Law Review* 1777 (2002). Lindgren and Heather repeatedly
charge Bellesiles with incompetence. According to Lindgren and Heather, the
very probate records examined by Bellesiles actually indicate guns present in
over half of the households inventoried. In a symposium on Bellesiles's *Arming America* recently featured in the *William and Mary Quarterly,* see 59 *WMQ* 3d
ser. 203, "Forum: Historians and Guns," Gloria T. Main, a highly respected
authority on probate records in colonial America, has similarly condemned
Bellesiles's methods; see Main, "Many Things Forgotten: The Use of Probate
Records in Arming America," 59 *WMQ* 3d ser. 211. Lindgren and Heather suggest Bellesiles may have falsified some of his evidence, 43, while Main stops
short of outright accusations of fraud, she calls Bellesiles's results "naïve," and
gives no credence to his statements concerning methodology; see Main, 59
WMQ 3d ser., at 212–213. However, other commentators in the *William and Mary
Quarterly* have defended Bellesiles; see, e.g., Jack N. Rakove, "Words, Deeds,
and Guns: Arming America and the Second Amendment," 59 *WMQ* 3d ser.
205. In the interest of fairness, it should be added that Bellesiles's conclusions
in *Arming America* do not depend entirely, or even chiefly, on his analysis of
probate data. His argument about the scarcity of guns in early America relies
very heavily on letters and reports by colonial, state, crown, and federal offi-

cials attesting to the need for weapons with which to arm militia units whose members had no guns of their own. For the early national period, Bellesiles relies principally on periodic militia censuses carried out by state adjutants general at the direction of the War Department under authority of Congress. We discuss the limitations of the militia censuses in some detail in note 78 to chapter 4. In the militia censuses, states reported figures on the numbers of citizens enrolled in their militia, and the number of arms available for service. These reports are reprinted in *American State Papers, Class V, Military Affairs,* Vol. I 159–162 (returns for 1802, incomplete), Vol. I 198–203 (returns for 1806), Vol. I 210–214 (returns for 1807), Vol. I 253–262 (returns for 1810), Vol. I 297–301 (returns for 1811), Vol. II 134–137 (returns for 1820), Vol. II 320–323 (returns for 1821), Vol. IV 687–691 (returns for 1830) (Vol. I published in 1832, Vol. II published in 1834, Vol. IV published in 1860), along with accompanying correspondence between executive officials and Congress. The militia censuses measured directly the percentage of the enrolled population who were armed with muskets or rifles as required by the Militia Act of 1792. The quality and frequency of returns differed from state to state, but hundreds of thousands of citizens and guns were counted during the early decades of the nineteenth century. The militia censuses therefore represent a much more comprehensive and accurate assessment of arms possession among members of the militia than has been attempted or is possible for the general population through extrapolation based on surviving probate inventories. According to the militia censuses, the percentage of militia members armed with either muskets or rifles ranged widely in the early nineteenth century, with about 80 percent representing the norm in New England, and 40 percent the norm elsewhere, before the militia system began to decay precipitously after the 1820 census. The first comprehensive census was conducted in 1806, before substantial federal money became available to the states to facilitate and augment the system of private, individual arms acquisition contemplated in the Act of 1792. It is reprinted in the *State Papers* alongside a revealing report by the House committee "instructed to inquire what measures are necessary to be adopted to complete the arming of the militia of the United States," from which we reprint the excerpt below. Mr. Varnum, from the committee made the following report:

That by the laws of the United States, each citizen enrolled in the militia is put under obligations to provide himself with a good musket or rifle, and all the other military equipments prescribed by law. From the best estimate which the committee have been able to form, there is upwards of 250,000 fire arms and rifles in the hands of the militia, which have, a few instances excepted, been provided by, and are the property of, the individuals who hold them. It is highly probable, that many more of the militia would have provided themselves with fire arms in the same way, if they had been for sale in those parts of the United States where the deficiencies have happened; but the wars in Europe have had a tendency to prevent the importation of fire arms from thence into the United States, which, together with the limited establishments for the manufacture of that implement in the United States has rendered it impossible for individuals to procure them. (*State Papers, Class V, Military Affairs,* Vol. 1, 193 (1832)).

According to our own tabulations, in 1806, the nation's militia included 475,487 infantry privates, who were equipped with 204,139 muskets and 45,043 rifles. *American State Papers, Class V, Military Affairs,* Vol. 1 pp. 198–203. The militia, then, was 52.40 percent armed. Thus, in 1806, the percentage of militia members who were armed in accordance with the Militia Act is somewhat lower than the percentage of probated inventories containing guns in Main and Lindgren's separate compilations, and substantially higher than the percentage of probated inventories containing guns in Bellesiles's compilations. It is possible that probate records suggest a different rate of arms possession than the militia censuses because households frequently contained more militia-obligated persons than guns (e.g. a household might contain one gun, a superannuated father, and three militia-obligated sons). It is also highly likely that the desire to comply with the Militia Act made militia members more likely to own arms than non-enrolled citizens. But whether Lindgren's determination of 40 percent to 65 percent or Bellesiles's estimate of little more than 10 percent comes closest to the actual percentage of early Americans who owned or held working guns ultimately does not bear on our thesis. For our purposes, what matters is that the Act of 1792 envisioned individual acquisition and maintenance of muskets and rifles to be held ready for militia duty consonant with the Second Amendment. Revolutionary era leaders recognized that this system of private arming had always proved problematic, but also understood that republican values pressed strongly for preservation of the private arming paradigm. Even before the end of the eighteenth century, state and federal governments were facilitating and supplementing private acquisition by spending public monies. In the early nineteenth century, assisted no doubt by increasing government aid, New England's citizen soldiers came into substantial compliance with the Militia Act. But New England's success was not replicated nationally, and by 1850, the old nexus of a universal, individually armed militia had collapsed everywhere on account of popular apathy and resentment.

55 Bellesiles, *Arming America* at 434.

56 Boorstin, *The National Experience* at 31–33. Whitney executed the contract during the third year of John Adams's presidency and did not make delivery of the last of the 10,000 muskets until Jefferson was preparing to leave office in January 1809. Boorstin, *The National Experience* at 32–33. Bellesiles insists Whitney's claim that his guns' parts could be interchanged was a hoax designed to dupe the government into awarding him contracts and putting up with his poor performance. Bellesiles, *Arming America* at 233–35.

57 The statements concerning modern administrative practice relating to arms

issuance in the Guard reflect Mr. Merkel's personal experience and observations as a reservist training with the U.S. Army and Maryland National Guard while an ROTC cadet at Johns Hopkins University in the 1980s.

58 But see Bellesiles's *Arming America* for the argument that local and central authorities played a determining role in arming the militia from the very beginnings of the Anglo-American experience.

CHAPTER SEVEN: TEXT AND CONTEXT

1 A flood of articles and book reviews have been published over the past decade (since January 1990) dealing in some way with interpretive devices like "originalism" and "textualism." We mention here only a few of the most recent entrants: Joseph Raz, "Intention in Interpretation," in *The Autonomy of Law: Essays on Legal Positivism* 264–65, 266 (Robert George ed., 1996); John F. Manning, "Textualism and the Role of the Federalist in Constitutional Adjudication," 66 *George Washington L. Rev.* 1337 (1998); Michael C. Dorf, "Integrating Normative and Descriptive Constitutional Theory: The Case of Original Meaning," 85 *Georgia L. J.* 1765, 1803 (1997); Raoul Berger, "Jack Rakove's Rendition of Original Meaning," 72 *Indiana L. J.* 619 (1997); Jack N. Rakove, "The Original Intention of Original Understanding," 13 *Constitutional Commentary* 159 (1996). And see Henry Monaghan, "Stare Decisis and Constitutional Adjudication," 88 *Columbia L. Rev.* 723 (1988). Three recent articles have looked critically at the problematic application of originalist interpretation methods in the Second Amendment arena, and, in particular, questioned the scholarly thoroughness of the standard modelers: Saul Cornell, "Commonplace or Anachronism: The Standard Model, the Second Amendment, and the Problem of History in Contemporary Constitutional Theory," 16 *Constitutional Commentary* 221 (1999); Jack N. Rakove, "The Second Amendement: The Highest State of Originalism," 76 *Chi. Kent L. Rev.* 103 (2000); Daniel A. Farber, "Disarmed by Time: The Second Amendment and the Failure of Originalism," 76 *Chi. Kent L. Rev.* 167 (2000).

2 By way of qualification, we must add that there are some provisions of the Bill of Rights that seem to invite just such perpetual reconstitution. Nothing in the linguistic or social context of the term "cruel and unusual" in the Eighth Amendment suggests just what punishments are prohibited, nor does the Fourth, by language or by social convention, decree what searches and seizures are to be deemed "unreasonable." For these, we suppose, it would be a mistake to define them according to ancient uses. Rather, the intent of the framers appears to have been to delegate to future generations the construction of the terms according to evolving notions of cruelty or reasonableness.

3 For assertions of constitutional fluidity, see William J. Brennan Jr., "The Constitution of the United States: Contemporary Ratification," in *The Debate over Original Intent* 23 (Jack N. Rakove ed., 1990); and Morton J. Horwitz, "The Supreme Court, 1992 Term Forward: The Constitution of Change: Legal Fundamentality Without Fundamentalism," 107 *Harvard L. Rev.* 30, 116 (1993) ("The

central problem of modern constitutionalism is how to reconcile the idea of fundamental law with the modernist insight that meanings are fluid and historically changing.").

4   H. Jefferson Powell, "The Original Understanding of Original Intent," 98 *Harvard L. Rev.* 885, 885 (1985).

5   Boris Bittker, "Interpreting the Constitution: Is the Intent of the Framers Controlling? If Not, What Is?" 19 *Harvard Journal of Law and Public Policy* 9 (1995).

6   In this we are in accord with Professor Lawrence Lessig, who takes "text" to mean "any artifact created in part to convey meaning," and "context" to be "the collection of understandings within which such texts make sense." "Text and context make meaning," he says and "Fidelity is the aim to preserve meaning." Lawrence Lessig, "Understanding Changed Meanings: Fidelity and Theory," 47 *Stanford L. Rev.* 395, 402 (1995). Fidelity requires understanding of the context of creation and the context of application. As Jefferson Powell states: "We can understand the original meaning of the Constitution . . . only by 'plunging [ourselves] into the systems of communication in which [the Constitution] acquired meaning.'" H. Jefferson Powell, "Rules for Originalists," 73 *Virginia L. Rev.* 659 (1987).

7   Garry Wills's provocative "To Keep and Bear Arms," XLII *N. Y. Rev. of Books* 62–73 contains a thoughtful and learned passage on the meaning of "bearing arms," id. at 66, which probably remains the most influential exegesis of the meaning of that phrase in the Second Amendment literature. Needless to say, standard modellers have their rejoinders, and even more staid members of the academe sometimes take Wills with a few caveats. While the respected and thoroughly dispassionate military historian Don Higginbotham has pointed out that Wills's "analysis of *to bear, well-regulated,* and *the people* is astute and helps rescue these terms from the distorted meanings ascribed to them by so many Standard Modellers," he adds that "[i]n his examination of the term to *keep* . . . Wills resorts to the same 'linguistic tricks' he repeatedly ascribes to Standard Modellers." Don Higginbotham, "The Second Amendment in Historical Context," 16 *Constitutional Commentary* 263, 278–79 (1999). Still, it remains highly difficult to make a credible case for a pervasive non-military meaning of "bearing arms," all the more so in the context of statutory or constitutional usage. As David Yassky remarks, "searching a Library of Congress database containing all official records of debates in the Continental and U.S. Congresses between 1774 and 1821 reveals thirty uses of the phrase "bear arms" or "bearing arms" (other than in discussing the proposed Second Amendment); in every single one of these uses, the phrase has an unambiguously military meaning." Yassky, "The Second Amendment: Structure, History, and Constitutional Change," 99 *Michigan Law Review,* 588, 618 (2000), citing A Century of Lawmaking for a New Nation: U.S. Congressional Documents and Debates, available at http://memory.loc.gov/ammen/amlaw/lawhome.html. The *Oxford English Dictionary* also attests unequivocally to the military implications of arms bearing in eighteenth century usage. 1 *Oxford English Dictionary*

634 (J.A. Simpson & E.S.C. Weiner eds., 2d ed., 1989). In Yassky's words "The *Oxford English Dictionary* defines 'to bear arms' as meaning 'to serve as a soldier, do military service, fight.' It defines 'to bear arms against' as meaning 'to be engaged in hostilities with.' As an exemplary use of the phrase in 1769, the *OED* gives 'An ample . . . pardon to all who had born arms against him,' and the exemplary use from 1609 is: 'He bure armes, and made weir against the king.' . . . Indeed, the word 'arms' itself has a primarily military connotation. According to the *OED*, the oldest established meaning of 'arms' (other than the plural of 'arm,' meaning limb) is 'armour, mail.' The next oldest meaning is '[i]nstruments of offence used in war; weapons.' The *OED* quotes a 1794 dictionary; 'By *arms*, we understand those instruments of offence generally made use of in war; such as firearms, swords, etc. By *weapons*, we more particularly mean instruments of other kinds (exclusive of firearms), made use of as offensive on special occasions.'" Yassky, 99 *Michigan Law Review* at 619, citing *OED* 633–34.

8   The two clauses of the Fourth Amendment provide a good example of joined but independent entitlements: "The right of the people to be secure in their persons, houses, papers, and effects, against unlawful searches and seizures, shall not be violated, and no Warrants shall issue, but upon probable cause, supported by Oath or affirmation, and particularly describing the place to be searched, and the persons or things to be seized."

9   And indeed the structure of the Fourth Amendment has generated just such debate.

10   Fowler (in his second edition) defines the absolute construction thus: ". . . [I]t consists in English of a noun or pronoun that is not the subject or object of any verb or the object of any preposition but is attached to a participle or an infinitive, e.g., *The play being over,* we went home. / Let us toss for it, *loser to pay.*" H. W. Fowler, *A Dictionary of Modern English Usage* 4 (Oxford University Press 2d ed. 1965); an eminent grammarian has this to add: "The absolute phrase has a great potential of polished economy. . . . but the ablative absolute is the supreme sophisticate of subordination. . . . And it is more common than you may suppose. . . . The . . . pattern, noun plus participle, marks the ablative absolute." Sheridan Baker, *The Practical Stylist* 51–52 (4th ed. 1977).

11   Jack Greenberg, *Crusaders in the Courts* 229–30 (1994).

12   H. Jefferson Powell, "The Original Understanding of Original Intent," 98 *Harvard L. Rev.* 885, 885 (1985).

13   H. Richard Uviller, "Forward: Fisher Goes on the Quintessential Fishing Expedition and Hubbell is Off the Hook," 91 *Journal of Criminal Law and Criminology* 311, (2001).

14   Ibid.

15   Schmerber v. California, 384 U.S. 757 (1966).

16   United States v. Hubbell, 530 U.S. 27 (2000); United States v. Doe, 465 U.S. 605 (1984).

17   United States v. Hubbell, 530 U.S. 27 (2000) (dissenting opinion).

18 The operative section of the Fifteenth Amendment to the Constitution, adopted in 1870, provides as follows: "The right of citizens of the United States to vote shall not be denied or abridged by the United States or by any State on account of race, color, or previous condition of servitude."

19 As Professor Monaghan puts it, "[T]hey [academic lawyers] have sought to sterilize the concept [of original intent], most typically, by conceptualizing original intent at a level of abstraction that, in effect, removes it as an interpretive constraint." Henry P. Monaghan, "Our Perfect Constitution," 56 *N.Y.U. L. Rev.* 353, 378 (1981).

20 The ages at which men were required to render militia service varied from time to time, colony to colony, and state to state before 1792, often set at sixteen to forty-five, or even at sixteen till death. Bellesiles, "Origins of Gun Culture" at 428. Under the Uniform Militia Act of 1792, which remained in force until 1903, men aged eighteen to forty-four were carried on the rolls.

21 Professor Levinson hints at this argument in the context of his metaphor regarding the New Yorker style map of the Bill of Rights, with the neo-rightist version of the map featuring the Second Amendment in the foreground and the First Amendment vanishing into the Pacific. Sanford Levinson, "The Embarrassing Second Amendment," 99 *Yale L. J.* 637, (1991).

22 18 U.S.C. § 3141 et seq. The provision was validated by the United States Supreme Court in United States v. Salerno, 481 U.S. 739 (1987), against a challenge under the excessive bail provision of the Eighth Amendment, among other grounds. The Court clearly held that the Constitution does not limit the grounds for pretrial detentions to the prevention of flight, nor does it entitle every defendant to a conditional release.

23 The Supreme Court has recently removed any doubt (created by themselves) concerning the paternity of the Fifth Amendment right in the genetic character of the *Miranda* right to helpful advice when interrogated in custody. Those who took the Court seriously, and began thinking of the *Miranda* warnings as a creature apart from the more conventional, "true," brute coercion, must now move back to a unified theory of the Fifth Amendment. Dickerson v. United States, 530 U.S. 428 (2000).

24 The question of what makes up the British Constitution is endlessly fascinating, and does not easily admit of short-form answers. For an outstanding and up-to-date historical and philosophical analysis of the British Constitution by an English legalist with strong comparative interests in American constitutional law, see Ian Loveland, *Constitutional Law* (2000).

25 Pocock, *Politics* at 80–103.

26 J. P. Sommerville, *Politics and Ideology in England, 1603–1640* 163–83 (1986).

27 On Locke's contributions to the development of political thought, moral theory, and rationalism, see generally John Dunn, *Locke* (1984).

28 Garry Wills, *Inventing America* at 170.

29 William Lee Miller, *First Liberty* at 95–96.

30 Thomas Jefferson, "A Summary View of the Rights of British America" (1774),

reprinted in 1 *The Papers of Thomas Jefferson* 121, 134 (Julian P. Boyd ed., Princeton University Press 1953).

31 The classic interpretation of the new structuralist departure of Madison's Constitution is of course Wood, *American Republic* at 593–615.

32 Sanford Levinson, "The Embarrassing Second Amendment," 99 *Yale L. J.* 637 (1991).

33 Halbrook, *That Every Man Be Armed;* Randy E. Barnett and Don B. Kates, "Under Fire: The New Consensus on the Second Amendment," 45 *Emory L. J.* 1139 (1996).

34 It is interesting to note that the right to arms (either linked to or divorced from duty in a militia) formed no part of the Universal Declaration of the Rights of Man promulgated by revolutionary France in 1789, and that it forms no part of the United Nation's Universal Declaration of Human Rights or the European Convention for the Protection of Human Rights and Fundamental Freedoms today.

35 Williams, "The Terrifying Second Amendment"; "The Militia Movement and the Second Amendment: Conjuring with the People," 81 *Cornell L. Rev.* 879 (1996), "The Unitary Second Amendment," 73 *N.Y.U. L. Rev.* 822 (1998); Robert E. Shalhope, "The Ideological Origins of the Second Amendment," 69 *Journal of American History* 599, 609 (1982).

36 Speaking of constitutional text, Professor Powell writes:

> to the extent that the interpreter needs or wishes historical illumination on their meaning, he is obligated as a historian to place them in a complex and unfamiliar setting: classical-republican thought about the autonomous and virtuous citizen, the British Country ideology that was developed in opposition to the Court administrations of the early 1700's, notions ultimately derived from ancient Greece concerning the inevitably redistributive tendencies of democracies, common law and Whig ideas about traditional English liberties, and so on.

H. Jefferson Powell, "Rules for Originalists," 73 *Virginia L. Rev.* 659 (1987).

37 Miller, *First Liberty* at 88–91.

38 Letter of Thomas Jefferson to James Madison (Aug. 30, 1785), in 8 *The Papers of Thomas Jefferson* 460 (Julian P. Boyd ed., Princeton University Press 1953) (enclosing voluminous manifest of books shipped); Letter of Thomas Jefferson to James Madison (Aug. 2, 1787), in 11 *The Papers of Thomas Jefferson* 662 (Julian P. Boyd ed., Princeton University Press 1953) (same).

39 See Akhil Amar, *The Bill of Rights: Creation and Reconstruction,* for the ingenious thesis that the entire Bill of Rights was essentially a structuralist creation, designed to protect states and localities rather than individuals against federal power. (Amar goes on to argue that the Fourteenth Amendment transformed the Bill of Rights and lent it its familiar individualist guise of today. See our discussion of this aspect of Amar's thesis in Chapter Eight, infra). We readily acknowledge that a republican animus continued to inform discourse about

the other provisions of the Bill of Rights in 1789, but we dispute Amar's suggestion that this was the only or the predominant mode of analysis applied to religious, intellectual, and procedural freedoms at the time the Bill of Rights was proposed and ratified. As we emphasize in the main text, the rights enshrined in the First, Fourth, Fifth, Sixth, Eighth (and Seventh) Amendments—unlike the Second Amendment right to arms—were also conceptualized as private liberties by leading politicians and wide segments of the population by 1789–91. (Rakove, *Original Meanings* at 312 on the First Amendment as a preserve of private liberties immune from government regulation; Miller, *First Liberty*, vii-viii and passim, regarding separation of church and state; and Rakove, *Original Meanings* on procedural liberties as restrictions on the manner of government action against individuals.) In contrast, those few radical anti-federalists who advocated a private right to arms outside the militia context were considered eccentrics, and even dangerous anarchists, and their views failed to resonate with the wider nation. Cornell, "Commonplace or Anachronism," 16 *Constitutional Commentary* at 238–45.

40 Joseph Story, *Commentaries on the Constitution of the United States* § 1896 at 607–608 (2d ed. 1851) (1833).

CHAPTER EIGHT: OTHER THEORIES
OF MEANING CONSIDERED

1 Sanford Levinson, "The Embarrassing Second Amendment," 99 *Yale L. J.* 637 (1991) (hereinafter, Levinson, "Embarrassing Second Amendment").

2 See Levinson, "Embarrassing Second Amendment."

3 Advocates arguing that the Second Amendment placed restrictions on gun control include Stephen P. Halbrook, Robert Dowlert, and Don B. Kates Jr., while those arguing that the Second Amendment did not seriously impair gun control legislation include Keith A. Ehrman and Dennis A. Henigan.

4 Lawrence Delbert Cress, "An Armed Community: The Origins and Meaning of the Right to Bear Arms," 71 *J. of Am. Hist.* 22 (1984); Robert E. Shalhope, "The Ideological Origins of the Second Amendment," 69 *Journal of American History* 599, 609 (1982).

5 See our discussion in the context of the case of *Emerson v. United States* in the next chapter.

6 Professor Tribe has since revised his assessment of the Second Amendment and adopted a position that resonates more closely with Levinson's. Laurence H. Tribe, 1 *American Constitutional Law* 897 n. 211 (3d ed. 1999).

7 Levinson, "Embarrassing Second Amendment" at 645–46.

8 Ibid. at 646–47.

9 In art. 1, sec. 10, and art. 1, sec. 9, cl. 8.

10 Levinson, "Embarrassing Second Amendment" at 641.

11 John R. Lott Jr., *More Guns, Less Crime: Understanding Crime and Gun-Control Laws* (University of Chicago Press 1998).

12 Levinson, "Embarrassing Second Amendment" at 656.

13 Ibid. at 656.

14 Ibid. at 657.

15 Plato, *The Republic* 568D-569C, on the desires of the *demos* (people) to end tyran-nical rule; Aristotle, *Politics* 1315b11–1316b27, on the impermanence of tyrannies and the scarcity of long-lived tyrannical states; Plutarch, *Life of Caesar* paras. 57–61, on the reasons justifying the assassination of Julius Caesar.

16 For commentary on the constitutional issues behind the Rye House Plot of 1683, see Aschcraft, *Revolutionary Politics and Locke's Two Treatises of Government* 338–407 (hereinafter, Ashcraft, *Revolutionary Politics*).

17 For a discussion of the constitutional implications of the Duke of Monmouth's Rebellion of 1685, see Ashcraft, *Revolutionary Politics* at 447–70.

18 Ibid. at 364–65.

19 John Locke, *Second Treatise of Government* § 212.

20 Ibid. at § 221.

21 Ibid. at § 240.

22 For an interesting discussion on whether the Second Treatise exercised direct influence on Jefferson's drafting of the Declaration of Independence, see Wills, *Inventing America* at 167–80 and passim, which excerpts Jefferson's own rebut-tal to the charge of plagiarism, leveled nearly forty years after the fact when Locke's Treatises had become more widely known in America than they were at the time of the Revolution. Wills takes the unorthodox position that Jeffer-son's phrasing owed more to mid-eighteenth-century Scottish writings (par-ticularly those of Francis Hutcheson) than to any manifestoes, pamphlets, or treatises from the Real Whig tradition. Our own view is in agreement with Jefferson's above referenced judgment that "[a]ll [the Declaration's] authority rests . . . on the harmonizing sentiments of the day, whether expressed in con-versation, in letters, printed essays, or in the elementary books of public right, as Aristotle, Cicero, Locke, Sydney, etc." See Wills, *Inventing America* at 172, quoting 10 *Writings of Jefferson* 343 (Paul Leicestor Ford ed.). In other words, Jefferson sounds like Locke not because he consciously echoes Locke, but be-cause they both spoke the language of Whiggery (leavened to differing de-grees by enlightened sentiments), and both developed fundamentals of Whig resistance theory that were as commonplace among the American patriots as they had been among the Real Whigs of Shaftesbury's, Sidney's, Ferguson's, Molesworth's, and Locke's day.

23 John Locke, *Second Treatise of Government* at § 225.

24 Joseph J. Ellis, *American Sphinx: The Character of Thomas Jefferson* 275–79 (1997) for a fascinating discussion of Jefferson and Madison's exchanges on constitu-tionalism after Jefferson's retirement. At times in old age, the "Constitution" apparently meant to Mr. Jefferson not Mr. Madison's Articles of 1787 and the subsequent Amendments, but the principals of the good old cause literature on resistance to the Stuarts! At these moments, for Jefferson real Whiggery still trumped ratification. To Madison, of course, the written Constitution was self-evidently the highest law of the land. It seems odd that Jefferson should "just

not get it," and deny the fundamental reality at the core of the American political system. The truth is that he obviously had grasped the situation back in 1787; indeed, it was Jefferson who argued to Madison that the Bill of Rights would be no mere parchment barrier because the federal courts would be able to exercise judicial review of government actions and enforce the Amendments. Letter from Thomas Jefferson to James Madison (Mar. 15, 1789), in 14 *The Papers of Thomas Jefferson* 659 (Julian P. Boyd, ed. 1953). But in retirement, Jefferson traveled back blissfully from the world of structuralism to the constitutionalism of his rebellious youth. There is a wonderful irony that the man who had been the most Francophile, most enlightened, most rational, most anti-English, most progressive, and most egalitarian of the American revolutionaries should at the end of his days rediscover that he was at heart still a seventeenth-century English Country Whig.

25 For the classic statement of the argument that the Constitution should not be conceived of as a counterrevolutionary reaction against the liberalism of the Revolution, but rather that the fundamental theoretical innovations embodied in Madison's structuralism and instrumentalism ushered in a revolutionary new style of democratic constitutionalism unlike anything known before, see Wood, *Creation of the American Republic* at 593–615 and discussion at 75–76.

26 Pocock, *Machiavellian Moment* at 372, 376–77 and discussion at 47–48.

27 Turk. Const. preamble; Turk. Const. art. 122; Ergun Özbudun, "Constitutional Law," in *Introduction to Turkish Law* 19, 22–25 (Tuğrul Ansay and Don Wallace Jr. eds., 1996) (discussing army interventions in the name of the preservation of constitutionalism carried out in 1960 and 1980 and leading to the establishment of new constitutional instruments in 1961 and 1982). Mr. Merkel thanks noted Ottomanist Can Erimtan of Istanbul and Lady Margaret Hall, Oxford, for bringing this aspect of Turkish constitutionalism to his attention.

28 John Locke, *A Letter Concerning Toleration* (1689).

29 Howard Peckham lists 6,824 battlefield deaths out of 25,324 deaths in service on the "American" side alone. *The Toll of Independence: Engagements and Battle Casualties in the American Revolution* 130 (Howard Peckham ed., 3d ed. 1974). Imperial losses (British and Irish, German, and free black) were listed as high as 70,000 by contemporary critics of the war, but this figure appears greatly exaggerated. Ibid. at 132. Peckham does not estimate Native American losses on the Imperial side. In terms of a proportion of the population, only the Civil War took a more gruesome toll on the nation.

30 Wood, *Creation of the American Republic* at 543–62.

31 Jack N. Rakove, "The Origins of Judicial Review: A Plea for New Contexts," 49 *Stanford L. Rev.* 1031, 1047 and passim (1997), and Rakove, *Original Meanings* at 81–82, 175–77, 345.

32 Benson noted on the House floor that writing a conscientious objector clause into the Bill of Rights would present "a question before the Judiciary on every regulation you [i.e. Congress] make with respect to organization of the militia, whether it comports with this declaration or not." I *Annals of Congress* 751.

33   Ashcraft, *Revolutionary Politics* at 521–89 and passim.

34   "On Monday, the 7th [of September 1789] . . . [t]he following propositions to add new articles of amendment were then successively made and decided in the negative. . . . 2. That government ought to be instituted for the common benefit, protection, and security of the people; and that the doctrine of non-resistance against arbitrary power and oppression is absurd, slavish, and destructive of the good and happiness of mankind." *Senate Journal* appearing in *History of Congress Exhibiting a Classification of the Proceedings of the Senate and the House of Representatives from March 4, 1789 to March 3, 1793,* reprinted in 2 Schwartz, *A Documentary History* at 1150–51.

35   Carl T. Bogus, "The Hidden History of the Second Amendment," 31 *U.C. Davis L. Rev.* 301 (1998) (hereinafter, Bogus, "Hidden History").

36   Bogus, "Hidden History" at 408. "The Amendment deals with keeping and bearing arms in the militia, subject to federal and state regulation. Therefore, to the extent original intent matters, the hidden history of the Second Amendment strongly supports the collective rights position."

37   Ibid. at 321.

38   Eugene D. Genovese, *Roll Jordan Roll: The World of the Slave Trade* (1972) at 596–97. Although slave rebellion was rare in America in the late eighteenth century, slave resistance was endemic, and resistance frequently took a violent turn. From "stealing" food to breaking tools to sabotaging crops to burning woodlands, violence against property formed part of the annual cycle on the plantation. Genovese, *Roll Jordan Roll* at 597–621; John Blassinghame, *The Slave Community: Plantation Life in the Ante-Bellum South* 225 (1979). The potential for escalation from vandalism into violence against people lurked, at least dully, in the back of every planter's mind. John Blassinghame, *The Slave Community: Plantation Life in the Ante-Bellum South* 225, 235–37 (1979); Genovese, *Roll Jordan Roll* at 595. Occasionally, when the newspapers reported that a slave was tried for murder of a white person, that unrest had flared in the West Indies, or that slaves aboard a slave ship had mutinied, Southern planters' awareness became keen and direct. Vigilance was heightened. Suspicion of poisonings became rampant. Genovese, *Roll Jordan Roll* at 615–17. Less enlightened planters feared the conjurers and medicine men. Blassinghame, *The Slave Community;* Genovese *Roll Jordan Roll* at 224–25. And occasionally, as when the refugees from the Haitian Revolution arrived in 1791–93, when Gabriel Prosser plotted in 1800, and when Nat Turner rose in 1831, whites reacted systemically, if not entirely consistently. Gabriel's plot hastened the repeal of Virginia's liberal revolutionary era manumission laws (accomplished 1806), William W. Freehling, *The Road to Disunion, Volume One: Secessionists at Bay, 1776–1854* (1990); Nat Turner's rebellion prompted Thomas Jefferson Randolph to introduce a post-nati emancipation measure in the Virginia Legislature that could well have passed had western counties been proportionately represented; Freehling, *Secessionists at Bay* at 188.

39   In his most systematic analysis of slave resistance in the New World, Eugene Genovese—probably the foremost authority on the history of American

slavery—acknowledges that full-blown slave rebellions were notably rare on the North American mainland; Eugene D. Genovese, *From Rebellion to Revolution: Afro-American Slave Revolts in the Making of the Modern World* 49–50 (1979) (hereinafter, Genovese, *From Rebellion to Revolution*). Notwithstanding his ideological identification with the heroism of the rebels, Genovese joins many other historians in taking issue with the tabulation of 250 American slave rebellions and conspiracies cited by Bogus. Those calculations, performed by Herbert Aptheker some fifty years ago, rated abortive conspiracies in the same column as revolts and rebellions. In William Freehling's words, "[h]istorians have rightly emphasized that Aptheker's History . . . is a history not of revolts achieved but of alleged plans gone awry." Freehling, *Secessionists at Bay* at 579 n. 6. According to Genovese, over the entire 243-year period of African slavery in mainland British North America and the United States, there are records of only four sustained violent slave uprisings involving large numbers of slaves or large-scale loss of white life (New York/Long Island 1712, approx. 25 slaves involved, eight whites killed; Stono, South Carolina 1744, approx. 100 slaves involved, perhaps 20 whites killed; St. John the Baptist Parish, Louisiana 1811, as many as 500 slaves organized into military units involved; Nat Turner's Revolt, South Hampton County, Virginia, 1831, 60–70 slaves involved, as many as 70 whites killed; omitted is the Seminole War of 1835–42, involving campaigns by U.S. Regulars against the Seminole Indians of Florida and their maroon allies, who had escaped from slavery in Georgia and South Carolina, often many years before, and costing the U.S. Army 1,600 dead and $30–40 million). Genovese, *Roll Jordan Roll* at 588, and Genovese, *From Rebellion to Revolution* at 41–50. He might also have noted the New York City/Long Island uprising of 1741, which resulted in massive property damage and the burning of the Governor's mansion but cost only one white life. But even if major revolts were uncommon in America, Southern fear of the potential for violence was pervasive, in part because of the example of the West Indies and South America, where violent resistance, and even war, was endemic. The comparatively much larger white population on the North American mainland stacked the odds in favor of the whites, and served as a deterrent to insurrection, while less oppressive conditions—at least outside of the Carolina rice coast—made the impetus to rebellion less desperate than in the islands or South America. Genovese, *From Rebellion to Revolution* at 49–50; Blassinghame, *The Slave Community* at 214–15. Ultimately, however, Genovese concurs with Bogus and Aptheker on the essential point that mainland Anglo-American whites were wary, and that they relied on their militia, the lynch mob, and disproportionate retribution to maintain security in the plantation districts.

40 Genovese, *From Rebellion to Revolution* at 117. But even Genovese makes the point that this realization did not acquire sufficient force to drive Southern political behavior until Haiti, Gabriel, St. John's Parish, Denmark Vessey, and Nat Turner had amplified the slave rebels' image in American planters' minds, that

is to say, until after the Second Amendment had been ratified. Genovese, *From Rebellion to Revolution* at 113–25.

41 Then again, the militia lost its nerve at Harper's Ferry in 1859 and stood by idly while Colonel Robert E. Lee and a detachment of marines from Washington stormed the arsenal. For an interesting account of the events surrounding the abortive slave insurrection led by John Brown, see *The Santa Fe Trail*, a 1940 feature film starring Errol Flynn (as Jeb Stuart), Ronald Reagan (as George Armstrong Custer), Olivia de Havilland (as Jefferson Davis's daughter, and the love interest of both the aforementioned), and Alan Hale (who later gained fame as the Skipper on *Gilligan's Island*) as a comical sutler turned field gunner.

42 Perhaps the explanation is Bogus's heavy emphasis on the debates of 1788 on the ratification of the main body of the Constitution and the animating fears behind them. He looks more to the call for the right to arms than the ratification of the Second Amendment as the critical bit of business. He thus ignores the state of mind that might have illuminated the meaning of the provision that the Virginian assembly adopted in the Bill of Rights.

43 Thomas O. Ott, *The Haitian Revolution, 1789–1804* (1973).

44 The influx of refugees from Haiti did not peak until the summer of 1793, when white resistance to the Revolution collapsed. But even as the Virginia Senate considered the Bill of Rights in the fall of 1791, Southern newspapers obsessed about what was already history's bloodiest revolution against white colonial rule. *Maryland Journal and Baltimore Advertiser,* October 14 and November 4, 1791 (describing the rebel leader Boukmann as a "ferocious voodoo priest"); *Maryland Journal and Baltimore Advertiser,* October 7, 1791, reprinting a letter extract from Le Cap François of September 7, 1791 (rebels "massacred a great number of the whites, and have taken as prisoners some females of that complexion"). Nor were Southern state governments silent on Haiti while ratification of the Second Amendment was under consideration. In September 1791, Governor Charles Pinckney of South Carolina dispatched the following to the "Colonial Assembly of St. Domingo":

> When we recollect how nearly similar the situation of the Southern States and St. Domingo are in the profusion of slaves — that a day may arrive when they may be exposed to the same insurrections — we cannot but sensibly feel for your situation (cited in Thomas O. Ott, *The Haitian Revolution, 1789–1804* at 53 [1973]).

Thus, by the time the Virginia Senate ratified the Second Amendment on December 15, 1791, the Senators were well aware that thousands of whites and tens of thousands of blacks had been killed in St. Dominque/Haiti. But when Madison drafted the Amendment in 1789, his nearest domestic reminder of the potential for slave insurrection of a scale sufficient to challenge the collective safety of white Southerners was indeed Stono, then 48 years distant.

45 I *Annals of Congress* at 1851–75.

46 In Staughton Lynd's words, "we *know* why the Founders did not use the words "slave" and "slavery" in the Constitution. Paterson of New Jersey stated in the Convention that when, in 1783, the Continental Congress changed its eighth Article of Confederation so that slaves would henceforth be included in apportioning taxation among the States, the Congress "had been ashamed to use the term 'Slaves' and had substituted a description." Iredell, in the Virginia ratifying convention, said similarly that the Fugitive Slave Clause of the proposed Constitution did not use the word "slave" because of the "particular scruples" of the "northern delegates"; and in 1798 Dayton of New Jersey, who had been a member of the convention, told the House of Representatives that the purpose was to avoid any "stain" on the new government. If for Northern delegates the motive was shame, for Southern members of the convention it was prudence. Madison wrote to Lafayette in 1830, referring to emancipation: "I scarcely express myself too strongly in saying, that any allusion in the Convention to the subject you have so much at heart would have been a spark to a mass of gunpowder." Staughton Lynd, "The Abolitionist Critique of the United States Constitution," in *The Anti-Slavery Vanguard: New Essays on the Abolitionists* 209, 215–216 (Martin Duberman, ed. 1965).

47 I *Annals of Congress* at 778–80, 795–96.

48 William M. Wiecek, *The Sources of Anti-Slavery Constitutionalism* 68 (1977) quoting South Carolina's Pierce Butler, who instructed the convention that "[t]he security the Southern States want is that their negroes may not be taken from them which some gentlemen within or without doors, have a very good mind to do," quoting Farrand, I *Records* 605 (13 July). As Wiecek comments, "[i]f Butler seriously thought any of his colleagues contemplated emancipation, he was hallucinating. But he had expressed an elemental slave-state response to real or imagined exogenous pressures on slavery that would characterize southern constitutionalism until the Civil War."

49 Wiecek identifies ten clauses of the Constitution "that directly or indirectly accommodated [eight aspects of] the peculiar institution" in 1787; William M. Wiecek, *The Sources of Anti-Slavery Constitutionalism* 62–63 (1977). Wiecek lists these as (1) art. 1, sec. 2, cl. 3 (apportionment of representation according to three-fifths ratio); (2) art. 1, sec. 2, cl. 3, and art. 1, sec. 9 (apportionment of direct taxes among the states according to the three-fifths ratio); (3) art. 1, sec. 9 (twenty-year moratorium on congressional action to abolish the international slave trade); (4) art. 4, sec. 2 (Fugitive Slave Clause); (5) art. 1, sec. 8 (Congress granted power to call forth state militias to suppress insurrections); (6) art. 4, sec. 4 (federal government required to protect states against domestic violence); (7) art. 5 (provisions of art. 1, sec. 9, cls. 1 and 4 [regarding slave trade abolition and direct taxes] made un-amendable); and (8) art. 1, sec. 9, and art. 1, sec. 10 (prohibition on taxing exports). William M. Wiecek, *The Sources of Anti-Slavery Constitutionalism* 62–63 (1977). Only the clauses listed at 1–4 on Wiecek's list address slavery directly, and none mentions slavery by name. Don E. Fehrenbacher, *The Dred Scott Case: Its Significance in American Law and*

Politics 19–27 (1978) (hereinafter, Fehrenbacher, *Dred Scott Case*) (identifying only three clauses addressing the existence of slavery). The euphemisms employed in the constitutional text are art. 1, sec. 2, "three fifths of all other persons"; art. 1, sec. 9, cl. 1, "such Persons as any of the States now existing shall think proper to admit"; and art 4, sec. 2, cl. 4, "Person held to Service or Labour in one State, under the Laws thereof." Fehrenbacher makes the point that by not sanctioning slavery by name, and only "dealing with peripheral features of the institution," the Constitution of 1787 cannot be said to have legitimized slavery. Fehrenbacher, *Dred Scott Case* at 27.

50   The crisis over counting slave population for purposes of apportioning states' representation in Congress and share of direct federal taxes was resolved by the "Great Compromise" at the Constitutional Convention, establishing the three to five ratio. Fehrenbacher, *Dred Scott Case* at 20.

51   The crisis over Missouri's application for admission as a slave state was resolved by the Compromise of 1820. Fehrenbacher, *Dred Scott Case* at 100–13.

52   The crisis over South Carolina's nullification of the so-called Tariff of Abominations eased when South Carolina acknowledged federal authority and Congress lowered the tariff rates. 1 Freehling, *Secessionists at Bay* at 272–86.

53   The crisis surrounding the annexation of Texas. Fehrenbacher, *Dred Scott Case* at 124–28, Leila M. Roeckell, "Bonds Over Bondage: British Opposition to the Annexation of Texas," 19 *Journal of the Early Republic* 257 (1999).

54   The crisis surrounding the status of slavery in the territories ceded by Mexico after its defeat in the Mexican-American War was resolved by the Compromise of 1850. Fehrenbacher, *Dred Scott Case* at 157–63.

55   The crisis surrounding Kansas' petition for admission under rival "free" and "slave" constitutions and the announcement of the Supreme Court's decision in the *Dred Scott* case festered until secession. Fehrenbacher, *Dred Scott Case* at 203–208.

56   The final constitutional crisis over slavery ushered in secession and the Civil War. Fehrenbacher, *Dred Scott Case* at 544–45, 555–56.

57   I *Annals of Congress* 778–80.

58   Freehling, *Secessionists at Bay* at 253–86 and passim for an interesting if slightly unorthodox analysis of the recurring pattern of secessionist posturing during the great antebellum constitutional crises.

59   Wood, *Creation of the American Republic* at 125–255, for an authoritative discussion of the pervasiveness of republicanism across all regions of the country (discussing the drafting of the state constitutions).

60   For exposition and examination of numerous documents relating to slave resistance of varying levels of violence, see Genovese, *From Rebellion to Revolution,* and the controversial Herbert Aptheker, *American Negro Slave Revolts* (1949), but see note 39 for this chapter cautioning about the accuracy of Aptheker's findings.

61   Bogus, "Hidden History" at 368, 407–408 (but recall "bet-hedging" variations of the argument set out by Bogus in "Hidden History" at 408 ["Whether Madi-

son personally shared this fear cannot today be known"] and at 366 ["We do not know why Madison chose to draft his provision this way."]).

62 Bogus, "Hidden History" at 358, 364.

63 See our discussion of militia-related anti-federalist critiques of the Constitution at 80, 87–88, demonstrating strong Northern support for amending the Constitution to support what Jefferson called the right "against standing armies."

64 Bogus asserts that the Virginia delegates to the ratifying convention in Richmond "knew the Northern states were increasingly disgusted by slavery" and he cites the egalitarian preamble to the Declaration of Independence along with Northern "abolitionist fervor." Bogus, "Hidden History" at 328, 329, 330.

65 Ibid. at 349.

66 Ibid. at 356.

67 Ibid.

68 Ibid. at 357.

69 Samuel Walker, *Popular Justice* 51 (Oxford University Press, 2d ed., 1998); Wilber R. Miller, *Cops and Bobbies* 73 (1973).

70 *Declaration of Independence* para. 29 (U.S. 1776) ("[The king of Great Britain] has excited domestic Insurrections amongst us").

71 The Fugitive Slave Clause provides:

> No Person held to Service or Labour in one State, under the Laws thereof, escaping into another, shall, in Consequence of any Law or Regulation therein, be discharged from such Service or Labour, but shall be delivered up on Claim of the Party to whom such Service or Labour may be due.

U.S. Const. art. 4, sec. 2, cl. 3.

72 Commonwealth v. Jennison (unreported) reprinted in Paul Finkelman, *The Law of Freedom and Bondage* 36 (1986), and discussion in Robert Cover, *Justice Accused: Anti-Slavery and the Judicial Process* 43–50 (1975). In a series of cases relating to Jennison's efforts to keep Quock Walker enslaved and avoid prosecution or liability for beating him, terminating in the above-referenced case, Massachusetts established the illegality of slavery. One of the grounds cited for this decision was that slavery violated Article 1 of the Massachusetts Declaration of Rights of 1780, which provided "All Men are Born Free and Equal." Thus, in Massachusetts, the same state Bill of Rights that protected the right to bear arms in language strikingly similar to Virginia's and that of the future Second Amendment (see following note) was responsible for *ending* slavery, not securing it.

73 The Massachusetts Constitution of 1780 provided:

> The people have a right to keep and bear arms for the common defense. And as in time of peace armies are dangerous to liberty, they ought not to be maintained without the consent of the legislature, and the military shall always be held in an exact subordination to the civil authority, and shall be governed by it.

The *Complete Bill of Rights: The Drafts, Debates, Sources and Origins* 183 (Neil H. Cogan ed., 1997).

74 Bogus, "Hidden History" at 366–69.

75 Ibid. at 368.

76 Ibid. at 367.

77 Veteran officers may well have despaired of the militia's fighting effectiveness, but, from the standpoint of political ideology as opposed to military policy, the perhaps "mythological" effectiveness of the militia as a bulwark against foreign invasion remained a powerful symbol. See, for example, Madison's invocation of the militia near of half a million men in Federalist No. 46.

78 In fairness, Professor Bogus says only that his exegesis is "consistent with" the purpose he suggests, not that it is compelled by it. Bogus, "Hidden History" at 368. But we think the argument is nonetheless mustered to support the thesis.

79 Letter of December 20, 1787, 12 *Papers of Thomas Jefferson* 438, 440 (Julian P. Boyd ed., 1953).

80 "But for the events at Richmond," Bogus writes, "it is doubtful that Madison would have included a right to bear arms in his proposed list of rights." Bogus, "Hidden History" at 364. Later he states "the events at the Richmond ratifying convention in June 1788 provided the impetus for embodying a right to bear arms in the Bill of Rights." Ibid. at 375.

81 I *Annals of Congress* 778–80, 796.

82 Ibid. at 779–80.

83 Ibid. at 779–80. Joshua Seney (Md.), Michael Jennifer Stone (Md.), John Vining (Del.), James Jackson (Ga.), William Smith (S.C.), Erasmus Burke (S.C.), ibid. at 749–52, 795–96. Note that these six Southerners included a member from Delaware and two from Maryland. Seney's remarks, moreover, were of a humorous rather than a political stripe. And while South Carolina's Erasmus Burke was indubitably a Deep South member with slavery's interests at heart, his commentary affords perhaps the clearest evidence that Congress was animated by civic-humanist concerns rather than fear of slave rebellion. Burke did not think the Second Amendment strong enough security against the dangers of standing armies, and "proposed to add to the clause just agreed to, an amendment to the following effect: 'A standing army of regular troops in time of peace is dangerous to public liberty, and such shall not be raised or kept up in time of peace, but from necessity, and for the security of the people, nor without the consent of two-thirds of the members present of both Houses; and in all cases the military shall be subordinate to the civil authority.'" Ibid. at 780.

84 Elbridge Gerry (Mass.), Roger Sherman (Conn.), Egbert Benson (N.Y.), Elias Boudinot (N.J.), Thomas Hartley (Penn.), Thomas Scott (Penn.), Ibid. at 778–80.

85 See table in Schwartz, *Great Rights of Mankind* at 157–58.

86 The argument for a trans-sectional Revolutionary era consensus on (anti-) slavery — or at least the widespread illusion of such a consensus — is set forth

cogently in Duncan J. Macleod, *Slavery, Race, and the American Revolution* 29–38 (1974). David Brion Davis, *The Problem of Slavery in the Age of Revolution, 1770–1823*, 41–49 (1975) (hereinafter, Davis, *Problem of Slavery*), on the emergence of worldwide antislavery opinion in the late eighteenth century.

87 Nevertheless, during the revolutionary period, significant numbers of Southerners endorsed with varying degrees of commitment private manumissions, slave trade abolition, and colonization-linked emancipation, MacLeod at 29–31, and took permissive stances on freedom suits. MacLeod at 109–126; see also Davis, *Problem of Slavery* at 196–212; Freehling, *Secessionists at Bay* at 121–43.

88 Davis, *Problem of Slavery* at 48.

89 The archetypal post-Haiti Jeffersonian variation of this theme was that while slave ownership was inherently immoral, rapid whole-scale emancipation without removal of the freedmen would lead to intolerably bloody social dislocation, or even racial Armageddon. Consider Jefferson's famous formulation of this position during the Missouri controversy, by which time more radically antislavery ideals he had entertained during the revolutionary era had been subsumed by temporizing and rationalization: "The cession of that kind of property, for so it is misnamed, is a bagatelle which would not cost me a second thought, if, in that way, a general emancipation and *expatriation* could be effected; and gradually, and with due sacrifices, I think it might be. But as it is, we have the wolf by the ears, and we can neither hold him, nor safely let him go. Justice is in one scale, and self-preservation in the other." Letter of Thomas Jefferson to John Holmes, Congressman from Massachusetts, District of Maine (Apr. 22, 1820), in 15 *The Writings of Thomas Jefferson* 248 (Andrew A. Lipscomb and Albert E. Bergh) (1905).

90 Rawlins Lowndes issued a classic exposition of this position during the South Carolina Legislatures' debates on ratification. He warned that Northerners would avail themselves of powers vested in the federal government to foist slave-trade abolition on South Carolina. According to the reporter's summary, Lowndes argued that "[w]ithout negroes, this state would degenerate into the most contemptible in the Union . . . [Lowndes] cited an expression that fell from General Pinckney on a former debate, that whilst there remained one acre of swamp-land in South Carolina, he should raise his voice against restricting the importation of negroes. . . . Negroes were our wealth, our only natural resource; yet behold how our kind friends in the north were determined soon to tie up our hand, and drain us of what we had!" 4 *Elliot's Debates* 272–73, cited in Bogus, "Hidden History" at 357.

91 Freehling, *Secessionists at Bay* at 121–31; Macleod at 41–49.

92 Davis, *Problem of Slavery* at 23–32, 84–89; Macleod at 98–99.

93 Davis, *Problem of Slavery* at 84. Far removed from Garrisonian immediatism, Franklin warned (in true Jeffersonian fashion) that "slavery is such an atrocious debasement of human nature, that its very extirpation, if not performed with solicitous care, may sometimes open up a source of serious evils." Davis, *Problem of Slavery* at 84, quoting Frederick Law Olmsted, *A Journey in the Seaboard*

Slave States, with Remarks on Their Economy 125 (1856). Franklin was Chairman of the Pennsylvania Abolition Society. Davis, *Problem of Slavery* at 100.

94 Davis, *Problem of Slavery* at 84.

95 Wood, *Creation of the American Republic* at 12–13.

96 Davis, *Problem of Slavery* at 48, regarding the emergence of an antislavery mainstream in the western world ("By the eve of the American Revolution there was a remarkable convergence of cultural and intellectual developments which at once undercut traditional rationalizations for slavery and offered new models of sensibility for identifying with its victims."); Robin Blackburn, *The Overthrow of Colonial Slavery, 1776–1848,* 121–22 (1988).

97 William M. Wiecek, *The Sources of Anti-Slavery Constitutionalism* 84–88 (1977).

98 Davis, *Problem of Slavery* at 215–22. But consider also the following commentary of Luther Martin at the Constitutional Convention. "[N]ational crimes . . . frequently are punished in this world, by national punishments; and . . . continuance of the slave trade . . . giving it a national sanction and encouragement, ought to be considered as justly exposing us to the displeasure and vengeance of Him, who is equally Lord of us all, and who views with equal eye the poor African slave and his American master."(eighteenth-century emphasis of nearly every word omitted). Davis, *Problem of Slavery* at 233, quoting Farrand, 3 *Records* at 211. To be sure, Martin feared that the Lord might take to washing away sins if America did not repent of its slaveholding ways, but this is not the same thing as bidding Him haste to do so in the later-day fashion of John Brown. It should also be noted that Martin was addressing the slave trade rather than slaveholding, and that his perspective was absurdly millennial by the deistic standards of the late eighteenth century. Davis, *Problem of Slavery* at 322–23. Thus, even the most extreme antislavery formulation of the constitutional period lacks the interventionist quality of late 1850s radical abolitionist rhetoric. It was also expounded—less threateningly from the Southern viewpoint—not by a New Englander but by a delegate from Maryland who was considered somewhat eccentric.

99 They soon would do precisely that, blaming "Jacobin" inter-meddlers for Haiti and the death of thousands of their fellow slave masters. MacLeod at 154–58.

100 Foner, *Free Soil, Free Men, Free Labor: The Ideology of the Republican Party Before the Civil War* (1970) at 76–80, 83–87.

101 William Van Alstyne, "The Second Amendment and the Personal Right to Arms," 43 *Duke L. J.* 1236 (1994) (hereinafter, Van Alstyne, "Personal Right to Arms"). Levinson goes so far as to suggest it could well be the worst written of the lot, Levinson, "Embarrassing Second Amendment" at 644, while Van Alstyne contents himself with the observation, "There is an apparent non sequitur . . . in midsentence"; Van Alstyne, "Personal Right to Arms" at 1236. As indicated throughout, we believe the Second Amendment, understood as it was to the founding generation, expresses well its internally harmonious intent.

102 Van Alstyne, "Personal Right to Arms" at 1241.

103 Ibid. at 1242.

104 The boundaries of the group including those "inclined to take the Amendment seriously" are left undefined. Does Van Alstyne mean to include among those "taking it seriously" writers who believe the amendment worth study (which would include, presumably, the present authors), or does he refer only to those who take the amendment to establish an immutable right of the people? Van Alstyne provides a hint when he tells us that "serious people" are those who decline to "trivialize" the Second and Fourteenth Amendments. Ibid. at 1254. Yet, he does not take it so "seriously" that he does not admit of circumscription by a "rule of reason." Ibid. at 250, 1251–52, and especially 1254. ("There is a rule of reason applicable to the First Amendment, for example, and its equivalent will also be pertinent here.").

105 Ibid. at 1242–43.

106 Ibid. at 1243.

107 We should note that insofar as Van Alstyne means only to note the original connection between an armed citizenry and an effective militia, we completely agree. Bolstering this interpretation is the sentence Van Alstyne writes somewhat further along: "The precautionary text of the amendment refutes the notion that the 'well-regulated militia' the amendment contemplates is somehow a militia drawn from a people 'who have no right to keep and bear arms.' Rather, the opposite is what the amendment enacts." Ibid. at 1249.

108 Ibid. at 1241.

109 Apart from and in addition to eighteenth-century legal practice, the militia could be, and was, explained and justified with reference to the "ancient" or "gothic" constitution favored by some opposition thinkers and radical Whigs. The argument here was that the militia was Saxon in origin, predated the imposition of feudal law under the Normans, and therefore had a quasi-common law legitimacy that transcended its statutory underpinnings. Logic of this sort became useful in explaining the local as opposed to royal command of the militia and in providing authority for summoning the legitimate militia when, to use the Lockean terms, the government under the Constitution was dissolved because of executive usurpation and the inability of Parliament to convene. Thus, even to the extent that eighteenth-century thinkers conceived of the militia as the "nation in arms," they did so to highlight its ancientness and to contrast it to the royal, Norman feudal array and to the standing army, and not to suggest that the militia's foundations lay outside the law, let alone that the militia required no legal foundations to begin with. And these champions of the gothic constitution laid particular emphasis on ancient regulations defining, according to class and station, who was obligated to serve in the militia and what arms each man was required to furnish. They were thus neither anarchists or universalists. They were also eccentrics. Jefferson and James Otis invoked gothic militia theory, but most American revolutionaries spent much more time in the state house reflecting on, modifying, and improving the statutory regime governing their provinces' militia, particularly from 1774 onward, when the

possibility of armed resistance to the imperial administration demanded that long dormant militia forces be revived.

110 Michael A. Bellesiles, "The Origins of Gun Culture in the United States, 1760–1865," *Journal of American History* 435, Sept. 1996, and "Gun Law in Early America: The Regulation of Firearms Ownership, 1607–1794," 16 *Law and History Review* 566 (1998).

111 Wills, "To Keep and Bear Arms" at 64.

112 Virgil, *Aeneid* 3 (John Dryden trans., Frederick Keenes ed., Penguin Books 1997). "Arms and a Man I sing" was the English usage of "arms" most familiar to the ratifying public.

113 Van Alstyne, "Personal Right to Arms" at 1245.

114 Somewhat further along, Van Alstyne notes that the adoption of the Bill of Rights in 1791 made the right to arms "doubly secure." Ibid. at 1247.

115 "We must be rigorously attentive to his political principles. You will recollect that before the revolution, Coke Littleton was the universal elementary book of law students, and a sounder whig never wrote, nor of profounder learning in the orthodox doctrines of the British constitution, or in what were called English liberties. You will remember also that our lawyers were all whigs. But when his black-letter text, and uncouth but cunning learning got out of fashion, and the honeyed Mansfieldism of Blackstone became the students' hornbook, from that moment, that profession (the nursery of our Congress), began to slide into toryism, and nearly all the young brood of lawyers now are of that hue. They suppose themselves, indeed, to be whigs, because they no longer know what whigism or republicanism means. It is in our seminary that the vestal flame is to be kept alive; it is thence it is to spread anew over our own and the sister States." Letter of Thomas Jefferson to James Madison (Feb. 17, 1826), 10 *Writings of Jefferson* 375–76 (Paul Leicestor Ford ed.), quoted in David N. Mayer, *The Constitutional Thought of Thomas Jefferson* 1–2, 10–11, 47–50 (1998) (hereinafter, Mayer, *Constitutional Thought*).

116 Van Alstyne, "Personal Right to Arms" at 1250.

117 Ibid. at 1253–54.

118 Ibid. at 1250. At another point, Van Alstyne again demonstrates his comfortable reliance on his constitutional intuition when he says, "It is difficult to see why they [those who decline to "trivialize" the Second Amendment presumably by construing it as according full individual entitlement] are less than entirely right in this unremarkable view." Ibid. at 1254.

119 Ibid. at 1250.

120 Foner, *Reconstruction* at 258. But see Raoul Berger, *Government by Judiciary* 182–85 (2d ed. 1997), for a powerful counterargument, presenting convincing evidence that Howard and Bingham spoke inconsistently, that they frequently contradicted themselves, that most members of Congress expressly rejected these views, and that Howard and Bingham did not command the respect of the mainstream of the Republican party.

121 Foner, *Reconstruction* at 258–59, 342–43, 425–44.

122 Ibid. at 258–59; Raoul Berger, *Government by Judiciary* 156–89, esp. 165–66 (2d ed. 1997); and see discussion of Senate Judiciary Chairman Lyman Trumball's later argument on this point in Presser, discussed at 19–21. A moderate Republican, Trumball did not make an individual rights argument in his Second Amendment defense of Mr. Presser. But see Berger, *Government by Judiciary* at 67–69 for the argument that Trumball's politics and theories of the Fourteenth Amendment changed after the amendment's ratification.

123 Raoul Berger, *Government by Judiciary* 30–56 (2d ed. 1997).

124 Van Alstyne, "Personal Right to Arms" at 1255.

125 Akhil Reed Amar, *The Bill of Rights: Creation and Reconstruction* (Yale University Press, 1998); Akhil R. Amar, "The Bill of Rights and the Fourteenth Amendment," 101 *Yale L. J.* 1193 (1992). Bruce Ackerman, *We the People: Foundations* (1991). Professor Ackerman posits three constitutional periods in American history ushered in by the founding, the Reconstruction, and the New Deal.

126 These commentators, less theoretical than Amar, did not rely expressly on Ackermanian notions. Robert J. Cottrol and Raymond T. Diamond, "The Second Amendment: Toward an Afro-Americanist Reconsideration," 80 *Georgia L. J.* 309 (1991); and Steven P. Halbrook "The Fourteenth Amendment and the Right to Keep and Bear Arms: The Intent of the Framers," in *Gun Control and the Constitution* 360–74 (Robert J. Cottrol ed., 1994).

127 Amar, *Creation and Reconstruction* 259.

128 Referring to Bingham, Professor Amar writes that, in 1866, "Over and over he described the privileges-or-immunities clause as encompassing 'the bill of rights'—a phrase he used more than a dozen times in a key speech on February 28." He notes that in 1867, while the amendment was pending before the states, Bingham again reminded an audience that his amendment would effectively overrule the Supreme Court case of *Barron v. Baltimore* that had held the Bill of Rights was not applicable to the states. Bingham is not, of course, Amar's only witness. "Two years before Bingham had introduced his amendment, Representative James Wilson made clear that he too understood the 'privileges and immunities of citizens of the United States' to include the guarantees of the amendments." Finally, he quotes Senator Jacob Howard at length to the effect that, among other things, the Privileges and Immunities Clause refers to the first eight amendments of the Constitution. Akhil Reed Amar, *The Bill of Rights: Creation and Reconstruction* 182–86 (Yale University Press 1998).

129 Raoul Berger, "Incorporation of the Bill of Rights: Akhil Amar's Wishing Well," 62 *University of Cincinnati L. Rev.* 1 (1993); Raoul Berger, *Government by Judiciary* (2d ed. 1997).

130 Berger might have noted further that Amar's conception of the common law as "notably adaptable" is the product of twentieth-century jurisprudence. In fact, in the mid-nineteenth century when the amendment was adopted, the common law was regarded as relatively fixed and immutable. See Grant Gilmore, *The Ages of American Law* (1977).

131 To those who, excusably, see the most likely vehicle of incorporation in the

last of the clauses, promising equal protection of the laws, to those who would say, why is not denial equal access to firearms an easy of denial of equal protection? We can answer only that full protection of the laws was never thought to include constitutional rights. The emphasis is on equal protection rather than full protection, and the clause has always had a nondiscriminatory implication. Raoul Berger, *Government by Judiciary* 198–220 (2d ed. 1997).

132   In Malloy v. Hogan, 378 U.S. 1 (1964).

133   Akhil Reed Amar, "The Consent of the Governed: Constitutional Amendment Outside Article V," 94 *Columbia L. Rev.* 457 (1994).

134   Palko v. Connecticut, 302 U.S. 319 (1937).

135   One of the earliest cases to articulate the incorporation effect of the Due Process Clause of the Fourteenth Amendment was Gitlow v. United States, 268 U.S. 652, decided in 1925, and finding the First Amendment binding upon the states.

136   David Yassky, "The Second Amendment: Structure, History, and Constitutional Change," 99 *Michigan L. Rev.* 588 (2000).

CHAPTER NINE: THE EMERSON CASE

1   Amicus curiae, or "friends of the court," filing briefs in support of Emerson's argument that the federal statute criminalizing gun purchase or possession in certain circumstances violated the Second Amendment included The Second Amendment Foundation; The Citizen's Committee for the Right to Keep and Bear Arms; The Independence Institute; The Independent Women's Forum and Doctors for Responsible Gun Ownership; The Gun Owners Foundation; The Congress of Racial Equality; The Ethan Allen Institute/Heartland Institute; Women Against Gun Control/Southern State Police Benevolent Association/Jews for the Preservation of Firearm Ownership; Texas Justice Foundation; Texas State Rifle Association; Academics for the Second Amendment; Law Enforcement Alliance of America; The National Rifle Association; The State of Alabama; The National Association of Criminal Defense Attorneys (supporting Dr. Emerson on grounds other than the Second Amendment). That amounts to fourteen briefs for affirmance on the Second Amendment issue. Supporting the government and arguing to reverse the District Court's construction of the Second Amendment, amicus curiae briefs were filed by The Center to Prevent Handgun Violence; The Potomac Institute; Professor David Yassky for himself and fifty-two individual co-signers (including one of the present authors, Richard Uviller); The Domestic Violence Network; Ralph Brock (an individual practitioner in the State of Texas); The Educational Fund to End Handgun Violence. Six briefs in all support the Government position.

2   The facts recited herein come from the Government's brief as well as the opinion of the United States District Court.

3   *Printz v. United States,* 521 U.S. 898, 939 n. 2 (1997) (Thomas, J. concurring).

4   *United States v. Lopez,* 514 U.S. 549 (1995).

5   *United States v. Pierson,* 139 F3d 501 (1998).

6 *Logan v. United States,* 144 U.S. 263, 276 (1892); *Miller v. Texas,* 153 U.S. 535, 538 (1893); *Robertson v. Baldwin,* 165 U.S. 275, 281–82 (1897); *Maxwell v. Dow,* 176 U.S. 581, 597 (1900).

7 165 U.S. 275 (1897).

8 144 U.S. 263 (1892)

9 176 U.S. 581 (1900).

10 Linda Greenhouse, "Justices Reject Cases on the Right to Bear Arms," *New York Times,* June 11, 2002.

CONCLUSION

1 President Lincoln's July 2, 1862, call to the states for 300,000 federal Volunteers inspired the popular recruiting song, "We Are Coming, Father Abraham." See Weigley, *United States Army* at 206. To that tune, thousands decamped from the training fields with their regiments, and left home for the front.

denied, 224; only exception to formerly unanimous judicial rejection of private rights reading of Second Amendment, 18

Enforcement Act of 1870, 17, 237 n.30

English Constitution. *See* British Constitution

Enlightenment: and American Bill of Rights, 163, 189; and American Revolution, 258 n.104; and individual rights, 40; and Thomas Jefferson, 302 n.24; and John Locke, 162, 164; and James Madison, 78, 165

Enrollment Act, 129

Enumerated Powers, Doctrine of, 88, 90, 252 n.32

Equal Protection Clause of the Fourteenth Amendment, 198, 237 n.30, 315 n.131

Europe: and American arms supply, 293–294 n.54; and origins of English phrase to "bear arms," 194; British involvement in, 46–47; in Cold War, 140; contrasted to England, 45, 175; contrasted to United States, 132, 175; World War I in, 134–135

Eustis, Dr. William, Secretary of War, 284 n.65

Exemptions (from militia service), 114, 119. *See also* Conscientious objection

Faubus, Orville, Governor, 151, 290 n.28

Federal Farmer (anti-federalist pamphleteer), 71; authorship of, 264 n.7

Federalism: in Articles of Confederation, 104; and *Baron v. Baltimore,* 29–30; in Constitution, 78, 92, 110, 252 n.32; and Fourteenth Amendment, 206; and Madison, 186, 252 n.32; and militia funding/arming, 126–127; and mobilization for World War I, 134–135; and National Guard,

33–34, 136, 138, 153; and power to compel military service, 128; and republican character, 55; and Second Amendment, 16–17, 30, 105

Federalist Papers, 88, 218; No. 25 (Hamilton), 66, 274 n.144; Nos. 25–29 (Hamilton), 89; No. 29, 278 n.29; No. 46 (Madison), 89–90, 121, 309 n.77; No. 84 (Hamilton), 90

Federalists (advocates of constitutional reform and ratification), 43; acknowledge necessity of professional army, 183; and crisis of 1780s, 72–75; English influence on, 48; and Federalist Papers, 88; militia disparaged by some leaders, 245 n.5; discuss right to arms in military/militia context, 249 n.23, 270 n.91; oppose private right to arms in Pennsylvania, 83–84; share many concerns of republicans, 76; and Shays' Rebellion, 118

Federalists (political party), 118

Fehrenbacher, Don E. (historian), 306–307 n.49

Feudal array, 45

Fidelity (in interpretation), 4, 158, 296 n.6

Fifteenth Amendment: compared to Second, 156; and political rights, 15; and Reconstruction, 177, 200–201, 235 n.15, 298 n.18

Fifth Amendment: applied in *Baron v. Baltimore,* 29; compared to Second Amendment, 11, 16, 37, 91, 159–160, 214, 300 n.39; Due Process Clause of, 18, 214–215; Grand Jury Clause not applied against states, 236 n.22; modern interpretation of, 155, 165–166, 207; Takings Clause of, 29, 39

Finkelman, Paul (constitutional historian), 246 n.9

Firearms: American acquisitions in Europe prior to War of Indepen-

under Constitution of 1799 and
Constitution of 1850, 242 n.80
Kenyon, Cecelia (historian), 78
Klopfer v. North Carolina, 235 n.17
Knox, Major General Henry, 69; and
*Plan for the General Arrangement of
the Militia of the United States,* 71–72,
112–113, 115, 123, 278 n.16
Korean War, 140
Ku Klux Klan, 17, 197, 203, 236–237 n.30

Lapierre, Wayne, 36
Laud, Archbishop William, 178
Lee, Richard Henry, 264 n.7
Lee, Robert E., 305 n.41
Lessig, Lawrence (law professor), 296
n.6
Letters of Marque and Reprisal, 169
Levinson, Sanford (law professor),
168–170, 191, 205, 214, 219, 233 n.5,
298 n.21, 311 n.101; and right to
insurrection, 170, 174–175, 178
Lewis v. United States, 235 n.12
Lexington and Concord (Battle of), 65,
82
Liberalism, 163–166, 248–252 n.23
Libertarian(s), and insurrection theory,
178; misinterpretation of historical
evidence, 38; and self-styled militia,
10, 70, 175, 263 n.6
Library of Congress: data base of con-
gressional proceedings features only
military uses of "bearing arms," 27
Lincoln, President Abraham: and Civil
War, 128, 228, 316 n.1; and conscrip-
tion, 209–211; on militia training of
his youth, 123–124
Lindren, James (law professor and
social scientist), 292–294 n.54
Little Rock, 151
"Living Constitution," 147
Lochner v. New York, 36
Locke, John, 10; compared to Jefferson,

163, 171–173, 301 n.22; compared to
Madison, 173–175; and conception of
rights, 164; in contemporary American thought, 251 n.23; and *Letter
Concerning Toleration,* 176; and radical
politics, 162, 252 n.23; and resistance
theory, 171–178; in revolutionary
American thought, 251–252 n.23; and
Second Treatise on Government, 41, 171–
173, 177, 252 n.23, 173, 301 n.22; and
dissolution of government, 64, 171,
177; and insurrection, 63
Logan v. United States, 219
Long Island (Battle of), 65, 67
Lopez, United States v.: assesses constitu-
tionality of Gun Free School Zones
Act of 1990 under Commerce Clause,
21–22; not applied by First Circuit
against Youth Handgun Safety Act,
234 n.10
Lott, John (social scientist), 1–2, 170
Louisiana, 17, 236–237 n.30, 304 n.39
Lowell (Massachusetts), 279 n.20
Lowndes, Rawlins, 310 n.90
Lowther, Sir John, M. P., 54, 257 n.101
Lucy, Autherine, 290 n.28
Lumpkin, Chief Justice (of Georgia)
Joseph Henry, 28–30
Lund, Nelson (law professor), 38
Lundy's Lane (Battle of), 121
Lynd, Staughton (historian), 306 n.40

Machiavelli, 44, 227, 252 n.38, 252 n.42;
Discourses of, 44
MacLay, Senator William, 103
Madison, Dolley Todd, 92, 270 n.96
Madison, James: and anti-federalists
in his constituency, 95, 266 n.46;
and Bill of Rights, 25, 40, 91–106,
187, 277 n.173; in Confederation
Congress, 69, 71; courtship of Kitty
Floyd, 91–92, 270 n.95; on emanci-
pation, 306 n.46; proposes military

Madison, James (*continued*)
draft, 209; and Constitution, 43,
176–177, 252 n.32; urges Congress to
"declare great rights of mankind,"
96; drafts Bill of Rights, 85, 91, 305
n.44; drafts Constitution, 73, 78, 173;
drafts Second Amendment, 3, 96–
98, 105–106; and Enlightenment,
165; and Federalist Papers, 88–90,
194; and Federalist, 46, 89–90, 121,
142–143, 309 n.77; and Jefferson, 25,
91–93, 95–96, 165, 187, 266 n.46, 270
n.97, 301 n.24; marriage of, 93, 270
n.95; and original intent, 148, 155; on
ratification struggle, 266 n.44; rejects
phrasing of Article 14 of English
Bill of Rights, 55; rejects resistance
theory, 173–178; and separation of
church and state, 55, 162, 257 n.102,
266 n.46; at Virginia Ratifying Convention, 85–86, 181, 185–187; and War
of 1812, 120–121, 209
Magna Charta (Carta), 90
Main, Gloria T. (historian), 292 n.54
Maine, 281 n.29
Malcolm, Joyce Lee (historian), 38, 53–
54, 214, 232 n.5, 246 n.9, 256 n.89, 263
n.6
Malloy v. Hogan, 235 n.17
Mapp v. Ohio, 235 n.17
Marbury v. Madison, 176–177, 273 n.140
Marshall, Chief Justice John, 29, 85, 177,
273 n.140, 283 n.53; on Madison as
great persuader, 96
Martial law, 86
Martin, Luther, 80, 311 n.98
Martin v. Hunter's Lessee, 177
Martin v. Mott, 120, 284–285 n.67
Maryland Ratification Convention,
80–81
Mason, George, 39, 79–80, 85, 91, 184
Massachusetts: abolition of slavery in,
185; and British Army, 74; and British

efforts to suppress militia training,
98–99; Constitution of 1780, 82,
308 n.73; 54th and 55th Regiments
(in Civil War), 130; Massachusetts
Government Act, 64; militia of,
281 n.29; petitions for amendments
to U.S. Constitution, 91; petitions
favoring private right to arms in
Massachusetts Constitution rejected,
82; Ratifying Convention of 1787, 25,
82, 85, 105, 273 n.142; and resistance
to British policy, 64, 74; and Revolution, 279 n.20; right to arms in, 82,
308 n.73; and Shays' Rebellion, 72,
117; and War of 1812, 120
Maxwell v. Dow, 219
McCulloch v. Maryland, 177
Meaning, 109. *See also* Interpretation;
and under individual terms
Mercenaries: reviled in republican
discourse, 45
Mexican War, 32, 120, 126, 134, 136, 227,
307 n.54
Middle Ages, 44–45
Military Industrial Complex, 141
Military revolution, 45, 252 nn.43–45
Military service: Power to Compel, 128
Militia: active, 134; anti-federalists fear
federal power over, 85; arming of,
85–86, 123, 126–127; Army supplants,
123; and Civil War, 128–129; common,
3, 20, 75, 88, 89, 112, 115–117, 119, 175;
common, abandoned, 125, 127–128,
227, 280–281 n.29, 286 n.78; compelled service in, 113, 119, 142, 159; as
Confederate Army, 210; Confederation Government fails to organize,
72; and Constitution, 76, 129, 239
n.51, 263 n.2; contrasted to standing
army, 57, 74, 116–118, 185; decline and
transfiguration of, 31, 57, 110, 115–
116, 119, 123, 150, 153, 156–158, 217,
286 n.78; dual state-federal character,

Political rights: distinguished from civil rights, 15, 200–201, 204

Posner, Judge Richard, 36, 206, 208

Powell, General Colin, 142

Powell, H. Jefferson (law professor), 148, 154, 296 n.6, 299 n.36

Preparedness Movement, 33, 134–135, 281 n.32

Prerogative (royal), 43, 46, 51

Presser, Hermann (litigant), 19, 238 n.43. See also *Presser v. Illinois*

Presser v. Illinois, 13, 19–21, 228, 239 n.52; reaffirms *Cruikshank*, 20; implies Supremacy Clause restriction on state disarmament of manpower pool of federal militia, 20–21, 219; restricts Second Amendment right to lawfully established militia, 131; Lyman Trumball's brief in, 239 n.53

Price, Richard, 57

Princeton, 71

Princeton (Battle of), 67

Princeton University, 165

Printz v. United States, 234 n.9

Privileges and Immunities Clause of Fourteenth Amendment: interpreted by Akhil Amar, 14–15, 204–206, 209, 314 n.128; Jacob Howard and, 197, 198; rejected as vehicle for incorporation, 16, 208; restrictive reading in *Cruikshank*, 237 n.30

Publius. *See* Federalist Papers

Puerto Rico, 138

Pym, John, 162

Quartering of troops, 11, 51, 62, 87, 164; Quartering Act, 64. *See also* Third Amendment

Quebec, 60

Quincy, Josiah, 57

Rahe, Paul (historian), 249

Rakove, Jack N. (constitutional histo-

rian), 80, 177, 246 n.9, 273 n.140, 292 n.54

Randolph, Thomas Jefferson, 303 n.38

Ratification controversy, 78–94, 112

Ratifying conventions, 78–79, 81, 96. *See also under names of individual states*

Reagan, Ronald, 141, 205

Reckord, General Milton A., 136, 290 n.17

Reconstruction, 14–18, 20, 197–205, 209–210, 236–237 n.30

Recruitment, 127, 129, 135, 141–142

Regulator Movement, 82–83, 267–268 n.60

Religious Sectarianism: and American political thought, 55, 273 n.137; politics of, in Britain and Ireland, 45–47, 50–52, 178, 282 n.37; and rivalry of Catholic and Protestant volunteer companies, 126; and revolutionary politics in Virginia, 257 n.102. *See also* Anti-Catholicism

Religious wars (in Renaissance Europe), 45–46

Renaissance: in Italy, 43–45, 227

Republicanism, republicans, 3, 42; and American Revolution, 67–68, 72; and anti-federalism, 141, 307 n.59; classical, 10, 40, 44–45, 76, 116, 141, 157, 187, 227, 248 n.22, 282 n.33, 299 n.36; object to classification, 113; defined, 247–248 n.22; Elbridge Gerry and, 98–99; historiography of, 248–252 n.23; partly gives way to individualism, 116; and mistrust of judicial construction, 154–155; favor legislative supremacy, 74; and militia, 40, 44, 111, 116, 119, 157, 203; republican character, 55–57, 75, 87; and resistance theory, 170, 175; and right to arms, 9, 40, 105–106, 141–142, 166, 183, 188, 299 n.39; and Society of Cincinnati, 117; and standing armies, 58, 78, 89, 125, 183

Waite, Chief Justice Morrison Remick, 237 n.30

Wallace, Governor George, 290 n.28

Walpole, Sir Robert, 56, 61, 259 n.110

War Department. *See* Department of War

War of 1812, 32, 115, 119–123, 134, 209, 281 n.32, 285 n.67

Warren, Chief Justice Earl, 235 n.17

Washington, D.C., 118, 120, 126

Washington, George: and Addison's *Cato,* 47–48; favors army over militia, 3, 227; in French and Indian War, 59; dim view of militia, 59, 65, 67, 89; and Newburgh Conspiracy, 116–117; presidential administration of, 111–113, 141, 148; and *Sentiments on a Peace Establishment,* 69–72; plays down danger of standing army, 67; favors select militia, 70, 112; on need for Regulars in War of Independence, 65–66; and Whiskey Rebellion, 118

Washington v. Texas, 235 n.17

Watts de Peyester, General J., 285 n.78

Weatherup, Roy G. (legal scholar), 238 n.41

Webster's Dictionary: cited in *State v. Aymette,* 27

Weigley, Russell F. (historian), 67–68, 284 n.65

West Point (United States Military Academy), 138

Whig (ideology), 42, 48, 51–52, 83, 94, 117–118, 161, 170, 172, 175–178, 195, 299 n.36

Whiggery (Political Movement/Party): in America, 42, 48, 61, 258 n.104; in England, 42, 48–49, 56, 63, 162, 171, 175, 259 n.110; Real Whiggery, 49, 56,

259 n.110, 280 n.27, 301 nn.22, 24, 312 n.109

Whiskey Rebellion, 118

White League. *See* Ku Klux Klan

Whitney, Eli, 143, 294 n.56

Wickersham, Attorney General George W., 284 n.64

Wiecek, William (constitutional historian), 288 n.16, 306 n.48, 306–307 n.49

Wiener, Frederick Bernays, 290 n.23

Wilkinson, Brig. General James, 283 n.53

William III (William of Orange), 50, 52–53, 90

Williams, David C. (law professor), 165, 242 n.76, 250–252 n.23

Williamsburgh (Massachusetts), 82

Wills, Garry (historian), 47–48, 301 n.22; on *Address of the Pennsylvania Minority,* 83; on meaning of bearing arms, 194, 296 n.7; on self-styled militia, 263 n.6; on standard modellers, 275 n.161

Wilson, James, 314 n.128

Wilson, President Woodrow, 136

Witherspoon, James, 165

Wood, Gordon S. (historian): *Creation of the American Republic,* 41, 72, 75, 258 nn.105, 106, 302 n.25; and "American science of government," 252 n.32

World War I, 120, 134–135

World War II, 137

Yassky, David (law professor), 209–211, 288 n.16, 296–297 n.7, 315 n.1

Yorktown (Battle of), 67

Youth Handgun Safety Act, 234 n.10